New Free Trade Agreements in the Asia-Pacific

Other books by the author

ASIA-PACIFIC ECONOMIC AND SECURITY CO-OPERATION (*editor*)

THE FOREIGN ECONOMIC POLICIES OF SINGAPORE, SOUTH KOREA AND TAIWAN

NORTHEAST ASIAN REGIONALISM: Learning from the European Experience (*co-edited with D. W. F. Huang*)

THE EUROPEAN UNION AND EAST ASIA: An Economic Relationship

THE EUROPEAN ECONOMY: The Global Context

New Free Trade Agreements in the Asia-Pacific

Christopher M. Dent

First published 2006 by
PALGRAVE MACMILLAN
Houndmills, Basingstoke, Hampshire RG21 6XS and
175 Fifth Avenue, New York, N.Y. 10010
Companies and representatives throughout the world

PALGRAVE MACMILLAN is the global academic imprint of the Palgrave Macmillan division of St. Martin's Press, LLC and of Palgrave Macmillan Ltd. Macmillan® is a registered trademark in the United States, United Kingdom and other countries. Palgrave is a registered trademark in the European Union and other countries.

ISBN 13: 978-0-230-00486-3   hardback
ISBN 10: 0-230-00486-5   hardback

This book is printed on paper suitable for recycling and made from fully managed and sustained forest sources.

A catalogue record for this book is available from the British Library.

Library of Congress Cataloging-in-Publication Data
Dent, Christopher M., 1965–
    New free trade agreements in the Asia-Pacific / Christopher M. Dent.
        p. cm.
    Includes bibliographical references and index.
    ISBN 0–230–00486–5 (cloth)
      1. Free trade–Asia.   2. Free trade–Pacific Area.   3. Asia–Commercial treaties.   4. Pacific Area–Commercial treaties.   I. Title.

    HF2294.D46 2006
    382'.915–dc22   2006044788

10   9   8   7   6   5   4   3   2   1
15   14   13   12   11   10   09   08   07   06

Transferred to Digital Printing 2007

To Thomas and Joel.
Thanks for entertaining me along the way.

Contents

List of Tables and Figures

Tables

Figures

List of Abbreviations

ACFTA	ASEAN–China Free Trade Agreement
ACTU	Australian Confederation of Trade Unions
AFL-CIO	American Federation of Labor–Congress of Industrial Organisations
AFTA	ASEAN Free Trade Area
ANZCER	Australia–New Zealand Closer Economic Relations
ANZSCEP	Agreement on a New Zealand–Singapore Closer Economic Partnership
APEC	Asia-Pacific Economic Co-operation forum
APT	ASEAN Plus Three
ASA	American Sugar Alliance
ASEAN	Association of Southeast Asian Nations
ASEM	Asia-Europe Meeting
AUSFTA	Australia–United States Free Trade Agreement
AWB	Australia's Wheat Board
BAFTA	Baltic Free Trade Area
BIMSTEC	Bay of Bengal Initiative for Multi-Sectoral Technical and Economic Co-operation
BIT	bilateral investment treaty
BOFT	Bureau of Foreign Trade
CACM	Central America Common Market
CAFTA	US–CACM FTA
CAP	Common Agricultural Policy
CARICOM	Caribbean Community and Common Market
CCFTA	Chile–China Free Trade Agreement
CEFTA	Central Europe Free Trade Area
CEPA	Closer Economic Partnership Arrangement
CEPT	Common Effective Preferential Tariff
CER	Closer Economic Relations
CGE	computable general equilibrium
CIE	Centre for International Economics
CIS	Commonwealth of Independent States
CISFTA	Commonwealth of Independent States Free Trade Area
CITIES	Convention on International Trade in Endangered Species
CLMV	Cambodia, Laos, Myanmar and Vietnam
CMI	Chiang Mai Initiative
CRTA	Committee on Regional Trade Agreements (of WTO)
CTC	change in tariff classification
DDR	Doha Development Round

DFAT	Department of Foreign Affairs and Trade (Australia)
DSB	Disputes Settlement Body
EAI	Enterprise for ASEAN Initiative
EAS	East Asia Summit
EC	European Community
ECA	Economic Complementary Agreement
EEA	European Economic Area
EEC	European Economic Community
EFTA	European Free Trade Area
EHP	Early Harvest Programme
EPA	Economic Partnership Agreement
ESCAP	Economic and Social Commission for Asia and the Pacific
ESRC	Economic and Social Research Council
EU	European Union
EVSL	Early Voluntary Sectoral Liberalisation scheme
FDI	foreign direct investment
FFNZ	Federated Farmers of New Zealand
FKI	Federation of Korean Industries
FKTU	Federation of Korean Trade Unions
FTA	free trade agreement
FTAA	Free Trade Area of the Americas
FTAAP	Free Trade Area of the Asia-Pacific
GAO	General Accounting Office
GATS	General Agreement on Trade in Services
GATT	General Agreement on Tariffs and Trade
GCC	Gulf Co-operation Council
GDP	gross domestic product
GKU	Green Korea United
GLC	Government Linked Company (Singapore)
HKCCEPA	Hong Kong–China Closer Economic Partnership Agreement
HRD	human resource development
HST	Harmonised System of Tariffs
IAPs	Individual Action Plans
ICT	information and communication technology
IMF	International Monetary Fund
IMSGT	Indonesia-Malaysia-Singapore Growth Triangle
IPR	intellectual property rights
ISI	Integrated Sourcing Initiative
ITA	Information Technology Agreement
ITC	International Trade Commission
JACEP	Japan–ASEAN Comprehensive Economic Partnership
JETRO	(Japan)
JKFTA	Japan–Korea Free Trade Agreement project
JMEPA	Japan–Malaysia Economic Partnership Agreement

JMFTA	Japan–Mexico Free Trade Agreement
JSCOT	Joint Standing Committee on Treaties
JSEPA	Japan–Singapore Economic Partnership Agreement
JTEPA	Japan–Thailand Economic Partnership Agreement
KBE	knowledge-based economy
KCFTA	Korea–Chile Free Trade Agreement
KFGA	Korean Farmers Group Association
KIEP	Korea Institute for International Economic Policy
KITA	Korea International Trade Association
KSFTA	Korea–Singapore Free Trade Agreement
LAIA	Latin American Integration Association
LDP	Liberal Democratic Party
MAFF	Ministry of Agriculture, Forestry and Fisheries (Japan)
MAS	Monetary Authority of Singapore
MCCEPA	Macao–China Closer Economic Partnership Agreement
METI	Ministry of Economy, Trade and Industry (Japan)
MFA	Ministry of Foreign Affairs (Singapore, Taiwan, Thailand)
MFAT	Ministry of Foreign Affairs and Trade (New Zealand)
MFN	Most Favoured Nation
MITI	Ministry of International Trade and Industry (Japan)
MNE	multinational enterprise
MOC	Ministry of Commerce
MOEA	Ministry of Economic Affairs (Taiwan)
MOFA	Ministry of Foreign Affairs (Japan, Taiwan)
MOFAT	Ministry of Foreign Affairs and Trade (South Korea)
MOFE	Ministry of Finance and Economy (South Korea)
MTI	Ministry of Trade and Industry (Singapore)
NAFTA	North American Free Trade Agreement
NCBA	National Cattlemen's Beef Association
NFF	National Federation of Farmers
NGO	non-governmental organisation
NGR	Negotiating Group on Rules (of WTO)
NIE	newly industrialised economy
NRT	new regionalism theory
OECD	Organisation for Economic Co-operation and Development
OP	outward processing
P3FTA	Pacific-3 Free Trade Agreement
PACER	Pacific Agreement on Closer Economic Relations
PBS	Pharmaceuticals Benefits Scheme
PECC	Pacific Economic Co-operation Council
PESC	Pan-European System of Cumulation
PICTA	Pacific Island Countries Trade Agreement
PRC	People's Republic of China
PRoO	preferential rules of origin

RoO	rules of origin
RTA	regional trade agreement
RVC	regional value content
SAARC	South Asian Association for Regional Co-operation
SACU	South African Customs Union
SADC	South African Development Community
SAFTA	Singapore–Australia Free Trade Agreement
SAPTA	South Asian Preferential Trade Arrangement
SAR	Special Administrative Region
SAT	substantially all trade
SECA	Strategic Economic Complementation Agreement
SEC	Singapore Environment Council
SECOFI	Ministry of Commerce and Industrial Development
SME	small and medium-sized enterprise
SPARTECA	South Pacific Regional Trade and Economic Agreement
SPS	sanitary and phytosanitary measures
TAFTA	Thailand–Australia Free Trade Agreement
TCF	textiles, clothing and footwear
TIFA	trade and investment framework agreement
TNZCEP	Thailand–New Zealand Closer Economic Partnership
TPA	Trade Promotion Authority
TPFTA	Taiwan–Panama Free Trade Agreement
TPSEPA	Trans-Pacific Strategic Economic Partnership Agreement
TRIPS	trade-related aspects of intellectual property rights
USCFTA	United States–Chile Free Trade Agreement
USSFTA	United States–Singapore Free Trade Agreement
USTR	United States Trade Representative
VC	value content
WTO	World Trade Organisation

Preface

This book is the culmination of over four years research into arguably the most important recent development in the Asia-Pacific's international political economy, namely the rapid proliferation of bilateral free trade agreement (FTA) projects within the region. I have tried to make as comprehensive a study as possible but have been particularly interested in how this new trade bilateralism could be an evolutionary step toward building a stronger regional community in East Asia and the Asia-Pacific, and therein make an important contribution to the development of international society generally. At first, I was optimistic that the emergence of stronger bilateral economic links amongst East Asian and Asia-Pacific states would help construct what I refer to as 'lattice regionalism', which draws upon the analogy of bilateral FTAs forming a latticed framework on which a broader regional community-building process could be founded. However, my initial optimism gave way to increasing concern the more I researched into the subject. Rather than make a positive contribution to regional community-building in the Asia-Pacific, this study concludes that intensifying bilateral FTA activity is more likely to have the opposite effect. In sum, the new bilateral FTA trend appears to be undermining the coherence and viability of existing regional organisations, and has the potential to significantly intensify inter-state rivalries, reinforce power asymmetries and exacerbate the development divide in the region.

The book is structured as follows. Chapter 1 provides a general overview of the new FTA trend in the Asia-Pacific, placing it in a global context and looking at the core determinants behind the trend, as well as discussing the main hindrances facing the development of Asia-Pacific free trade agreement projects. Chapter 2 then examines the FTA policies of the various Asia-Pacific countries in which field-research was conducted by the author (see below). This is followed by Chapter 3's case studies on eight high-profile FTA projects in the Asia-Pacific. Chapter 4 then presents the main conclusions and arguments of the book's study within an analytical framework devised to test the lattice regionalism hypothesis.

I am very grateful to the Economic and Social Research Council (ESRC), which awarded a research grant (award number R000 223 715) to help develop this book project. The ESRC grant funded a number of field-research trips across the Asia-Pacific region (to Australia, Japan, New Zealand, Singapore, South Korea, Taiwan, Thailand and the United States) and also to the WTO community at Geneva, Switzerland. In total, 175 research interviewees from 144 agencies took part in field-research for this study. I would like to thank all the research interviewees who kindly participated in this project. Special thanks to Jiro Okamoto, Mignonne Chan, Dario Guzman, Roberto Fiorentino, Rachel Fry, Rowena Hume, Stuart Horne, Mike Hearn, Deborah Peterson, Helen Oakey, Niran Niranoot, Greg Doud and to all my colleagues in the Department of East Asian Studies at the University of Leeds. A special mention of thanks also to Fair Trade's dark roast coffee for the caffeine-inspired moments of lucidity it provided during my writing of this book. Thanks also to Amanda Hamilton and Katie Button at Palgrave Macmillan for their cheerful help and encouragement through the book's development and publication process. Finally, extra special thanks to my family for their love, patience and support.

Christopher M. Dent
Leeds, UK
February 2006

1
Free Trade Agreements in the Asia-Pacific: An Introduction

1.1 The significance of New Asia-Pacific FTA trend

The proliferation of bilateral free trade agreement (FTA) projects in the Asia-Pacific since the late 1990s has arguably been the most important recent development in the region's international political economy. This book presents a comprehensive study of the phenomenon. We can think of the Asia-Pacific as a 'trans-region' that comprises three separate regions, namely:

- *East Asia*: that itself consists of *Southeast Asia* (Brunei, Cambodia, East Timor, Indonesia, Laos, Malaysia, Myanmar, Philippines, Singapore, Thailand, Vietnam) and *Northeast Asia* (Japan, China, South Korea, North Korea, Hong Kong SAR, Macau SAR, Mongolia and Taiwan).
- *Oceania*: Australia, New Zealand, Pacific Island Country (PIC) group, and Papua New Guinea.
- *Pacific America*: United States, Canada, Mexico, the Central American states (e.g. Costa Rica), Columbia, Ecuador, Peru and Chile.

The Asia-Pacific accounts for around half the world's trade and production/gross domestic product (GDP). Significant developments in the trans-region's (hereafter referred to as a region itself) trade policy and trade diplomacy, like the new FTA trend, thus have major global implications. As we shall note, the intensification of FTA activity in the Asia-Pacific impacts upon other global regions such as Europe, as well as the multilateral trading system. Figure 1.1 and Table 1.1 show that by 1997 there were relatively few FTAs in the Asia-Pacific by global comparison. The region's first full FTA was signed in 1983, the Australia–New Zealand Closer Economic Relations (ANZCER) agreement. In 1994, the US, Canada and Mexico had formed the North American Free Trade Agreement, or NAFTA.[1] In the same year, the Central America Common Market (CACM) countries – Costa Rica, El Salvador, Honduras, Guatemala and Nicaragua –

2

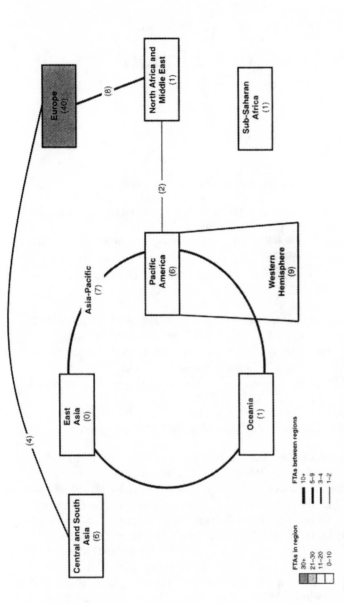

Figure 1.1 Global Map of FTAs by Region (by end of 1997)

Notes:

1. Figures relate to FTAs signed under WTO Article XXIV and do not include 'preferential agreements' under the WTO's 'enabling clause' for developing countries, or 'service agreements' under WTO Article V.

2. Pacific America comprises those Western Hemisphere countries with a Pacific Ocean coastline. Central and South Asia includes the Russia and Asian ex-Soviet republics, as well as the Commonwealth of Independent States FTA. Europe includes the ex-Soviet republics of Belarus, Moldova and Ukraine.

3. Figures include customs unions. By this time, Europe was host to five customs union agreements (European Community, EC–Malta, EC–Cyprus, EC–Andorra and Czech Republic–Slovak Republic) and the EU/EC also had a customs union with Turkey. Similarly, the Western Hemisphere region was host to three customs unions (CACM, CARICOM and Mercosur), Central Asia to one (EAEC), and Sub-Saharan Africa to one (SACU).

Source: WTO and author's own research.

signed the Central American Economic Integration Protocol that revitalised a regional FTA arrangement between them. Chile and Mexico signed a FTA becoming effective in 1992, the Mexico–Costa Rica FTA came into force in 1995, and both the Chile–Canada FTA and the

Table 1.1   Global FTAs by Region, 1990–2005

FTAs by Region	1990	1997	2003	2005
Intra-Regional	[12]	[58]	[103]	[98]
Europe	7	40	65	43*
North Africa and the Middle East	0	1	1	8
Sub-Saharan Africa	1	1	2	2
Western Hemisphere	3	9	20	24
[Pacific America]	[1]	[6]	[8]	[14]
East Asia	0	0	5	8
Oceania	1	1	2·	2
Central and South Asia	0	6	8	11
Inter-Regional / Trans-Regional	[4]	[14]	[59]	[55]
Europe – North Africa and Middle East	3	8	35	16
Europe – Sub-Saharan Africa	0	0	1	1
Europe – Pacific America	0	0	4	4
Europe – East Asia	0	0	1	2
Europe – Central and South Asia	0	4	6	6
Central and South Asia – North Africa and Middle East	0	0	0	1
Pacific America – North Africa and Middle East	1	2	4	7
Pacific America – Oceania	0	0	0	1
East Asia – Central and South Asia	0	0	1	2
East Asia – North Africa and Middle East	0	0	1	2
East Asia – Oceania	0	0	3	4
East Asia – Pacific America	0	0	3	8
East Asia – Pacific America–Oceania	0	0	0	1
[Asia-Pacific]	[2]	[7]	[21]	[38]
Total	16	72	162	153

Notes: End of year figures for FTAs where their negotiations have been concluded. These figures appear generally lower than the WTO official 'notified RTA' figures because they only take into account Article XXIV 'free trade agreements' (on merchandise trade) and not 'service agreements' that, for broader band FTAs that include services liberalisation, have to be notified separately under Article V of the WTO rules and lead to these FTAs being effectively double-counted on the WTO notification list. Partial scope and non-reciprocal agreements, under the WTO's 'Enabling Clause', are also not counted in these figures, but it does include certain full FTAs that have been signed but not yet officially notified to the WTO, as determined by the author's research. It also includes customs unions (e.g. Mercosur) and common markets (e.g. the EU) as they contain de facto FTAs within their frameworks. * After the EU's May 2004 enlargement involving 10 East European states, a number of preceding FTAs were subsumed into the European Economic Area arrangement as a consequence, which explains the drop in the actual number of FTAs in Europe. This peaked at 65 leading up to the May 2004 enlargement. *Sources*: WTO, various government and media sources.

4

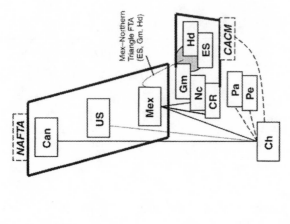

Figure 1.2 Asia-Pacific FTA Projects (before 1998)

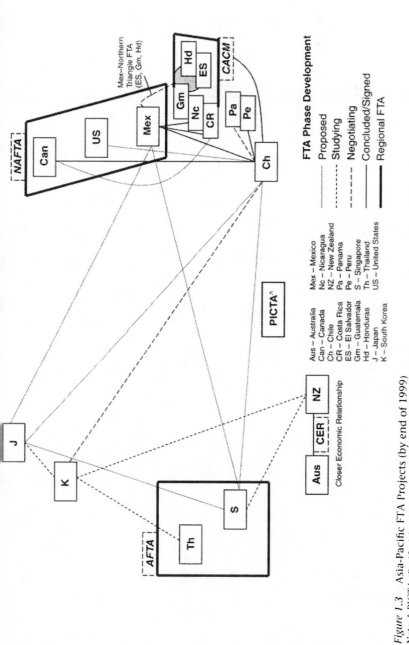

Figure 1.3 Asia-Pacific FTA Projects (by end of 1999)

Note: ^ PICTA (Pacific Island Countries Trade Agreement) involves the 14 Pacific Island Countries. PICTA has been afforded relatively less RFTA box 'boldness' due to the fact it was only proposed in October of this year. PICTA has been afforded relatively less RFTA box 'boldness' due to the fact it was only proposed in October of this year.

6

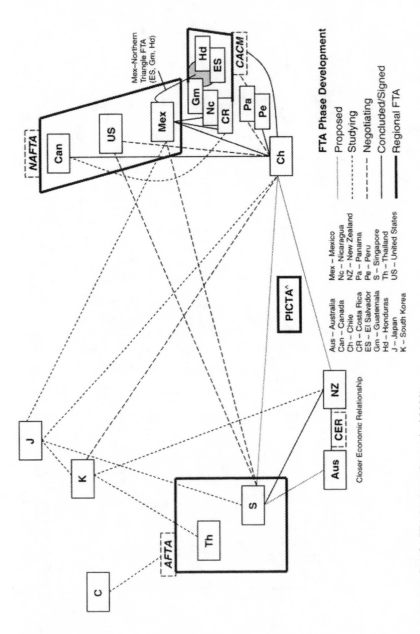

Figure 1.4   Asia-Pacific FTA Projects (by end of 2000)
Note: ^ PICTA (Pacific Island Countries Trade Agreement) involves the 14 Pacific Island Countries. Negotiations on establishing PICTA commenced in April 2000.

FTA Phase Development

— Proposed
······ Studying
--- Negotiating
— Concluded/Signed
━━ Regional FTA

Aus – Australia
Can – Canada
Ch – Chile
CR – Costa Rica
ES – El Salvador
Gm – Guatemala
Hd – Honduras
J – Japan
K – South Korea

Mex – Mexico
Nc – Nicaragua
NZ – New Zealand
Pa – Panama
Pe – Peru
S – Singapore
Th – Thailand
US – United States

Mex–Northern Triangle FTA (ES, Gm, Hd)

Closer Economic Relationship

PICTA^

NAFTA
Can
US
Mex

CACM
Hd
ES
Gm
Nc
CR

Pa
Pe
Ch

J
K
NZ
CER
Aus
S
AFTA
Th
C

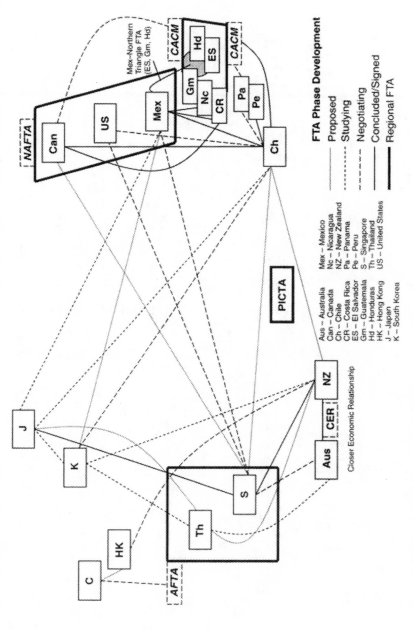

Figure 1.5   Asia-Pacific FTA Projects (by end of 2001)

8

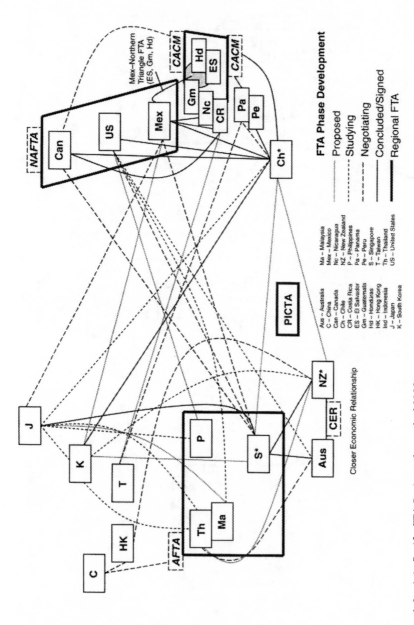

Figure 1.6 Asia-Pacific FTA Projects (by end of 2002)

Notes: * Pacific-3 FTA negotiating parties, later expanding to quadrilateral Trans-Pacific Strategic Economic Partnership (TPSEPA) arrangement in 2005.

FTA Phase Development

- Proposed
- Studying
- Negotiating
- Concluded/Signed
- Regional FTA

Aus – Australia
C – China
Can – Canada
Ch – Chile
CR – Costa Rica
ES – El Salvador
Gm – Guatemala
Hd – Honduras
HK – Hong Kong
Ind – Indonesia
J – Japan
K – South Korea

Ma – Malaysia
Mex – Mexico
Nc – Nicaragua
NZ – New Zealand
P – Philippines
Pa – Panama
Pe – Peru
S – Singapore
T – Taiwan
Th – Thailand
US – United States

9

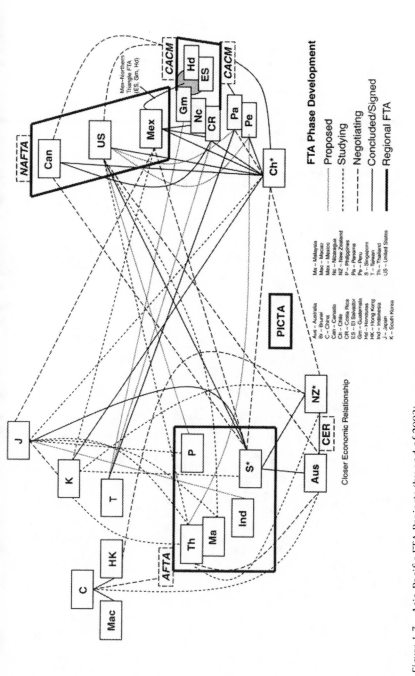

Figure 1.7   Asia-Pacific FTA Projects (by end of 2003)
Notes: * Pacific-3 FTA negotiating parties, later expanding to quadrilateral Trans-Pacific Strategic Economic Partnership (TPSEPA) arrangement in 2005.

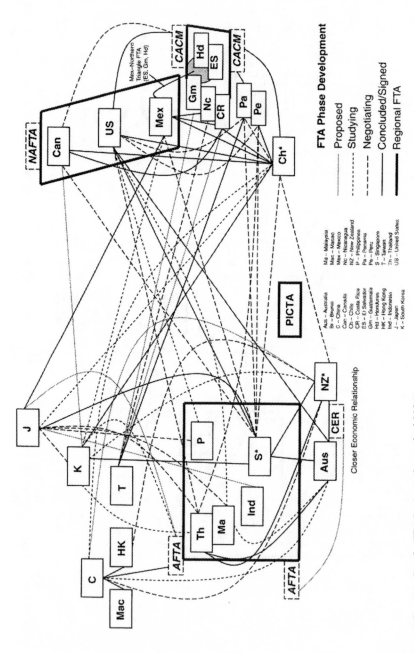

Figure 1.8 Asia-Pacific FTA Projects (by end of 2004)

Notes: * Pacific-3 FTA negotiating parties, later expanding to quadrilateral Trans-Pacific Strategic Economic Partnership (TPSEPA) arrangement in 2005.

FTA Phase Development

- ⋯⋯ Proposed
- ⋯⋯ Studying
- ----- Negotiating
- ----- Concluded/Signed
- —— Regional FTA

Aus – Australia
Br – Brunei
C – China
Can – Canada
Ch – Chile
CR – Costa Rica
ES – El Salvador
Gm – Guatemala
Hd – Honduras
HK – Hong Kong
Ind – Indonesia
J – Japan
K – South Korea

Ma – Malaysia
Mac – Macao
Mex – Mexico
Nc – Nicaragua
NZ – New Zealand
P – Philippines
Pa – Panama
Pe – Peru
S – Singapore
T – Taiwan
Th – Thailand
US – United States

PICTA

NAFTA

CACM

CACM

Mex–Northern
Triangle FTA
(ES, Gm, Hd)

Can
US
Mex
Gm
Nc
CR
Hd
ES
Pa
Pe
Ch*

J
K
C
Mac
HK
T

NZ*
S*
Aus
P
Th
Ma
Ind

CER

AFTA

AFTA

Closer Economic Relationship

11

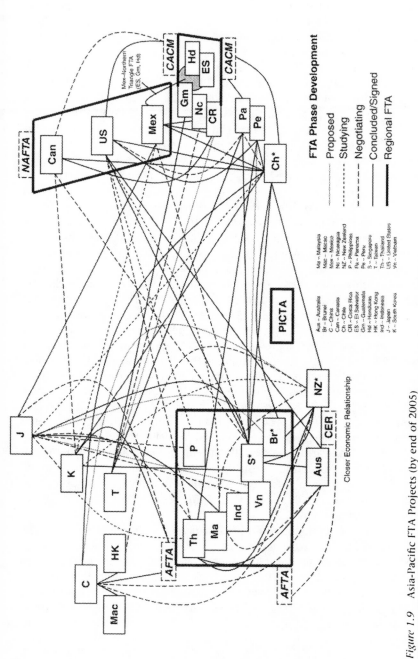

Figure 1.9 Asia-Pacific FTA Projects (by end of 2005)

Notes: • Pacific-3 FTA expands to quadrilateral Trans-Pacific Strategic Economic Partnership (TPSEPA) project including Brunei as full negotiating partner from April 2005.

Mexico–Nicaragua FTA became operational in 1997. Meanwhile, the Association of Southeast Asian Nations (ASEAN) member states began implementing its Free Trade Area (AFTA) project from 1993 onwards. A few other Pacific America FTA projects were in development by this time as indicated in Figure 1.2.

At seven concluded FTAs in total by 1997 this represented a very small number by global region comparison (Table 1.1). East Asia was the only region by this date to have no concluded FTA in force at all (Figure 1.1). However, since the late 1990s the Asia-Pacific has been host to the world's fastest growing concentration of new FTA projects. Figures 1.3 to 1.9 show the growing density of FTA project activity in the region. The origins of the expanding Asia-Pacific FTA trend dates from the late 1998. In November of that year, South Korea–Chile, Japan–South Korea, and South Korea–Thailand FTA projects had all been formally proposed (Appendix A, which numbered projects correspond to those in Table 1.2 for reference purposes). Appendix A details other FTA project developments that were meanwhile occurring between Pacific America states, but it was the fact that East Asian states were for the first time initiating bilateral FTA policies that was the most significant.

Further momentum behind the trend gathered in 1999, which saw eight new FTA projects initiated, six of which involved an East Asian country with Singapore also now participant (Table 1.2, Figure 1.3). The city-state soon made up for lost time: in August 2000 it had concluded bilateral FTA negotiations with New Zealand, the agreement (formally known as the Agreement on a New Zealand–Singapore Closer Economic Partnership, or ANZSCEP) coming into force in January 2001. This was East Asia's first FTA link established with a trade partner outside the region. In 2000, four more FTA projects were started, bringing the total number of FTA projects initiated or concluded to 28, up from 13 in 1997. At the 2000 Asia-Pacific Economic Co-operation (APEC) forum 2000 summit in Brunei, Singapore's Prime Minister Goh Chok Tong expressed his belief that such new "cross-regional free trade areas", as he called them, signified a new development in Asia-Pacific regional integration. The Asia-Pacific FTA trend was to intensify further still over the next few years. Eight new projects were proposed in 2001 and nine in 2002. By the end of this year 19 FTAs had been signed within the region (Table 1.2).

An important development during this period was the emerging bilateral FTA policy of the United States. Aside from NAFTA, the US only had bilateral FTA links with Israel and Jordan, the motivation and rationale behind which were largely political rather than economic. Negotiations on the long proposed US–Chile FTA commenced in late 2000, as did those for an US–Singapore FTA. A number of other Asia-Pacific states were requesting similar talks with Washington in the early 2000s, these being Australia, Malaysia, New Zealand, Philippines, South Korea, Taiwan and Thailand. Australia made the earliest breakthrough, with the first round of FTA negotia-

Table 1.2   Asia-Pacific FTA Projects: Time Phase Development, 1997–2005

No.	FTA
1	US–NAFTA (1988)
2	Chile–Mexico (1992)
3	ACM (1993)
4	NAFTA (1994)
5	Mexico–Costa Rica (1995)
6	Chile–Panama
7	Chile–Canada (1997)
8	Mexico–Nicaragua (1997)
9	Chile–Peru FTA
10	Chile–CACM
11	ASEAN Free Trade Area
12	US–Chile
13	Mexico–Northern Triangle
14	South Korea–Chile
15	Japan–South Korea
16	South Korea–Thailand
17	South Korea–New Zealand
18	New Zealand–Singapore
19	Japan–Singapore
20	Singapore–Mexico
21	Japan–Mexico
22	Canada–Costa Rica
23	PCTA
24	Japan–Chile
25	Taiwan–CACM
26	Singapore–Australia
27	ASEAN–China
28	US–Singapore
29	Thailand–New Zealand
30	Hong Kong–New Zealand
31	South Korea–Mexico
32	Canada–CACM
33	Thailand–Australia
34	Singapore–Canada

Column headers (years with quarters 1Q, 2Q, 3Q, 4Q): 1997, 1998, 1999, 2000, 2001, 2002, 2003, 2004, 2005

Key: Pre-proposal study | Proposal phase | Proposed/stalled from | Study phase (post proposal) | Proposed / Negotiating from | Negotiating | Negotiations stalled | Concluded

Table 1.2 Asia-Pacific FTA Projects: Time Phase Development, 1997–2005 – *continued*

No.	FTA	1997	1998 1Q 2Q 3Q 4Q	1999 1Q 2Q 3Q 4Q	2000 1Q 2Q 3Q 4Q	2001 1Q 2Q 3Q 4Q	2002 1Q 2Q 3Q 4Q	2003 1Q 2Q 3Q 4Q	2004 1Q 2Q 3Q 4Q	2005 1Q 2Q 3Q 4Q
35	Hong Kong–China									
36	Japan–Thailand									
37	Taiwan–Panama									
38	Australia–US									
39	Malaysia–US									
40	Philippines–US									
41	Singapore–South Korea									
42	P5 FTA									
43	Japan–Philippines									
44	Taiwan–Costa Rica									
45	Taiwan–Malaysia									
46	US–CACM									
47	Taiwan–Guatemala									
48	Thailand–US									
49	Macao–China									
50	Japan–Indonesia									
51	US–Panama									
52	Thailand–Peru									
53	China–Australia									
54	US–Peru Andean Community									
55	Singapore–Panama									
56	South Korea–ASEAN									
57	China–New Zealand									
58	China–Chile									
59	Malaysia–Australia									
60	Japan–Nicaragua									
61	South Korea–Canada									
62	Singapore–Peru									
63	Japan–ASEAN									
64	ASEAN–CER									
65	Malaysia–New Zealand									
66	Japan–Vietnam									
67	Japan–Brunei									

Key:
- Pre-proposal study
- Proposal phase
- Proposed/stalled focus
- Study phase (post proposal)
- Proposed/Negotiating focus
- Negotiating
- Negotiations stalled
- Concluded

Source: Author's research

tions with the US taking place in March 2003. Meanwhile, China began to fast develop its FTA policy after acceding to the World Trade Organisation (WTO) in November 2001. In 2002, China signed the basis of its FTA with the ASEAN group, and in the following year secured agreements with Hong Kong and Macao. China's fourth FTA was signed with Chile in 2005, and continued to negotiate agreements with Australia and New Zealand. By December 2005 a total of 67 FTA projects (in various stages of development) had been initiated in the region, 38 of which had been signed or negotiations concluded. Of these, 47 projects involved East Asian states with 17 within East Asia itself, of which eight have been concluded (Figure 1.9, Table 1.2).

The proliferation of FTA projects in the Asia-Pacific is significant for a number of reasons. First, it has brought about important changes to the macro-structure of international economic relations in the region, contributing to a broader shift towards 'high politics' economic agreements particularly for East Asian countries. Second, FTAs have become a centrepiece of trade policy for most key Asia-Pacific states, and in many cases have further exposed the linkages between domestic politics and international trade, especially concerning sensitive industry issues such as agriculture. Third, FTAs have the potential to significantly affect trade and investment flows within the Asia-Pacific not only by removing economic barriers between nations but also through how these agreements can shape the region's commercial regulatory environment. Fourth, the intensification of FTA activity in the Asia-Pacific has significant implications for other regions and the multilateral trading system. Other regions and regional powers (e.g. the EU, Mercosur) will be concerned if the Asia-Pacific FTA trend disadvantages their commercial interests, through trade diversion and other adverse welfare effects. As we later note, the WTO and others have expressed concern over Asia-Pacific FTAs and the further complexity they add to rules that govern international trade flows. Fifth and finally, the increasingly dense pattern of FTA activity within the Asia-Pacific region raises questions concerning the relationship between economic bilateralism and regionalism. Whether or not this pattern of trade bilateralism is making positive contributions to regional community-building in the Asia-Pacific is the core hypothesis of this study, what shall be referred to as 'lattice regionalism', the discussion of which culminates in the concluding Chapter 4.

1.2   Free Trade Agreements: The Global Picture

1.2.1   An introduction to FTAs

What is a free trade agreement?

In simple terms, a *free trade agreement* is an undertaking by signatory parties to remove the trade barriers that exist between them. Each party retains the ability to formulate their own trade policy towards third countries, i.e. non-parties. A *customs union* is the next stage of trade integration, which in addition to an FTA framework operates a common external tariff and other unifying trade policy measures that are applied to non-parties. A *common market* in turn builds on a customs union framework but extends it beyond simply trade integration into the realm of wider economic integration by eliminating the remaining barriers that impede the flow of goods, services, labour and capital between signatory parties. In addition, businesses enjoy the same rights of establishment irrespective of their own national identity or where they wish to conduct business activity within the common market. The WTO collectively refers to these three types of integrative arrangements as regional trade agreements (RTAs). Within this WTO nomenclature, certain FTAs are termed 'preferential arrangements', these falling into two broad categories, these being:

- *Non-reciprocal agreements*, where developed countries offer developing country partners free access to their markets but these concessions are not returned in kind, the aim being to realise a development assistance objective through trade, e.g. Australia's trade arrangement with Papua New Guinea.
- *Partial scope agreements*, which usually involve developing countries only, whereby an exchange of preferences on a limited range of products is agreed between them. Reasons for this can include the lack of technocratic and institutional capacity to implement a comprehensive FTA, as well as political inertia on liberalising 'sensitive' industry sectors.[2]

At the other end of the spectrum, many countries have a predilection for 'FTA plus' or 'broad band' agreements that extend beyond the elimination of import tariffs and other conventional trade barriers to include measures on 'new' trade issues, such as investment, intellectual property rights, competition policy, government procurement, mobility of natural persons, labour and environment clauses, scientific and technical co-operation, e-commerce and so on. A main reason for this is that average import tariff levels have gradually fallen over time, especially on manufactured goods, and consequently the marginal benefits of conventional trade liberalisation from an FTA have correspondingly fallen. 'Broad band' elements compensate for this somewhat by presenting additional areas where FTA parties are looking to open up and integrate their economies closer together. However, FTAs also often carry many sectoral or sub-sectoral exemptions from trade liberalisation, and these invariably concern agriculture, usually the most sensitive sector in FTA negotiations and certainly so in the Asia-Pacific's case. As we discuss later, there are WTO rules that in theory oblige FTA partners to include 'substantially all trade' in the agreement. To date, only very few of the world's FTAs have eliminated all duties and other restrictions on agricultural trade.[3]

Issues of FTA project development and implementation

The implementation of FTAs also invariably entails transition periods, typically 'phase-in' schedules for trade liberalisation in particular sectors (agriculture again figures predominantly here) that allow producers to gradually adjust to new competitive conditions. Overall, the transition periods in FTAs notified to the WTO have become both shorter and more narrowly applied to the whole product line range over time. For those that entered into force from the mid-1990s, less than four years has become the transition period norm, whereas earlier that decade it was around ten years (WTO 2002a). Both the Singapore–Australia FTA and Singapore–New Zealand FTA have no transition period whatsoever, the agreements enacting duty-free trade with immediate effect of coming into force (Appendix B). In global terms, only in rare cases do transition periods exceed ten years, yet there have been many Asia-Pacific FTAs where this has been the case, the most high profile being the Australia–US FTA (AUSFTA) whereby Australian farmers face 18-year phase-in periods for dairy and beef market access to the US.[4] Asymmetry in transition period arrangements between FTA partners may occur for two main reasons. The first relates to similar development assistance objectives in a developed country FTA policy noted above under non-reciprocal agreements. The second reason for this asymmetry concerns relative power differentials between negotiating parties, the stronger being able to secure a better deal on market access *per se*. This is often because the stronger party has a much larger domestic market (e.g. the US) and argues that the net market access gains for weaker (i.e. smaller market) party are greater (see Chapter 4 for further discussion on this issue).

FTA projects usually follow similar phases of development. The project is first officially *proposed*, which entails leaders or high government officials from each FTA partner agreeing to proceed at some point to FTA negotiations, FTA feasibility studies, or exploratory talks between officials from the parties concerned. This is normally followed by a *feasibility* or *scoping study* phase in which commissioned trade research bodies examine procedural and impact factors relating to the proposed FTA. In some cases governments will commission feasibility studies before they proceed to a formal proposal, such as in AUSFTA's case. In other instances there may appear to have been no official study phase (e.g. Singapore–Canada FTA project), and sometimes only one FTA partner government appears to have initiated an official feasibility study (e.g. New Zealand in its FTA project with Hong Kong). Most FTA scoping studies recommend the initiation of negotiations without qualification, although the results from some may not be promulgated because they predict lop-sided trade effects in favour of one partner, or identify too many obstacles to opening up highly protected sensitive industries (e.g. agriculture), as occurred for example in the Thailand–South Korea FTA project.

The length of the *negotiating* phase of FTA project development can vary enormously. Table 1.2 shows that the China–Macao FTA took only a few months to conclude negotiations, mainly due to it being templated on China's prior concluded FTA with Hong Kong. In contrast, some FTA projects can take well over two years to negotiate and may even be stalled for a period owing to certain impasses, e.g. Korea–Chile FTA. Stalled negotiations may lead to some FTA projects being effectively 'mothballed', such as the Singapore–Mexico and Singapore–Canada projects. FTA negotiations often take many rounds of talks to conclude: for instance, the US–Chile FTA and Japan–Mexico FTA both involved 14 rounds of negotiations. The negotiation phase is then followed by the *signing* of the FTA, normally by the premiers or trade ministers of the FTA partners. Thereafter, the agreement is *ratified* by the legislatures of each country, although this process is not required in certain cases, e.g. Australia. The ratification process can take some time, depending on legislative procedures and the extent of domestic political opposition. In South Korea, legislators opposed to the country's FTA signed with Chile managed to delay the passage of the FTA bill for well over a year (see Chapter 3). Once the FTA has been ratified, it then *enters into force* becoming a legally binding agreement between the signatory parties.

Certain FTA projects in the Asia-Pacific have not followed the above norms of phased development. The most important of these is the ASEAN–China FTA (ACFTA) in which both sides first signed a partial scope agreement in 2002 on a range of agri-products – referred to as the Early Harvest Programme – and then signed a more comprehensive FTA that included industrial products two years later. However, negotiations on how to implement what was signed up for came after the signing of the agreement itself. We mentioned earlier the fact that certain FTA projects may skip the scoping study phase altogether, as Singapore has increasingly done with smaller scale FTA partners such as Panama. Finally, Table 1.2 shows that FTA project development can vary significantly in duration. We discuss the many reasons for this throughout the book. Taking the Japan–South Korea FTA project as an illustrative example of how long bilateral FTAs can take to gestate, this was first officially proposed at the very early stages of the new Asia-Pacific FTA trend back in late 1998 but it took a full five years before negotiations commenced in December 2003, and talks were still far from concluded two years later. Many other FTA projects in the region have been proposed and studied for a number of years and yet still awaited a specified date to initiate formal negotiations, e.g. Japan–Chile.

FTA heterogeneity

Furthermore, each bilateral FTA is different to another, being crafted in accordance to the particular political economic interaction of the two trade partners involved. Typically, the variance between different FTAs is mostly evident in the following areas:

- *Scope of liberalisation*: to restate an earlier point, the vast majority of FTAs do not achieve complete free trade between signatory parties. Almost all contain trade liberalisation phase-in schedules,[5] and some sectors may be completely exempt or neutralised from trade liberalisation, e.g. agriculture in the Japan–Singapore FTA; rice, apples and pears in South Korea's FTA with Chile (Appendix B). These arrangements can be very complex involving various differentiated and subdivided classifications of the harmonised system of tariffs (HST), and take up hundreds of pages in the appendices of the FTA text itself. The WTO's rules stipulates that each FTA must liberalise 'substantially all trade' (Article XXIV, clause 8b) between signatories parties, the objective being to deny countries protecting those industries where trade creation (i.e. efficiency-enhancing, and hence welfare-enhancing, trade competition arising from FTAs) opportunities may be greatest. Yet as we later discuss, the rules do no specify what 'substantially' actually means, either quantitatively or otherwise, thus providing countries with considerable latitude to shape the trade liberalisation (and retained protectionism) arrangements of each FTA different to others.
- *Rules of origin regime*: this can add considerable complexity to the FTAs arrangements, especially where product-specific rules of origin apply. Rules of origin (RoO) seek to establish the geographic location of value-adding production, and are thus used to determine whether a product has sufficient production content from the FTA party country to qualify for FTA treatment. Like differentiated trade liberalisation phase-in schedules, product-specific RoO are primarily determined by domestic industry protectionism whereby more restrictive RoO (e.g. higher local content ratios) apply to the most protected industries. Moreover, FTAs create *preferential* rules of origin where they confer a production sourcing or other advantage to an FTA partner over third parties.
- *Content and emphasis of 'broad band' elements*: as noted earlier, developed economy trade partners have a special penchant for 'broad band' FTAs, reflecting their more extensive commercial and economic interests in trade agreements generally. While such variance poses less of a challenge with regard to merging different bilateral FTAs into wider plurilateral agreements, especially with regard to technical standards (e.g. on sanitary and phytosanitary measures), different preference of 'broad band' approach (i.e. some elements afforded priority over others) is often evident, and this is indicative of different FTA models being championed by particular countries, e.g. Japan and the US (see Appendix C). The difficulties of coalescing different FTA model arrangements into one

unified arrangement has important implications for the lattice regionalism hypothesis (see Chapter 4).

- *Implementation schedules, modalities and other arrangements:* following on from the point on scope of liberalisation, each FTA will have its own schedules of implementing the agreement, with some not enacting complete liberalisation for up to 20 or 25 years after the FTA comes into force, e.g. the Thailand–Australia FTA. As we later note, WTO rules dictate that the majority of the FTA's provisions must be implemented within ten years (Article XXIV, clause 5c) but, as with sectoral coverage, the rules are sufficiently vague to permit much variation here too. Different modalities or methods of commercial liberalisation may arise between FTAs. For example, if a 'negative list' modality is applied then all sectors and services are to be liberalised except for those explicitly stated in the agreement. Under this approach, yet to be invented new services or sector areas (e.g. in telecoms) will be automatically covered, and moreover it is assumed that negative list items will be gradually eliminated over time. Both aspects thus work to gradually widen market access, and the US is particularly insistent on using negative list modalities (see Chapter 4). Where a 'positive list' approach is adopted, only those sectors and services listed in the agreement are liberalised, and hence adding further items to this list therefore requires further negotiation under the agreement's periodic review mechanisms. Regulatory conformity is another area where implementation modalities may vary significantly. Some FTAs may carry special provisions in certain areas (e.g. on intellectual property rights) that extend beyond existing WTO agreements while other FTAs simply seek to be WTO consistent. Some FTA partners may adopt mutual recognition provisions or even harmonise aspects of their commercial policies in particular areas that are different to those chosen in other FTA partnerships.

Given the technical policy variance in FTAs noted above, the merging of bilateral FTAs into a unified sub-regional and regional rationalised agreement is not an easy process and requires substantial and perhaps even lengthy re-negotiations of pre-existing bilateral arrangements between participating countries, an issue further discussed in Chapter 4.

The economic effects of FTAs

Static effects.   Assessing the net economic welfare effects of FTAs has usually centred on the twin concepts of trade diversion and trade creation, as derived from Jacob Viner's seminal work from the 1950s (Viner 1950). Negative welfare effects arise from *trade diversion*, which occurs when non-member country producers, who offer a more competitively priced product than producers within the FTA area, are subsequently disadvantaged by relative tariff changes incurred by the FTA's internal liberalisation (i.e. free trade) that is not matched by similar external liberalisation. In this scenario, relatively less efficient producers (located within the FTA) are able to expand production at the expense of more efficient non-member located producers. This must be weighed up against the positive welfare effects borne from *trade creation*, which arises when the same internal trade liberalisation allows more competitive FTA-based producers to expand their own share of the FTA's markets once held by their less competitive rivals inside the FTA area. This process leads to greater productive and allocative efficiencies being captured, lower consumer prices and a greater specialisation in the economy's comparative advantages. The extent of these changes will depend on what levels of trade protection the FTA is removing. Moreover, the net welfare effect will also depend upon what level of external barriers remain imposed on third countries (Kemp and Wan 1976).

It also follows that the higher the level of intra-industry trade (i.e. the simultaneous import and export of goods from the same industries) within the FTA, the wider the scope for trade creation opportunities. Put alternatively, if FTA members possess comparative industrial profiles, this fosters a more intensified engagement of competitive free trade between producers and buyers located in the FTA countries. On the other hand, contrasting industrial profiles associated with a pattern of inter-industry trade narrows the scope for potential trade creation. Taking the South Korea–Chile FTA as an example, there is arguably little scope for trade creation from the agreement as the two countries only really compete in textiles, while seasonal differences between the two countries make for limited trade competition-induced efficiency gains in agri-sectors. In contrast, the high degree of complementarity between the South Korean and Chilean economies yields substantial scope for trade diversion as firms from both countries now enjoy a non-tariff advantage over their 'third country' rivals across a wide range of sectors, e.g. Chilean wine in the South Korean market, South Korean electronic products in the Chilean market. A Japan–South Korea FTA presents a different case. The highly competitive interaction between South Korean and Japanese industry in autos, consumer electronics, industrial machinery and other sectors provide significant opportunities for trade creation, but also for reactive domestic opposition to intensified foreign competition. Conversely, South Korean tyre manufacturers were complaining in 2005 that their export sales in the Mexican market had fallen drastically as a result of the Japan–Mexico FTA that came into force that year, whereby more expensive pre-tariff priced Japanese products were entering tariff-free and allegedly gaining market share at their Korean rivals' expense.[6] In June 2003, the Philippines called upon South Korea to narrow the tariff differential between imports of copper cathodes from its own producers and those from Chile during the South Korea–Chile FTA (KCFTA) negotiations. South Korea's import tariff on Chilean copper products was scheduled for phasing out by 2009 under the KCFTA, and in the meantime

Philippine producers were faced with a five percent MFN tariff. The Philippines was South Korea's second most important source of copper cathode imports after Chile.[7] Further a field, German car manufacturers expressed concern about similar trade diversion effects from an anticipated Japan–Thailand FTA, Japan being Asia's largest producer and Thailand Southeast Asia's largest producer of autos.[8]

Dynamic or 'second order' effects.   Free trade agreements must also be judged on the dynamic or 'second order' effects they have upon signatory parties. There are four broad areas of dynamic effects to consider that relate to FTAs and deepening trade integration:

- *Economies of scale*: As FTA area integration deepens, the opportunities for firms to exploit economies of scale become more frequent. The conditions for internal specialisation created within an FTA area will lead to cost efficiencies that in turn engender welfare gains. Each FTA partner country specialises according to its own comparative advantages, being able to expand production within a larger FTA integrated market.
- *Increased competition and efficiency*: FTAs intensify the competitive pressures exerted on domestic producers from rival firms from FTA partners over the long-term, disciplining firms to invest in new technologies and improve efficiency in order to survive and prosper in the new competitive environment. In theory, monopoly power will either be undermined by increased competition or consolidated by broadened opportunities to exploit scale economies. Third countries can benefit from the structural changes brought about by both economies of scale and intensified competition: efficiency gains will lower the prices of their imports from the FTA area, while FTA area demand for their exports could rise from the increased growth rates induced from those changes.
- *Closer collaboration in general*: FTAs can help network together firms in joint ventures and other forms of strategic alliances through the market integration effects noted above or by government sponsored co-operative programmes that may be incorporated into the FTA. This collaboration should result in a greater transfer of technology and skills across the FTA and additional synergetic effects.

These effects are more difficult to quantify because changes in such factors are open to many other determining variables. The above dynamic effects will also more probably arise with deepening trade or economic integration. Thus, they are more likely to be captured in a common market than an FTA.

Empirical Economic Studies on FTAs.   Extensive econometric studies have been undertaken on the trade and welfare effects of FTAs. These studies are usually *ex ante* in nature (i.e. based on pre-FTA economic data) based on either general or partial equilibrium models. Both assume a particular model structure with specific parameter values and functional forms in relation to a base year prior to the FTA entering into force. The model is then subjected to the removal of tariffs between the FTA parties and the welfare effects calculated. Computable general equilibrium (CGE) analyses on the estimated net welfare effects of FTAs within the Asia-Pacific generally conclude that their positive effects are quite small, especially if large economies are not involved (Lee and Park 2005; McKibbin *et al* 2004; Scollay and Gilbert 2001; Urata and Kiyota 2003; Wang and Coyle 2002). Given that, in most cases, the net trade creation effects are minimal, this begs the question why so many Asia-Pacific states have become increasingly participative. The answer lies partly in wider commercial, politico-economic and strategic objectives and motives rather than 'pure' economic gains, an issue discussed throughout this book. For example, both Ethier (1998) and Brown *et al* (2003) suggest that smaller countries may seek FTAs with much larger ones to attract inward FDI or develop stronger 'alliance' ties with states like the US and Japan. Ethier (1998) further argues that FTAs can help 'lock in' economic reforms in a country by harnessing foreign pressure to break down the domestic industry resistance to reform. 'Broad band' FTAs offer greatest scope for this, depending on the extent of their economic policy coverage.

Dee and Gali (2003) and Ravenhill (2003) have, however, questioned the usefulness of CGE modelling on FTAs, arguing that it suffers from certain theoretical and practical difficulties, including the assumption that the terms of trade are fixed, which is not easily reconcilable with the assumption of product differentiation at the national level. CGE modelling also tends to assume that FTAs introduce complete trade liberalisation between members, which in reality rarely occurs. Moreover, they do not consider various trade-restrictive, non-tariff measures (e.g. rules of origin) that remain after the FTA has been negotiated, nor the impact of 'broad band' measures on trade flows such as IPR (Lloyd and MacLaren 2004). Hence, CGE modelling is useful to an extent but their findings should be treated with caution.

Ex post econometric studies on FTAs measure the net welfare effects by establishing links between actual FTA formation and actual trade outcomes. The gravity model is a useful *ex post* econometric technique for examining the determinants of bilateral trade flows. With analogous reference to gravitational laws in physics, the model assumes that trade between two countries is positively related to their size, and inversely related to the distance between them. Hence, large market economies like the US, Japan and China exert the greatest gravitational pull upon other economies. In its augmented version, bilateral trade is determined by domestic supply conditions and demand conditions at the destination, as well as by other stimulating or restricting variables. Frankel and Wei (1997) conducted gravity model tests on possible FTAs in the Asia-Pacific. They found that geographic distance has an economically and statistically significant effect on trade, with trade flows declining by one percent for every two percent increase in distance between trade partners. However, as with CGE modelling, this approach cannot accommodate the importance of broader economic, political and strategic factors in evaluating both the causes and consequences of free trade agreements (Anderson and van Wincoop 2004). Despite its own limitations, the multi-disciplinary approach inherent within international political economy analysis can make a comprehensive evaluation of the new Asia-Pacific FTA trend.

1.2.2   Recent global trends in FTA activity

The dramatic rise in FTA activity in the Asia-Pacific is constituent to the significant recent growth of FTAs globally. By 1990 around 40 FTAs had been notified to the WTO's predecessor, the General Agreement on Tariffs and Trade (GATT), although at this time only 16 full FTAs were actually in force (Table 1.1).[9] By 1997 the number of FTAs worldwide had increased to 72, and by 2005 this total has risen to 153. The vast majority, approaching 90 percent, are bilateral in nature, and FTAs generally accounted for 84 percent of all RTAs (i.e. all trade integration agreements) in force by this time and 96 percent of those believed to be proposed, studied or in negotiation (WTO 2005a). With the intensification of FTA activity has come the increased scope of world trade covered by FTA rules and regulations. The ratio of preferential trade to the world total grew from around 40 percent in 1992 to nearly 50 percent by 2000 (WTO 2000), and was probably somewhere between 55 to 60 percent by the mid-2000s if the trend is extrapolated. Yet the geographic pattern of RTA activity is notably asymmetric: Europe alone is linked to around half of all RTAs currently in force, hosts over a quarter of the global total of FTAs, and these account for around 40 percent of total world trade (Figure 1.10). While Europe remains a centre of gravity for RTAs, the most important change in the global geographic pattern since the mid-1990s has been the growth of FTAs in the Asia-Pacific, which by 2005 had almost as many intra-regional FTAs as Europe, albeit it could not match the same trade flow coverage nor the level of trade integration as found within the European Union in particular.

Some long-standing FTAs have been superseded by more modern ones between the same signatories, or by their consolidation into wider regional groupings. Of the 124 RTAs originally notified under the GATT period (1947–1994) only 38 were in force by 2005 (WTO 2005a). Other significant points to note include the global increase in developed–developing country FTA linkages, bringing a decreasing reliance by certain developing countries on non-reciprocal systems of preferences (Bilal 2003). There has also been a growth in FTAs exclusively between developing countries themselves, e.g.

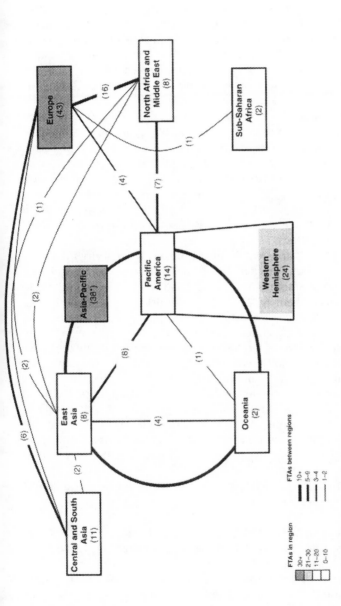

Figure 1.10 Global Map of FTAs by Region (by end of 2005)

Notes:

1. Figures match those in Table 1.1 (page 3) and relate to FTAs signed under WTO Article XXIV and do not include partial scope agreements under the WTO's 'enabling clause' for developing countries, or 'service agreements' under WTO Article V.

2. Pacific America comprises those Western Hemisphere countries with a Pacific Ocean coastline. Central and South Asia includes the Russia and Asian ex-Soviet republics, as well as the Commonwealth of Independent States FTA. Europe includes the ex-Soviet republics of Belarus, Moldova and Ukraine.

3. Figures include customs unions. By this time, Europe was host to four customs union agreements (European Union, EU–Malta, EU–Cyprus and EU–Andorra) and the EU also had a customs union with Turkey. Similarly, the Western Hemisphere region was host to four customs unions (CAN, CACM, CARICOM and Mercosur), Central Asia to one (EAEC), and Sub-Saharan Africa to one (SACU).

* Trans-Pacific Strategic Economic Partnership (TPSEPA) FTA between Singapore, Chile, New Zealand and Brunei counted as additional FTA link.

Source: WTO and author's own research.

ACFTA. The geographic reach of FTA linkages is increasing too, consistent with the 'distance-shrinking' dimension of globalisation. For much of the GATT period, FTAs were mostly signed by countries in close geographic proximity to each other, this perhaps explaining the origins of the GATT/WTO preferred referent of 'regional' trade agreement. In more recent times the configuration of FTAs has become more complex and geographically ambitious. Globalising forces have led countries to seek relatively distant FTA partners outside their home region. Many new Asia-Pacific FTAs are indicative of this global trend. For example, South Korean and Chilean trade diplomats had to traverse antipodean distances between Seoul and Santiago when conducting bilateral FTA negotiations. Somewhat ironically, US and Singapore trade officials did not travel across the Pacific at all for seven of the 11 rounds of their bilateral FTA talks, but decided to meet in London instead because it avoided one side having to undertake a long jet-lagged flight across the other side of the planet. Furthermore, some Asia-Pacific states have sought FTA partners well outside the region itself, such as Thailand with the Gulf state of Bahrain, and the US with Israel, Jordan, Morocco and others.

A concomitant trend is apparent for even mutually low priority trade partners entering into FTAs. For example, Bangladesh and Morocco, whose annual bilateral trade amounts to around US$3 million, were looking to sign an FTA between them in 2005. This was despite reservations from Bangladesh's Tariff Commission whose research suggested that the deal would hardly serve any marginal benefit for the country given the small trade flows involved and the cost of negotiating and implementing the agreement.[10] Less extreme but quite similar examples can be found in the Asia-Pacific. For example Appendix D indicates that the total bilateral trade for the FTA pairing of Taiwan and Panama in 2004 was just US$33 million, and for prospective FTA partners Singapore and Peru a mere US$41 million. While trade economists have contested the economic value of these micro-FTA projects, their advocates contend that they form part of a wider strategy of establishing bridgeheads for expanding FTA linkages with larger market nations of the partner region.

In a 2003 report, the WTO highlighted the following factors in explaining the growth of RTAs (WTO 2003a):

- *Recent setbacks at the WTO Ministerial Meetings*: FTAs are seen as an insurance policy in light of recent problems experienced by the WTO in advancing multilateral trade liberalisation.
- *Access to large markets*: especially important to small, highly trade-dependent nations. The most important large markets are the European Union (EU), Japan, China and the US.
- *Promoting deeper economic integration in areas than is presently available through the WTO*: for example in trade and investment, competition

policy, environment, services trade, and therefore applies to 'broad band' FTAs.

• *Promoting deeper regional integration between countries*: in Europe, bilateral and sub-regional FTAs have been precursors to candidate member states' accession to the EU as (see Europe section below). As we discuss throughout this book focusing on the Asia-Pacific, dense bilateral FTA patterns within a region may more generally build in various ways a sub-structural foundation on which region-wide integration develops i.e. lattice regionalism.

• *Attracting inward FDI*: this is often a primary objective amongst developing countries engaged in FTA activity, both bilaterally and regionally. Free trade agreements create larger and more integrated market spaces that help lure multinational enterprise (MNE) investment.

• *Politico-diplomatic reasons*: FTAs help promote peace and security between nations, as well as cement diplomatic ties between security partners, e.g. AUSFTA. The WTO has observed the growing importance of this latter factor and noted concern of basing RTA partnerships on political and security criteria, thus 'potentially undermining or diluting the economic rationale' of the RTAs in question (WTO 2003a: 10). This book's research findings from the Asia-Pacific concurs with the WTO's observations. We later discuss how the relative importance of 'strategic diplomacy' factors in explaining the region's new FTA trend.

In addition to these factors there is the *changing geoeconomic context* to consider, from the bipolar world system period (1950s to 1989), in which adversarial lines were drawn between capitalist and communist power blocs, to the post-Cold War period (1990 to present) whereby the combination of globalising economic forces, the rapproachement between old geopolitical foes, and a more open international trading environment have led to the worldwide expansion of new commercial linkages and agreements. The more specific factors in addition or connection to the above that have driven the new Asia-Pacific FTA trend are discussed later in this chapter. We now place developments in the Asia-Pacific in a comparative context by briefly surveying recent FTA activity in other global regions.

Europe.   Europe has been the historic centre of RTA activity and has had more FTAs than any other region, with 43 in total by 2005 (Figures 1.1 and 1.10). Over the five decades of antecedent evolution, the EU stands as the world's most sophisticated regional integration arrangement by far. Albeit with a gradually diminishing membership, the EFTA group (comprising Switzerland, Norway, Iceland and Liechtenstein) has also existed since the early 1960s. Not only do the EU and EFTA have close and long-standing RTA linkages with each other – coalesced under the European Economic Area (EEA) arrangement – but both entities have extensive FTA linkages with East European countries. However, many of the region's

Table 1.3 Europe's FTAs and other RTAs by 2005

	EEA		CEFTA			Other Europe										
	EU	EFTA	Bul	Cro	Rom	AndF	Fl	BH	Kos	Mcd	SrbM	Alb	Bel	Mol	Ukr	Turk
EU	^	•	•	•	•	*				•	•	•		•		*
EFTA	•		•	•	•		•			•	•	•		•		•
Bulgaria	•	•		*	•			•		•	•	•		•		•
Croatia	•	•	*		•			•		•	•	•		•		•
Romania	•	•	•	•				•		•	•	•		•		•
Andorra	^															
Faroe Islands	•	•								•						•
Bosnia Herz										•						
Kosovo										•				•		
Macedonia (FYR)	•	•	•	•	•			•	•		•	•		•		•
Serbia and Montenegro			•	•	•			•	•	•		•		•		•
Albania			•	•	•			•		•	•			•		•
Belarus														•		
Moldova	•		•	•	•			•	•	•	•	•	•		•	•
Ukraine		•	•	•	•			•		•				•		
Turkey	*		•	•	•			•		•				•		
Algeria	•	•														•
Egypt	•	•														•
Israel	•	•			•											•
Jordan	•	•														•
Lebanon	•	•														•
Morocco	•	•														•
Palestinian	•	•														•
Syria	•	•														•
Tunisia	•	•														•
Mexico	•	•														
Chile	•	•														
Singapore		•														
South Africa	•															
South Korea		•														
CISFTA														•		
EAEC															•	
Georgia														•		•
Russian Fed.														•		•
Turkmenistan															•	

Key   • FTA   * Customs union   ^ Economic union

Notes: CEFTA (Central European Free Trade Area), EEA (European Economic Area), EFTA (European Free Trade Association), EU (European Union). CISFTA (Commonwealth of Independent States Free Trade Area), EAEC (Eurasian Economic Community).
Sources: WTO, various government and media sources.

bilateral FTA links were subsumed into the EEA arrangement after the May 2004 accession of ten countries to the EU (Cyprus, Czech Republic, Estonia, Hungary, Latvia, Lithuania, Malta, Poland, Slovak Republic and Slovenia) to the EU. As a consequence a large number of Europe's intra-regional FTAs as well as extra-regional FTAs (especially with North Africa and the Middle East) were abrogated in the process (Table 1.1). The geographic scope of Europe's FTA linkages has, of course, remained undiminished and trade integration in the region has strengthened as a consequence of the 2004 EU enlargement. Moreover, there remains a network of bilateral FTAs between the EEA bloc and sub-integrating Balkan economies that further develops an emerging pan-European regional economy with the EU at its core (Table 1.3). In addition, Europe retains strong and growing FTA linkages with North Africa and the Middle East. These are a foundation for the planned Euro-Mediterranean Free Trade Area, aimed for completion by 2010. The European Commission, which oversees EU trade policy, has indicated that it will not be initiating any new FTA projects before the completion of WTO's Doha Development Round (DDR) of global trade talks.[11] The EU also has a few bilateral FTA links with countries from other regions (Mexico, Chile and South Africa) and the EFTA group has FTAs with two East Asian countries (Singapore and South Korea), unlike the EU that as yet has no FTA links with the region.

Western Hemisphere. The Americas, or Western Hemisphere, is another important historic centre of FTA activity. Figure 1.10 shows that the region had the third highest number of RTAs after Europe and the Asia-Pacific, with 24 in total by 2005. In 1994, the US, Canada and Mexico formed the North American Free Trade Agreement (NAFTA), the world's largest FTA in terms of GDP. Other key FTA developments at the sub-regional or plurilateral level include Mercosur (Argentina, Brazil, Paraguay, Uruguay), the Central American Common Market (CACM – Costa Rica, El Salvador, Honduras, Guatemala and Nicaragua), the Caribbean Community (CARICOM) that comprises over a dozen small island states, and the Andean Community between Bolivia, Columbia, Ecuador, Peru and Venezuala. There also exists a dense network of bilateral FTA links between Western Hemispheric states, with Chile and Mexico being particularly active here (Table 1.4). These two countries have also cultivated FTA partnerships outside the region (e.g. with the EU) and between them they have signed FTAs involving around 30 trading partners to date. On a continental level, official negotiations on establishing a Free Trade Area of the Americas (FTAA) began in 2002 with the initial aim of concluding talks by 2005, but this deadline has slipped. The FTAA project includes 34 countries, the whole region bar Cuba. The Mercosur group were exploring their FTA options with the EU (in negotiatons by 2005), India and China by the mid-2000s.

Table 1.4 Western Hemisphere's FTAs and other RTAs by 2005

	NAFTA				CACM					CACM group	Pan	CARI		Andean Community (CAN)					MERCOSUR			
	US	Can	Mex	Chl	CR	ES	Gtm	Hnd	Nic	group	Pan	COM	Dom	Bvr	Col	Ecd	Peru	Vnz	Arg	Brz	Par	Urg
United States		•	•	•																		
Canada	•		•	•																		
Mexico	•	•		•		MNT	MNT	MNT														•
Chile	•	•	•								•			•		•	•	•	•	•	•	•
Costa Rica			•	•		*	*	*	*	•		•										
El Salvador			MNT	*	*		*	*	*													
Guatemala			MNT	*	*	*		*	*													
Honduras			MNT	*	*	*	*		*													
Nicaragua			•	*	*	*	*	*														
CACM (as group)	CAFTA																					
Panama				•															•	•	•	•
CARICOM																						
Dominican Rep.	CAFTA											•										
Bolivia			•												•	*	*	*	*	*	*	*
Colombia			•	•										•		*	*	*	*	*	*	*
Ecuador														•	*		*	*	*	*	*	*
Peru			•											*	*	*		*	*	*	*	*
Venezuela			•											*	*	*	*					
Argentina														*	*	*	*	*		*	*	*
Brazil														*	*	*	*	*	*		*	*
Paraguay														*	*	*	*	*	*	*		*
Uruguay			•											*	*	*	*	*	*	*	*	
Australia	•	•																				
Bahrain	•	•																				
Brunei				TPSEPA																		
China				•																		
EU	•	•	•	•	•	•	•	•	•		•				•	•	•	•	•	•	•	•
EFTA			•	•																		
Israel		•	•	•																		
Japan			•	•																		
Jordan	•																					
Morocco	•																					
New Zealand			•	TPSEPA																		
Oman	•																					
Singapore	•	•		TPSEPA																		
South Korea	•	•		•																		
Taiwan								•														
Thailand				•													•					

Key

  • FTA   * Customs union

Notes: NAFTA (North American Free Trade Agreement). CACM (Central American Common Market), CAFTA (FTA between US, CACM and Dominican Republic), CARICOM (Caribbean Community and Common Market), MERCOSUR (Southern Common Market). MNT relates to the Mexico – Northern Triangle (El Salvador, Guatemala, Honduras) FTA arrangment. TPSEPA relates to the quadrilateral Trans-Pacific Strategic Economic Partnership Agreement between Brunei, Chile, New Zealand and Singapore.

Sources: WTO, Organisation of American States trade database (http://www.sice.oas.org/tradee.asp), various government and media sources.

Table 1.5 East Asia's FTAs by 2005

	ASEAN (AFTA)										ASEAN group	Other East Asia					
	Brun	Camb	Indon	Laos	Malay	Myan	Phil	Sing	Thai	Viet		China	HK	Macao	Japan	S Korea	Taiwan
Brunei		•	•	•	•	•	•	•	•	•							
Cambodia	•		•	•	•	•	•	•	•	•							
Indonesia	•	•		•	•	•	•	•	•	•							
Laos	•	•	•		•	•	•	•	•	•							
Malaysia	•	•	•	•		•	•	•	•	•					•		
Myanmar	•	•	•	•	•		•	•	•	•							
Philippines	•	•	•	•	•	•		•	•	•							
Singapore	•	•	•	•	•	•	•		•	•					•	•	
Thailand	•	•	•	•	•	•	•	•		•							
Vietnam	•	•	•	•	•	•	•	•	•								
ASEAN (as group)												•			•	•	
China											•		•	•			
Hong Kong SAR												•					
Macao SAR												•					
Japan					•			•			•						
South Korea								•			•						
Taiwan																	
Australia								•	•								
New Zealand	TPSEPA							TPSEPA	•								
Chile	TPSEPA							TPSEPA				•				•	
Guatemala																	•
Mexico															•		
Panama								•									•
Peru									•								
United States								•									
India								•	•								
Bahrain									•								
Jordan								•									
EFTA								•								•	

Notes: AFTA (ASEAN Free Trade Area). TPSEPA relates to the quadrilateral Trans-Pacific Strategic Economic Partnership Agreement between Brunei, Chile, New Zealand and Singapore. EFTA (European Free Trade Association).

Sources: WTO, various government and media sources.

North Africa and the Middle East.   The North Africa and Middle East region was host to only one FTA in 1997 but by 2005 this number has risen to ten. A Turkey–Israel FTA came into force in 1997, while Turkey signed other bilateral FTAs with Morocco, the Palestinian Authority and Syria in 2004, and with Egypt and Tunisia in 2005. The Gulf Co-operation Council (GCC) group also signed an FTA with Lebanon in 2004, and in the same year Egypt concluded it FTA negotiations with Sri Lanka, the agreement entering into force in January 2005. Towards the end of 2005, Jordan signed an FTA with the Palestinian Authority. As noted earlier, many North African and Middle Eastern states have signed FTAs with the EU, and also EFTA, as part of the Barcelona Process of establishing a Euro-Mediterranean Free Trade Area by 2010. The region also has a growing number of bilateral FTAs with Asia-Pacific countries, totalling nine by 2005 – seven with Pacific American countries (Table 1.4) and two with East Asian countries (Table 1.5). Various other RTA projects have been initiated in North Africa and the Middle East, including a proposal to create an Arab Free Trade Area by 2007 between the 18 Arab League countries, and the GCC group's working towards creating a customs union and then monetary union by 2010. In addition, Egypt, Jordan, Morocco and Tunisia signed the Agadir Agreement, which commits them to signing an FTA by 2006.

Sub-Saharan Africa.   Sub-Saharan Africa has too witnessed a recent intensification of RTA project activity, although trade agreements notified to the WTO thus far have generally been partial scope agreements rather than full FTAs. Of the region's two comprehensive operational RTAs the most prominent is the South African Customs Union (SACU) that was first established in 1970 then later fortified in the late 1990s.[12] Meanwhile, the South African Development Community (SADC) moved beyond its original 1980 partial scope trade agreement to create a regional FTA in 2000.[13] There exist a number of ambitious RTA projects in progress at the sub-regional level, such as the West Africa Economic and Monetary Union (WAEMU), the Central African Economic and Monetary Community (CEMAC), and the Common Market for Eastern and Southern Africa (COMESA), although the realisation of their objectives remain elusive. There is even a more ambitious plan to achieve long-term continent-wide integration through establishing African Economic and Monetary Union by 2028 under the auspices of the African Economic Community. Finally, South Africa – the predominant member state in both SACU and SADC – has also sought FTA partners outside the region, most importantly the EU (an agreement in force since 2000), EFTA, United States, China, Mercosur and India.

Central and South Asia.   Central and South Asia had 11 signed FTAs in place by 2005, and a number of FTA links with other regions, especially Europe (Figure 1.10). Most of these are accounted for by the ex-Soviet

Table 1.6 Central and South Asia's FTAs and other RTAs by 2005

	EAEC					CIS FTA	Other Central and South Asia							South Asia Free Trade Agreement						
	Bel	Kazk	Kyrg	Rus	Tajik	FTA	Arm	Azer	Geor	Mold	Tur	Ukrl	Uzh	Bang	Bhut	India	Mald	Nepal	Pakis	Sri L
[Belarus]		*	*	^	*		*			|•|										
Kazakhstan	*		*	*	*		•	CISFTA	CISFTA	[CISFTA]			CISFTA							
Kyrgyz Republic	*	*		*	*		•	CISFTA	CISFTA	CISFTA		[•]	CISFTA							
Russian Federation	^	*	*		*		•	CISFTA	•	[•]		[•]								
Tajikistan	*	*	*	*			•	CISFTA	CISFTA	[CISFTA]			CISFTA							
CISFTA						•														
Armenia		•	•	•	•			•	•	•		[•]								
Azerbaijan		CISFTA	CISFTA		CISFTA		•		CISFTA	CISFTA			CISFTA							
Georgia		CISFTA	CISFTA	CISFTA	CISFTA		CISFTA	CISFTA		CISFTA	•	[•]	CISFTA							
[Moldova]	|•|	[CISFTA]	[CISFTA]	[•]	[CISFTA]		[•]	[CISFTA]	[CISFTA]		[•]	[•]	[CISFTA]							
[Ukraine]							[•]		[•]	[•]										
Uzbekistan		CISFTA	CISFTA					CISFTA	CISFTA	[CISFTA]										
Turkmenistan																				
Bangladesh															•	•	•	•	•	•
Bhutan														•		•	•	•	•	•
India														•	•		•	•	•	*
Maldives														•	•	•		•	•	•
Nepal														•	•	•	•		•	•
Pakistan														•	•	•	•	•		*
Sri Lanka														•	•	*	•	•	•	
Egypt																				
Morocco														•						
Singapore																•				*
Thailand																				

Key   • FTA   * Customs union   ^ Economic union

Notes: Belarus, Moldova and Ukraine are counted as European countries, notwithstanding their close economic and trade agreement ties with other ex-Soviet republic states listed here. |•| represents an FTA of these countries with a Central and South Asian country and ||•|| an FTA between these European ex-Soviet republics. CISFTA (Commonwealth of Independent States Free Trade Area, whose membership overlaps with the EAEC's and which comprises Moldova, Kazakhstan, Uzbekistan, Kyrgyz Republic, Azerbaijan, Tajikistan and Georgia), EAEC (Eurasian Economic Community).

Sources: WTO, TACIS database (http://www.aris.ru/WIN_E/), various government and media sources.

republics of Central Asia, which have been busy establishing FTA links between themselves in recent years. In addition to the Commonwealth of Independent States (CIS) free trade agreement (between Moldova, Kazakhstan, Uzbekistan, Kyrgyz Republic, Azerbaijan, Tajikistan and Georgia) and Eurasian Economic Community (EAEC) customs union agreement (between Belarus, Kazakhstan, the Kyrgyz Republic, the Russian Federation and Tajikistan) various other bilateral FTAs have been signed (Table 1.6). These developments are in many ways reconstructing pre-existing economic links between the ex-Soviet Republics. In South Asia, Bangladesh, Bhutan, India, Maldives, Nepal, Pakistan and Sri Lanka were signatories to the South Asian Preferential Trade Arrangement, or SAPTA, a partial scope agreement that came into force in 1995.[14] In January 2004, these countries signed an agreement to supersede SAPTA with the South Asia Free Trade Agreement, which began to be implemented between member states from 2006.[15]

1.2.3   The WTO and FTAs

An uneasy relationship?

The intellectual debate over FTAs and the multilateral trade system has raged for some time (Andriamananjara 2003; Bagwell and Staiger 2004; Baldwin 1999; Bhagwati 1968, 1993; Bond *et al* 2004; Deardorff and Stern 1994; Ethier 1998; Kemp and Wan 1976; Krishna 1998; Krugman 1991, 1993; Panagariya 2000; Westhoff *et al* 1994; Zissimos and Vines 2000). The success of the GATT framework in particular in the post-1945 period of significantly reducing average import tariff rates (on industrial products, down from around 40 percent in 1945 to just four percent by 1995) and other forms of trade barriers helped avert the kind of adversarial bilateral and regional economic relations that marked the inter-war period. The development of a generally robust multilateral trade order had, then, created the conditions for more 'benign' forms of trade bilateralism and regionalism to emerge through progressive 'most favoured nation' (MFN, i.e. reciprocated and non-discriminatory) liberalisation reducing the preferential tariff margins between trade alliances and blocs.

Today, GATT's institutional successor, the WTO acknowledges that FTAs are a feature of the global trading system and will persist no matter how well the multilateral trade system functions. The question is how to "maximise their compatibility with the WTO while minimising their negative effects" (WTO 2003a: 12). Furthermore, the WTO concedes that, depending on how they are done, FTAs can make positive contributions to the development of the multilateral trading system. For example, "The promotion of free trade at a preferential level may help developing economies to implement domestic reforms and open up to competitive market pressures at a sustainable pace, thus facilitating their integration in the world economy. This may also benefit the multilateral process by exerting leverage for openness and competitive liberalisation in international trade relations" (WTO 2005a: 1). Moreover, "RTAs can be laboratories for change and innovation and may provide guidance for the adoption of new trade disciplines at the multilateral level" (WTO 2005a: 16). On the other hand, the same WTO report notes that although FTAs can help developing countries in particular develop valuable negotiating skills on trade agreements, they are also resource-intensive in terms of relative gains secured when compared to negotiating multilaterally and may seriously stretch the institutional capacities of even large developed nations such as the US (see Chapter 2). The report continues to argue that FTAs can create vested interests in which certain industry groups will resist the erosion of preferential benefits conferred. Furthermore, complex rules of origin that are used to safeguard these benefits can also add significant complications and costs to firms involved in international trade. These issues highlighted by the WTO are discussed at greater length in Chapter 4 when we evaluate the costs and benefits of Asia-Pacific FTAs in more detail.

Long-standing critics of free trade agreements such as Jagdish Bhagwati have called for stricter WTO rules on FTAs, arguing that their trade diversion effects are often underestimated, and multilateralised or global free trade presents the 'first best' or optimum welfare choice for trading countries. At a more conceptual level, such critics often refer to FTAs as *preferential* trade agreements. They contend this is more accurate because it accounts for their impact upon third parties. In other words, FTAs are essentially contracts in which each signatory party is conferred reciprocated sets of preferences that, by their nature, exclude non-signatories and are therefore discriminatory. Bhagwati (1995) likens the phrase 'free trade agreements' to Orwellian newspeak, because in his view FTAs are "embody both free trade and protection" (p. 2). The choice of *preferential* as the determining referent of the agreement allows consideration of the insider-outsider relationship, and this is at least a useful argument to keep in mind when especially examining the impact of FTAs upon the WTO and the multilateral trading system. Chapter 4 further discusses Bhagwati's argument that an expanding number of FTAs causes the so called 'spaghetti bowl' problem by this proliferation of agreements adding greater regulatory and preferential complexity to the governance of international trade, thus undermining WTO multilateralism.

WTO Director-General Supachai Panitchpakdi himself became increasingly critical of the growing FTA trend during his term in office, from 2002 to 2005. At the November 2002 informal WTO ministerial meeting convened in Sydney, Supachai warned that if some small countries pursued bilateral or regional accords they might have to divide their time "more delicately" as the Doha Round progressed towards the WTO's 2003 Cancun Ministerial.[16] He later stated in January 2004 that bilateral and regional deals were no substitute for global trade liberalisation because, "They are by their very nature discriminatory. None has really succeeded in opening markets in sensitive areas like agriculture", and that, "They add to the complexities of doing business by creating a multiplicity of rules, and the poorest countries tend to get left out in the cold."[17] A 2005 report commissioned by the WTO to evaluate the organisation's achievements over its first ten years expressed particular concern about the intensification of FTA activity globally, stating that it was creating confusion in the world trading system, with complex and inconsistent rules of origin, costly administrative rules, and opportunities for corruption (WTO 2005b). Reports published by the IMF and World Bank around the same time came to similar conclusions about the potential dangers that FTAs posed to the multilateral trading system (Feridhanusetyawan 2005; World Bank 2005).

WTO rules on FTAs/RTAs

Broadly speaking, WTO rules on RTAs are designed to maximise trade creation and minimise trade diversion effects. These rules originate in the early GATT period and there has been relatively little change made to them during this time. They are covered under three provisions – *Article XXIV* (on free trade areas and customs unions), *Article V* (on economic integration) and the *1979 'Enabling Clause'* on developing countries and RTAs. Taking the first of these provisions, Article XXIV of GATT sets out four main basic requirements for an RTA, these being:

- RTA parties should not raise trade barriers against non-members (*clauses 4 and 5b*);
- Plans and schedules to establish an RTA should be completed within a reasonable period (*clause 5c*), generally accepted since the 1994 Uruguay Round 'understanding' to mean ten years;
- Member countries should immediately notify the WTO, and hence other members, of the RTA project (*clause 7*);
- Import tariffs and other restrictive trade rules and regulations should essentially be abolished for "substantially all trade" (*clause 8b*), intended to deny countries protecting those industries where trade creation opportunities may be greatest.

Likewise, Article V of the General Agreement on Trade in Services (GATS) stipulates the following main points of compliance if an RTA involves services trade liberalisation:

- The agreement has "substantial sectoral coverage" (*clause 1a*), hence mirroring Article XXIV: 8b;
- Implementation of the agreement within a "reasonable time-frame" (*clause 1bii*), thus mirroring Article XXIV: 5c;
- More favourable treatment may be conferred to developing countries (*clause 3b*).

The 1979 Enabling Clause on RTAs allows derogations to MFN treatment in favour of developing countries. This relates the earlier point made on what the WTO refers to as 'preferential agreements', these being either partial scope or non-reciprocal in nature, although the latter requires a waiver in accordance to Article IX of the 1994 Marrakesh Agreement, which formally established the WTO.

Problems with FTA/RTA rules

The WTO's rules on FTAs and other RTAs are generally thought to be failing, perhaps more than in any other area of WTO governance (Bagwell and Staiger 2004; Lloyd 2003). There are both institutional and technical dimensions to this. Firstly, it is accepted even by the WTO itself that it has lacked both the technocratic and judicial capacity to enforce these rules effectively, conceding that for example that its Committee on Regional Trade Agreements (CRTA), which oversees notified RTA cases, "has enjoyed no success so far in assessing the consistency of more than 100 RTAs notified to the WTO due to political and legal difficulties" (WTO 2002b: 12).[18] The CRTA is a permanent committee that meets only three times a year, publishing an Annual Report to the WTO's General Council. Furthermore, the WTO's RTA office is relatively small and has to deal with an increased workload owing to the intensifying global FTA trend, which has led to a lengthening backlog of uncompleted RTA reports.

Such institutional weaknesses are linked to the more technical problems facing the WTO on RTA rules compliance. For example, the GATT/WTO system has only been able to produce a few clarifications on its RTA-related rules in recent years,[19] and mounting pressure a wide-ranging review of these rules came to a head at the WTO's 2001 Doha Ministerial Meeting. Consequently, paragraph 29 of the Doha Ministerial Declaration called for negotiations aimed at clarifying and improving the disciplines and procedures under the existing WTO provisions applying to RTAs, taking due account of the developmental aspects of these agreements (WTO 2001). These talks have took place within the WTO's Negotiating Group on Rules (NGR), which began in early 2002 and continued through the duration of the Doha Round. The NGR classified the technical problems or contestations pertaining to RTA rules into two issue areas, namely *procedural* and *systemic*. Procedural issues have mainly concerned the timing and content of RTA notifications, and developing a more transparent and efficient RTA review process. For example, no draft CRTA examination report has been finally endorsed since 1995 mainly owing to a lack of consensus within the CRTA membership about RTA consistency with WTO rules. More critically important discussions, however, have centred on key systemic issues, namely:

- Contested interpretation over an RTA's supposed coverage of "substantially all trade" (or SAT) as stipulated in Article XXIV: 8b;

- Other (restrictive) regulations on commerce, especially matters relating to preferential rules of origin introduced into the international trading system by RTA arrangements;
- The primacy of the multilateral system and possible negative effects caused by RTAs on third parties;
- The 'grandfathering' of existing RTAs and retroactive application of any new rules;
- RTAs and development, especially in relation to the 1979 Enabling Clause.

The first two of these points generated by far the most intense debate within the NGR on RTA rules,[20] and these are particularly relevant to the development of FTA projects in the Asia-Pacific, as will become clear as we examine each of these in more detail below.

The 'substantially all trade' (SAT) issue.   Achieving greater clarity on what is actually meant by 'substantially all trade' as stated in clause 8b of Article XXIV in quantitative or qualitative terms has proved a highly contentious issue.[21] Cho (2003) refers to this as the prime 'legal vacuum' in the WTO's rules on RTAs. The idea behind an RTA's sectoral coverage having to be 'substantial' is to optimise its trade creation gains and minimise trade diversion losses, and this is best achieved by exposing relatively inefficient industry sectors to FTA-induced increases in foreign competition. Excluding these sectors from FTA liberalisation also makes it more difficult to achieve progress here at the multilateral (i.e. WTO) level by FTAs setting precedents on sector inclusion and exclusion with regard to trade liberalisation generally. This especially relates to agriculture in the Asia-Pacific's case, yet various political, social and cultural sensitivities can arise over opening up inefficient industries more to foreign competition, and this exerts considerable pressure upon governments to seek their omission from FTAs.

It is not surprising that Australia, one of the world's efficient agricultural producers, was very proactive within the NGR in pressing for quantitative or qualitative clarity on the SAT issue. In July 2002, the Australian Government tabled a proposal for discussion that laid out a numerical test for the definition of 'substantially all trade', suggesting that trade agreements should cover a percentage of trade expressed as six digit HST lines. Although it did not specify the exact number, Australia had suggested earlier in an 1998 CRTA meeting that such a percentage be set at 95 percent of trade among parties, with members free to determine what products to fit into the five percent exclusion. Australia argued that this definition would prevent members from undertaking agreements that sought to exclude large sectors of trade.[22] There has also been debate here concerning whether any percentage criteria should apply to the number of HST tariff lines or to the money value or volume of trade flows. The WTO meanwhile observed that FTA coverage rarely falls below 50 percent, was usually higher than 75 percent but with most notified under Article XXIV having over an estimated 85 percent coverage (WTO 2002a).

Other WTO members to have demonstrated proactive interest on SAT clarification include New Zealand, China, India, Japan and South Korea, but from different interest perspectives. While Japan and South Korea – who both have inefficient agricultural sectors – have an according interest in pressing for a much larger exclusion margin to be allowed within RTA rules, they have both long sought a tightening of the rules generally given their past predilection for multilateralism over bilateral or regional trade agreements, although of course this now has changed somewhat. As Chapter 2 examines in detail, there are complex domestic political factors at play here: the trade ministries of both countries are strong advocates of agricultural sector reform back home, and were influential in what their respective governments brought to NGR discussions in Geneva. In the meantime, neither the US or EU has shown much interest in revising Clause 8b, with one report suggesting the US is more interested in challenging RTAs through the WTO's Disputes Settlement Body rather than seeking to clarify existing rules.[23] The EU had, though, proposed in July 2002 that any attempts to clarify Article XXIV should permit developing countries flexibility and derogations, for example on sectoral coverage and phase-in periods of liberalisation. Having a generally inefficient and highly protected agriculture sector itself, this may have been an EU ploy to deflect moves towards SAT clarification. After three and a half years of talks, the NGR Chair's Report published in November 2005 conceded that little progress had been made on the SAT issue, with significant differences of opinion still persisting amongst WTO members (WTO 2005c). As one WTO-related interviewee commented on the matter, "everyone knows what the problem is but nobody wants to deal with it."[24]

The preferential rules of origin (PRoO) issue. The second important area of NGR debate on RTA rules during the Doha Round period concerned preferential rules of origin. Establishing a product's country of origin has become increasingly difficult in a globalising world economy. The content of multi-component goods, such as cars or computers, can originate from a large number of countries within an international production systems organised by multinational enterprises, although the final product will be assembled in one particular country. The national identity of even simply made traded products may be difficult to determine if a country's rules of origin regime is weak. Rules of origin seek to establish the location of value-adding production, and they have become an increasingly important element of FTA negotiations in the Asia-Pacific region and worldwide. Using a hypothetical example, if Country A is not able to assure Country B that its exports are substantively made within its own territory, then

Country B may see this as compromising the whole bilateral FTA arrangement, as firms based in third countries enjoy free trade access to its markets by using Country A as a conduit. This may take the form of *trade deflection*, where in this case goods from third countries are transhipped through Country A to Country B under free trade conditions. As noted in Appendix A, FTA negotiations between New Zealand and Hong Kong broke down in 2002 because of concerns that goods from China could be transhipped through Hong Kong to New Zealand without being subjected to rigorous rules of origin examination.

While RoO are helpful insofar that they help establish whether traded goods are eligible for FTA treatment, they may also be viewed as a protectionist mechanism by introducing certain restrictions on commerce (Krishna and Krueger 1995; Kruger 1997). The WTO (2002b) has noted the lack of transparency and significant complexity found in many RoO regimes that can incur considerable administrative and operational costs for producers. This may especially apply to transnational business operations by imposing new stipulations on local content sourcing and hence restricting the scope to trade inputs within their international production networks.

Moreover, various complications can arise where *preferential rules of origin* (PRoO) are created as an outcome of FTA negotiations. The preferential aspect derives from one FTA partner being conferred a RoO advantage over another, whether this is another separate FTA partner or non-FTA partner. For example, one FTA partner may be conferred greater flexibility in RoO compliance (e.g. lower local content ratios) than others, and this is more likely to occur when a large number of product-specific RoO are contained within an FTA that allows for preferential differentiation between trade partners. This can be seen for instance in the US's FTAs with Singapore and Australia (see Appendix E) where exporters to the US market face different rules on the certain product sectors, e.g. textiles. Significant additional complexity can be brought here to a country's trade policy regime, leading to convoluted regulations governing international trade generally, and making RoO compliance even more costly for producers. Indeed, some exporters may decide to forgo the preferential FTA tariff rates if the margin of preference is not deemed sufficient to offset the administrative burden of compliance.[25]

Some WTO members, such as South Korea, Australia and India, have raised the question in NGR talks as to whether or not PRoO should come under the rubric of "other regulations of commerce" (ORCs) or "other restrictive regulations of commerce" (ORRCs) under Article XXIV, and therefore must comply like tariff lines to the WTO's rules on RTAs[26] (Mathis 2003). As with the SAT issue, there are ambiguities here that many NGR parties are seeking clarity on: in this case, Article XXIV offers no definition of ORCs. Certainly, PRoO can have the effect of regulating the entry of imported products in an FTA to a significant degree, and potentially have an adverse (i.e. trade diversionary) effect upon third party imports just as tariffs can. At the same time, it is widely acknowledged that the complete harmonisation of PRoO is extremely difficult to achieve. Furthermore, FTA negotiating parties may lack the motive to do so given PRoO allow governments to conciliate domestic industry interest groups that are resistant to trade liberalisation, for instance by having stricter rules (e.g. high minimum local content) in those sectors where competition from the FTA partner is particularly intense.

Moreover, as the WTO Agreement on Rules of Origin currently stand, the harmonisation of PRoO lies outside the ambit of multilateral (i.e. WTO) negotiation. While attempts at the harmonisation of *non-preferential* RoO under the existing WTO Agreement have made little progress to date, the continued fragmentation of global production would seem to make this objective more critically important (Estevadeordal and Suominen 2003). There has been, at least, a consensus in NGR talks that the harmonisation of PRoO, notwithstanding the difficulties, is a desirable long run objective (WTO 2002c). Whether this will be achieved will, though, ultimately depend on whether PRoO are commonly viewed as generating significant trade diversion effects to present a cause of concern. As with the SAT issue, no real consensus had been achieved on this matter in NGR talks by the end of 2005 (WTO 2005c). Chapter 4 presents a broader discussion on RoO related issues.

1.3   Core determinants of the Asia-Pacific's new FTA trend

Earlier in this chapter we considered those factors identified by the WTO that explained the global proliferation of FTAs. These help explain the new Asia-Pacific FTA trend to a degree but there are specific core determinants that particularly apply to the region, namely: (i) trade policy paradigm shift; (ii) trade institution inertia; (iii) FTA 'catch-up' with other regions; (iv) the impact of the 1997/98 East Asian financial crisis; and (v) strategic diplomacy motives. There are overlaps between these core determinants, and additional specific determinants apply to different countries as Chapter 2 discusses in extensive detail. These core determinants examined below apply to either all Asia-Pacific countries or subsets of them, for example East Asian countries.

1.3.1   Trade policy paradigm shift

There are two main aspects or types of this core determinant. The first relates to the change in the economic ideology underlying the trade policies of certain Asia-Pacific countries, especially those from East Asia that had been long-time ardent practitioners of neo-mercantilism: that is, the dualistic protection and promotion of strategic export industry development.

However, the gathering forces of globalisation compelled many East Asian states to steadily adopt a more neo-liberal approach to trade policy from generally the 1980s onwards, and thus becoming more receptive to the idea of FTAs by the 1990s. Japan and South Korea are stand-out examples in this respect, and moreover FTAs provided an external pressure mechanism that has been harness to catalyse domestic economic reform. The Anglo-Pacific countries (Australia, Canada, New Zealand and the US) plus Singapore, Chile and perhaps also Mexico had, though, been overt neo-liberal advocates on matters of the trade policy, so the economic ideology shift aspect does not apply to this important group of nations that have been amongst the most FTA active in the Asia-Pacific. Furthermore, whether neo-liberalism has actually supplanted neo-mercantilism and its underpinning economic nationalist impulses in East Asian trade policy practice is a matter of some debate (Beeson and Islam 2005). Japan, South Korea and other East Asian countries like Malaysia and Thailand have remained, for example, very resistant to opening up traditionally protected industry sectors to their FTA partners.

The second aspect or type concerns the *modus operandi* of how a country advocates trade liberalisation should be achieved. Many Asia-Pacific states had placed great emphasis and faith on multilateral trade diplomacy in this regard, eschewing bilateral and regional FTAs on account that they offered only a second-best outcome on market access and, moreover, served to undermine efforts at the multilateral level as previously discussed. This particular shift in trade policy paradigm is often referred to as a progression from a multilateral to a multi-track approach. It can be applied to many Asia-Pacific states owing to their undeveloped FTA policy in general by the mid-1990s but especially to those nations that had singularly advocated multilateralism as the only effective route to achieving trade liberalisation. We can place Japan, South Korea, Australia, New Zealand, and to some extent the US and Canada, into this category. Moves towards a multi-track approach signified by FTAs have been, though, more an outcome of other determinants outlined below rather than a determinant in itself. Having said this, for certain countries (e.g. New Zealand) the origins of this shift predated many key determinant events and developments, such as the 1997/98 financial crisis and the WTO's Seattle Ministerial debacle of 1999, but these countries are in a minority. In sum, the actual relevance of both aspects of this core determinant is questionable for the reasons noted.

1.3.2 Trade institution inertia

The trade institutions in question are the WTO, APEC and the ASEAN Free Trade Area (AFTA). Their respective problems experienced since the late 1990s in advancing trade liberalisation within the Asia-Pacific led many of the region's states to look to an alternative path, namely bilateral FTA projects. We shall examine each of these trade institutions in turn.

The WTO

Both the WTO's agenda and membership have continually expanded and become more diverse. Reconciling the different trade interests arising from these twinned developments has been the fundamental cause of the WTO's inertia on advancing trade liberalisation, and it is the rift between developed and developing countries where the main problem lies. Most observers cite the failed launch of the much heralded New 'Millennium' Round (NMR) at the WTO's December 1999 Seattle Ministerial Meeting as a critical juncture. Up till this point, differences of interest arising between developed and developing country members had become apparent to some extent, but it was at Seattle that these came to a head. In essence, developed countries were advocating the inclusion of 'new' trade issues such as competition policy and environment more firmly onto the WTO agenda, i.e. often referred to as the 'Singapore issues', arising from the 1996 Ministerial Meeting that was hosted by the city-state. Meanwhile, developing countries were unhappy that many labour-intensive industries such as agriculture and textiles (where they possessed a competitive advantage) were still heavily protected by the developed world. In addition to this, civil society groups were complaining about the WTO's alleged lack of accountability and transparency, and the elite governed nature of the organisation itself. While the civil society protests on the streets of Seattle during December 1999 dominated the popular media's coverage of the meeting, it was the growing rift between developed and developing countries that posed the more serious predicament for the WTO. It was thus not the civil society protests that primarily caused the aborted launch of the NMR.

Although a number of Asia-Pacific states (e.g. Japan, South Korea, Thailand, Singapore) had initiated new bilateral FTA policies before the WTO's 'Seattle debacle', this setback on the multilateral front played some part in intensifying the new Asia-Pacific trend thereafter. Chapter 2 explores the varying degrees of impact that post-Seattle WTO inertia had on catalysing the FTA policies of different countries from the region as each looked to bilateral routes as alternative insurance on securing market access. As Dobson (2001) remarked, "East Asia's export-led growth has been highly dependent on trade liberalisation in the major OECD economies. If this source of growth momentum declines or is uncertain, other sources must be found" (p. 1004). Despite the successful launch of the rebranded Doha[27] 'Development' Round in November 2001, subsequent difficulties leading up to and after the September 2003 Cancun Ministerial Meeting seems to have made the WTO inertia motive stronger still. This applies even to ardent supporters of the multilateral process such as New Zealand, whose trade minister, Jim Sutton, was of the view that while the multilateral route to free trade was 'Plan A', recent troubles at the WTO has made the bilateral route the increasingly significant 'Plan B' (presumably B for 'Bilaterals').[28]

As the December 2005 deadline for concluding the DDR at the Hong Kong Ministerial approached, the divide between developed and developing countries was as wide as ever. At Cancun, a newly formed coalition of developing countries emerged, the G20 group,[29] led by the big emerging developing countries of China, India and Brazil. While many countries in this group maintained quite high tariffs on agricultural imports themselves, the G20 has pressured the EU, US, Japan and other developed countries to relinquish their export subsidies and other market-distorting measures affecting farm product trade. The G20 demanded this concession before it was prepared to tackle its own trade barriers[30] and substantively address the 'new' trade issues being pushed by developed countries, who themselves were unwilling to move significantly on farm trade issues until significant progress in other areas was achieved. Standoffs in other areas such as services trade and industrial tariffs also persisted through 2005. At the December 2005 Hong Kong Ministerial it was agreed that all export subsidies (which made up just two percent of all farm product subsidies) would be eliminated by 2013. It was also agreed at the Hong Kong Ministerial to grant improved market access to the world's 49 poorest countries and provide more assistance to West African cotton farmers but a complete DDR agreement remained some way off. WTO members agreed to extend the deadline by a year to December 2006 to conclude negotiations. Failure to do so could prove critical. This is because the fast-track negotiating authority of the US Government runs out in July 2007, and there is a strong chance it will not be renewed (see Chapter 2, US section). Given that it normally takes around six months to a year for trade negotiators to finalise and 'legally scrub' a global trade agreement once reached in talks, this provides very little room for overshooting if this extended deadline is missed. Without fast-track negotiating authority, any WTO accord to which the US is party is open to scrutiny and questioning by US Congress before any negotiated outcome is attained. The prospect of a failed DDR will only stimulate the further development of FTA activity in the Asia-Pacific and elsewhere.

Asia-Pacific Economic Co-operation (APEC) forum

Inertia experienced by the Asia-Pacific's most comprehensive regional economic grouping on trade liberalisation also played a part in stimulating FTA activity in the region. APEC was established in 1989 between 12 member economies with three prime objectives: (i) promoting regional economic growth, development and co-operation; (ii) upholding an open multilateral trading system; (iii) engendering a sense of regional economic community in the Asia-Pacific in general. These were to be realised through inter-governmental consultations and, where appropriate, convergent directions in economic policy-making between APEC member states. It thus sought to avoid EU-style forms of institutionalised, treaty-driven regional economic co-operation and integration (Dieter 1997; Ravenhill 2001; Yamazawa 2000). There was hence no intent to construct a Pacific trade bloc but rather to foster a constructive economic interdependence and economic policy dialogue between members. Membership expanded to 18 member economies by the early 1990s by which time APEC had found a bold centrepiece project, this being to create a free trade and investment zone across the Asia-Pacific. It was first formally proposed at the 1993 APEC summit convened in Seattle based on recommendations made from the organisation's Eminent Person's Group (EPG). The American EPG chair, Fred Bergsten, had allegedly first advocated the creation of a Pacific free trade area, or PAFTA, but most Asian and Oceanic EPG members argued the case for a free trade and investment zone based on the principles of 'open regionalism', this being a non-discriminatory process in which APEC members open up their economies unilaterally not just to each other but also to non-members, i.e. on an MFN basis.[31] Such an approach was seen as WTO-consistent, and at the following year's summit at Bogor in 1994 this objective was formally agreed.

At the 1995 summit in Osaka, Individual Action Plans (IAPs) for how to realise the 'Bogor goals' (as they became known) were laid out. Each APEC member was obliged to declare in its own IAP how it was to achieve its free trade commitments on a unilateral and voluntary basis by 2010 for developed economy members, and 2020 for developing economy members. However, this first strategy of APEC's to advance trade liberalisation is widely acknowledged to have been an abject failure from the very beginning (Bergsten 2000; Findlay *et al* 2003; Ravenhill 2001; Yamazawa 1998). The main problem was that each member was reluctant to undertake 'concerted unilateral liberalisation' without direct reciprocal concessions made by others, as occurred in FTA negotiations. The issue of 'reciprocity choice' is discussed further in Chapter 4. A second APEC strategy soon emerged, this being *sectoral liberalisation*, strongly advocated by the US in particular and which was kick-started by the successful launch of the Information Technology Agreement (ITA) at the 1996 summit convened at Subic in the Philippines, that was then forwarded to the WTO where it became a plurilateral trade accord signed by a number of non-APEC parties including the EU. Following on from the ITA's success, at the 1997 APEC summit in Vancouver the US led the proposal for an Early Voluntary Sectoral Liberalisation (EVSL) scheme that aimed to liberalise trade in 15 targeted sectors (nine of which were conferred special priority) by the time of the following summit held at Kuala Lumpur in 1998.

In the chosen EVSL sectors a balance was sought between primary and manufacturing industries, and hence broadly between developing and developed country interests. However, Japan's proposal to include transportation equipment (including automobiles) was not supported, and Tokyo was also frustrated by American opposition to include textiles on the

EVSL list, a sector that Japan thought was important to developing East Asian members. More importantly, Japan was from the start opposed to the inclusion of forestry and fishery sectors, the first being mainly advocated by the US and the second being championed by Australia, Indonesia, New Zealand and Thailand (Aggarwal and Ravenhill 2001; Krauss 2004; Rapkin 2001). Despite being more or less isolated on this issue, Japan's steadfast refusal to concede anything in these sectors brought EVSL negotiations to a stalemate. It was decided to pass the issue to the WTO for further discussion, thus further undermining APEC credibility on trade liberalisation (Berger 1999; Okamoto 2004; Ravenhill 2000; Wesley 2001).

In addition to the collapse of the EVSL talks tensions also arose between APEC members at the 1998 Kuala Lumpur summit over East Asia's financial crisis. Member economies from the region were disappointed by the response from other members (especially the United States), and APEC itself as a regional economic organisation, at providing timely and substantive assistance to those East Asian members most in need. The 1997/98 financial crisis is explored in more detail later in the chapter, but suffice to say here that it exacerbated rifts between certain East Asian members and their Anglo-Pacific counterparts. It was primarily APEC's Anglo-Pacific member states – sharing a common market-liberal tradition – that had championed the organisation's trade liberalisation programmes. In contrast, East Asian states had been more interested in APEC's trade facilitation schemes as well as its economic and technical co-operation (ecotech) programmes. This was natural given that most East Asian members were still developing countries, with some lacking adjustment capacities to cope with comprehensive trade liberalisation. Furthermore, many retained the vestiges of a neo-mercantilist approach to trade policy and were therefore less inclined towards a trade liberalisation agenda within APEC largely determined by the Anglo-Pacific states (Ravenhill 2001).

The 1998 APEC summit clearly exposed these political economy differences, and it was the consequent rifts within its membership that led to FTA coalition-building. The important point here was that it was not just APEC's failure to advance its trade liberalisation agenda that stimulated the development of FTA activity within the Asia-Pacific: conflicts of interest between different subsets of APEC membership also provided strategic diplomacy motives for doing so. At the 1998 summit, as the EVSL talks were heading towards stalemate, a coalition of Anglo-Pacific members – namely the US, Australia and New Zealand – and two other pro-trade liberalisers, Singapore and Chile, raised the idea of establishing a 'Pacific-5' FTA between them. This was further discussed at the September 1999 APEC summit at Auckland[32] and, although this never came to fruition, from this derived the Singapore–New Zealand FTA project (the ANZSCEP being a key milestone new Asia-Pacific FTA trend as it was the first FTA signed by an East Asian country) and eventually the quadrilateral Trans-Pacific Strategic

Economic Partnership Agreement (TPSEPA) signed by Singapore, New Zealand, Chile and Brunei in June 2005. Chapter 3's case study on the TPSEPA project examines more closely how the motives for the derivative Pacific-5 FTA idea were to catalyse trade liberalisation movement within APEC after the EVSL scheme had failed.[33]

More generally, APEC's trade liberalisation inertia to date could be partly explained by its lack of institutional or regime capacity to see through ambitious projects. This is an inherent problem with large international groupings like APEC in that its agenda often has to work at the lowest common denominator level in order to bring all members into agreement on particular issues, like on trade. Similarities can be made with the WTO here in that expanding membership, with the ensuing accommodation of more complex interests and diversity, can ultimately restrict what an organisation can achieve. APEC was perhaps always too large and diverse a grouping to ever venture on the Bogor Goals project, and that smaller sub-regional groupings in the Asia-Pacific was always going to be more viable. Bilateral FTAs were thus seen as more viable routes to realising trade liberalisation and strengthening economic co-operation within the Asia-Pacific as lowest common denominators only need to be found between pairs of countries, and moreover countries can beforehand select less problematic trade partners with which to do FTA business with. The impact of the new Asia-Pacific FTA trend on APEC itself is discussed in Chapter 4.

ASEAN Free Trade Area (AFTA)

We have established that trade liberalisation inertia at the WTO was relevant to all Asia-Pacific states that had initiated FTA policies at the turn of the millennium, while APEC's own problems with advancing towards into free trade goals had particularly impacted upon it's most ardent trade liberalisation advocates. At the Southeast Asia sub-regional level, similar difficulties experienced within ASEAN made certain member states – in particular Singapore and Thailand – look closer at their FTA options (Sen 2004). ASEAN was established in 1967 between the five original member countries of Malaysia, Singapore, the Philippines, Indonesia and Thailand. Brunei joined in 1984 and during the 1990s ASEAN's membership increased to ten countries after Cambodia, Laos, Myanmar and Vietnam (the CLMV group) joined the organisation. Under the conspicuous promotion of the US, ASEAN was originally conceived as a group of ideologically compatible regimes in Southeast Asia that could together act as a bulwark against a further communist advance in the region. Thus, there was initially a strong underlying political rationale behind ASEAN's formation. Although there were attempts at cultivating regional economic co-operation within the ASEAN group, these achieved limited success during the Cold War period. With the ending of the Cold War and ensuing diminishment of the 'invading' communist threat, ASEAN was compelled to find a new economic rationale in order to retain a sense of regional organisational purpose. This could be understood in the broader global context of a shift from geo-political to geo-economic competition in the new post-Cold War era. Plans to create AFTA, first proposed at ASEAN's 1992 summit, thus provided the organisation's new economic *raison d'etre* (Dosch *et al* 2004).

The ASEAN group had been implementing AFTA since the early 1990s, with an aim of realising the core trade liberalisation objectives by the end of 2002 (see Appendix A), but the 1997/98 financial crisis severely tested member states' commitment to the process as they became increasingly preoccupied with domestic economic problems. This especially applied to Indonesia and the Philippines – two of the largest ASEAN economies – whose crisis-induced economic and political turmoil was particularly pronounced (Ruland 2000; Stubbs 2000). Singapore's proposal in 1998 to actually accelerate the pace of AFTA trade liberalisation was opposed by Indonesia, and the general chairman of Indonesia's Chamber of Commerce and Industry, Aburizal Bakrie, even called for the implementation of AFTA between core ASEAN states to be postponed from 2002 to 2005. Meanwhile, the Philippine government expressed concern over how the AFTA-induced loss of tariff revenue would significantly compromise its fiscal position. Both Indonesia and the Philippines unilaterally delayed AFTA liberalisation of their respective petrochemical trade regimes, to the particular annoyance of Singapore.[34] Furthermore, tensions arose between Malaysia and Thailand over the former's decision to delay the phase out of its tariffs on automotive product imports in the AFTA schedule by three years.[35]

Not only did the 1997/98 financial crisis lead many ASEAN states to drag their feet on AFTA trade liberalisation, but it also made AFTA itself a relatively less attractive proposition given the subsequent decline of the sub-region's overall regional market value. Singapore's highly active bilateral FTA strategy was seen by many of its fellow ASEAN member states – and Malaysia especially – as in some way compensating for AFTA downward-revised market potential. Moreover, Malaysia took Singapore to task over its 2001 proposal to extend AFTA to Australia and New Zealand, which was then perceived by Kuala Lumpur as undermining AFTA's rationale, integrity and key purpose, that is to consolidate a Southeast Asian economic community.[36] As Ramon Navaratnam, a former Malaysian Government minister, argued in a letter to the *New Straits Times* in July 2001, "Even if Singapore's Free Trade Agreements are consistent with AFTA and WTO, the real issue is whether Singapore's unholy haste is consistent with the ASEAN spirit of optimising co-operation, consultation and fraternal goodwill, in the longer term."[37] Malaysia had been further critical of Singapore's readiness to omit agriculture from its FTA talks with Japan, and include measures linking trade to labour and environment clauses in negotiations with the US.[38] However, Thailand soon followed Singapore's lead in developing bilateral FTA projects with a number of trade partners outside with Southeast Asia (Desker 2004; Dent 2006a). This particular aspect of trade liberalisation inertia was only really relevant to these two ASEAN member states in the early phase of the new Asia-Pacific FTA trend, other member states – including the once critical Malaysia – were compelled to participate as the trend intensified. The reasons for this are discussed under theme of 'isolation avoidance' in the strategic diplomacy section below. In addition, the emerging relationship between FTA bilateralism and economic regionalism (e.g. AFTA) within Southeast Asia has lessons for the wider Asia-Pacific region, a matter examined in some detail in Chapter 4.

1.3.3 FTA 'Catch-up' with other regions

Chapter 2 discusses in specific detail how this was one of the most important motivating factors behind the FTA policies of Asia-Pacific countries. We have already examined the explosive growth of FTAs globally during the 1990s and how the Asia-Pacific was a relative latecomer to this development. Many of the region's states were concerned, then, of being denied the same trade preferences that rival economies had to big markets (e.g. East European nations' FTA links to the EU; Mexico's access to the US market through NAFTA), as well as missing out on the other economic and political benefits (e.g. trade economies of scale, strengthened diplomatic and security alliances) that FTAs were believed to confer. How the trade diversion of other FTAs was negatively impacting upon the region was also a key concern. Frankel and Wei (1997) surveyed various empirical studies on the effect of NAFTA on East Asian economies. Work undertaken by both Braga *et al* (1994) and Noland (1994) predicted that Asian labour-intensive producers would lose significant market share in the US and Canada to Mexican firms as a result of trade diversion. Noland (1994) suggested this could amount to between a one to three percent share for South Korean firms in these industries by 2000. Meanwhile, Hufbauer and Schott (1993) estimated that NAFTA could divert around US$300 million worth of manufactured exports annually for South Korea and Taiwan each, and for Southeast Asian NIEs around US$350 million annually, with machinery, transport equipment, consumer goods and clothing sectors particularly hit. Kreinen (1992) and McCleery (1993) looked at the investment diversion effects of NAFTA on East Asian economies. For instance, McCleery (1993) estimated that Indonesia would lose four to five percent of its inward FDI levels as a result of NAFTA, equating to 2.2 percent of its GDP, while Singapore would lose two to three percent of its inward FDI that in turn would lead to a 1.3 percent drop in its GDP. Similarly, Thailand would experience an FDI loss of around four to five percent of its total inward flow and a consequently a one percent fall in its GDP. American foreign investment in Mexico did indeed rise substantially during the 1990s but it is difficult to ascertain whether this FDI would have been destined for East Asia had NAFTA never came into existence. Nevertheless, predictions of substantial trade and investment diversion effects from NAFTA and other major RTAs (e.g. the Single European Market, Mercosur) caused some disquiet amongst East Asian nations as the 1990s progressed. As previously noted in this chapter, East Asia (above all Northeast Asia) and Oceania especially lagged behind in the global FTA trend, and so for these regions the 'catch-up' factor was particularly relevant. Research fieldwork for this book also suggests it strongly applied to the US too, which felt it should keep up with the expanding FTA network of the EU, its main economic rival.

1.3.4   The impact of the 1997/98 East Asian financial crisis

The influence of the 1997/98 East Asian financial crisis has already been commented upon, at least regarding its indirect effect upon the new Asia-Pacific FTA trend, for example on causing underlying frictions within APEC that played some part in derailing its trade liberalisation projects, most notably the EVSL scheme. As one would expect, the main indirect and direct effects of the crisis, however, has been on East Asian countries. The core issue here is how the crisis contagion exposed both the extent of regional economic interdependence that had developed by this time, and the lack of co-operative mechanisms between the region's states to deal with such serious region-wide predicaments. This connects with *co-operative diplomacy* discussed under the section theme of 'strategic diplomacy motives' below. Japan's endeavours to rectify this, primarily through new initiatives aimed at improving regional financial governance but also its own model of FTAs (see Chapters 2 and 4), should be particularly noted. This model, in which free trade was embedded within a wider 'economic partnership agreement' devised to enhance co-operative ties with its trade partners, was evident at an early post-crisis stage in the Japan–Korea FTA project (JKFTA), first proposed in 1998. Other intra-regional East Asian FTAs followed in a similar vein. The Japan–Singapore and Singapore–South Korea bilateral FTAs emulated the JKFTA's approach on fostering economic co-operation. Furthermore, the ASEAN–China FTA is embedded within a Framework Agreement on Comprehensive Economic Cooperation that seeks to develop a sense of economic community between all signatory parties. In addition to the intent found within the text of these agreements to better manage the economic interdependence between East Asian states, the FTAs concerned have also been driven by the motive of strengthening politico-diplomatic ties generally, thus leading to a situation whereby future economic crises should be, in theory, more effectively addressed. FTAs were seen as potentially very important in this respect because they were the most comprehensive and significant international economic agreements that East Asian states had signed between themselves, and for that matter with other Asia-Pacific states (Pangestu and Gooptu 2004).

There are additional points to consider. First, the 1997/98 financial crisis caused some disturbance regarding market access security in the region, and thus FTAs could from one perspective be seen as sending a signal that key East Asian countries like Japan and South Korea were not going to retreat to defensive protectionism but rather continue to open up their markets to each other and countries outside the region. Second, and in connection with previously made points, FTAs were used to help expedite the process of post-crisis economic reform. For both Japan and South Korea, free trade agreements were a means to harness 'foreign pressure' to help overcome entrenched domestic opposition to economic reform, restructuring and opening up the economy generally. For South Korea specifically, FTAs were conceived to help achieve such ends and make the country an 'open trading nation'. While Japan did not directly succumb to the 1997/98 financial crisis, its moribund economy was indirectly affected (e.g. through loss of export revenue), and moreover the regional crisis raised the imperative to push through new economic reform and restructuring policies. The development of an FTA policy was a high profile element of this. Singapore and Thailand's governments used a similar argument that FTAs were a way of pulling their national economies, as well as the wider region, out of the crisis quagmire through actualising economic openness and reform.

1.3.5 Strategic diplomacy motives

This core determinant is mostly concerned with politico-diplomatic or geopolitical motives for FTAs but that also can include underlying economic motives. Here, strategic diplomacy is broadly concerned with how free trade agreements are used to primarily strengthen relations with key trade partners, and related to a question posed to research interviewees in fieldwork research conducted for this book. There answers given generally fell into one of the four sub-categories of strategic diplomacy outlined below.

The first concerns *co-operative diplomacy*, which has already been discussed in the context of 1997/98 East Asian financial crisis. This derives principally from the neo-liberal institutionalist view that intensifying FTA activity is a means to better manage the growing economic interdependence that is binding states within the region closely together. Interdependence creates situations where states face increasingly common economic challenges, problems and shared destinies generally. According to neo-liberal institutionalists, this necessitates the development of co-operative mechanisms between states (such as FTAs, potentially) so that this interdependence may be more effectively managed. Of course, East Asia is just one constituent element of a wider, increasingly economic interdependent Asia-Pacific region, hence co-operative diplomacy motives apply in this broader geographic sense but it has nevertheless been most relevant to East Asia in its post-crisis aftermath.

The second category is *security alliance diplomacy*, which is informed more by a neo-realist view that FTAs – like all international economic agreements – are ultimately subordinate to underlying security objectives shared by alliance partners, such as the US, Singapore, Australia and Thailand. This is particularly relevant to the US in maintaining its security interests, and politico-diplomatic influence generally, in the Asia-Pacific, the imperative of which has strengthened since the 11 September 2001 terrorist attacks on the United States. For many of its partners in the region, the security context of their FTAs with the US has been a crucial aspect, the FTA itself being seen as a reward for assisting the Bush Administration with its 'war on terror', with AUSFTA being a clear case of this, but also more importantly a free trade agreement can help consolidate a security alliance with the US. By July 2005, Singapore remained the only Southeast and East Asian country that had an FTA with the United States, and in this month it signed an enhanced security agreement with Washington, henceforth bestowed with security alliance privileges not enjoyed by other Southeast Asian states.[39]

Competitive bilateralism derives from another neo-realist perspective in that FTAs are a function of inter-state competition for economic and political influence. This may be particularly relevant amongst hegemonic contenders, such as China and Japan within East Asia, or China, Japan and the US within the Asia-Pacific. It is widely accepted, for instance, that Japan's proposal for establishing an FTA link with the ASEAN group was a strategic counter-reaction to China's earlier proposed FTA with ASEAN. Competitive bilateralism may also involve the use of FTAs to extend a major power's influence over the trade regulatory environment or shape trade diplomacy norms within the region. Previous illustrative reference has been made regarding these matters to competing rules of origin regimes. Competitive bilateralism also extends to the notion of contesting FTA models in the Asia-Pacific, for example between Japan's 'developmental–industrial', or 'economic partnership agreement' FTA model and the US's 'asymmetric neo-liberal' FTA model, as later discussed in Chapter 4.

Isolation avoidance, the fourth category, is related in some way to competitive bilateralism, and may be also linked to Baldwin's (1999) 'domino effect' of FTA activity in that as this intensifies so the does the incentive for non-participating countries to themselves engage in the FTA trend: the costs of being an outsider increase as the number of insiders grows. If we take Southeast Asia as an example, Singapore's securing of free market access to the US, Japan, Australia and New Zealand – with Thailand close behind Singapore's lead – meant that other ASEAN member states were placed at a commercial disadvantage because they lacked preferential access to such key markets. This was reinforced by rivals from outside Southeast Asia, such as Chile and Mexico, making similar gains. As previously noted, Malaysia was compelled to reverse its criticism of bilateral FTAs and engage in the trend so that its exporters could compete on level terms with its rivals based in Singapore and Thailand as their FTA links expanded. The same principle of different states seeking the same parity treatment of others in foreign markets can be applied to the wider Asia-Pacific region. For instance, New Zealand has tried desperately hard to initiate FTA negotiations with the US to match the trade preferences conferred in AUSFTA, and by the same token minimise the trade diversion impact AUSFTA had on the New Zealand economy, especially its critically important agricultural sector where export competition with Australia was extensive. These twin factors of matching trade preferences and minimising is diversion effects are the key drivers of isolation avoidance, and that have provided the new Asia-Pacific FTA trend with a self-propelling momentum. Competitive bilateralism has worked in a similar fashion, motivated more though by geopolitical reasons. In essence, the dynamics of both primarily arise out of counter-reactions to preceding FTAs signed within the region, although proactive strategic diplomacy can explain certain aspects of competitive bilateralism as suggested above.

1.4   Main hindrances to FTA projects in the Asia-Pacific

In addition to identifying the main determinants behind the new Asia-Pacific FTA trend, this chapter also highlights the main hindrances that have confronted the region's states in developing FTA projects in the region. As with the 'determinants' section, the purpose of this section is to preface discussions on these matters specific to each country's FTA policy.

1.4.1   Agriculture

Agriculture has proved by far the most problematic area in the development of Asia-Pacific FTA projects overall. The main challenge has been for countries to either liberalise their own long protected agricultural sectors, or to convince their FTA partners to do the same. Often, these challenges arise simultaneously. As previously noted, only a very few of the world's FTAs have eliminated all duties and other barriers in agricultural trade, e.g. the ANZSCEP. Most FTAs have only succeeded in removing existing tariff peaks in the trade of agricultural products, moreover the widespread use of the 'positive list' approach in granting concessions on agricultural goods in the majority of FTAs negotiated has limited the scope of potential concessions. The converse applies in FTA negotiations on industrial products where a 'negative list' approach is generally used (WTO 2002a). It is not only conventional trade barriers that are a problem but also the substantial and various forms of domestic support (e.g. subsidies) given to farmers – especially in developed countries – that provide them with a significant commercial advantage in world markets.

The WTO reported that in 2001 the total support for agriculture in developed countries came to US$311 billion, and that the prices received by farmers in these countries were on average 31 percent above world price levels (WTO 2002a). In terms of producer support as a share of farmers earnings, Switzerland came top with 69 percent, South Korea second with 64 percent, Japan third with 59 percent, the EU fourth with 35 percent, and the US fifth with 21 percent. At the global level, the EU is invariably labelled as the biggest offender owing to both the sheer operational scale of Europe's Common Agricultural Policy (CAP) and its annual US$80 billion budget. Yet certain Asia-Pacific states also provide high levels of market-distorting support and trade protection to their farmers. Japan, South Korea and Taiwan, on a per capita basis, give the highest levels of support and are the most agri-protectionist in the region. The US too offers very high levels of support and protection in certain agri-sectors, like cotton (where each farmer receives on average around US$150,000 in subsidies per annum) and sugar. Addressing protectionism embodied in domestic support systems on agriculture can only be effectively done at the multilateral level. For example, if a country concedes to reduce its domestic subsidy levels then all trade partners will benefit: single trade partners cannot be singled out for preferential treatment through FTAs in this case. Most developing countries in the Asia-Pacific also place high import tariffs on many agricultural products, making it a highly sensitive and difficult issue in FTA negotiations. Even where agriculture trade flows represent a miniscule share of total trade between countries, disputes over just a few farm products can often jeopardise the whole FTA deal. The row between high-tech trading Japan and South Korea over gim seaweed, leading to the stalled JKFTA talks for many months from late 2004 into 2006, is a good illustration of this.

In Chapter 2, we examine how FTA-led attempts to liberalise and reform a country's agriculture sector reveals the often complex interface between domestic politics and the negotiation of international trade agreements. Those resistant to liberalisation and reform tend to make similar defensive arguments about the uniqueness of agriculture. They contend that agriculture is not just an industry or business, like other sectors of the national economy, as it performs multiple functions valued by society. A recent OECD report considered the defining aspects of the *multifunctionality of agriculture* as being: "(i) the existence of multiple commodity and non-commodity outputs that are jointly produced by agriculture; and (ii) the fact that some of the non-commodity outputs exhibit the characteristics of externalities or public goods, with the result that markets for these goods do not exist or function poorly" (OECD 2001: 7). In addition, Japan's Ministry of Agriculture, Forestry and Fisheries (MAFF) outlines this multi-functionality in the following constituent elements: (i) land conservation (including the prevention of floods and soil erosion); (ii) fostering water resources; (iii) the preservation of the natural environment (including the maintenance of bio-diversity and wildlife habitat); (iv) the preservation of traditional culture, communities and amenities in rural areas; and (v) the formation of scenic landscapes (MAFF 2004). Agriculture's importance to a nation's environment, heritage and culture make it politically a very difficult sector of the economy to open up to foreign competition. A 2003 Pacific Economic Co-operation Council (PECC) paper on Asia-Pacific FTAs argued that, "we have to estimate the marginal loss (gain) of the social value caused by multifunctionality as agricultural production shrinks (expands), if multifunctionality is to be placed at the centre of the proposal for the agricultural trade negotiations" (PECC 2003a: 8). However, estimating such social values is notoriously problematic in both scientific and political terms.

The other main defensive argument from agri-protectionists concerns *food security*, which may be defined as, "a situation in which all households have both physical and economic access to adequate food for all members and where households are not at risk of losing such access" (PECC 2003a: 9). This is an issue for many developed and developing Asia-Pacific countries alike, but especially for the natural resource-poor Northeast Asian economies of Japan, South Korea and Taiwan who already currently import around 60 to 70 percent of domestically consumed foodstuffs. These food import ratios have steadily risen over the years, and hence the caution regarding FTA-induced foreign competition compromising the indigenous food production capacities of the economies further still. However, natural resource paucity is not the only reason for this food security predicament. Inefficient production methods are also to blame, although this is partly owing to the lack of large, cultivatable flat open fields in Japan, South Korea and Taiwan that does not make it easy to capture productive economies of scale. Nevertheless, these economies do have considerable technological and capital resources at their disposal to better address domestic production capacity issues, and their FTA policies have helped focus in on this and other matters of agriculture sector reform, e.g. see the Korea–Chile FTA project case study in Chapter 3.

1.4.2   Other 'sensitive' industry issues

There are a number of other industries that have proved notably 'sensitive' to FTA trade liberalisation in the Asia-Pacific, and these may be categorised into four main types. The first concerns those in *structural decline*. These are usually labour-intensive industries in developed countries whose competitive advantage in such sectors has gradually diminished owing to rising labour costs and the extensive transfer of underpinning mature technologies to developing countries, where the competitive advantage now firmly lies. Prominent industry examples are textiles, clothing and footwear (TCF), steel and simple manufactured products, e.g. toys, kitchenware. Although developed country employment in these sectors has shrunk considerably over time, it tends to be geographically concentrated in industrial districts, for example steel in certain West Virginian and Pennsylvanian towns in the US. Further contractions of the industry, whether through the impact of foreign competition or other factors, hence lead to further income and prosperity losses in already depressed areas of the country, making it a politically sensitive issue. Many if not most FTAs signed within the Asia-Pacific thus have an elaborate scheme of tariff liberalisation phase-ins (often with long time frames) specific to particular 'sensitive' industries to allow them time to gradually adjust to FTA competitive conditions.

The second type of 'sensitive' industry is that with a strong *socio-cultural dimension*, especially if they are integral to social, culture-arts and health policies. One high-profile example is Australia's Pharmaceuticals Benefits Scheme (PBS), a system that offers below market priced pharmaceuticals to the Australian public. American drug companies such as Pfizer had complained during AUSFTA negotiations that the PBS significantly reduced their profit margins in the Australian market and wanted according changes to the system. Chapter 3's case study on AUSFTA examines Australian public and political opposition to this based on an unwillingness to trade-off health and social policy objectives against market access concessions offered by US negotiators. Australia and also South Korea have resisted US demands to open up its entertainment media industries (e.g. film and television) to American firms, primarily because these are deemed important conduits for expressing national culture and identity, and therefore not to be compromised. There are some links with agriculture in this respect, as noted in one of its multifunctional elements. In addition, Singapore's resistance to American demands in USSFTA negotiations to comprehensively lift its ban on chewing gum was based on a social policy argument, this being the anticipated littering of disposed gum in the famously and proudly clean city-state (see Chapter 3).

Those industries believed to *uphold national security* forms the third type of 'sensitive' industry. For example, Singapore resisted American pressure in USSFTA negotiations to relinquish its capital controls based on this argument. Being able to still mediate speculative transactions in the Singapore dollar remained a critically important foreign economic policy priority for Southeast Asia's most important financial centre, especially after the region's 1997/98 financial crisis. More generally, national security imperatives can also limit the scope in FTA negotiations on lifting investment restrictions in certain infrastructural and service industries, e.g. telecommunications, news media, banking (or finance generally) and energy. These kind of sectors are thought to underpin both the basic functions of the economy and the fundaments of a modern nation-state's security overall in times of crisis, whether caused by domestic or international factors.

The fourth type relates to *strategic industries*, which themselves to fall into high-tech industry or big global market industry sub-categories. Some connection may be made with national security here in that such strategically important 'sensitive' industries are thought vital to the nation's long-term economic security (Dent 2006b). In JKFTA negotiations, for example, Korean firms and business associations have expressed significant concern over intensified Japanese competition – domestically and globally – in core strategic industry sectors like autos and consumer electronics. While South Korea's growing trade deficit with Japan may considerably deepen with the implementation of a JKFTA deal, tariff levels tend to be relatively low in these sectors, and disputes have been generally rare or low-key here, thus making it the less relevant 'sensitive' industry type.

1.4.3 Diplomatic over-stretch

Limited diplomatic resources as a constraining factor on the development of a country's FTA policy may seem a rather incongruous theme for discussion. However it is certainly a relevant hindrance factor, though it principally applies to limiting the number of FTAs a country can negotiate simultaneously. Compared to multilateral or WTO trade negotiations and agreements, bilateral FTAs are a very diplomat resource-intensive process. Even countries with considerable government resources, such as the US and Japan, do not possess enough trained and suitably experienced trade diplomats to negotiate more than around three or four FTAs at any one time. For smaller countries like New Zealand – whose Ministry of Foreign Affairs and Trade only had 15 trade negotiators up to 2003 – this number is normally one to two. Given that it takes around a year to a year and a half on average to negotiate a bilateral FTA, this has significantly restricted the FTA policy ambitions of probably all participative Asia-Pacific states. This being said, Chapter 2 notes how many countries have boosted the ranks of their trade diplomacy corps to help facilitate expanding FTA negotiating capacity. Part of this process has involved seconding private sector professionals (mostly lawyers) to fill 'expertise gaps' in government negotiating teams. The increasing use of video conferencing in FTA negotiations[40] has also helped address budgetary constraint and negotiator jet-lag fatigue problems. Technology can only, though, provide partial solutions to these problems. Moreover, criticism persists, especially amongst WTO multilateral purists, that bilateral FTAs use scarce diplomatic resources in a relatively inefficient way to achieve free trade outcomes.

1.4.4 Deficient technocratic and institutional capacities

While diplomatic over-stretch limits the ability of many Asia-Pacific states to develop their FTA policies to the extent they would wish, many developing countries from the region lack the basic technocratic and institutional apparatus or capacity to operationalise an effective FTA policy in the first place. By technocratic and institutional capacity we are generally referring to whether a nation possesses the following elements:

- *Sufficient technical expertise*: as previously discussed, FTA negotiations require a minimum number of trained and experienced trade diplomats. This number will be higher for more complex 'broad-band' agreements.
- *Policy coherence*: similarly, the complexities of issues often involved in FTAs require different elements of a nation's foreign economic policy-making apparatus to work in a coherent manner.
- *Robust institutional arrangements*: the ability of a nation's institutions (e.g. agencies, rules, laws) to operationalise a free trade agreement once negotiated in terms of implementation and compliance to its provisions.

Weaker developing countries in the Asia-Pacific (e.g. Cambodia, Laos, Myanmar) lack the above, and middle-order developing countries like Indonesia and Philippines have experienced difficulties in these areas. Overall, the deficient capacity problem is a serious one for developing countries because they are effectively marginalised in the new Asia-Pacific FTA trend, leading to the potential risk of exacerbating the development divide in the region, and Chapter 4 discusses this issue in some detail. Suffice to say here that the deficient capacity problem hinders the ability of many developing countries to initiate bilateral FTA projects, especially with demanding developed country partners.

1.5 Conclusion

The proliferation of free trade agreements (FTA) in the Asia-Pacific since the late 1990s has not just significant implications for the international political economy of the region but also for the global political economy. We have examined how the Asia-Pacific's new FTA trend is part of a wider expansion of FTA activity at the global level. However, the relative dearth of FTA activity in the region before this time, the region's subsequent acceleration of FTA activity since then, and the geoeconomic weight of the Asia-Pacific itself make the global significance of this trend very important.

This chapter has provided a broad context or macro perspective for the analysis that follows in other chapters. It has examined the nature of free trade agreements, the phased development of FTA projects, and how considerable heterogeneity exists between signed agreements. This is because each FTA is crafted in accordance to the particular political economic interaction of the trade partners involved. Consequently, each agreement is a bespoke product in terms of its scope of liberalisation, rules of origin regime, the inclusion (or not) and emphasis of 'broad band' elements (e.g. IPR, competition policy, economic co-operation measures), its implementation schedules, modalities and other technical policy measures. We have also discussed both the static and dynamic economic effects of FTAs, including debates about trade creation and trade diversion, and the longer-term impact of FTA integration amongst signatory parties. Some observations on empirical economic studies have too been made, noting their usefulness and limitations when assessing FTAs, especially now that the extra-trade elements found in 'broad band' agreements adds greater complexity to the assessment exercise. Recent global trends in FTA activity have also been examined, comparing the Asia-Pacific's experience with that of other global regions such as Europe and Latin America. How the global expansion of FTA activity poses critical challenges to the WTO and the multilateral trade system has been another key issue of debate in this chapter. Issues pertaining to the WTO's rules on FTAs and other 'regional trade agreements' were conferred particular attention. It was noted that while the rules and the enforcement of them remain weak, little progress had been made in improving either aspect in Doha Development Round negotiations by the end of 2005.

An overview of the core determinants of the Asia-Pacific's new FTA trend was also made. The importance of FTAs being indicative of a fundamental ideological shift in the trade policy paradigm of many Asia-Pacific countries was questioned given that the most active FTA protagonists in the region were long-standing and ardent free trade advocates (e.g. the US, Singapore and Australia), and that those that have fallen well short of their FTA policy ambitions (e.g. Japan and South Korea) have been hindered by a residual neo-mercantilism that remains deeply embedded within their national political economies. It was argued that trade institution inertia at various levels, especially at the WTO – multilateral level, has been a more critical factor. The failures experienced by the WTO, APEC and ASEAN at advancing their respective trade liberalisation agendas caused Asia-Pacific countries to look to bilaterals as an alternative insurance policy with respect to securing market access. Another core determinant related to Asia-Pacific states playing 'FTA catch-up' with other global regions, especially with Europe. The 1997/98 East Asian financial crisis also played a part in spurring FTA activity in the region by exposing both the degree of economic interdependence amongst East Asian states and the weak co-operative diplomacy architecture between them to deal with such regional crises. Free trade agreements were thus part of broader endeavours to improve regional economic governance in East Asia, and FTAs that East Asian states signed with other Asia-Pacific economies could too be seen as crisis-averse initiatives by diversifying market access risk. Co-operative diplomacy was one of four 'strategic diplomacy' motives identified, the others being security alliance diplomacy, competitive bilateralism and isolation avoidance. Chapter 2 examines the country-specific relevance of these four motive factors.

Lastly, we considered what have been the main hindrances to FTA project development in the Asia-Pacific. The first of these hindrances, relating to the agriculture sector and more specifically agri-protectionism, has overall been the most problematic area of FTA negotiations. The general reasons for persisting agri-protectionism in the Asia-Pacific were explored, including multifunctionality and food security issues, and Chapter 2 explores the different aspects of domestic politics at play from various country-specific perspectives. The second main hindrance concerned other 'sensitive' industry issues and these were sub-categorised into the following: (i) those industries in structural decline, such as textiles; (ii) those with a strong socio-cultural dimension, such as the entertainment, media and health sectors; (iii) those deemed vital to upholding national security, such as finance; and (iv) 'strategic' industries, such as high-tech sectors or big global market industry sectors on which the future lifeblood of the economy depended. Diplomatic over-stretch was identified as the third main hindrance, whereby the ability of a country to develop its FTA policy is constricted by limited diplomatic resources, especially trained trade negotiators. The fourth and last main hindrance – deficient technocratic and institutional capacities – is closely related to the third hindrance factor and particularly concerns wider 'capacity' problems facing developing countries when trying to both effectively negotiate FTAs and implement them. The issues introduced in this chapter are discussed further in those that follow. The next two chapters offer different micro perspectives on the new Asia-Pacific FTA trend. Chapter 2 analyses the development of eight different Asia-Pacific states' FTA policies, while Chapter 3 makes case study analyses of individual FTA projects based on a representative sample across the region. Finally, in the concluding Chapter 4, we consider the relationship between bilateral FTAs and regional community-building in the Asia-Pacific, in particular discussing the prospects for an emergent 'lattice regionalism' based on the foundation of an increasingly dense pattern of FTAs within the region.

Notes

1 The US and Canada had signed a sectoral FTA on autos in 1965 that was superseded by full bilateral FTA between them introduced in 1988, which was in turn subsumed into NAFTA in 1994.
2 By 2005, there were around 50 partial scope RTAs notified to the WTO.
3 The earliest FTAs were primarily concerned with trade liberalisation in industrial products only, with agriculture being omitted (WTO 2002a).
4 Other such examples from the Asia-Pacific include the Canada–Chile FTA (14.5-year, 15.5-year and even 19.5-year transition periods for certain industrial and agricultural products) and the Korea–Chile FTA, which carries 13-year and 16-year transition periods on a few tariff lines.
5 These will typically involve gradual tariff reductions and quota limit increases.
6 The matter was not helped when after South Korea's own exploratory FTA talks with Mexico broke down in 2003, the Mexican government raised tariffs on Korean tyres, which previously were 23 percent, to more than 50 percent. Under a later agreement, though, Mexico agreed to reduce the tariff to 35 percent in September 2004 (*Joong Ang Daily*, 25.06.2005).
7 *Manila Bulletin*, 03.06.2003.
8 *Bangkok Post*, 05.05.2005.
9 This included a number of customs unions.

10 *China View News*, 28.10.2004.
11 *Financial Times*, 18.11.2002.
12 SACU member states are Botswana, Lesotho, Namibia, South Africa and Swaziland.
13 SADC member states are Angola, Botswana, Congo, Lesotho, Malawi, Mauritius, Mozambique, Namibia, Seychelles, South Africa, Swaziland, Tanzania, Zambia, Zimbabwe.
14 In the meantime, India and Sri Lanka concluded a bilateral FTA in 2001.
15 These countries were also members of the South Asian Association for Regional Co-operation (SAARC) grouping.
16 *Reuters*, 14.11.2002.
17 *New Zealand Herald*, 06.01.2004.
18 The CRTA has failed to reach consensus on all but one RTA that has been referred to it for examination (Scollay 2003).
19 For example, NAFTA helped instigate the '10 year completion' rule introduced in 1994.
20 Other WTO rules-related issues that were prominently discussed by the NGR during the Doha Round included anti-dumping duty and countervailing duty regimes.
21 This also applies to the "substantial sectoral coverage" statement of Clause 1a of Article V of GATS on services trade agreements, as previously noted.
22 Research interview with official from the Australian Embassy to the WTO in Geneva, September 2002.
23 *Inside US Trade*, 30.08.2002. Only one RTA has been challenged thus far by use of the DSB mechanism, however, this being made by India against the EU–Turkey customs union.
24 Research interview, Geneva, September 2002.
25 More generally, RoO can reduce both trade diversion and trade creation effects of FTAs. They can reduce trade diversion by requiring FTA-based firms to use inputs from more expensive internal sources to qualify for tariff preference and hence raise the production cost above the tariff inclusive price of competitive outsider suppliers. By the same token, trade creation will be reduced from RoO that similarly raise the input costs of more efficient FTA-based suppliers in intra-FTA trade (Panagariya 1999).
26 The ORC term is used in Article XXIV, clauses 5 and 8(a)(ii) and the ORRC term in 8(a)(i) and (b), and there is some dispute over whether the terms are synonymous or distinctly different, thus leading to a separate argument concerning whether RoOs should be considered ORCs or ORRCs.
27 The Qatari capital where the Fourth WTO Ministerial Meeting was convened.
28 Gleaned from *New Zealand Herald*, 21.04.2005.
29 Originally comprising Argentina, Bolivia, Brazil, Chile, China, Costa Rica, Cuba, Ecuador, Egypt, El Salvador, Guatemala, India, Mexico, Nigeria, Pakistan, Paraguay, Philippines, South Africa, Thailand and Venezuela. The group has been in a state of flux, with some small Latin American countries soon leaving as a result of US pressure on them to break away or jeopardise their ties with Washington (*Financial Times*, 23.10.2003), while others (e.g. Indonesia, the Philippines, Egypt and Nigeria) have reportedly joined the coalition. The G20 has also predecessors. In 1964, developing countries formed the G77, which has since expanded to over 130 countries. In the 1970s, the G77 called for a new international economic order that would redress the global economic balance in favour of the poor, but failed to make much progress.

30   The reason given by China, Thailand and other G20 members for this was that, unlike developed countries, they could not afford huge programmes of domestic support to help their farmers, instead depending on tariff-based safeguard measures to help address food security and farmer income security issues.

31   Research interviews, Canberra, August 2003. According to Ravenhill (2001), the concept of 'open regionalism' initially came from a Japanese trade study group in 1981. It appeared in official APEC documentation for the first time in the Joint Statement of the Fifth Ministerial Meeting held at Seattle in November 1993, in which member states expressed their commitment to attain regional trade liberalisation "through consultation in a manner consistent with the principles of GATT and open regionalism" (APEC 1993, paragraph 6). Ravenhill maintains, however, that APEC as an organisation has never really fully articulated what open regionalism means. Yet there was a general consensus amongst officials and analysts working in Pacific Trade and Development Conference (PAFTAD) and PECC circles about what open regionalism generally implies, this being "a continuation of the process of unilateral liberalisation that has characterised the economic policies of countries in the region for several decades, a market-driven process rather than one directed by government officials to construct formal free trade areas" (Ravenhill 2001: 141).

32   *Far Eastern Economic Review*, 09.09.1999.

33   Research interview with a former APEC member-state trade minister in attendance at the 1998 summit, July 2003.

34   *The Economist*, 06.11.2002.

35   Thailand provides an export platform in Southeast Asia for many foreign automotive producers, while Malaysia wished to delay the phasing out of trade barriers to allow its national Proton car manufacturers more time to adjust to new AFTA-induced competitive conditions.

36   Both Indonesia and the Philippines have also like Malaysia been critical, though not to the same degree, of Singapore's bilateral FTA strategy for similar reasons. *International Herald Tribune*, 22.02.2001.

37   *New Straits Times*, 16.07.2001.

38   Malaysia even wanted its fellow ASEAN member states to gain approval at ASEAN-level for any bilateral FTAs they wished to sign with those outside the group. *Straits Times*, 06.07.2001.

39   *Channel News Asia*, 13.07.2005.

40   Singapore and the United States have been pioneers in this area.

2
Asia-Pacific FTAs: Country Profiles

2.1 Introduction

This chapter examines the FTA policies of eight Asia-Pacific countries visited by the author in which extensive research interview fieldwork was conducted. The field-research country group comprises Australia, Japan, New Zealand, Singapore, South Korea, Taiwan, Thailand and the United States.[1] These were chosen because they were amongst the first wave of important FTA protagonists when the Asia-Pacific FTA trend initially emerged. In total, 175 research interviewees from 144 agencies across the eight countries (plus the WTO community in Geneva) took part in field-research for this study, these being from amongst the government, business, civil society, research institute and foreign ambassadorial communities of the field-researched countries, and thus with a stakeholder or an analytical interest in FTA policy. Depending on the agency, each research interviewee was asked a series of questions that covered the following fundamental issues:

- What are the main determining factors behind the FTA policy?
- What are the main hindrances faced in advancing FTA policy? This forms part of a wider examination of the key challenging areas and contentious issues of the country's FTA policy.
- What are the main consequences from the substantive development of FTA policy?
- How FTA policy fits into a wider economic and trade policy strategy?
- How is FTA policy itself formulated, including how the government works with different stakeholder groups in this process?

Under many of the questions, interviewees were given a number of possible 'explanatory factors' to which they were asked to: (i) assign a 'significance-rating' to each explanatory factor so that their importance may be judged relative to others, with 5 being 'high significance' and 0 being 'low significance' (see Table 2.1 for details of the relevant questions and associated explanatory

Table 2.1   Research Interview Survey

	Australia	Japan	New Zealand	Singapore	South Korea	Taiwan	Thailand	United States
Main determining factors								
Helping consolidate domestic economic reforms	1.8	3.0	2.0	2.7	3.4	2.7	3.3	1.9
APEC trade liberalisation inertia	2.4	2.2	3.5	3.0	2.2	–	2.4	2.0
WTO trade liberalisation inertia	2.8	2.6	4.1	3.1	2.9	–	3.2	3.4
Instigating a new trade policy direction	3.1	3.1	2.8	3.2	3.5	2.7	3.6	3.3
Strengthening diplomatic relations with key trade partners	3.9	3.6	4.1	4.6	3.8	3.8	3.9	3.6
Toward wider regional trade arrangements	2.4	3.1	4.1	3.4	3.7	3.2	2.9	2.5
Strengthen regional economic cohesion	3.0	3.3	3.6	3.3	3.1	3.2	3.2	3.2
Response to regional/global FTA trend	3.1	3.4	2.5	1.9	3.9	3.8	3.4	3.5
Helping achieve global free trade/help WTO	2.4	2.4	3.8	3.0	2.3	2.0	2.2	3.5
Consolidate security alliances – Australia/US	4.1	–	–	–	–	–	–	2.6
As a response to 1997/98 financial crisis – Japan	–	4.5	–	–	–	–	–	–
Exploiting the benefits of WTO membership – Taiwan	–	–	–	–	–	3.3	–	–
'Isolation avoidance' diplomacy – Taiwan	–	–	–	–	–	3.9	–	–
ASEAN's problems implementing AFTA – Thailand	–	–	–	–	–	–	2.5	–
Recent securing of Trade Promotion Authority – US	–	–	–	–	–	–	–	3.3
Main hindrances								
Agriculture	4.8	4.8	4.3	–	5.0	2.8	3.5	3.3
Opposition from (other) domestic industries	2.2	2.7	2.9	2.9	2.2	2.1	3.2	2.2
Opposition from civil society groups/NGOs	1.7	1.4	2.4	1.1	2.7	1.0	1.5	2.2
Lack of business sector support	1.8	1.6	1.6	1.7	2.4	1.7	1.9	1.6
Low foreign economic policy priority of government	1.3	3.0	1.7	1.1	2.5	1.2	1.8	1.7
Diplomatic over-reach/scarce diplomatic resources	1.1	1.6	2.9	2.3	1.8	1.7	2.9	3.1
Greater domestic problems of FTA partner(s)	–	1.7	–	3.2	3.2	2.0	3.1	2.3
Opposition from other countries or international organisations	1.3	1.6	1.2	1.8	1.2	4.8	1.5	1.1

Table 2.1   Research Interview Survey – *continued*

	Australia	Japan	New Zealand	Singapore	South Korea	Taiwan	Thailand	United States
Non-tariff barriers or other technical issues – *Aus/NZ*	3.5	–	2.7	–	–	–	–	–
State bureaucratic inertia or opposition – *Japan/S. Korea*	–	2.6	–	–	2.3	–	–	–
Lack of priority afforded by trade partners – *Taiwan, Thailand*	–	–	–	–	–	3.6	2.2	–
Government working with stakeholders								
Agriculture lobby	5.0	4.2	5.0	1.0	3.8	2.8	4.5	4.0
Other industry groups	4.0	4.4	3.3	4.0	3.3	2.8	4.5	3.5
Trade unions	3.0	1.4	3.0	2.2	2.0	1.6	1.7	2.1
Environmental groups	2.5	1.4	3.0	1.7	1.0	1.4	1.5	1.9
Other civil society groups	3.0	1.4	2.5	1.7	1.3	1.0	1.7	1.9
Main consequences (*net positive/negative*)								
Domestic economic policy reform	1.0	3.4	1.3	2.9	3.4	3.4	3.2	1.5
Domestic economic restructuring	0.8	2.8	2.0	3.0	3.5	3.6	3.4	1.5
For APEC	–0.3	0.6	3.0	1.6	1.9	–	1.0	1.5
For the WTO	0.5	1.2	1.6	1.6	1.8	–	1.4	2.1
Relations with bilateral FTA partners	3.2	4.0	4.2	4.1	3.7	3.9	3.9	4.2
Country's influence in the East Asia/ Asia-Pacific region	1.5	3.8	2.4	2.9	2.7	2.9	3.2	2.9
Developing wider regional trade agreements	1.2	2.8	2.5	2.9	3.5	3.3	3.2	2.3
International relations in the region	0.7	3.4	2.2	3.2	2.7	2.5	2.6	2.6
Countries and regions outside the Asia-Pacific	0.2	1.6	0.8	2.4	2.1	2.3	1.7	1.4
Taiwan's relations with China – *Taiwan*	–	–	–	–	–	1.7	–	–
For AFTA	–	–	–	–	–	–	2.6	–
The 'war on terror'	–	–	–	–	–	–	–	1.7

Notes: Based on author's field research. Figures relate to average 'significance ratings' of 0 to 5, with 5 the highest significance rating.

factors); (ii) explain why they had assigned the significance-rating they had to each explanatory factor. While this 'significance-rating' method is admittedly a rather inexact scientific approach to evaluating the relative importance of each explanatory factor, it did at least allow for some analytical assessment of this kind to be made, augmented by the further qualified explanation noted above under (ii). In addition, research interviewees had the opportunity under 'other' sections to add explanatory factors not listed and comment upon their relative importance.

Each country analysis is structured along the following lines, in accordance to research questions asked. The first section considers the origins, determining factors and development of the country's FTA policy. This includes at the beginning an international political economy overview of the country concerned to provide important contextual background. The second section then examines how FTA policy is formulated within the country's wider trade policy framework. In the third section, the main challenging areas and contentious issues of the country's FTA policy are discussed. Finally, the impacts and consequences of the policy are considered. Particular comment is reserved for those questions and issues that were assigned higher significance ratings. Each country analysis follows in alphabetical order, and the field-research material provides the substantive basis of the chapter's analysis overall.

2.2   Australia

2.2.1   The origins, determining factors and development of Australia's FTA policy

Australia: an international political economy overview

Australia is one of the Asia-Pacific's developed countries, but like New Zealand agriculture plays a key role in the nation's economy and trade. It has been one of the fastest growing economies in the OECD group, with an annual average economic growth rate of 3.9 percent over the 1992–2003 period. Before Britain joined the European Community (EC) in 1973, Australia had very close economic ties with the mother country through the British Commonwealth trade preferences system. Britain was a major export destination for Australian agri-products but when Britain joined the EC it had to apply high tariff rates and other trade barriers on Australian farm imports, as dictated by the EC's highly protectionist Common Agricultural Policy. In anticipating Britain's accession to the EC, Australia was already looking to foster a new Pacific identity for itself and strengthen economic relations with fellow Asia-Pacific countries. In conjunction mainly with Japan, Australia did much to develop and promote the idea of a Pacific economic community from the 1960s. It was an Australian initiative under the leadership of Prime Minister Bob Hawke that led to the creation of APEC in 1989.

Australia's politico-economic position in the Asia-Pacific has, though, been a source of much contentious debate amongst the countries' leaders. In the early 1990s under the premiership of Paul Keating, Australia pursued a more Asia-centric foreign economic policy than his predecessors, strengthening ties with Japan in particular. However, this changed somewhat when John Howard became Prime Minister in 1996, whose administration sought closer links with the United States. This became even more so after Australia's attempts to forge a trade and economic agreement with ASEAN in 2000 failed largely owing to opposition from Malaysia. Australia's relationship with the US strengthened considerably after the September 2001 terrorist attacks, as Australia assumed the position of America's main alliance partner in the region. This culminated in the signing of the Australia–US Free Trade Agreement (AUSFTA) in February 2004, as discussed in this section and case studied in Chapter 3. However, Australia knows that it must also avoid marginalisation from a dynamic integrating East Asia, and that its economic future also lies in forging links with the region. In this context, subsequent FTA projects initiated with China and ASEAN (after a change in Malaysia's leadership) are seen as critical to this end by Canberra, as was securing Australia's participation in the inaugural East Asia Summit held in December 2005.

Australia's foray into FTAs represents both continuity and change in the nation's trade policy and diplomacy. It signed the Asia-Pacific's first full bilateral FTA, with New Zealand in 1983, the Australia–New Zealand Closer Economic Relations (ANZCER) agreement. This formed part of Australia's broader shift towards trade liberalisation from the early 1980s onwards, making it by the 1990s one of the most liberalised trading nations in the world. Unlike most other OECD countries, this applies to Australia's agricultural trade sector as well as its industrial trade sector, and explains why it has offered comprehensive import tariff liberalisation in negotiations with certain FTA partners, n.b. mostly developed states like the US and Singapore. Hence, FTAs may be viewed as an extension of Australia's trade liberalisation policy, and yet in another sense they marked a significant methodological change. Australia was part of a set of Asia-Pacific countries (the others being Japan, South Korea and New Zealand) that were staunchly multilateralist in their approach to negotiating trade liberalisation. The economic security of all four countries depended on the expansion of an increasingly open multilateral trading system, albeit for different reasons: Japan and South Korea were industrial export-oriented while Australia and New Zealand were agricultural export-oriented. Global trade deals brokered through the GATT/WTO process were deemed particularly vital to the fortunes of these countries. Today, agriculture still accounts for around 20 percent of Australia's total exports.

In August 1986, leading up to the start of GATT Uruguay Round negotiations, Australia formed the Cairns Group, a coalition of 17 big agricultural producers that account for 23 percent of the world's agricultural exports.[2] The primary aim of the Cairns Group at GATT was to persuade the main trading powers (i.e. the US, EU and Japan) to reduce their agri-protectionism. In May 2002, the Cairns Group condemned the US Farm Bill, which brought increased levels of income support to American farmers, and called on the Bush Administration to "demonstrate the necessary leadership for the attainment of an ambitious and comprehensive programme of agricultural liberalisation and reform in the current WTO negotiations."[3] More recently, the Cairns Group welcomed the decision made by WTO members in July 2004 to negotiate on eliminating agricultural export subsidies as part of the Doha Round. While the Cairns Group's endeavours within the GATT/WTO system have been a prime focus of Australia's efforts on agri-trade diplomacy, the country's adherence to the multilateral trade negotiation process in general is held in great importance to many in Australia's trade policy elite (Bisley 2004; Findlay 2002). Thus, to them Australia's shift towards FTA bilateralism is of some considerable concern as we discuss later in detail.

The origins and development of Australia's FTA policy

Apart from ANZCER, Australia's FTA policy remained more or less dormant up until the late 1990s. The 1997 White Paper on Australia's Foreign and Trade Policy published by the Department of Foreign Affairs and Trade (DFAT) under John Howard's National Party Government signalled a shift from the country's staunch multilateralism to a more multi-track approach on trade liberalisation diplomacy (DFAT 1997). According to Capling (2001), Howard made bilateralism a central plank of his foreign policy platform in the run up to the country's 1996 general election, mainly to differentiate National Party policy from the preceding Labour Government's idealist internationalism and Asia-centricity. The idea for negotiating an FTA with the US was afforded special priority by Howard's trade policy advisors.[4] However, a preoccupation with domestic over international policy, and a certain degree of bureaucratic continuity within DFAT on Asia-centric policies, explained why little was done to develop Australia's bilateral FTA policy, and more specifically an Australia–US FTA (AUSFTA) project. Indeed, efforts during 1999 and 2000 to form an FTA with the Association of Southeast Asian Nations (ASEAN) constituted the first real developments of this policy. Malaysia's veto on an AFTA–CER link at an ASEAN Economic Ministers Meeting in October 2000 spurred Australia to develop alternative separate bilateral FTA projects with Singapore, formally proposed just a month later in November 2000, and with Thailand, formally proposed in July 2001.

Australia's rebuff on the AFTA–CER project in October 2000 also led to a decision made at an Australian Government Cabinet meeting to pursue an FTA with the US. In December 2000, Australia's Ambassador to the US, Michael Thawley, proposed in a speech made in Washington DC that formal talks on AUSFTA should be initiated. The subsequent development of the AUSFTA project is case studied in Chapter 3 but just to briefly note here that it was not formally proposed by both sides until November 2002, with the first round of negotiations occurring in March 2003. By then, the Singapore–Australia FTA (SAFTA) had been signed and Thailand–Australia FTA (TAFTA) negotiations were well under way (see Appendix A). A DFAT

White Paper published in February 2003 stated the Government's intentions to further enhance Australia's FTA policy (DFAT 2003) that bought into the 'competitive liberalisation' ethos also driving US FTA policy, which as Australia's Trade Minister Mark Vaile himself explained was based on the view that "bilateral and regional liberalisation can complement and stimulate multilateral liberalisation."[5] Despite the AUSFTA project seemingly dominating Australia's FTA policy during the early 2000s, East Asia remained of critical importance, not least because the region accounted for over half of the country's exports. Apart from SAFTA and TAFTA (concluded in April 2004), Australia had by 2005 formally initiated bilateral FTA projects with Malaysia, China and ASEAN as a group with New Zealand. Thus, by this time Australia had concluded four FTAs within the Asia-Pacific region and was in the negotiation phase of three other projects (Table 2.2).

Table 2.2   FTA Projects within the Asia-Pacific Region by Trade Partner (by end of 2005)

FTA Party	Proposed	Studying/ Studied	Negotiating	Concluded/ Implementing	TOTAL
Australia	0	0	3	4	7
Brunei	1	0	0	3	4
China	0	0	2	4	6
Canada	0	0	2	3	5
Chile	0	1	0	8	9
Costa Rica	1	0	0	2	3
Guatemala	0	0	0	3	3
Hong Kong	0	0	1	1	2
Indonesia	0	0	2	3	5
Japan	0	1	5	3	9
Macao	0	0	0	1	1
Malaysia	0	1	2	4	7
Mexico	0	1	1	6	8
Nicaragua	0	0	1	2	3
New Zealand	0	1	3	4	8
Panama	0	0	1	3	4
Peru	1	0	0	3	4
Philippines	0	1	1	3	2
Singapore	0	1	2	9	12
South Korea	0	3	2	3	8
Taiwan	1	0	1	2	4
Thailand	0	0	2	6	8
United States	0	2	2	6	10
Vietnam	1	0	0	0	1

Notes: Includes plurilateral and regional FTAs such as AFTA, NAFTA and TPSEPA, as well as 'country-to-region' FTAs such as ACFTA. Where these apply, separate bilateral FTA projects have been factored out. For example, the Thailand – South Korea bilateral FTA project with respect to the ASEAN – South Korea FTA. *Source:* Author's research.

Main determining factors

The two highest 'significance-rated' determining factors underpinning Australia's FTA policy identified by research interviewees were *consolidate security alliances* and *strengthening diplomatic relations with key trade partners* (Table 2.1). These motives are closely related, and moreover this is consistent with the general trend across the field-researched country group concerning the primacy afforded to politico-diplomatic motives over those of a more overt economic nature. For Australia, the AUSFTA project could to some extent be considered a policy framework in itself owing to how it dominated various aspects of the country's trade policy apparatus during the early-to-mid 2000s. A considerable number of research interviewees across the stakeholder constituency spectrum made a point of highlighting the Australia–US security nexus regarding AUSFTA. Intimate security ties between both the two Anglo-Pacific countries have existed for some time, bound by the ANZUS treaty signed in 1951 whereby each country is obliged to support the other in the event of one coming under attack. Australia invoked ANZUS provisions on security co-operation in response to the September 2001 terrorist attacks on the US. Of particular concern to Canberra was Australia's geographic proximity to Indonesia, the world's largest Muslim country and host to many *Jemaah Islamiyah* radical terrorist groups. The Bali bombing incident of October 2002, in which 88 Australians died, confirmed Canberra's security fears and helped augment pro-US sentiments in Australia with an ensuing encroachment of security objectives into the nation's foreign economic policy. The Australian Government had strongly supported the US's 'war on terror' from the start, sending troops to both Afghanistan and Iraq, as moreover was subsequently labelled as America's 'deputy-sheriff' in the Asia-Pacific region.

The security imperatives behind AUSFTA predate the September 2001 terrorist attacks. Australia's involvement in the East Timor crisis of 1999, where the US military was allegedly on standby in case Australia's own forces became over-stretched, led many of country's foreign policy elite to believe that a substantial upgrading of the Australia–US relationship was needed at the millennial eve. The aforementioned Ambassador Michael Thawley, who had first officially proposed AUSFTA, was himself a security specialist with (allegedly) no real expertise in trade policy, and became increasingly concerned about the East Asian security threat after the East Timor crisis.[6] The AUSFTA project was seen to realise wider politico-diplomatic objectives. As then US Trade Representative Robert Zoellick commented at the project's launch, "an FTA further deepen the ties between our societies and strengthen the foundation of our security alliance... An FTA would facilitate the building of new networks that enhance our Pacific democracies' mutual interests, shared experiences and promotion of common values so that we can work together more effectively with third countries."[7] There was clearly an intention, then, for AUSFTA to perform multiple functions beyond simply a trade liberalisation demonstration effect to other Asia-Pacific nations. Furthermore, the security dimension to Australia's FTA policy extended to other projects such as SAFTA and TAFTA. The network of FTA projects between Australia, the US, Singapore and Thailand could be viewed as helping consolidate a US-led coalition of security partners in a strong post-9/11 context.[8] As a research interviewed Singapore Embassy official based in Canberra commented, "the close security relationship between Singapore and Australia, which became even closer after September 11, was a crucial determining factor behind SAFTA."[9]

The next ranked determining factors were similarly significance-rated, these being *instigating a new trade policy direction, response to regional/global FTA trend* and to *strengthen regional economic cohesion* (Table 2.1). We have already explored the background behind the first of these factors, and the second was discussed in Chapter 1. These determining factors are also closely related. A key motive for Australia developing a more multi-track trade policy and diplomacy was to keep pace with intensifying global FTA activity, which the country was hitherto lagging behind. While AUSFTA was seen to serve important politico-diplomatic and economic ends, Australia's various other bilateral FTA projects with East Asian countries also helped integrate it into a still dynamic and increasingly coalescent regional economy.

Research interviewees ranked *WTO trade liberalisation inertia* not far behind the above determining factors, although Australia's significance-rating here was at the low end for the field-researched country group. Notable points made on this matter included that the US's recent trade unilateralism and lack of leadership at the WTO was instrumental in Australia's trade policy shift to bilateralism. Disappointing outcomes from Cairns Group diplomacy at recent WTO Ministerial Meetings were also cited. At the September 2003 Cancun Ministerial, the Australian Government was heavily criticised for not making a formal public position on agri-trade liberalisation before the meeting, and then suffered a further setback when a number of Cairns Group members (including Thailand, Indonesia and the Philippines) joined the new G20 coalition of developing countries, at least partly owing to disappointing progress achieved by the *de facto* Australian-led Cairns Group. Although securing multilateral trade deals remains a priority to Australia, the WTO's recent inertia on trade liberalisation adds some critical imperative to FTA policy in providing alternative market access avenues. Australia's FTAs as *helping achieve global free trade/help WTO* was conferred a slightly lower significance-rating. Most research interviewees were not convinced by the Australian Government's 'competitive liberalisation' strategy, believing it was simply a policy marketing exercise.

From one perspective, the relatively low significance-rating assigned to *APEC trade liberalisation inertia* – in comparison to other factors here and to other field-researched countries (Table 2.1) – is surprising given that APEC was originally an Australian initiative and that the country was a core advocate of the organisation's endeavours to advance trade liberalisation in the region. However, APEC's failures to make progress here were not deemed that important a stimulus to bilateral FTA policy. The main reason cited by research interviewees here concerned the previously mentioned issue of the new Howard Administration wishing to differentiate policy from the preceding Labour Governments under Prime Ministers Bob Hawke (who hosted the inaugural APEC meeting in Canberra) and Paul Keating. Other low significance-rated factors were *toward wider regional trade arrangements* and *helping consolidate domestic economic reforms*. In line with other market-liberal countries (i.e. the US and New Zealand), the latter determining factor was not deemed relevant given the already open nature of the Australian economy. Thus, FTAs would make only marginal difference in terms of locking in economic reform.

2.2.2   The formation of Australia's FTA policy

The principal agency of Australian trade policy formation is DFAT. As one would expect from in a well established democratic country like Australia, DFAT consults widely with various stakeholding constituencies from the business, civil society and academic sectors. High significance-ratings in government–stakeholder consultation on FTA policy (Table 2.1) confirm this to be the case. It is also worth noting here that, like New Zealand, agricultural groups were conferred the highest significance-rating possible, the peak organisation – the National Federation of Farmers – being the most important. Consultative mechanisms used by DFAT include the Agricultural Trade Consultative Group, the Automotive Council, and various Export Advisory Panels. The Trade Policy Advisory Council, whose membership consists mainly of business representatives from major Australian companies, provides advice from various commercial perspectives. The Department also takes public submissions on its negotiations of FTAs that may come not just from non-government actors but also state and territorial governments within Australia's federal system of governance.[10] National Trade Consultations form another framework for intra-Government dialogue on trade policy matters, and the Senate Enquiry process fields wider public opinion on government policy in general.[11] A high degree of inter-agency co-operation also takes place within the Federal Government structure involving numerous trade-related ministries.

In 1996, the new Howard Administration established a Joint Standing Committee on Treaties (JSCOT), whose membership includes senators and other parliamentarians. The JSCOT provides parliamentary scrutiny on FTAs and other types of international agreement but cannot stipulate changes, rather only recommends them. Furthermore, it is the executive arm of the government rather than its legislative arm (i.e. the parliament) that ratifies international agreements such as FTAs simply by signing them with partner countries. Parliament can, though, block or amend any legislation thought by government to be required to fully implement the agreement. For example, the Labour Party motion tabled in parliament to amend part of AUSFTA on proposed changes to Australia's Pharmaceutical Benefits Scheme (PBS), which the government duly did, much to the annoyance of certain American drug companies.

Even though many civil society groups have been critical of Australia's FTA policy, most have been generally happy with the government's consultative process in formulating that policy.[12] One research interviewee noted that transparency and the consultation process on trade policy formation had improved considerably since the Uruguay Round negotiations of the early 1990s, although in his opinion the consultative process was still skewed considerably more in the business community's favour[13] – a common complaint amongst civil society representatives across the Asia-Pacific region.

2.2.3 Challenging areas and contentious issues

For most field-researched countries the highest significance-rated hindrance factor to the development of their FTA policies was *agriculture*. While for many countries this concerned overcoming domestic protectionist interests, in Australia's case the problem lay in the agri-protectionism of FTA project partners. Table 2.1 shows that agriculture was well ahead of any other hindrance factor for Australia. The AUSFTA study in Chapter 3 provides useful illustrative examples of how Australia's FTA partners have sought to extensively protect their own farmers from their competitive Australian rivals in various product sectors, especially dairy, beef, sugar and fruit. Thailand insisted on long tariff liberalisation phase-in schedules in various agri-sectors in TAFTA, and China is likely to request the same in its FTA negotiations with Australia. In March 2005, Beijing blocked the publication of a scoping study report on the China–Australia FTA project because it showed that China would benefit by far the most from an agreement. This was to avoid undermining Beijing's position when negotiating with Canberra on agri-trade issues.

The hindrance factor with the second highest significance-rating noted by research interviewees was *non-tariff barriers or other technical issues*. The most important aspects highlighted here was Australia's quarantine regime, foreign investment laws and the PBS. Australia's rigorous quarantine regulations are cited by most of FTA partners as a challenging area. Although not as critical as to New Zealand, bio-security is highly prioritised by Australia given the importance of agriculture to its export trade, and this approach receives strong public and civil society group (e.g. Greenpeace) support. Some of Australia's quarantine rules have been challenged at the WTO (e.g. Tasmanian salmon, with Canada as the complainant party) and

Thai trade diplomats negotiating TAFTA argued that a developing country such as itself should not have to comply with developed country standards on quarantine, but these efforts were largely in vain. In brief coverage of other relevant points here, the PBS provides a system for offering below market priced pharmaceuticals to the Australian public. Under the PBS, producer suppliers have to accept marginal profit returns, and this was a particular issue for American drug companies in AUSFTA negotiations (see Chapter 3). The US also wanted Australia to remove certain regulations on foreign investment, for example on foreign takeovers.

Table 2.1 shows that the responses of research interviewees were considerably skewed towards the two hindrance factors noted thus far. In a relatively low third place was *opposition from (other) domestic industries*. The textile, clothing and footwear (TCF) sector was a difficult area of negotiation in TAFTA as did autos, which Thailand-based Japanese producers like Toyota became especially involved. Australia maintains relatively high tariffs in the automotive sector to protect companies like Holden, a subsidiary of General Motors. A number of other hindrance factors were assigned low significance-ratings. Of these, *opposition from civil society groups/NGOs* attracted most comment from research interviewees. Notwithstanding the low significance-rating assigned here, many of Australia's civil society groups vehemently opposed the AUSFTA project in particular, mainly because US demands in negotiations connected with various embedded domestic policy issues such as health, media and culture. Greenpeace Australia raised concerns over how AUSFTA may lead to a weakening of laws on genetically modified (GM) foodstuffs (e.g. labelling or state-level moratoria on growing GM crops commercially), and also expressed some unease regarding North American Free Trade Agreement (NAFTA) style investment chapters whereby FTA rules could potentially compromise Australia's environmental and social laws (see US section).

While research interviewees assigned a low significance-rating for *low foreign economic policy priority of government*, some noted that a lack of bipartisan support for FTAs amongst Australia's political parties has at times been a notable hindrance factor. Labour, the main opposition party, has been sceptical of the National Government's priority afforded to FTAs, whilst the Democrats and the Greens have been the most critical of the policy generally. They have drawn upon the critiques articulated by Australia's civil society groups that FTAs, and particularly AUSFTA, compromise the country's social policies. The AUSFTA project generally remained a highly contentious issue both during negotiations and well after a final deal was signed. Many of Australia's pre-eminent political economists, such as Ross Garnaut, Peter Drysdale and Linda Weiss, were highly critical of AUSFTA and the country's new trade bilateralism generally. Garnaut and Drysdale's arguments particularly centred on the bilateralism/regionalism versus multilateralism debate, while Weiss, along with co-authors Elizabeth

Thurbon and John Mathews, focused more on AUSFTA's compromising of Australia's social institutions and national state capacity (Weiss *et al* 2004).

2.2.4 Impacts and consequences

The general consensus amongst research interviewees was that the net benefits of Australia's FTA policy for the country and Asia-Pacific region would be relatively small. Table 2.1 shows that the country's significance-ratings across the 'main consequence' category were the lowest on average of the field-researched group. *Relations with bilateral FTA partners* was Australia's highest significance-rating under 'main consequences' of FTA policy but this was the lowest top-rating achieved by any country. Moreover, Australia's second ranked factor – *country's influence in the East Asia/ Asia-Pacific region* – was well below the first, although these findings were consistent with the regional trend that politico-diplomatic rather than economic consequences were believed to be notably more important. There are inevitable similarities to be drawn with New Zealand here in that bilateral FTA linkages with East Asian and other Asia-Pacific nations augment Australia's ties to a bigger 'home' region than just the South Pacific, or Oceania. It is difficult to establish the exact extent to which Australia's FTA projects with ASEAN group countries and China assisted Canberra's efforts to secure membership of the East Asia Summit, or how exactly has AUSFTA prioritised Australia in the US's foreign policy objectives. Relatively speaking, however, these kinds of outcomes were seen by many as the most important contributions that FTAs were making in advancing Australia's own national interests.

In some contrast, the research interviewee consensus on the net impact of Australia's FTAs upon *domestic economic policy reform* and *domestic economic restructuring* was not that significant. Some linked the economic impact effects to social policy concerns discussed earlier and conferred a negative significance-rating accordingly, while others gave positive significance-ratings based mainly on the belief that FTAs would reform protected sectors like TCF and autos. However, trade multilateralists like Ross Garnaut contended that undertaking this on a preferential bilateral basis weakened support for multilateral liberalisation and fractured the trade liberalisation process on sectoral trade generally.[14] The impact upon the WTO and APEC, including their own trade liberalisation processes, was generally thought to be minimal, with the overall impact on APEC actually negative. Regarding *international relations in the region*, AUSFTA was singled out by some interviewees as causing fractures in regional diplomacy in that it brought greater definition to an Anglo-Pacific alignment of powers. However, as noted earlier, Australia has initiated a number of FTA projects with East Asian countries that provides some counterbalance to AUSFTA. Casting a wider global perspective, certain research interviewees noted in relation to the impact on *countries and international regions outside the*

Asia-Pacific that Australia's FTA policy has further cemented the shift away from the EU. This should be placed in the wider context of disagreements with continental European countries over the Common Agricultural Policy and Iraq, as well as the Howard Government's preference for the US economic and social role model.

2.3   Japan

2.3.1   The origins, determining factors and development of Japan's FTA policy

Japan: an international political economy overview

Japan has been central to East Asia's economic development and international economic relations. It was the region's first modern industrialised country and has been its largest national economy by far for many decades. Japan's post-1945 export-oriented industrialisation, emulated by many other East Asian countries, was made possible by the development of a strengthening multilateral trading system. This largely explains the country's traditional ardent support of, and faith in GATT/WTO led multilateralism (Drifte 1998; Hughes *et al* 2001; Mikanagi 1996). Up to the end of the 20th century, Japan remained the world's most important trading nation not to have signed an FTA or any other preferential trade agreement. While it has gradually removed its own conventional trade barriers, mainly through GATT/WTO multilateral negotiations and parallel bilateral negotiations with the US, Japan has retained elements of its long-standing neo-mercantilist approach to trade and industry policy. Neo-mercantilism entails measures undertaken by the state to both protect and promote the development of key industries. The protectionist aspects of this policy approach have especially applied to agriculture and strategic base industries such as petrochemicals and steel. The development of an FTA policy has thus brought some degree of paradigm shift in both Japan's trade diplomacy and trade policy formation, as we shall discuss in some detail.

From the 1950s to the 1990s, Japan's foreign economic policy was based on the two pillars of GATT multilateralism and US 'security' bilateralism (Hughes *et al* 2001). As Japan became stronger economically, other aspects became increasingly relevant as well. Its burgeoning financial surpluses have facilitated the development of a substantive aid and economic co-operation diplomacy over time. This especially applies to developing East Asian countries, and hence as part of a wider reconciliatory diplomacy towards nations brutally damaged by pre-1945 Japanese colonialism and military aggression. There are not just moral but also geopolitical and commercial motives underlying Japan's assumed responsibility for fostering East Asia's regional economic development. A strong region could in theory confer Japan, as East Asia's pre-eminent economic power, with wider geopolitical power and influence in the world system. Japan's recent economic malaise and the concomitant rise of China have, though, raised doubts about this prospect. Concerning commercial motives, East Asia's dynamic economic development has been made partly possible by the transnational activities of Japan's large companies, the *keiretsu*, in which host nations have benefited from transfers of capital and various forms of technology. The improving techno-industrial capabilities of Japan's regional neighbour economies have in turn played a significant part in enabling Japanese firms to undertake the necessary restructuring required to compete in global markets (METI 2005a). Free trade agreements are seen as increasingly relevant to the extensive regionalised production and distribution systems managed by Japanese firms in East Asia and the wider Asia-Pacific as they help minimise the international transaction costs incurred by operating these systems, for example in trade between different nodes of the *keiretsu's* inter-firm networks.

Japan's penchant of embedding a free trade agreement within a wider 'economic partnership agreement', or EPA, represents a particular conflation of the country's trade and aid policies, and moreover in some way a projection of the country's national developmentalism onto a broader regional or international canvas (METI 2005b). Japan's championing of a particular FTA model is indicative of its shift from a 'reactive state' to a more proactive actor on the international stage. The idea of Japan as a 'reactive state' has its roots in the country's past isolationism, especially during the 17th to 19th century, which has followed through in more contemporary times to its deference to the United States in the post-1945 era in various foreign relations issues (Calder 1988). By a 'reactive state' we mean one that simply waits until other states or international actors undertake actions before making foreign (economic) policy decisions themselves. Japan's hesitance at undertaking bold proactive measures itself in its foreign relations partly derives from an aversion to any manoeuvres that may be construed as 'post-colonial', and hence particularly applies to East Asia. This to some degree explains why Japan was tentative over approaching the ASEAN group with an FTA proposal, for fear of imposing its economic dominance, and had to 'react' to China's own FTA proposal with ASEAN before it felt able to fully commit to making one itself. The 1997/98 East Asian financial crisis has generally speaking, though, spurred Japan to take a more proactively responsible position on matters of regional economic diplomacy, and its FTA policy has played a central role in this respect (Terada 2001). In a Japanese Government statement on its 'basic policy' on FTAs, the 'fostering of an East Asian community' was placed high on its list of aims (MOFA 2004).

The origins and development of Japan's FTA policy

Japan's switch from a pure multilateralist to a multi-track approach to trade liberalisation (and hence taking on an FTA policy) first emerged in the second half of 1998, and it appeared a relatively sudden shift. In the 1998 edition of the Ministry of International Trade and Industry's (MITI) annually published *White Paper on International Trade*, priority was placed on the "steady implementation of WTO rules, and constant surveillance of and countermeasures for protectionist behaviours of foreign countries" (MITI 1998: 322). Moreover, comments on the global FTA trend were referred to only in negative terms, noting for example how FTAs carried certain "dangers" like "discriminatory treatment through sophisticated techniques such as substantial tightening of rules of origin", and the "substantial increase of trade barriers when expanding the area coverage of an RTA" (MITI 1998: 142). Later on that year, though, discussions within MITI's International Trade Policy Bureau on regional economic integration resulted in a proposal to explore new FTA policy options. South Korea, Mexico, Singapore and Chile were chosen as Japan's first FTA partners, and moves towards initiating these bilateral projects were made from late 1998 through to late 1999 (see Appendix A).

MITI's 1999 *White Paper on International Trade* published in May that year marked an important turning point in Japan's trade policy by acknowledging that FTAs could also have positive effects upon the multilateral trading system, e.g. the provision of new models of rule-making in multilateral fora (MITI 1999). There remained, however, elements within the Japanese Government that argued for maintaining a multilateral purist approach to trade liberalisation and trade agreement diplomacy generally, and hence resisted the development of an FTA policy. This view was especially prevalent within the Ministry of Foreign Affairs (MOFA), which became at odds with the main advocate of Japan's FTA policy, MITI and its transmogrified successor the Ministry of Economy, Trade and Industry (METI, formed in 2001). This inter-ministerial contestation over the future direction of Japan's trade policy had philosophical, ideological and practical dimensions. In October 2000, MOFA Deputy Minister, Yoshiji Nogami, commented that, "I am concerned that excessive expectations towards FTAs have been built up... It is important to draw a line between what we can do and what we cannot do as well as what we should do and what we should not do."[15] This was partly in response to a MITI report published a month earlier that argued bilateral FTAs would serve Japan's foreign economic policy objectives, particularly with regard to furthering the country's market access interests, as well as the improved diplomatic influence it would confer upon Japan.[16]

By the end of 2000, scoping study phases with Japan's first four FTA projects noted had all been initiated, and in January 2001 FTA negotiations commenced with Singapore. These went relatively smoothly with a deal struck after only four rounds of talks, leading to the Japan–Singapore Economic Partnership Agreement (JSEPA) being formally signed between the leaders of both countries in January 2002, and the Agreement entering into force in November that year. The signing of JSEPA marked an historic event in Japan's trade policy, being the first FTA signed by the country. Singapore was, though, an easy FTA partner for most because of the already very open nature of its economy, and substantive problems arose in the development of Japan's other FTA projects during 2002. In the case of those with Mexico and Chile this related especially to agriculture, and regarding South Korea a wide range of issues from agriculture to various industry sectors where competition between the two nations was intense, e.g. autos, consumer electronics. Continued in-fighting between METI and MOFA over FTAs and WTO multilateralism, and between METI and the Ministry of Agriculture, Forestry and Fisheries (MAFF) over agri-trade liberalisation was not conducive to an effective and progressive overall management of Japan's FTA policy.

New FTA projects initiated with Thailand from late 2001, and with Malaysia and the Philippines from late 2002 also brought additional burdens upon Japan's FTA policy-making cadres. Responding to these pressures, METI formed its own special FTA Task Force in October 2003 in an effort to better strategise and co-ordinate FTA policy, as well as to manage simultaneous negotiating processes with different trade partners. A few months later in February 2004 the number of METI staff working on FTA projects was over doubled from 35 to 80, spurring other ministries such as MOFA and MAFF to increase the number of their own FTA-related staff.[17] As we later discuss, continuing inter-ministerial fractions and disputes led to the Prime Minister's Office intervening in November 2003 to assume a central co-ordinated role in Japan's FTA policy. This move by Prime Minister Koizumi achieved some success at moving various projects forward, with Japan–Philippines FTA negotiations being substantially concluded by December 2004. Around the same time came final confirmation that broader ASEAN-wide FTA talks would commence in early 2005. In December 2005, Japan signed a bilateral FTA with Malaysia and in the same month initiated new bilateral FTA projects with Brunei and Vietnam. By this time, Japan had overall signed three FTAs within the Asia-Pacific region and was negotiating five others (Table 2.2).

Main determining factors

Most research interviewees acknowledged there was a strong regional dimension to Japan's bilateral FTA policy, and this is clearly evident in both METI and MOFA policy papers (METI 2005b; MOFA 2004). There are two elements to this. The first relates to establishing market access and other commercial linkages with large or emerging regional markets. This would hence help explain the FTA project with Mexico in the context of NAFTA, and with Chile in terms of the emerging South American market. The second element, and the stronger of the two, concerned Japan's role and links within the East Asia region. Many interviewees noted that Japan's

FTA policy could in many ways be understood *as a foreign economic policy response to the 1997/98 financial crisis* in that it formed part of the country's broader endeavour to develop new mechanisms and frameworks for better managing East Asia's regional economic interdependence. Developing FTA links with other East Asian countries was believed to be integral to this strategy, as did leading contributions to improving regional financial governance through actions such as the 1998 New Miyazawa Initiative (NMI) which was a precursor to the 2000 Chiang Mai Initiative, itself a key component of the then new ASEAN Plus Three (APT) framework. The 'post-crisis response' factor can be linked back to the earlier made point about the apparent sudden introduction of Japan's FTA policy in the second half of 1998, which closely coincided the launch of the NMI.

Both *strengthening economic relations with key trading partners* and *strengthening regional economic cohesion* – two top significance rated determining factors – should mostly be understood in this post-crisis context. The general view amongst research interviews that then Japanese Prime Minister Obuchi, as well as MITI, wanted to use FTAs to strengthen economic co-operative arrangements with other East Asian states so as to avert another regional crisis. For some this marked a further step towards the 'Asianisation' of Japan's foreign (economic) policy in that, in the past, the country had thought itself separate from East Asia, being instead a global player with stronger links outside the region, e.g. bilaterally with the US, and as a G7, OECD and GATT/WTO member. Given the virtual lack of East Asia wide economic regionalism before the 1997/98 crisis, an interviewed METI official remarked that "building up region-wide links through bilateral means appeared the practical way to begin with for us."[18] These above points also underline the relatively high significance rating assigned to *towards wider regional trade arrangements*. Another high rated determining factor was *response to regional/global FTA trend*. In both this case and Japan's response to the 1997/98 financial crisis, many research interviewees noted the relevance of country's 'reactive state' economic diplomacy. METI officials openly conceded that the ASEAN–China FTA (ACFTA) proposal accelerated Japan's actions to conclude more FTAs in East Asia.[19] Furthermore, the EU's free trade agreement with Mexico is widely acknowledged to have been instrumental in spurring the Japan–Mexico FTA project.

An additional key area of debate concerned how FTA projects constituted a new *gaiatsu* ('foreign pressure') mechanism to *help consolidate domestic economic reforms*, which research interviewees ranked as a mid-rated determining factor. Reform-minded government leaders and bureaucrats have a tradition of using *gaiatsu* to help realise their economic restructuring and policy reform objectives in the face of resistance from domestic interest groups. Bilateral economic diplomacy with the US had been a prime instrument of *gaiatsu* in the past but this had diminished in importance by the 1990s, mostly because Japan had complied with many US demands on trade and commerce policy issues (Hughes *et al* 2001; Mikanagi 1996). Multilateral *gaiatsu* through the WTO has also diminished in recent years, as already hinted and discussed further below. The extent to which FTAs could provide a new source of *gaiatsu* was a contentious point amongst research interviewees, although most agreed it would depend upon the extent agriculture was incorporated into the FTA liberalisation process. Also related to this is how FTAs helped *instigate a new trade policy direction* for Japan with particular regard to the shift from a multilateral to a multi-track trade agreement approach noted earlier.

Opinion was quite evenly split between research interviewees regarding the importance of *WTO trade liberalisation inertia* in spurring the development of Japan's FTA policy. Around a third attached high significance to it, notably citing the catalytic effects of the 1999 'Seattle debacle' (see Chapter 1), whereas another third assigned it very little significance, stating that Japan has recently become more interested in trade facilitation rather than trade liberalisation in its economic diplomacy generally and the response to 1997/98 crisis was more deterministically significant. The emphasis on trade facilitation over liberalisation also explains the low rating conferred to *APEC trade liberalisation inertia*, as Japan's dispute with the US and other APEC member states over the EVSL scheme clearly revealed, as discussed in Chapter 1. This hence begs the question is Japan's FTAs being used to advance the cause of trade liberalisation or rather achieve some other foreign economic policy objective or objectives? Our discussions on Japan's 'developmental–industrial' FTA model are relevant owing to its embedding of free trade arrangements within a broader 'economic partnership agreement' as Tokyo prefers to call them. Furthermore, this confirms the priority attached to strengthen politico-diplomatic ties and cultivating new frameworks of economic co-operation through this type of FTA approach. In addition, the 'co-operative' broad band elements of this FTA type can bring domestic economic restructuring effects (e.g. from collaboration in promoting the small and medium-size enterprise sector) in addition to trade liberalisation elements.

2.3.2   The formation of Japan's FTA policy

Economic policy-making in Japan has traditionally centred on the so called 'iron triangle' relationship between the central government bureaucracy, big business (*zaikai*), and the Liberal Democratic Party (LDP), and from this we can understand how Japan's FTA policy is formulated. The central government bureaucracy provides the main technocratic expertise that in turn relies on human networks (*jinmyaku*) between its own constituent elements and other influential agencies, e.g. research institutes such as the Institute of Developing Economies. The state bureaucracy's relationship with the business sector is augmented by *amakudari*, in which retired government officials are recruited to senior positions on the boards of companies or quasi-governmental special corporations. In the bureaucratic division of labour, METI is primarily responsible for managing Japan's trade negotiations and most aspects of trade policy, and as one would expect is the government agency with the closest relationship with the business sector. MOFA is mainly responsible for Japan's diplomatic policy, and therein its remit includes the creation and implementation of overall foreign political, economic and security policy. It is also charged with co-ordinating Japan's international relations, yet its own managerial control over the country's foreign policy is constrained both by its own limited technocratic resources and the contesting influence exerted by other ministries, e.g. METI in Japan's foreign economic policy formation. Other relevant ministries include MAFF (which maintains a strong interest-alignment with Japan's agricultural lobby) and the Ministry of Health, Labour and Welfare (MHLW), although it has only been involved in relatively marginal issues such as labour standards and human resource development co-operation. Japan's Ministry of Finance also has FTA stakeholder interest primarily in relation to tariff customs and financial sector issues.

The LDP has held almost continuous political power in Japan since the 1950s. It has traditionally deferred to the central government bureaucracy on matters of foreign (economic) policy, generally preferring to focus on constituency politics rather than Japan's international affairs. Debates over whether the origins and development of new economic policy initiatives derive more from the ruling LDP leadership or from state bureaucrats have raged for some time (Hughes *et al* 2001; Johnson 1996; Mikanagi 1996; van Wolferen 1988). Generally speaking, it is a highly interactive process that is also significantly influenced by consultations with Japan's business sector, this being a core aspect of Japan's developmental statism. The business sector itself remains dominated by the *keiretsu* big business groups whose common interests are championed by four main business associations. The most powerful of these is the Federation of Economic Organisations, or *Keidanren*, which represents around 800 of Japan's largest corporations. It is also makes substantial donations to the LDP and participates extensively on various government special advisory committees (*shingikai* and *chosakai*). The *Keidanren* has been an influential advocate of Japan's FTA policy from the very beginning. For example, it was calling upon the government to explore FTA policy options some time before its initiation,[20] and was instrumental in the early development of the JKFTA project (Keidanren 2000; Yoshimatsu 2005). The other three main business associations comprise the Japan Council for Economic Development (*Keizai Doyukai*), Japan Federation of Employer's Associations (*Nikkeiren*), and the Japan Chamber of Commerce and Industry, and these too have played FTA advocacy roles. For instance, the *Keizai Doyukai* was instrumental in establishing the country's Free Trade Council group in October 2000 that comprised mainly business leaders and with the prime aim of pushing forward the free trade agenda in Japan.[21]

As previously noted, the Prime Minister's Office assumed a more central co-ordinating role in Japan's FTA policy from November 2003 after PM Koizumi's frustrations over inter-ministerial disputes that were hampering the progress of most FTA projects.[22] Matters came to a head after the breakdown of a Japan–Mexico FTA negotiation round a few weeks earlier, and after Mexican Economy Secretary Fernando Canales complained of having to face three Japanese ministers: Foreign Minister Yoriko Kawaguchi (MOFA), Trade Minister Shoichi Nakagawa (METI) and Agriculture Minister Yoshiyuki Kamei (MAFF). Each of the ministerial players in Japan's FTA policy has close links with their associated domestic stakeholder groups. Apart from METI's ties with the business sector, MAFF's connection with the farming lobby is another particularly strong link in the policy-making chain. Research interviewees ranked these two groups substantially ahead of other domestic stakeholders in terms of their influential relationship with the government on FTA related matters (Table 2.1). The country's trade unions, environmental movement and other civil society groups have not, though, been that engaged in influencing FTA policy, partly out of it being of peripheral interest to them but perhaps mostly because their own ministerial advocates (e.g. the MHLW in the case of trade unions) have themselves only been involved at the margins of FTA policy formation.

2.3.3   Challenging areas and contentious issues

By far the most contentious issue in the development of Japan's FTA policy has been that of *agriculture*, as confirmed by research interviewees who rated this by far the most significant hindrance factor (Table 2.1). Close comparisons can be made here with South Korea in terms of opening up an economically weak but politically very sensitive sector to greater foreign competition. Japanese farms are very small in size, averaging only 1.6 hectares (compared to an average 190 hectares for the US and 20 for the EU), and are therefore not easily able to capture scale economy advantages. One consequence of this is that the country produces only 40 percent of its own food, and hence food security issues arise with any policy initiative or actions deemed to undermine Japan's agricultural production.[23] In contrast to many other developed nations, Japan's food self-sufficiency ratio has fallen.[24] While the country's average import tariff rate on agri-products is only 12 percent, and rates of below five percent apply to around a fifth of these, tariffs on certain key products are very high, e.g. 490 percent equivalent rate on rice and 210 percent on wheat.

Although agriculture represents just over one percent of Japan's GDP, the farm lobby remains politically very powerful. The reasons for this lie in historic links between the farmers and the LDP. The origins of the LDP are rooted in an alliance formed with the *daimyos*, rural-based magnates who dominated much of the country from about the 11th to the 19th century. The Party maintained strong ties with the rural elite and their associates

through to the post-1945 era in a coalition aligned against the urban industrialised labour supported Socialist Party. This age-old alliance with rural
groups forms an important cultural and traditional background of the LDP.
Moreover, most current LDP members of the Diet (Japan's Parliament) are
the descendants of first-generation parliamentarians, providing a further
seam of continuity in the Party's links with farming communities. The
LDP's sense of political obligation to the farmers is hence strong, and additional political power stems from the proportionately high concentration
of Diet constituencies in rural areas of the country.

The triangular relationship between core LDP elements, Japan's farmers
and MAFF is the basis of formidable opposition to opening up the nation's
agriculture sector to foreign competition, through FTAs or any other
means. Historic parallels can be drawn between the current political debate
in Japan over agri-sector liberalisation and Britain's Corn Law controversy
of the early 19th century in which similar discussions over food security and
free trade raged both inside and outside parliament for some time. In
October 2003, Prime Minister Koizumi remarked that, "In light of the need
to conclude FTAs with as many countries as possible in the near future, we
can't avoid squarely addressing farm trade problems. The nation can no
longer maintain an isolationist policy in terms of agricultural matters."[25]
On the one hand there remain political risks for Japanese government
leaders in pressing too hard too fast for agricultural trade reform. On the
other hand a number of policy options are left open to them, such as
making compensatory side-payments (e.g. grants for rural redevelopment)
to the nation's farmers as part of the bargain of liberalising and reforming
the agriculture sector. Another would be to increase the average size of
Japan's farms to capture scale economies. The Government had explored
some of these options by 2005 but the farm lobby remained largely uncon-
vinced, maintaining their general opposition to domestic market opening.
Furthermore, both MAFF and the main farming association – JA Zenchu –
continue to argue that WTO rules currently dictate that only "substantially
all trade" (clause 8b of Article XXIV) be covered in an FTA, thus allowing
for relatively minor trade flows to be exempted (see Chapter 1). In part
attempt to draw support from MOFA, they have further contended that
negotiations on agricultural trade liberalisation should be confined to the
WTO, and that, "it is not appropriate that further reduction and/or elimination of tariffs to be done within bilateral agreements."[26] The farm lobby
also continue to make the 'multifunctionality of agriculture' argument in
relation to the various functions Japan's agriculture industry performs, as
discussed in Chapter 1.

An early demonstration over Japan's FTA policy problems regarding agriculture came in the JSEPA project. Singapore's virtually non-existent
agricultural sector was a prime reason why it was chosen as Japan's first
negotiating FTA partner. Despite the extremely limited competitive threat

that the city-state's agri-producers posed to their Japanese counterparts (constrained to the micro-sectors of ornamental fish and flowers), Japan's farmers insisted on exemptions in their sector. This was mostly, though, to set the precedent for Japan's other FTA projects in development with relatively much larger and more competitive agri-producing countries like Mexico, Chile and Thailand. As Kagami (2003) noted, Singapore's goldfish exports in particular was a major issue in JSEPA talks. Tokyo's position was guided by advice given by the LDP's Research Commission on Trade in Agriculture, Forestry and Fishery Products made in September 2001 that any tariff liberalisation on these products should be agreed through multilateral rather than bilateral negotiations. In the final agreement only 486 agri-product lines were selected for tariff liberalisation in JSEPA from a sector total of 2,227 but these 486 were in effect already traded duty-free between the two countries beforehand.[27] So agriculture was included in JSEPA but only in neutralised terms as no new agri-trade liberalisation was achieved.

Although not ranked anywhere near as highly as agriculture, *opposition from other Japanese domestic industries* was rated the third most significant hindrance factor by research interviewees, with particular reference to sectors where some degree of structural decline was evident such as petrochemicals, plastics, textiles and steel. The textiles sub-sector of leather products is a particularly sensitive issue for Japan because of its sociocultural dimension. Small-scale leather goods manufacturing are essential to the livelihoods of the *buraku-min*, descendants of former social outcasts that are still economically and socially marginalised in Japanese society. Japan maintains high levels of trade protection in this sector. The second highest rated hindrance factor overall, though, was *lack of foreign economic policy priority of Government*. Most research interviewees associated this with two main factors. The first concerned the apparent lack of a coherent FTA policy strategy to have emerged from Tokyo, which itself was attributed to the aforementioned inter-ministerial bickering and poor leadership shown by PM Koizumi on this matter. The second related to lack of political will to take on agricultural sector reform. Following on from this point, *state bureaucratic inertia or opposition* also scored highly among research interviewees (Table 2.1), with special reference to MAFF bureaucrats and more mercantilist minded METI officials. In many ways, this is confirming earlier points made on the various obstacles to the development of Japan's FTA policy, as well as the country's trade policy formation process.

Many potential hindrance factors were assigned relatively low significance ratings. Japan had the lowest rating for *opposition from civil society groups/NGOs* amongst the OECD countries in the field-research group (Table 2.1). This can be explained by the comparative weak contesting influence of civil society on matters of Japan's trade policy, and by the fact that the NGO group with the most interest in FTAs – the trade union movement – can see the benefits to Japanese workers of these agreements being pursued, with the proviso of their attention to job security. To a large extent this stemmed from a confidence in Japan's trade competitiveness, although the nation's largest trade union, Rengo, accepted that job losses may occur in certain sectors.[28] Rengo and other trade unions have nevertheless expressed concern over how FTAs could allow low-skilled workers to enter Japan and cause disruptions in the country's labour market. This issue particularly arose in FTA negotiations with the Philippines and Thailand, both of which earned substantial sums of foreign exchange from the 'export' of care workers to foreign countries. In both sets of talks, Tokyo agreed to open up its labour markets to some extent under certain conditions, e.g. quota limits, required language training.[29]

2.3.4   Impacts and consequences

Amongst the top significance rated 'consequence' factors concerning Japan's FTA policy were *relations with its bilateral FTA partners, country's influence in the East Asia/Asia-Pacific region* and *international relations in the region*. In the context of China's rise within the East Asian region, one research interviewed MOFA official commented that, "Japan has to develop more FTA projects just to maintain its current influence."[30] The impact of these projects on *domestic economic policy reform* was also thought relatively significant if comprehensive FTAs were signed by Tokyo. Foreign ambassadorial officials seemed most sceptical about this from amongst the research interviewee group. This also applied to *domestic economic restructuring process*, which attained a mid-ranked rating. Both agriculture and other aforementioned FTA-problematic industries were most relevant here. The same rating was conferred to *developing wider regional trade agreements* with many research interviewees believing that key FTA projects such as the JKFTA could be a starting point to plurilateral FTA networks.

The impact of Japan's FTA policy on the WTO was thought to be minimal. Having said this some research interviewees believed this could be significant, some in positive terms and some negative. A foreign ambassadorial representative remarked that, "anything that helps Japan think more in free trade terms will prove useful to the WTO process, and it could also make Japan a more predicable, reliable trade negotiator in the multilateral process."[31] Another commented that, "FTAs are an important free trade conditioning process for Japan, and this is useful in the WTO context."[32] However, one MOFA official was of the opinion that, "FTAs lead to an undermined multilateral discipline."[33] The believed impact effects upon APEC were less equivocal, these being quite insignificant but this was more to do with APEC's own diminishing significance in the Asia-Pacific regional political economy. There were nevertheless important connections to note, such as that the FTA policies of large economy states like Japan had particularly overshadowed APEC's own initiatives on trade liberalisation. Finally, the impact on *countries and international regions (e.g. EU) outside the Asia-Pacific* was thought to be low, which given the significance of the Japanese economy both regionally and globally was somewhat surprising. Most research interviewees assigned a low rating to this factor, though, because they believed Japan's FTA policy would develop in a relatively slow manner.

2.4 New Zealand

2.4.1 The origins, determining factors and development of New Zealand's FTA policy

New Zealand: an international political economy overview

New Zealand is a small, trade dependent developed country. It has one of the world's most developed agricultural industries, having particular competitive advantages in the dairy and lamb product sectors. New Zealand also bucks the general OECD trend for advanced industrial countries in that agriculture has in recent years taken an increasing share of GDP, rising from seven percent in 1998 to around nine percent in 2003. Commensurate with this is the rise of agriculture's share of total exports, standing at about 58 percent by 2003, with dairy exports alone accounting for approximately 20 percent of the total. The dairy industry has long been of vital importance to the New Zealand economy. New Zealand's largest company, Fonterra, is the world's largest producer of dairy exports, selling its products in over 140 countries. Agricultural protectionism operated by New Zealand's major trade partners is therefore a major issue for the country given its high dependence on farm product exports.

Major changes occurred in New Zealand's international political economy during the 1970s and 1980s. For some time, New Zealand's farmers had traditionally relied on the British market for a significant proportion of their agricultural exports, and hence exports *per se*. Britain's joining of the EC in 1973 caused similar problems for New Zealand as noted earlier for Australia, with New Zealand farm exports consequently placed at a price competitive disadvantage after CAP tariff effects. This led to a broader shift in New Zealand's once British Commonwealth orientated trade to a more Asia-Pacific trade orientation from around this time. Following on from this geographic shift in trade policy, New Zealand like Australia made the ideological shift from having a generally protectionist trade policy to one based on unilateral trade liberalisation. The deepening of market economy politics during the 1980s and 1990s further entrenched this trend (Nixon and Yeabsley 2002).

New Zealand signed the ANZCER with Australia in 1983, and was also at the forefront of the new Asia-Pacific FTA trend, initiating bilateral FTA projects with Singapore and South Korea from 1999. New Zealand's new FTA policy was introduced by Jenny Shipley's National Government but was replaced by a Labour Government in 2001 under Helen Clark's leadership. While still ascribing importance to trade liberalisation in its economic policy approach, the Clark Government has been more qualified than its predecessor about what kind of free trade it wishes to promote. For example, when Clark herself addressed the heads of some of the world's biggest companies at the 2003 APEC summit in Bangkok, she noted both the potential social inequalities brought about by free trade as well as the economic benefits.[34]

New Zealand's strong support for an open and strong multilateral trading system has been a constant factor in its trade policy and diplomacy. Research conducted by the country's Ministry of Agriculture and Forestry on the quantitative benefits of the Uruguay Round suggested that its beef, sheep-meat, and dairy sectors gained around NZ$590 million (approx US$400 million) in export growth in the US and EU markets in the year 2000 alone. In addition, other government research concluded that New Zealand gained from at least NZ$9 billion (approx US$6 billion) in benefits over the ten-year implementation period of the Uruguay Round.[35] Membership of the Cairns Group has been of critical importance to New Zealand in its multilateral trade diplomacy at the GATT and WTO. Yet like other staunch multilateral supporters in the Asia-Pacific, New Zealand has been frustrated by the recent lack of progress at the WTO front and has thus turned to FTAs for additional market access options.

The origins and development of New Zealand's FTA policy

The ANZCER has been the cornerstone of New Zealand's trade policy for many years (Nixon 2000). Australia and New Zealand actually signed a precursorial NZ–Australia FTA in 1965 but this was never fully implemented. The weaknesses and failures of this agreement led to the improved 1983 ANZCER arrangement. A decade later a key Ministry of Foreign Affairs and Trade (MFAT) strategist, Tim Groser, developed a multi-track, four-dimension framework (unilateral, bilateral, regional, multilateral) for New Zealand's trade policy, where all aspects were, though, subordinate to advancing multilateral trade liberalisation. The US and Chile were the first FTA partners targeted by the NZ Government during the mid-1990s, but the domestic politics of these countries at the time were not conducive to launching FTA projects. In the US case, this was due to the lack of 'Fast Track' trade policy authority, and in Chile's case sensitivity over opening up the dairy sector to NZ imports. New Zealand did, however, sign a bilateral investment treaty (BIT) with Chile and also Hong Kong in 1995, these being seen as precursors to negotiating FTAs. A model for negotiating an FTA with Hong Kong followed on from this in 1996 but negotiations were not initiated until 2001, these themselves becoming stalled just a year and five rounds of talks later over rules of origin issues.

In 1999, New Zealand initiated two bilateral FTA projects, with South Korea in July and with Singapore in September. The former never progressed owing to political opposition in South Korea to liberalising the country's agricultural trade. The Agreement on a New Zealand–Singapore Closer Economic Partnership (ANZSCEP) project was a distillation of the 'Pacific-5' FTA proposal that would have also involved Australia, Chile and the US in the arrangement (see Chapters 1 and 3). Linkage aspects of the ANZSCEP also extended to a possible AFTA–CER arrangement where this bilateral FTA would serve as a foundation on which a wider free trade agreement between Southeast Asia and Oceania could be built.[36] Other ideas of wider strategic objectives being realised by New Zealand's FTA policy were fermenting amongst its trade policy-makers. Tim Groser, in a speech entitled 'Beyond CER: New Trade Options for New Zealand' given in March 2000 at the NZ Institute for Policy Studies, described FTAs as the Trojan Horse within APEC to help reach the regional organisation's Bogor Goals of creating a free trade and investment zone in the Asia-Pacific. As an interviewed NZIER analyst commented, small countries such as New Zealand have only ideas on trade policy to offer rather than market appeal. Hence, New Zealand could be considered 'policy-traders' in this respect.[37] Similarities can be made with Singapore here in that both set out to bring trade policy innovation to the Asia-Pacific. Indeed, both countries were at the original leading edge of the new Asia-Pacific FTA trend in the late 1990s.

Other bilateral FTA project proposals involving New Zealand quickly followed, including those with Chile (later subsumed into the Trans-Pacific Strategic Economic Partnership Agreement, or TPSEPA, also involving Singapore and Brunei), Thailand, Hong Kong and the Pacific Agreement on Closer Economic Relations (PACER), which also involved Australia in a extended 'most favoured nation' arrangement with the Pacific Island Countries. After the signing of the ANZSCEP in November 2000, New Zealand then moved on to commence negotiations with Hong Kong a few months later in May 2001. At the beginning, New Zealand wanted to include labour standards in the talks but Hong Kong's position was that this was inappropriate.[38] However, New Zealand's demands for the application of strict rules of origin (RoO) proved far more contentious. Through rounds of Wellington was concerned about re-routed imports from China through Hong Kong gaining free market access to NZ markets, especially after Hong Kong and China were set to commence their own bilateral FTA negotiations in January 2002. More specifically, New Zealand was circumspect about the inclusion of an outward processing arrangement whereby an element of processing would be permitted in China. Hong Kong would not concede on this issue because of the precedent it would set in the nomenclature of its trade relations with key partners like the US and EU.[39] Negotiations reached an impasse after five rounds of talks by 2002 with no subsequent developments since then, except perhaps for the initiation of New Zealand–China FTA talks from December 2004. The conclusion of this bilateral agreement could potentially lead to its extension to Hong Kong in a TPSEPA type arrangement, particularly since the Hong Kong–China CEPA came into force in January 2004.

The next action New Zealand's bilateral FTA negotiating team saw was in July 2003 with the start of TPSEPA talks hosted in Wellington. Both New Zealand and Australia had made concurrent attempts to initiate FTA talks with the US, and the launch of the AUSFTA project heightened a sense of FTA competition between New Zealand and Australia. In December 2002, Wellington suggested that New Zealand should be included in trilateral FTA negotiations with the Australia and the US. However, both Canberra and Washington rebuffed the proposal, and it is widely thought that security policy related issues have been the prime hindrance to the development of a NZUSFTA project. New Zealand's decision to opt out of the ANZUS security treaty in the 1980s, and Prime Minister Helen Clark's comments in April 2003 that the US would not have gone to war with Iraq if Al Gore had been elected US President are particularly relevant.

New Zealand did, however, beat Australia to initiating bilateral FTA talks with China, an initial round of negotiations taking place in December 2004, a few months ahead of Australia's first round of talks with China (see Appendix A).[40] Developing FTA links with other East Asian countries has been strongly promoted by the Wellington based Asia–New Zealand Foundation, whose 2002/03 annual report claimed that the country's trade and other commercial links with the region underpinned roughly 20 percent of the national economy (Asia–New Zealand Foundation 2003). The conclusion of a substantive FTA agreement with Thailand on the sidelines of October 2004 APEC summit was soon followed by the official launch of the long sought ASEAN–CER free trade agreement project at the APT summit the following month. While persisting sensitivities over agricultural trade liberalisation make the prospect of FTAs with either Japan or South Korea a long-term goal for New Zealand, its prospective FTA links with China and Southeast Asia provide New Zealand with the opportunity for a more comprehensive integration into East Asia's regional economic dynamics. By the end of 2005, New Zealand was a signatory to four FTAs within the Asia-Pacific region and was conducting negotiations in three other projects (Table 2.2).

Main determining factors

Three main determining factors behind New Zealand's bilateral FTA policy were assigned equal top rating by this country's group of research interviewees (Table 2.1). The first of these – *strengthening diplomatic relations with key trading partners* – is in line with the high rating afforded this factor generally across the field researched country group. In New Zealand's case, a key relevant point here concerns the country's feeling of geographic isolation, with even its 'sister nation' Australia being almost 3,000 kilometers away. Certain research interviewees remarked that, in this context, FTAs provide New Zealand with both important symbolic and psychological links to its key but 'distant' trading partners and the wider Asia-Pacific. Some also specifically noted the 'isolation avoidance' motive in that New Zealand had to keep pace with the new FTA trend in order to avert its economic marginalisation in the region (see Chapter 1). The second of the equal top-rated factors – *towards wider regional trade arrangements* – follows from this in that these bilaterals would hopefully broaden out to wider sub-regional linkages, as seen with the ANZSCEP in relation to the TPSEPA. This also explains why *strengthen regional economic cohesion* was assigned a relatively high rating.

The third and last top factor – *WTO trade liberalisation inertia* – is not surprising given the importance of the multilateral trade system to small trade-dependent nations like New Zealand. The vast majority of research interviewees concurred that bilaterals offered a 'plan B' insurance policy against a collapse of that system, and many noted that the 'Seattle debacle' gave substantial impetus to the country's new FTA policy, as have subsequent troubles in the Doha Round of talks. There was also a strong view amongst many research interviewees that 'competitive liberalisation' principles partly underpinned New Zealand's FTA policy in that it was intended to *help stimulate progress of the WTO/multilateral trade liberalisation*, the next highest rated factor. As MFAT states in its approach to FTAs, "[FTAs] enable New Zealand... to set a faster pace towards opening markets by linking up with economies that share the same level of ambition. In this way, these agreements can make a useful contribution to generating momentum for the WTO process by highlighting the benefits of liberalisation."[41] This is consistent with the country's demonstrated interest in free trade alliance-formation discussed earlier. Although this was only limited to the Asia-Pacific regional sphere rather than the global-multilateral, this is probably seen the most viable means by which New Zealand could contribute to a competitive liberalisation process.

Amongst the field research country group New Zealand has the highest rating given for *APEC trade liberalisation inertia*. Disappointments over the failure of the EVSL and IAP schemes to deliver trade liberalisation gains were certainly instrumental in New Zealand's push for new FTA options, such as the Pacific-5 FTA idea and the eventual ANZSCEP project.[42] According to one research interviewee, the New Zealand Government saw APEC as an effective mechanism for levering in the country's interests into the WTO, hence APEC's own failures were seen as having significant ramifications for New Zealand trade diplomacy at the global-multilateral level.[43] In contrast, New Zealand has one of the lowest ratings for *response to the regional/global FTA trend* in the group, with only Singapore having a lower rating. This maybe expected since both were pioneers of the Asia-Pacific's new FTA trend. Research interviewees also specifically noted the ANZCER agreement as evidence of even earlier FTA pioneering, as well as the strategic planning behind New Zealand's multi-track trade policy from the early 1990s that predating both the global level intensification of FTA activity. Other low rated factors were *instigating a new trade policy direction* and *helping to consolidate New Zealand's economic reforms*, these being linked in some way. New Zealand had embarked on a programme of unilateral trade liberalisation many years beforehand. Hence, FTAs were not going to have a significant liberalisation impact upon the economy, nor bring a notable change to technical aspects of trade policy.

2.4.2   The formation of New Zealand's FTA policy

The Ministry of Foreign Affairs and Trade is the core agency of the New Zealand's FTA policy. Its staff has been central to both formulating its philosophical basis, has consulted with both counterparts from other government offices and NGO representatives on FTA-related issues, and has been primarily responsible for managing all aspects of the FTA negotiating process itself. As a well established democratic nation, a society-centric approach has been a defining feature in New Zealand's foreign economic policy-making, where the government has sought a relatively comprehensive inclusion of societal interests in its FTA policy formation. The relatively high ratings the country scored in government– stakeholder consultation on FTA policy strongly suggests this to be the case (Table 2.1). Finding a workable societal consensus has been easier for New Zealand than most. It is a small country with a relatively narrow range of domestic interests, and moreover these are generally aligned in the support of FTAs, the most important alignment here being between the agriculture and industry lobbies that both strongly support the trade liberalisation cause *per se*. Such strong alignments are not found in countries like the US and Japan.

The importance of agriculture to New Zealand's trade and economy has meant that its farmers are embedded in the country's 'business' community rather than being seen as a separate domestic political entity. Research interviewees were of the opinion that the government consulted more closely with the farming lobby than any other, but this may be because of the wide range of sensitive and complex issues (e.g. quarantine) confronting MFAT officials when negotiating FTAs with their foreign counterparts. The country even has an 'Ambassador of Agriculture' who travels the world championing New Zealand's farming interests. The main agriculture organisation, the Federated Farmers of New Zealand (FFNZ), while being more supportive of the WTO has increasingly recognised the importance of the country engaging in the new FTA trend, and has worked very closely indeed with MFAT negotiating teams. In the words of an interviewed senior

FFNZ official, "we are well integrated into the trade policy process."[44] A similar assessment can be made of other 'business' interest groups. Representatives from both the New Zealand Business Roundtable and the American Chamber of Commerce meet regularly with government to discuss FTA issues, and have furthermore made efforts to build transnational business lobby groups to advance particular FTA projects, especially between New Zealand and the US. These groups invariably spend more time lobbying foreign governments than the NZ Government.[45]

The country's main labour movement, the New Zealand Congress of Trade Unions (NZCTU), has become increasingly involved in FTA-related matters, especially from the development of the Hong Kong FTA project. A research interviewed NZCTU official noted that the Government was "insistent that our organisation got more involved in trade policy matters generally", and also that the NZCTU had "excellent access to politicians and the government bureaucracy."[46] The NZCTU's generally pro free trade stance changed after the WTO Seattle Ministerial of 1999, becoming more critically evaluative thereafter and exploring new trade-linked issues (e.g. FDI, environment, migration) in more substantive detail. This was an analytical response to the issue-linkage bound up in globalising processes more than anything else, and led to the NZCTU working more closely with other NGOs, such as Greenpeace. Indeed, because of New Zealand's agri-dominated export structure, there is significant cross-over between the farming and environment lobbies. However, New Zealand's green movement, like most of its counterparts around the Asia-Pacific, are more focused on domestic issues (e.g. waste emissions from the dairy industry) rather than on international trade, and have not taken too much interest to date on FTA matters. The interest taken by New Zealand's Maori community in FTA policy has mainly centred on foreign investment related issues, as we later discuss.

2.4.3 Challenging areas and contentious issues

Research interviewees identified agricultural issues as the most significant hindrance to developing New Zealand's FTA policy, especially concerning the agri-protectionism of its trade partners. Japan, South Korea and Taiwan would therefore make problematic FTA partners, and New Zealand face challenges here too in FTA negotiations with China. In 2004 for example, China imposed import tariffs of 38 percent on wool (ex-quota), 20 percent on kiwifruit and 15 percent on lamb. That year, China's Commerce Minister commented that free trade in agricultural products "would be something very difficult for the Chinese Government to bear."[47] Foreign trade partners, especially developing country partners, cited New Zealand's strict quarantine regulations as a significant agri-related trade they themselves faced when exporting to the country. New Zealand's government and farmers are unlikely to compromise on this in any FTA negotiations given the critical importance of bio-security to the nation's agricultural industry.

Second equally rated hindrance factors identified were *opposition from certain New Zealand industry groups* and *scarce diplomatic resources*. Regarding the former, most research interviewees noted that the TCF sector was particularly relevant. Production of TCF goods is concentrated around the provincial centres of the country, which makes it a sensitive issue to some extent in terms of political geography. The decline of the TCF sector would hit certain local communities hard, although one research interviewee was of the opinion that, "unless you are making boots and clothes for sheep, there is not much point in New Zealand producing in this area over the long-term."[48] Regarding the latter, New Zealand only had 15 trade negotiators working on FTAs in 2003, which meant that it could only undertake a limited number of FTA negotiation schedules simultaneously, around two or possibly three at most. In comparison, Australia at this time reportedly had around 80 or so trade negotiators and another 60 more staff in trade diplomacy support, with 30 negotiators alone working on the AUSFTA project. However, MFAT's Trade Negotiating Department did receive a budget increase that year to help expand its operations.

Quarantine (or sanitary and phytosanitary measures, SPS) and RoO related issues arose under the fourth ranked hindrance factor, *non-tariff barrier or other 'technical' issues*. The fifth ranked was *opposition from civil society groups*. Trade unions figuring especially high here, and a notably strong alignment exist between themselves and the TCF industry in particular. An FTA with China is deemed to pose a considerable job security risk in this area. The NZCTU has also identified intellectual property rights (IPR) with China as another problematic issue for New Zealand industry, especially after a high profile case of a Canterbury based tools manufacturer revealing evidence of a Chinese producer directly copying one of its designs.[49] In addition, the NZCTU has also taken a strong stance on the inclusion of labour standards in FTAs New Zealand signs with other countries.

Although New Zealand's environmental movement have been generally more preoccupied with domestic issues, it has nevertheless been critical of the country's FTA policy, seeing projects like AZNSCEP as a vehicle for consolidating transnational economic liberalism and the environmental risks carried therein.[50] In addition, activists at the Campaign Against Foreign Control of Aotearoa expressed concern over the ANZSCEP's investment-promotion measures, claiming it would allow Singaporean firms to buy up more of New Zealand's corporate assets.[51] Furthermore, the Maori community have insisted that all trade agreements signed by the New Zealand government should include the Treaty of Waitangi, which *inter alia* protects Maori land rights, in investment-related and other provisions. In addition, New Zealand's human rights activists highlighted the poor working conditions on Batam Islands, where much of Singaporean firms' labour-intensive production has been relocated as part of the Indonesia-Malaysia-Singapore Growth Triangle (IMSGT) arrangement.[52]

Low ratings were assigned to factors such as *lack of business sector support, lack of foreign (economic) policy priority afforded by New Zealand Government* and *opposing pressure from other countries or international organisations*. A number of additional 'other' hindrance factors were, though, noted by research interviewees. This included New Zealand's small market size and hence trading value (Appendix D) as well as its security policy, especially in relation to its 'nuclear-free zone' legislation passed in 1987, which in effect withdrew the country from the trilateral ANZUS security pact as it forbids the entry of the US's nuclear-powered or nuclear-armed ships into its territorial waters. This, together with Helen Clark's aforementioned vocal criticism of the US-led invasion of Iraq in 2003, is often cited as the most significant impediment to New Zealand advancing its FTA project with the US. As early as February 2001, MFAT officials expressed public concerns about Australia playing the 'security card' with the US to sign an FTA ahead of New Zealand.[53]

Yet even if the security issue is factored out, there are other notable commerce-related issues that pose a challenge to negotiating a NZ–US FTA. New Zealand's farmers would not be that encouraged by the limited gains secured by their Australian counterparts under AUSFTA, and the US is unlikely to offer any improvement on what it offered Australia on agritrade liberalisation. Moreover, the US is likely to insist on a similar set of wide-ranging 'behind the border' liberalisation demands in negotiating with New Zealand as it did with Australia. Many of these may be discerned from an April 2002 US Trade Representative (USTR) Office report on a list of trade barriers facing American exporters to New Zealand. Quarantine was a key issue, citing bans on certain US food imports as unscientific. Foreign investment and telecommunication laws were also noted, as were local content quotas for radio and television, and the pharmaceutical pricing system in the public health sector, similar to Australia's PBS arrangement.[54]

2.4.4 Impacts and consequences

Research interviewees were of the general opinion that the main impact and consequences of New Zealand's FTA policy were more of a politico-diplomatic nature than of an economic one, with *relations with its bilateral FTA partners* the highest ranked factor. The prime reason given for this concerned New Zealand's potential for marginalisation in the regional political economy given its geographic location and relative small size. There is, of course, an economic dimension to this as discussed earlier when the importance of a trade-dependent nation like New Zealand of maintaining good access to 'distant' key markets. This economic dimension did not, however, extend the same way into the realm of domestic economic policy reform and restructuring, where the impact of FTAs was deemed insignificant.

Consistent with a previous debate, there is a consensual view that some significant restructuring of the country's TCF sector should, though, be expected as a consequence of various FTA projects.

While a small member-state of APEC, the demonstration effects of New Zealand's 'pioneering' new FTA policy from the late 1990s was believed to have had a notable demonstration effect for other APEC countries in the development of their own FTA policies. Our analysis of how the ANZSCEP and TPSEPA projects developed are cases in point here, although this has more to do with APEC as a group of separate states rather than the organisation itself. Some research interviewees followed this up by commenting that New Zealand's contribution to the early development of the new Asia-Pacific FTA trend will help APEC realise its 'free trade zone' objectives, i.e. the Bogor Goals. Chapter 4 debates the wider relationship between Asia-Pacific FTAs and APEC in some detail. New Zealand scored the highest significance rating in research interviewee responses for the impact of its FTA policy on APEC for the above main reasons. This also explained the relatively high rating afforded to *New Zealand's influence in the Asia-Pacific region* from its FTA policy, although compared across the field researched country group this rating was quite low (Table 2.1).

Many research interviewees noted how New Zealand's FTA policy has impacted on Australia's and vice versa. One raised the point that New Zealand should have waited until Australia was ready to join its FTA project with Singapore, demonstrating CER solidarity. Subsequently Australia used the same argument against New Zealand in its FTA projects with the US and Thailand, with deals in both instances secured ahead of its sister nation.[55] Especially with respect to AUSFTA there were a number of concerns from a New Zealand perspective relating to trade and investment diversion (MFAT 2002). In a speech given to the US Chamber of Commerce in New York in December 2002, NZ Prime Minister Helen Clark stated that trade and investment diversion would ensue if the US only concluded an FTA with Australia and not New Zealand.[56] A study undertaken by Robert Scollay at Auckland University estimated that New Zealand's trading income would be reduced by 0.3 percent, equal to about NZ$39.5 million (US$19.5 million) as a result of AUSFTA but this was a conservative estimate.[57]

2.5 Singapore

2.5.1 The origins, determining factors and development of Singapore's FTA policy

Singapore: an international political economy overview

Singapore is Southeast Asia's most advanced newly industrialised economy and possesses the region's most impressive state economic bureaucracy with a predilection for geo-strategising. It is also Southeast Asia's premier entrepot hub economy through which around half of ASEAN's trade passes. It's industrialisation strategy has been principally based on attracting increasingly technology-intensive investments from foreign multinational enterprises (MNEs) who use the city-state as a platform from which to export to other markets in East Asia, and also worldwide. Singapore's position as a regional hub economy further extends to its hosting of regional MNE headquarters and for the research, development and design centre activity for foreign MNEs. Singapore is thus a key node in regional and global circuits of capital. Securing FTAs with major trade partners is part of the same strategy, as from the city-state foreign MNEs can export their Singapore-made products tariff-free to a growing number of FTA partner markets. Singapore has therefore always been a fervent advocate of free trade in various levels and channels of economic diplomacy, e.g. regional, multilateral (Daquila and Huy 2003; Desker 2004; Low 2003; Rajan *et al* 2001).

The soft authoritarian, mono-regime style developmentalism of Singapore's ruling People's Action Party (PAP) has been a fundamental determinant of the city-state's economic policy formation since it gained full independence in the 1960s. The PAP Government has long adopted a 'distant horizon', strategic approach in formulating Singapore's foreign economic policy (Dent 2001, 2002). This relates to both the long-term and strong geoeconomic perspectives that shape this policy, which in turn is largely attributable to a combination of Singapore's developmental statism and a deep security complex. Taking the first of these factors, FTA projects help realise the objectives of broader transformative economic projects (e.g. creating a 'knowledge-based economy', or KBE) managed by the Singapore developmental state. Regarding the second of these factors, Singapore's deep security complex derives from the city-state's long perceived, inherent vulnerability within its regional situation. Although advanced and prosperous, Singapore is a small economy with virtually no natural resources or economic hinterland, and has experienced periods of difficult political diplomacy with its two much larger neighbours, Malaysia and Indonesia. Cultivating economic security linkages with key trade partners outside the region – whether through FTAs most recently or by other means (e.g. inward foreign investment) – has been an important geo-strategic objective of Singapore's foreign economic policy. There are thus broad security connotations to Singapore's FTA projects as the government sees these as further advancing the city-state's economic prosperity.

The origins and development of Singapore's FTA policy

Singapore had long sought some kind of FTA for Southeast Asia well before the introduction of the ASEAN Free Trade Area (AFTA) programme. It had proposed an ASEAN free trade agreement at the first ASEAN Economic Ministers Meeting held at Jakarta in 1975 but other member states (especially

Indonesia) were opposed to the idea. The eventual proposal for AFTA itself mainly derived from Singaporean initiatives to find a new geo-economic rationale for ASEAN in the emerging post-Cold War era of the early 1990s (see Chapter 1). The prospect of a Southeast Asia wide FTA very much appealed to the Singapore Government at a time when it was also trying to consolidate and develop the city-state's 'hub economy' position in the regional locale through its 'Regionalisation 2000' programme and other schemes. However, when the 1997/98 financial crisis severely hit the Southeast Asian economy, Singapore re-evaluated its economic security strategy.

Consultations between Singapore's Ministry of Trade and Industry (MTI) and Ministry of Foreign Affairs (MFA) on initiating a bilateral FTA policy began around the time of the 1997/98 crisis.[58] Soon thereafter, then Minister of Trade and Industry, George Yeo, made a proposal at a higher ministerial level that Singapore should explore its bilateral FTAs options.[59] This coincided with the aforementioned Pacific-5 FTA proposal emerging within APEC circles during 1997 and 1998 that envisaged a plurilateral FTA between Singapore, the US, Australia, New Zealand and Chile. As we know from Chapter 1, although this proposal faltered both Singapore and New Zealand decided to proceed instead with a bilateral FTA project, the ANZSCEP (see also previous section). This was East Asia's first FTA signed with a country outside the region. At the 1999 APEC summit, Singapore also announced its intention to start negotiating bilateral FTAs with Chile, Japan and Mexico, making it from the start a key protagonist in the new Asia-Pacific FTA trend.

Indeed, Singapore has initiated and concluded more bilateral FTA projects with other Asia-Pacific economies than any other country in the region. By the end of 2005, it had concluded nine FTAs within the Asia-Pacific, was negotiating two more and was in the study phase of one other (Table 2.2). Many Asia-Pacific states chose Singapore as an FTA partner because it was deemed easy to negotiate with given its small size (hence limited competitive threat to domestic industries), virtually non-existent agricultural sector (no threat to domestic farmers) and already very open commercial regime (not many difficult protectionist barriers to negotiate on). The city-state thus presented a good litmus test or 'practice swing' FTA partner, especially to those countries with limited FTA experience and sensitive domestic industry interests to address, e.g. Japan and South Korea. Singapore had to play on these advantages to counteract the disincentives of choosing it as an FTA partner, most critically its small and already very open home market. The Government has thus had to stress the strengths rather than the weaknesses of these factors in FTA terms, and also to highlight the importance of 'FTA-plus' measures in any negotiated agreement to entice partners. Promoting the Singapore commercial hub functionalities has been another key factor here in that an FTA with the city-state can act as a 'bridge' to the Southeast and East Asia region.

Main determining factors

According to research-interviewed stakeholders, by far the most important determining factor behind Singapore's bilateral FTA policy was *strengthening diplomatic relations with key trading partners*. The most commonly cited reasons for this were to secure access to key markets and to enhance Singapore's wider security relations with key allies in the Asia-Pacific. The city-state's FTA with the US, and also with Australia and Japan were particularly relevant. One interviewed believed that "locking in key trade partner interests to Singapore" was especially relevant.[60] The second most important factor was *towards wider regional trade arrangements*. Singapore scored the highest from the field researched country group (Table 2.1). Singapore's political leaders have often prescribed to the 'lattice regionalism' thesis that bilateral FTAs are creating a sub-structural basis for wider regional trade agreements to form (see Chapter 4). The third most important factor cited, *to strengthen regional economic cohesion generally in East Asia and the Asia-Pacific*, follows on from this above point. Like Japan and other East Asian states, Singapore's bilateral FTA policy is seen, at least in the city-state itself, as a means to better manage regional economic interdependence in post-crisis East Asia. The decision taken by Singapore and Japan in JSEPA negotiations to include an accession clause in the final agreement – thus giving an option for third countries to later join it – was made with the above idea in mind.[61] *Instigating a new direction in Singapore's trade policy* also came high in research interview ratings. For the Government, bilateral FTAs were "new in the sense of being a new mechanism", and they "gave new substance to our trade policy".[62]

Trade liberalisation failures of APEC and the WTO also scored relatively highly as determining factors behind Singapore's FTA policy (Table 2.1). As discussed elsewhere, the city-state has been a vocal advocate of free trade in its economic diplomacy, and the recent faltering of both organisations stirred some alarm in Singapore's foreign economic policy-making circles. Yet, as with the field-researched countries in general, Singapore's expectations about what APEC could actually deliver on trade liberalisation were low, or 'realistic' as one interviewed government official euphemistically put it. Another interviewed official remarked that, "APEC is not expected to be a negotiating arena, but its failure on trade liberalisation was nevertheless a stimulus to Singapore's FTA development".[63] Research interviewees generally held the view, though, that inertia at the WTO was a more important factor behind the development of Singapore's FTA policy. According to one government official, "if Seattle had not failed we probably would not have gone down the bilateral FTA track. FTAs were our insurance policy".[64] One MNE representative observed that, "the Government held that WTO multilateralism was philosophically correct but FTAs were more practically viable".[65] Multilateral trade liberalisation remains the ideal objective or route of Singapore's trade diplomacy, and this largely explains why the government tries to sell its FTA projects as 'WTO-plus', or at least WTO consistent, i.e. compliant with the organisation's rules on FTAs (Thangavelu and Toh 2005). In the words of an interviewed chief FTA negotiator, "We are highly dependent on trade for our survival and prosperity. Hence our commitment to the WTO is primary. Our bilateral and regional and inter-regional trade agreements are secondary to the WTO. They are intended to complement and reinforce the WTO system."[66] This largely explains why *helping achieve global free trade* was afforded a relatively high rating also by research interviewees when assessing the intended objectives underlying Singapore's FTA policy.

In the 'other' category, a number of interviewees specifically stated that Singapore's FTAs could be understood as a competitive response to China's economic ascendancy. According to an interviewed MNE representative, "the initiation of Singapore's FTA policy in the late 1990s was all part of the government's millennial *feng shui*".[67] At this time, the government was examining all aspects of policy to ensure Singapore maintained geopolitical and geoeconomic advantages, especially in relation to China's rise in the region. Singapore's Economic Review Committee (ERC) – on which this MNE representative participated in one of its sub-committees – was an integral part of this progress and submitted its final report, entitled *'New Challenges, Fresh Goals – Towards a Dynamic Global City'*, in February 2003 and made a number of policy and development recommendations, including to press ahead with its bilateral FTA policy. The Singapore Government is particularly concerned about China's growing techno-industrial capabilities and its attraction of key sector foreign investments. This not only relates to higher-tech production but also more value-adding corporate functions, such as research and development (R&D) centres and regional headquarter offices. Philips and various other long embedded Singapore-based companies are relocating some activities from the city-state to China. In a speech made in August 2003, Singapore Prime Minister Goh Chok Tong acknowledged that Singapore faced increasing competition from lower-cost countries, particularly noting that for the cost of hiring one Singaporean worker, a company could employ 13 in China and 18 in India.[68] As previously discussed, bilateral FTAs are now central to the Singapore Government's strategy of retaining and attracting high value-added foreign investment.

2.5.2   The formation of Singapore's FTA policy

Among the field researched country group, Singapore has the most *state-centric* approach to foreign economic policy formation. Government officials have formulated Singapore's FTA policy in a relatively autonomous manner, and in the process being comparatively immune to competing private industry interests. The MTI is the most relevant state agency here, although FTA policy has been developed at the Cabinet level also, where it has been afforded high priority on the economic policy agenda. While the state is the most important independent and intervening variable in Singapore's FTA policy formation, government agencies have used various channels of communication with the business community and civil society groups to gather market intelligence and other forms of information when making FTA policy. According to research interviewees from the business sector, the government prefers to work with their own selection of business representatives chosen to sit on state-managed committees such as the ERC. This 'cross-sectional' approach is in contrast to other field-researched countries where the government mostly prefers to dialogue with the key business organisations on trade policy matters. We should note, however, that Singapore-based MNEs exercise transnational contesting influence over the city-state's FTA projects (Dent 2002, 2003a). For example, a US–Singapore FTA Business Coalition was formed that consisted of around 200 firms and partly facilitated by the ASEAN–US Business Council, with the main aim of lobbying US Congress to support the USSFTA project. This business coalition, though, had more influence over the US's FTA policy formation than Singapore's.

While Singapore remains a semi-democratic state, civil society groups are increasingly engaged in economic policy-making processes. The government has consulted with key civil society organisations like the National Trade Union Congress (NTUC) and Singapore Environment Council (SEC), seeking their views and opinions on FTA issues. It should be noted, however, that state influence and control over these groups remains substantial. Interviewed NTUC officials confirmed that both the MTI and the Ministry of Manpower (MOM) regularly updated and consulted them on FTA matters. The NTUC has been supportive of Singapore's FTA policy owing to the prosperity and job creating effects they expect it will bring, but at the same time expressed their concerns about how to tackle the impact of adjustment and change also brought on by FTAs. While the NTUC accepted the call from Japan's main trade union, Rengo, for core labour standards to be incorporated into JSEPA, the NTUC did not demand this from its own government, being ultimately more concerned with how FTAs could improve job security for its members. For the SEC, the main issues from their environmental viewpoint concerned the transhipment of endangered species and products through Singapore's vast port complex. There exists some contention between the government and the SEC over whether this is actually happening to a significant extent or not but the SEC's main concern is that FTAs will lead to an increase in this illegal trade.

2.5.3 Challenging areas and contentious issues

Although as previously noted Singapore's lack of an agricultural sector has eased the development of its FTA policy, it was also noted under the Japan section that Singapore's micro-scale ornamental flower producers and goldfish breeders were a contentious issue in JSEPA negotiations. This of course was essentially a problem area for Japan rather than for Singapore. On the whole, research interviewees did not rate any factor that highly as a major hindrance to Singapore's FTA policy (Table 2.1). On the domestic side, the highest rated factor was *opposition from Singapore industry groups*. Singapore's restrictions on foreign entry into certain professional service sectors (e.g. law, architecture) and the financial sector, and also the Government Linked Company (GLC) sector have been particular areas of contention. These especially came to the fore in USSFTA negotiations where the US was demanding market access beyond what it saw as the *status quo*: that is above and beyond what Singapore had conceded previously at the WTO (e.g. in services trade liberalisation under the General Agreement on Trade in Services), or AFTA or indeed other bilateral FTAs such as with Japan and New Zealand. On more specific issues, Japan pushed Singapore to further open up its petrochemicals sector market, while other FTA partners (Mexico, the US and New Zealand) wanted tighter rules of origin in the TCF sector in order to avert trade deflection from China and other low-cost East Asian producers.

Consistent with the state-centric approach to economic policy formation in Singapore, it is not domestic industry groups themselves that have been resisting FTA-related liberalisation as such, rather how the government has dealt with opening up these domestic sectors to more foreign competition is most relevant. Many of the regulatory controls maintained by the government here were initially developed in the broader context of pursuing economic security objectives (e.g. in strategic sectors such as telecommunications and finance), and the government has stressed its relative openness in these sectors compared to other Asian states. Research interviewees assigned a relatively high rating to *diplomatic over-reach/scarce diplomatic resources* in comparison to both other 'hindrance' factors and to other field researched countries. Small states like Singapore do have relatively limited diplomatic resources, and yet the Singapore Government has managed to maintain a number of FTA projects in development simultaneously, comparing favourably with much larger countries. This has been quite a feat, and the Singapore Government's decision to recruit increasing numbers of personnel from the private sector (e.g. trade lawyers) onto FTA negotiating teams is indicative of the priority afforded to FTA policy generally. Other possible 'hindrance' factors barely registered amongst research interviewees. These included *opposition from civil society groups/NGO movements*, *general lack of support from Singapore's business sector* (although some FTA negotiating partners, such as Mexico and New Zealand, have been somewhat disappointed about the lack of interest from Singaporean firms in their markets), and *lack of foreign (economic) policy priority afforded by top Singapore Government officials*, which as we have already established has not been a problem for Singapore's FTA policy development.

Because Singapore is such an open economy with relatively very few conflicting domestic industrial or political interests to reconcile, *greater domestic problems confronting FTA partner* was given the highest 'hindrance factor' rating by research interviewees. Although *opposing pressure from other countries or international organisations* was assigned a much lower rating, many interviewees noted the once vehement criticism Singapore's bilateral FTA policy attracted from Malaysia. This is detailed in Chapter 1, which examines how tensions arising within ASEAN over trade bilateralism and regionalism. Briefly to comment here that there were both technical and diplomatic aspects to Singapore's highly active FTA policy that Malaysia took issue with, both of which concerned the potential undermining of Southeast Asia's regional economic projects and community-building generally.

2.5.4 Impacts and consequences

In line with the field-research country group trend, *relations with its bilateral FTA partners* was deemed the most important area of consequence from Singapore's FTA policy (Table 2.1). This too was consistent with the strong diplomatic motives driving this policy in the first place. In a similar vein, many interviewed Singapore diplomats and foreign ambassadorial staff assigned relatively high significance to *international relations in the region,* and to *Singapore's influence in the East Asia/Asia-Pacific region.* According to one government official, Singapore's active bilateral FTA policy "improves our leverage in AFTA-related issues" but this was due more to how this policy had changed the broader context of Southeast Asian trade diplomacy (in line with Singapore's interests) rather than exerting direct influence over other ASEAN member states, or the group as a whole. For example, Singapore's various FTA projects have compelled other states to join Singapore in extending AFTA's linkages with ASEAN's main extraregional trade partners (e.g. China, Japan) through bilateral and region-level deals (Dent 2006a; Sen 2004). This issue is discussed further in Chapter 4. Interviewees also afforded *developing wider regional trade agreements* a relatively high rating, the main reasons for this being discussed in the following section, but a comparatively low rating for *countries and international regions outside the Asia-Pacific* mainly because of Singapore's small size.

Research interviewees also rated the consequences for Singapore's domestic economic policy reform and domestic economic restructuring some significance (Table 2.1). The impact here of certain FTAs (e.g. USSFTA and JSEPA) in Singapore's hitherto quite restricted service industries and GLC sector was particularly noted, as previously highlighted. However, the vast majority of interviewees believed the economic impacts would be primarily positive yet minimal. Research interviewees gave low 'consequence' ratings for the impact of Singapore's FTAs upon APEC and the WTO but for quite different reasons. While mostly Singapore Government officials argued that their FTAs would help APEC's trade liberalisation objectives, some believed it could actually have a detrimental effect on the organisation by further consolidating the bilateral FTA route as an alternative to APEC's 'open regionalism' route (see Chapter 4's discussion on this issue). Many others believed there would be little impact whatsoever. Nevertheless, the Singapore Government hopes that its bilateral FTAs will contribute to both regional and multilateral trade liberalisation, thus buying into the idea of competitive liberalisation. Singapore Prime Minister Goh Chok Tong argued for example in October 2003 that, "FTAs in a sense serve as a pressure point or a fast track of the WTO process."[69] Just a few months later in January 2004, PM Goh also commented that, "The best route is to have the WTO getting a new round of negotiations started. We came to the conclusion that that new round is not going to come about so quickly... The alternative, therefore, is to pursue a freer trading regime through bilateral agreements".[70] While we may situate these comments in Singapore's prescribed to competitive liberalisation argument, some may also construe this to indicate a preference for bilateralism over multilateralism at a time when the multilateral trade order was experiencing severe difficulties.

2.6   South Korea

2.6.1   The origins, determining factors and development of South Korea's FTA policy

South Korea: an international political economy overview

South Korea is East Asia's third largest economy and is strategically located between China and Japan. It has also become one of the world's most important trading nations. The export-oriented industrialisation strategy, first introduced by the Park Chung-hee Government in the 1960s, gradually transformed a predominantly agrarian economy into a modern industrial state within the space of three decades. South Korea has drawn heavily upon the lessons of the Japanese economic development experience, most crucially the role played by the (developmental) state, business and industry sector organisation, and the exercise of neo-mercantilist policies. This was socio-culturally underpinned by strong levels of economic nationalism, which still strongly pervade South Korean society. The country remains highly trade-dependent with exports accounting for around 40 percent of GDP. American financial and technical aid dispensed to South Korea in the 1950s and 1960s was of critical importance to the nation's early economic development, as was the US market to Korean exporters. As, though, South Korea began to register growing trade surpluses with the United States, it came under increasing American pressure to liberalise its neo-mercantilist trade policy. At the same time the US, the EU and other trade partners were raising their trade barriers on competitive Korean exports.

Both these external pressures to liberalise, and the growing influence of domestic neo-liberal advocacy groups within the country led to the gradual liberalisation of South Korea's trade policy and economic policy from the 1980s. Import tariffs on industrial products were reduced to relatively low levels by the late 1990s (on average to around eight percent) although the agriculture sector remained highly protected. The economic reform and liberalisation process was accelerated somewhat after the 1997/98 financial crisis, where the then new Kim Dae-jung Administration were obliged to accept the neo-liberal policy conditions attached to the IMF's US$58 billion 'bailout' package. President Kim Dae-jung was generally compliant to the IMF's demands, seeing it as an opportunity to exact a paradigm shift in the South Korean political economy. However, his government's attempts to move the country out of its entrenched economic nationalism to embrace globalism, and in the process establish South Korea as an 'open trading nation', had limited success. As we discuss below, significant obstacles have hindered the progress of country's FTA policy that relate to South Korea's resilient economic nationalism and neo-mercantilist policy tradition.

The origins and development of South Korea's FTA policy

South Korea was at the forefront of the new Asia-Pacific FTA trend, initiating new FTA projects with Chile, Japan and Thailand as early as 1998 (see Appendix A). A fourth project with New Zealand followed the year after in 1999 so that by the end of that year it shared the position with Singapore of having the most active new FTA policy in the region. These new FTA projects were deemed integral to the Kim Dae-jung Government's post-crisis restructuring agenda, here in specific relation to trade policy and diplomacy (Sohn and Yoon 2001; Cheong 2002). Other potential FTA partners both inside and outside the Asia-Pacific were also considered at this time, including the US, Australia, South Africa and Turkey (as suggested by South Korea's Ministry of Foreign Affairs and Trade, or MOFAT),[71] as well as Israel (as proposed by the Ministry of Commerce, Industry and Economy, or MOCIE).[72] Like Japan, South Korea had hitherto based its 'market access' trade diplomacy primarily on the multilateral GATT and WTO routes. It was after all the development of an increasingly open multilateral trade system that had been instrumental in facilitating the country's impressive export-oriented industrialisation. The development of a bilateral FTA policy thus marked a notable philosophical shift in South Korea's trade diplomacy, although FTAs were still seen as the 'second best' option to WTO and multilateralism.

However, South Korea's first phase of FTA projects moved at a relatively glacial pace or soon entered into a state of arrested development. Those with New Zealand and Thailand had not moved passed the study phase stage by early 2006, mainly because of political sensitivities over opening up South Korea's agriculture markets to these two competitive agri-producers. South Korea and Japan did not initiate FTA negotiations until late 2003, five years after the project was first officially proposed, and had become mired in political and agricultural disputes by March 2005. Negotiations with Chile, while commencing some time beforehand in 1999, were stalled for a year and a half, and the passage of the Korea–Chile FTA (KCFTA) bill had a protracted and bumpy ride through South Korea's legislative enactment process (see Chapter 3). However, South Korea's more recently initiated projects with Singapore, ASEAN (as a group) and Canada have developed with some speed. An agreement with Singapore was concluded within two years, amongst the shortest time-frames in the Asia-Pacific FTA trend. Negotiations with the ASEAN group and with Canada were commenced within a year of first being proposed respectively, and within only two months in Canada's case. Outside the Asia-Pacific, FTA projects with the EFTA group and with India have also quickly developed, an agreement with EFTA signed in December 2005. An important fillip to these developments was the introduction of an 'FTA Roadmap' by the new Roh Moo-hyun Government in September 2003, which brought both greater strategic definition, technocratic resources and overall foreign economic policy priority to South Korea's FTA policy. This drew upon important lessons that had been learned from the KCFTA project experience, which had caused delays in the development of other projects noted above. By the end of 2005, South Korea had signed three FTAs within the Asia-Pacific region, was negotiating two others and engaged in the study phase of three more (Table 2.2). A proposal for commencing FTA negotiations with the US was being talked about in early 2006. In its 2005 annual report, MOFAT stated the objective of signing FTAs with 15 countries by 2007.

Main determining factors

A number of main determining factors attained a similar high significance rating from research interviewees. The highest rating was given to *response to regional/global FTA trend*, and South Korea also had the highest rating here amongst the field researched country group. South Korea was one of only four WTO members (the others being Japan, Hong Kong and Mongolia) that by 2000 was not party to any free trade agreement. Many interviewees specifically noted in relation to this that 'isolation avoidance' motives (see Chapter 1) were relevant from the outset of the country's FTA policy from the late 1990s. This remained pertinent during the period in the early 2000s when South Korea made slow progress in advancing its first phase of FTA projects. As one interviewed foreign ambassadorial representative commented, "it is harmful to South Korea's self-image of being left behind international trends."[73] President Roh Moo-hyun has himself often expressed concerns that his country risked becoming "a loner" if it could not secure FTAs with key trade partners in the near future.[74]

Strengthening economic relations with key trading partners was assigned the second highest rating, with many research interviewees citing the strong post-crisis context to this factor. There were two elements to this. Firstly, South Korea's strong economic recovery after the crisis was largely export-based, which in turn confirmed that maintaining good terms of access to key export markets remained a crucial economic security objective for the country. Mexico was chosen as an early FTA partner as a first initial step into NAFTA (and because of its new FTA link with the EU), and Thailand for similar reasons with respect to Southeast Asia. Secondly and like for other East Asian countries, FTAs were integral to the broader endeavour to better managing regional economic interdependence in the crisis aftermath. As noted earlier in the Japan section of this chapter, the JKFTA project is particularly relevant in this respect. Another high rated factor – *towards wider regional trade arrangements* – connects closely to this latter point. Both the Kim Dae-jung and Roh Moo-hyun governments, as well as the Korean business community, have promoted the idea of creating an East Asia Free Trade Agreement. Notwithstanding difficulties in negotiating it, the Roh Government viewed the JKFTA project as a key foundation for this wider regional FTA.[75]

The role of FTAs in *instigating a new trade policy direction* was awarded a high significance rating also by research interviewees, although for many this depended on how many FTAs the country managed to sign. As alluded to earlier, there are two main dimensions to this. The first relates to moves towards a more risk-averse and multi-track trade diplomacy (away from uni-track multilateralism), and the second to trade liberalisation. This factor should hence be considered together with *helping consolidate domestic economic reforms*, which too was rated relatively highly, in that FTAs also provided an external pressure mechanism that could be harnessed by domestic neo-liberal advocates to realise certain reform objectives.

WTO trade liberalisation inertia was a mid-rated determining factor in the development of South Korea's FTA policy according to research interviewees. One Korean trade policy-maker explained in the context of moving from multilateral to multi-track diplomacy on market access issues, "Our decision to embark on FTAs was more a question of method rather than principle in that trade liberalisation remains the objective."[76] Other interviewees noted the WTO's Seattle Ministerial Meeting debacle of 1999 as a key catalyst in South Korea's FTA policy development after 1999, but at the same time that 'FTA catch-up' and the impact of the 1997/98 financial crisis were relatively more important. In keeping with the general field-researched country trend, *APEC trade liberalisation inertia* was afforded a low rating. A Korean trade policy official stated that, "South Korea viewed APEC usefulness in WTO-plus terms, but ultimately perceived it more in political than economic terms."[77]

2.6.2   The formation of South Korea's FTA policy

South Korea has one of the most complex inter-ministerial dynamics for trade policy formation amongst the field-researched country group. There are three main government agencies apart from the President's Office (the Blue House) responsible for South Korea's trade policy, namely the Ministry of Foreign Affairs and Trade (MOFAT), the Ministry of Commerce, Industry and Energy (MOCIE) and the Ministry of Finance and Economy (MOFE). MOFAT is the most important of these, being responsible for most trade policy strategy formation and primary trade diplomacy functions. It leads and co-ordinates the country's FTA negotiation teams working closely with other ministries, especially MOCIE which has competence for various sectoral trade issues as well as trade and FDI related issues. MOFE's most important trade policy function concerns import tariffs and general customs procedures, these being financial management aspects of South Korea's trade policy. Aside from the inter-ministerial competition between these three ministries in the country's trade and foreign economic policy, other ministries have become increasingly involved in South Korea's FTA policy (Dent 2002). These particularly include the Ministry of Agriculture and Forestry (MAF), the Ministry of Maritime Affairs and Fisheries, and the Ministry of Culture and Tourism (MOCAT).

The more neo-liberal oriented MOFAT has come into frequent conflict with MAF over agri-trade liberalisation and with MOCAT on the 'screen quota' system – designed to insulate the domestic film industry from foreign competition – where MOCAT has opposed pressure from MOFAT and other sources (e.g. the US Government and the Hollywood lobby) to scrap the system. Owing mainly to conflicts over agri-trade liberalisation issues, the President's Office has assumed more of a central co-ordinating role in FTA policy, especially in the actual negotiation process. It was the differences between MOFAT and MAF that was deemed largely responsible for the 20-month impasse in the KCFTA talks during 2001 and 2002. Both Presidents Kim Dae-jung (1998–2002) and Roh Moo-hyun (2003–2007) have also attempted to involve greater civil society engagement in the FTA policy process. This forms part of a broader endeavour of deepening democratisation in South Korea's polity in which creating a more society-centric model of economic policy formation has been sought.

Most of South Korea's NGOs have, though, either shown little interest or indeed opposition to the country's FTA policy, and have been forced into protracted domestic-level negotiations with farmers groups in particular in order to establish firm enough public support to proceed with FTA negotiations with foreign trade partners. This is borne out in the relatively high significance ratings afforded by research interviewees to the farmers groups in terms of government–stakeholder consultation in comparison to other civil society groups (Table 2.1). South Korea's farmers have a quite a strong ally and advocate within the government executive in the form of MAF, and also within its legislative branch as a more than proportionate number of National Assembly constituencies are concentrated in rural areas. Furthermore, there is considerable public support for the farmers groups. Many older Koreans were once farmers themselves before the country rapidly industrialised from the 1960s onwards and younger Koreans, in Confucian filial respect for their elders, have too shown strong backing for the farmers' cause. Government–business group dialogue on FTAs has been far less problematic, and the Federation of Korean Industries (FKI, the *chaebol* conglomerates' main representative body) particularly has engaged with South Korea's FTA policy from the very beginning. This notably relates to the development of the JKFTA project whereby the FKI has worked closely with its Japanese counterpart – the *Keidanren* – in both FTA study activities and promoting the project generally. The *chaebol* big business groups dominate the national economy, and hence the FKI has significant political clout. The Korea International Trade Association (KITA) has too worked closely with the government through similar channels, and actually suggested the idea of creating an 'FTA Roadmap' back in 2001.[78]

2.6.3   Challenging areas and contentious issues

Every research interviewee assigned 'agriculture' the highest significance rating possible with regard to factors hindering the progress of South Korea's FTA policy. No other country field-researched group attained this but then South Korea has the most protected farming sector of the group this. South Korea's agriculture sector has many similarities to that of Japan, having a slightly smaller average farm size (approximately 1.5 hectares) and an even lower food self-sufficiency ratio at around only 30 percent. The case study of the KCFTA project in Chapter 3 offers valuable insights into the nature of South Korea's agricultural politics and how this has hampered the development of the country's FTA policy. Korean farmers groups criticised the Government for not sufficiently consulting them at the outset of the KCFTA project, and also for not publishing the results of other FTA scoping studies (e.g. with New Zealand), charges generally accepted by the South Korean Government in retrospect.[79] In November 2002, around 70,000 farmers gathered in front of the National Assembly building in Seoul to protest against the KCFTA, as well as demand a freeze on minimum market access levels for agricultural imports and an extended tariff grace period on rice in WTO negotiations.[80] As the KCFTA case study in Chapter 3 details, South Korea's farmers also secured a substantial package of short and long-term support measures as a placating side-payment for coping with FTA-induced foreign competition in domestic agri-markets. This generous concession revealed just how important agriculture remains in the South Korean political economy, despite the relatively small proportion it has of nation's GDP, at four percent in 2004. It is a highly emotive issue for the South Korean public and for the farmers themselves it is a question of maintaining not just their businesses but also local and family traditions, livelihoods and community cohesion.

The second most significant hindrance factor to South Korea's FTA policy according to research interviewees was *opposition from civil society groups/ NGOs*. The country's labour movement in particular has been a vocal critic of FTAs, and South Korea's largest trade union, the Federation of Korean Trade Unions (FKTU), is against free trade agreements on a matter of principle, this being to resist the penetration and growth of transnational capital within the national economy. A key concern of the FKTU was that foreign firms would compromise Korean worker rights and job security more readily than Korean firms. It was thus a matter of the foreign investment inducing effects of FTAs (e.g. their infusion of Western 'flexible' labour market practices into Korean industrial relations) that was the main basis of their opposition.[81] The FKTU is also part of an anti-globalisation coalition of NGOs in South Korea that collectively oppose FTAs. This coalition, which also includes consumer groups, environmental NGOs and cultural industry (e.g. film) groups, is to a significant degree bound together by Korean economic nationalism, as already illustrated by the FKTU's position on foreign capital. Another coalition member and the country's largest environmental movement, Green Korea United (GKU), states its opposition to FTAs in eco-metaphorical terms: the world comprises a series of diverse economic, social and cultural paradigms, and the convergence brought about by FTAs and other globalising developments would lead to unwelcome diversity loss, in South Korea's case undermining its unique national economic system.[82] Apart from concerns regarding endangered 'economic species' in the world system, the GKU have pushed the Government to make FTAs at least more 'environment compatible', especially on maintaining strong quarantine measures.

Table 2.1 shows that a number of hindrance factors were 'significant rated' just below the above. The highest of these – *lack of foreign (economic) policy priority of Government* and *state bureaucratic inertia or opposition* – are closely related, and explanations from research interviewees mostly related to political anxieties amongst government officials to opening up South Korea's agriculture markets through FTAs, and also to economic nationalist reactions within the government to market opening to foreign commerce generally. *Greater domestic problems confronting FTA partner(s)* was thought particularly relevant to Japan and the JKFTA project, again with agriculture figuring highly. In relation to *lack of business sector support*, many research interviewees thought that businesses in general had not shown much interest in South Korea's FTA policy. As one interviewed research analyst put it, "The business sector has been curiously indifferent to the FTA policy issue. It has publicly supported FTAs but have not become very involved in practical FTA advocacy, which has disappointed the Government."[83] This comment was made in July 2002 and applied more to the business community in general rather than business associations. Nevertheless, the FKI and KITA have made greater endeavours to interest *chaebol* company groups about the benefits offered by FTAs.

South Korea has long sought an FTA with the US but initiating this project has been beset by a series of persisting bilateral trade and other commerce-related disputes. These actually intensified during the early 2000s, culminating in the USTR's decision in January 2004 to elevate South Korea from Special 301 Watch List to the Priority Watch list status. The main areas of contention lie in a wide range of IPR issues (most notably pharmaceuticals, computer software, music and film), government procurement (especially in the telecommunications sector), tariff and non-tariff barriers in South Korea's automobile markets, and the screen quota issue. The screen quota system, first introduced in 1967, required all cinemas to play Korean movies for 40 percent (146 days) of their operating days annually.[84] At the behest of Hollywood lobby, the US Government had pressed South Korea to scrap or significantly reduce the quota limit, stating this was a precondition for initiating bilateral FTA talks with Seoul. Both MOFE and MOFAT supported the US's demands but MOCAT and general public opinion in South Korea opposed any dismantling of the screen quota system, arguing it was necessary to further develop and strengthen the national film industry, which has been successfully developing under state 'infant industry' protection in recent years as films like *Shiri* (1999), *Joint Security Area* (2002) and *Old Boy* (2004) testified. This was too a further manifestation of South Korea's economic nationalism. However, in January 2006 the South Korean Government announced its decision to half the quota limit to 20 percent, or 73 days a year, in order to expedite an FTA project with the United States.[85]

2.6.4 Impacts and consequences

As with the field-researched country group trend, research interviewees believed the main impact of South Korea's FTA policy would be more politico-diplomatic than economic in nature, with *relations with bilateral FTA partners* conferred the highest significance rating. This particularly applied to the East Asia regional context and South Korea's ambitions to play a more prominent role in regional economic diplomacy, as well as more specifically an intermediary 'brokering' power between Japan and China in Northeast Asia. Research interviewees did, though, rank the economic impact of South Korea's FTAs not too far behind the above (Table 2.1). Both *domestic economic restructuring process* and *domestic economic policy reform* were rated relatively highly on the basis that FTAs had the potential to bring about a paradigm shift in the country's neo-mercantilist tradition. This was under the proviso, however, that the FTAs in question were comprehensive in scope and substantially incorporated agri-trade liberalisation.

As we have thus far seen, this is by no means assured, and South Korea's resilient economic nationalism provides further cause for doubt. Projects with large competitive countries like Japan would also lend itself to significant economic restructuring and policy reform impacts from the intra-industry competitive effects derived from trade creation. By the same token, FTA partners like Chile offer limited intra-industry competitive contact, as discussed in Chapter 1. Returning to the politico-diplomatic impacts of South Korea's FTA policy, both *South Korea's influence in the East Asia/Asia-Pacific region* and *impact on international relations in the region generally* received mid-ranked ratings, with one research interviewee specifically commenting that given South Korea's neo-mercantilist tradition, its FTA policy may have significant demonstration effects for other countries with a similar trade and economic policy past.[86]

2.7   Taiwan

2.7.1   The origins, determining factors and development of Taiwan's FTA policy

Taiwan: an international political economy overview

Taiwan is East Asia's fourth largest economy and a major producer and investor in the region. Taiwan's path of economic development bares many similarities to South Korea, Japan and Singapore in terms of its export-oriented nature and the developmental guidance provided by the state. Of equal if not greater importance in the determination of Taiwan's foreign economic policy is its 'contested statehood' predicament. Its ambiguous position in the international community derives from the Peoples Republic of China's (PRC) insistence that Taiwan is a Chinese province and not a sovereign nation-state, a view formally accepted by the large majority of national governments. Despite the extensive internationalisation of Taiwan's economy, its trade policy-makers are nevertheless confronted by significant external constraints that primarily derive from this predicament. It has thus had comparatively limited 'diplomatic space' in which to manage its foreign economic relations, and moreover convince its trade partners to sign substantive economic agreements such as FTAs. Another corollary of this is that the 'mainland China' variable looms large in Taiwan's trade policy. The burgeoning growth of trade and investment links between Taiwan and the PRC adds a further dimension to this, as we discuss in relation to Taiwan's FTA policy. Taiwan's accession to the WTO in January 2002 marked a crucial development in its trade diplomacy. It was able to achieve this because members only need to be a custom's authority rather than a nation-state. Like China, Taiwan could not effectively develop FTA projects with trade partners until it acceded to the WTO: other member countries wanted Taiwan and China within the ambit of WTO trade rules and norms first before initiating any FTA negotiations with them. Both the accession process and subsequent WTO membership has required Taiwan to further liberalise it trade policy regime, which had traditionally leaned towards a neo-mercantilist approach although not to the same extent as South Korea.

Taken these factors together, then, Taiwan's FTA policy fulfilled a number of foreign economic policy objectives. Firstly, FTAs help realise market access security that are crucial for such an export-oriented economy, especially if much anticipated market access gains from WTO membership do not materialise for some time yet. Secondly, signing FTAs with trade partners help further delineate and expand Taiwan's 'diplomatic space' by conducting trade diplomacy on similar terms as nation-states. Thirdly, it has become increasingly imperative for Taiwan for both economic and politico-diplomatic reasons to engage in the new FTA trend given that non-engagement could further marginalise Taiwan. Taiwan's limited foreign policy options were not so much of a constraint in its economic relations with East Asian neighbours before the 1997/98 financial crisis. Up to then, East Asia's regional economic integration had been primarily developed through the process of *regionalisation* rather than *regionalism*. As discussed in Chapters 1 and 4, very few international economic agreements of any real significance (e.g. FTAs) had been signed by the mid-1990s in East Asia or by East Asian states within the Asia-Pacific, and Taiwanese firms were furthermore well integrated into the region's international business networks. Taiwan had also become in 1991 a member of APEC, the only substantive regional economic grouping at the time, and then looked to reap the benefit from the organisation's planned 'free trade and investment zone'. Thus, Taiwan's commercial interests in the region were not by this time that disadvantaged by the politico-diplomatic constraints of 'contested statehood', but of course this changed with the advent of the Asia-Pacific FTA trend.

The origins and development of Taiwan's FTA policy

In October 2001, Taiwan indicated it would pursue bilateral FTAs soon after formally joining the WTO. The Taiwanese Government established an FTA Task Force in November 2001, formed between the Ministry of Foreign Affairs and Ministry of Economic Affairs, and it also announced that Singapore, New Zealand, Japan and the US were the most probable candidates for Taiwan's initial FTA partners.[87] At first Taiwan's FTA policy made a promising start, with substantive interest demonstrated by all these trade partners, and it was not long before Beijing sought to constrain Taiwan's FTA options (Dent 2005a). In June 2002, China's Minister of Foreign Trade and Economic Co-operation, Shi Guangsheng, stated his government's opposition to any of its diplomatic partners signing FTAs with Taiwan, warning that they would encounter serious political troubles, with their trade and economic relations with the mainland being adversely affected.

He repeated this thinly veiled threat in November 2002 at a news conference in Beijing.[88] This seems to have had an immediate effect on Singapore, which reportedly sought thereafter to slow the pace of development of its FTA project with Taiwan. By June 2003, the Taiwan–Singapore project was suspended after Singapore reportedly introduced a new precondition that the negotiations and the FTA be carried out under the 'one China' principle, a position not acceptable to Taiwan.[89] The prospects of Taiwan's other FTA projects with Japan and New Zealand also diminished after the warning statements made by Beijing during 2002.[90] The US was the only diplomatic partner of China that did not appear to take much notice of these, although discussions between Washington and Taipei on any future FTA had become mired by disputes over IPR and other issues pertaining to Taiwan's compliance to its WTO accession commitments (e.g. on agriculture and pharmaceuticals) that are discussed in more detail later on.

Taipei did manage, though, to launch FTA negotiations with Panama in October 2002, leading to a successful conclusion of talks in August 2003. This first FTA signed by Taiwan entered into force in January 2004. Panama is an insignificant trading partner for Taiwan, with total bilateral trade at just US$33 million in 2004 (Appendix D), and the economic benefits of the Agreement were far outweighed by the political benefits. Taipei had gained experience at learning how to negotiate and construct an FTA, and moreover had set a diplomatic precedent by signing an FTA. Bilateral FTA projects with other Central American diplomatic partners were also initiated, with Costa Rica from October 2002, with Guatemala from March 2003, and with Nicaragua from August 2004 (Appendix A). However, taken together, the 26 relatively small states that Taiwan's enjoys full diplomatic relations with account for only four percent of its total trade. In terms of specific FTA projects, Panama ranked as Taiwan's 59th largest trading partner in 2004, Costa Rica as 71st, Guatemala as 75th and Nicaragua as 96th. Appendix D shows that Taiwan's bilateral trade with these nations only amounts to a few hundred million US dollars a year (US$324 million total in 2004), and this has to be offset by the very high proportionate cost of actually negotiating these FTAs.[91] Thus, Taiwan's FTA options with the Central American region offer very marginal net economic benefits overall.

Moreover, progress on FTA projects with more important trade partners, such as Japan and Singapore, slowed significantly after 2002. Attempts have been made by Taipei to initiate new FTA projects with the Philippines and the Association of Southeast Asian Nations (ASEAN) as a whole, but little progress has been achieved here too. The announcement from the Taiwanese Government in October 2003 that it is flexible on the title conferred to Taiwan (e.g. 'Chinese Taipei', as used in APEC) in any prospective FTA failed to achieve the desired effect amongst its trade partners. Or at least this is what appears to be the case from the relative lack of media reports on Taiwan's FTA project activity since then. One could conclude that since Beijing's threatening statements to prospective FTA partners of Taiwan in 2002, Taipei has adopted a more clandestine approach to developing FTA projects. Government press release reporting on the progress Taiwan's FTA policy, other than those relating to the Taiwan–Panama FTA, has gradually diminished. Although Taiwan is likely to made some 'secret progress' with its FTA projects,[92] it is still confronted with the prospect of being marginalised in the new Asia-Pacific FTA trend.

Main determining factors

The most important determining factor of Taiwan's FTA policy according to research interviewees was *isolation avoidance*, which is not surprising given the geopolitical circumstances outlined above. A number of pertinent comments were made on this subject. An interviewed Taiwan Ministry of Foreign Affairs (MFA) official remarked that, "for us it is often difficult to distinguish between trade and security objectives in our foreign policy-making", and that, "FTAs help Taiwan's business and society feel more secure."[93] According to an interviewed research analyst, "Taiwan's FTA policy is an integral part of our endeavours to subvert China's oppression of Taiwan's status in international organisations."[94] As one would expect, the discourse on Taiwan's geopolitical and geoeconomic peripheralisation has intensified as the Asia-Pacific FTA trend has deepened. In October 2003, the influential Taipei Mayor, Ma Ying-jeou, stated that, "Taiwan fears very much that we will be marginalized as a result of our inability to participate in all the regional integration programmes", and that, "we do not want to be left in the cold when regional integration is taking place."[95] He also made specific reference to the ACFTA project in this respect, commenting that, "Although it will take place seven years from now, still you can see that goods... in the ASEAN countries can enter the Chinese mainland without tariffs. Taiwan will still have to pay tariffs, which will put Taiwanese businesses at a competitive disadvantage."[96] Anxiety over the trade diversionary and other potential adverse effects of ACFTA on Taiwan prompted the Government in December 2004 to undertake a wide-ranging assessment of the Agreement, involving the Industrial Development Bureau, the Bureau of Foreign Trade (BOFT) and the Industrial Development and Investment Centre.[97] This culminated in an October 2005 government report that estimated that Taiwan would suffer losses of around US$150 million annually a year, or 0.05 percent of GDP, from the implementation of ACFTA. However, another report published by the Chung Hua Institution for Economic Research earlier that year in January was far more pessimistic, predicting that ACFTA could lead to almost a one percent fall in Taiwan's GDP through trade diversion and other adverse economic effects.[98]

The relatively high (joint second) rank assigned to *strengthening diplomatic relations with key trade partners* is inextricably linked to the *isolation avoidance* factor. An interviewed BOFT official remarked that, "we think FTAs are essentially exercises in promoting economic co-operation with our trade partners."[99] The other joint second ranked factor – *response to regional/global FTA trend* – is also strongly linked to isolation avoidance. A significant trading economy like Taiwan (the world's 16th largest) cannot afford to be left behind in this trend. The next ranked factor, *exploiting benefits of WTO membership*, should be viewed in the facilitative terms previously noted. In addition, the WTO's recent inertia on advancing global trade liberalisation pushed Taiwan further towards strengthening its FTA policy. An interviewed research analyst observed that, "people had much expectations about WTO membership but have been somewhat disappointed."[100] By the same token, the politico-diplomatic constraints facing Taiwan's FTA policy means that Taipei should continue to highly prioritise its WTO diplomacy. In an assessment of this situation Director-General of the MFA's Economic and Trade Department, Liu Jung-chuo, stated that, "Taiwan has encountered difficulties about signing bilateral trade agreements with other countries due to pressure from China. Therefore, Taiwan should play it safe and work to help other WTO members reach agreement on various issues during future WTO meetings."[101]

Research interviewees placed *strengthen regional economic cohesion* and *toward wider regional trade arrangements* as the next most significant determining factors behind Taiwan's FTA policy. The subtext of practically all responses here was that bilateral FTAs were the only way open for Taiwan's engagement in East Asian economic regionalism given Beijing's opposition to it joining either the ASEAN Plus Three (APT) or East Asia Summit (EAS) regional arrangements. In this sense, it was Taiwan's own non-participation in deepening regional economic integration – or the prospect of being blocked out of it – that was the prime issue at stake. Research interviewees generally agreed that the already well established regionalisation of Taiwanese business activity in East Asia did help mitigate the potential risks of being marginalised in the region's FTA trend albeit with certain caveats. A main one was that FTAs could make vital contributions in reducing international transaction costs for Taiwanese firms in those sectors where regional or global competition was especially intense. Another was that the regionalisation of Taiwanese business activity had become increasingly skewed towards the PRC economy. Thus, as an MFA official argued, "FTAs are a way of diversifying Taiwan's economic dependence away from mainland China."[102]

2.7.2 The formation of Taiwan's FTA policy

The BOFT is the principal government agency responsible for Taiwan's trade policy and diplomacy. It is technically a division of the MOEA but also works closely and in a generally harmonious fashion with the MFA. The BOFT regularly consults with private sector representations and convenes cross-authority meetings with other government agencies on trade-related issues. It has also managed and co-ordinated the various 'task forces' on FTAs assembled by the Government that have required relatively high-levels of inter-ministerial co-operation and private sector involvement. In many ways these arrangements followed through from the WTO accession process, although this switch in focus to FTAs may have distracted 'task force' personnel from implementing Taiwan's WTO accession agreements somewhat according to certain observers.[103]

While Taiwan's foreign economic policy formation has traditionally been quite state-centric, this has changed with the onset of democratisation. The business sector especially has seen its contesting influence strengthen over recent years. The Government's formalised consultation with business and civil society groups on its FTA policy began in late 2001.[104] There was a general consensus amongst research interviewees that Taiwanese society have been quite receptive to the idea of FTAs, as revealed by public surveys conducted on the issue, because of the significant politico-diplomatic and economic advantages they were thought to confer upon Taiwan. At the same time, there was a view that Taiwan's NGOs had not done much to mobilise themselves or the public on FTA issues yet, though this may be because Taiwan had yet to sign or even negotiate an FTA with a major trade partner. It should also be noted that Taiwan has by far the lowest significance ratings overall on government–stakeholder consultation (see Table 2.1), probably for this very reason that extensive consultation has not yet been required owing to this relative lack of FTA policy progress.

2.7.3   Challenging areas and contentious issues

By far the highest significance rated factor thought to hinder the progress of Taiwan's FTA policy was *opposing pressure from other countries or international organisations*, i.e. China (Table 2.1). Prior discussions on this matter provide an explanation for this, and also for the second ranked factor – *lack of priority afforded by Taiwan's trade partners* – which is closely linked to the first. Relating back to the clandestine nature of Taiwan's FTA policy, a BOFT official commented that, "our trade partners must be subtle in how they prioritise Taiwan on their FTA list because of opposition from China."[105] Another reason given by other research interviewees on the 'lack of priority afforded' issue included that, "Taiwan joined the region's new FTA trend comparatively late and is therefore towards the back of many FTA project queues for other Asia-Pacific states", which is some way contradicts the above view from the BOFT.[106] Under current circumstances it is also inconceivable that Taiwan would be able to fully initiate FTA projects with trade partners that had already signed an agreement with China. The ACFTA project would therefore seem to shut off Taiwan's FTA options with Southeast Asian countries.

Agriculture was the third ranked hindrance factor. Taiwan's agricultural politics and economics share many similarities with Japan and South Korea, possessing a relatively inefficient agri-industry sector that has high levels of protection. The sector's contribution to Taiwan's GDP has fallen from around 30 percent in the 1950s to just under two percent currently. It's average farm size is even smaller than Japan and South Korea's at just 1.1 hectares. Many of Taiwan's farmers work on a part-time basis to the extent that only 20 percent of the income of farming households derives from agricultural activities.[107] Regarding the food security issue, Taiwan's food self-sufficiency rate is around 50 percent and imports huge amount of wheat, corn and soya beans (largely for livestock).[108] Before WTO membership, Taiwan put complete bans or very strict quotas on certain sensitive products such as rice, pork, chicken, garlic, mushrooms, grapes, citrus fruits. As part of Taiwan's WTO accession obligations tariff levels on many of these were reduced to between 20 and 25 percent by 2005, and a tariffication process was implemented from January 2003. When research interviewed in 2003, Taiwan farmer group representatives did not seem that anxious or even cognisant of the agri-trade liberalisation implications from signing FTAs. The Panama FTA project had made very minimal impact upon Taiwanese farmers who were far more preoccupied by WTO accession related matters, on which they have made public protestations against. Taiwan's Ministry of Agriculture is somewhat circumspect on negotiating FTAs with the US in particular, and also with Australia and New Zealand.[109]

Table 2.1 shows that all other general hindrance factors were assigned low significance ratings by research interviewees in comparison to the research country groups aggregates. One prospective FTA project that did, though, generate much debate about more particular hindrance factors was that with the US. The US and Taiwan had signed a trade and investment framework agreement (TIFA) in September 1994, which provided a basis for enhanced consultations on commercial policy matters. These were suspended, however, in October 1998 owing to the US's dissatisfaction with Taiwan's progress on addressing the following outstanding issues: (i) the illegal restrictions on rice imports; (ii) slow approval procedures on US pharmaceutical products; (iii) lax implementation and enforcement of IPR regulations on copyrights and patents; and (iv) lack of market access in the telecommunications sector. In its bilateral WTO accession negotiations with Taipei, Washington insisted that Taiwan should commit to satisfactorily resolving these issues on entering into membership. The US subsequently indicated that progress here was a prerequisite for the resumption of TIFA-level consultations that in turn could be a precursor to commencing FTA negotiations. However, in May 2004 it was announced that Taiwan remained on the US's 'Special 301' priority watch list for a fourth successive year, which meant that sanctions could be applied if Taiwan failed to make significant improvements in the above specified areas. Although the Taiwanese Government has implemented much of the legislation demanded by Washington, American trade diplomats were still arguing by 2005 that these new laws were being weakly enforced.

2.7.4 Impacts and consequences

Research interviewees had little generally to say in this area, mostly because Taiwan is the only one from the field researched group not to have signed, or even started to negotiate an FTA with a major trade partner. The highest significance rated factor was *relations with bilateral FTA partners*, with particular regard to Taiwan's endeavours to break the circle of diplomatic isolation (Table 2.1). An FTA with the US was believed to make the biggest potential impact for reasons already discussed. In relation to both *domestic economic policy reform* and *domestic economic restructuring process*, FTAs were seen as either an extension of or running parallel to Taiwan's WTO accession commitments in this area. *Developing wider regional trade agreements* also scored relatively highly, mostly in connection with how Taiwan's bilateral FTAs may link them into a wider East Asian arrangement if it transpired. This point was closely associated with the *Taiwan's influence in the East Asia/ Asia-Pacific region* factor, which also achieved a relatively high ranking.

Research interviewee opinion on the impact of Taiwan's FTA policy upon Cross-Strait relations was rather mixed. One the one hand there was the view that if progress was made with this policy it could be seen as a defeat by Beijing and lead to more antagonist behaviour towards Taiwan. On the other hand, many believed it could give Taipei a useful bargaining chip, especially if an FTA with the US or Japan was secured. One research interviewee even thought it could give new imperative to reinitiate Cross-Strait dialogue, which has been dormant since the early 1990s.[110] There has been talk of a Taiwan–China FTA itself, although ideas on the subject have come more from Beijing than Taipei. In November 2003, for example, Beijing proposed that both sides should start talks on a Closer Economic Partnership Arrangement (CEPA) similar to those then recently signed with the special administrative regions of Hong Kong and Macao.[111] However, the same 'one country, two systems' principle underlying such an agreement was unacceptable to Taipei. There exists strong support amongst Taiwan's business community for a conventional FTA with China, as part of liberalising the restrictions on Cross-Strait commerce, and Taipei had become more positive towards the idea by 2005. In May that year, Minister of Economic Affairs, Ho Mei-yueh, announced Taipei's willingness to negotiate an FTA on a country-to-country basis but refused to consider Beijing's insistence on establishing a more integrative CEPA within a 'one China' political framework.[112]

At the heart of this dilemma lies managing Taiwan's increasing economic dependence on mainland China that has occurred as a result of expanding commercial interactions between both sides. Taipei has always feared that the growth of Cross-Strait commerce would provide Beijing with greater political leverage by the territorialised 'capture' of Taiwanese assets. Taipei has especially tried to restrict Cross-Strait transfers of strategically significant technological and capital assets over the years, which has frustrated especially those elements of Taiwan's business community seeking to relocate operations to the mainland for cost efficiency and improved market access (to China) reasons. Despite Taiwanese Government restrictions, Cross-Strait commerce expanded rapidly during the 1990s. By 2005 there were over 40,000 Taiwanese companies operating in mainland China with an estimated total cumulative investment that varied between US$50 billion to US$80 billion. Meanwhile, Cross-Strait trade had risen from an annual level of US$2.7 billion in 1988 to US$78.3 billion by 2004 (Appendix D). Although Taipei has gradually liberalised its Cross-Strait commerce policy many product-specific and industry-specific restrictions are still applied for national security reasons. For example, it has been resisting pressure from Taiwan's information technology firms to lift mainland investment bans on higher-tech product lines, and remains hesitant to fully establish the so called 'three direct links' (i.e. transport, mail, trade) across the Strait (Dent 2005a).

2.8 Thailand

2.8.1 The origins, determining factors and development of Thailand's FTA policy

Thailand: an international political economy overview

Thailand emerged in the aftermath of the 1997/98 East Asian financial crisis as the premier economy of Southeast Asia. This is somewhat ironic as it was Thailand's de-pegging of its currency, the baht, from the US dollar that initially triggered the onset of the region's financial crisis. Thailand's strong post-crisis recovery and dynamic leadership under Prime Minister Thaksin Shinawatra from 2001 has placed it more firmly centre-stage in ASEAN affairs generally. As discussed here and elsewhere, what is also increasingly apparent is an emerging bilateral economic partnership or alliance with Singapore. In recent years both countries have sought together to shape the agenda and set the pace of Southeast Asia's intra-regional and extra-regional economic integration. In the intra-regional context this could be seen by their attempts to accelerate the implementation of AFTA and their joint proposal to establish an ASEAN Economic Community by 2020. These endeavours have largely stemmed the Singapore–Thailand Enhanced Economic Relationship framework that was established in 2003.

In extra-regional terms, Thailand has, like Singapore, shown a penchant for developing a broad network of bilateral economic partnerships beyond

Southeast Asia, and FTAs have been a principal instrument of this strategy (Dent 2006a). In December 2000, the Thai Government announced plans to explore FTA projects with a global spread of trade partners. The strategic element of this partner selection process was that many of them were core members of other regional trade arrangements: India and the South Asian Association for Regional Co-operation, Brazil and Mercosur, South Africa and the South African Development Community, the Czech Republic and the Central European Free Trade Agreement, Bahrain and the Gulf Co-operation Council, the United States and NAFTA. These bilateral FTA links are seen as bridgeheads into other global regions, while bilateral FTAs with other East Asian states would help consolidate Thailand's position as an emerging national hub economy within ASEAN. There are similarities here with Singapore's broad geo-strategic approach in that bilateral FTAs were viewed as a relatively quick and effective method to globalise Thai economic diplomacy and diversify its market access interests.

The origins and development of Thailand's FTA policy

Thailand became a member of GATT in November 1982. As a small developing country adopting an export-oriented industrialisation strategy it relied on the development of an increasingly open multilateral trading system. The conventional wisdom in Thailand well into the 1990s was that bilateral FTAs were not in the country's interest, as they would allow larger more powerful trade partners to dictate the terms of such agreements. This was in contrast to the GATT/WTO where small and large were, in theory, treated as equal partners. However, Thailand began to take a different view as the global FTA trend intensified during the decade. Plans arose in 1994 and 1995 for a proposed FTA with the Czech Republic.[113] In December 1996, Israel and Thailand held tentative discussions on initiating FTA talks,[114] although these never actually transpired. In the latter months of 1997, Thailand had indicated its interest in negotiating bilateral FTAs with other countries, namely Australia, Chile, Croatia, India and South Korea (Nagai 2002). Of these, South Korea showed most interest at initiating an FTA project with Thailand, this being formally proposed in November 1998, one of the first in the Asia-Pacific's new FTA trend (see Appendix A). However, this bilateral project faded away after its scoping study completed in March 2001 revealed the potential adverse effects an FTA would have for a number of sensitive industries, in particular on South Korea's agriculture sector. Thailand is one of East Asia's major producers and exporters of rice and other farm products, this posing a challenge to its FTA negotiators when dealing with agri-protectionist countries like South Korea, Japan and the US.

Signs of other possible and actual FTA projects emerging came over 2000 and 2001. In November 2000, the ACFTA project was proposed, and a month later the Thai Government held informal discussions with Croatia, the Czech Republic and Bahrain. After entering office in 2001, Prime Minister Thaksin announced a new direction in Thailand's FTA policy whereby large or key markets in Asia and the Western Hemisphere would be targeted. New FTA projects were subsequently commenced with Australia, Japan, the US, India, New Zealand and Peru. As a legacy of the previous administration, Thailand signed its first bilateral FTA with Bahrain in 2003. Thailand also secured fast track bilateral negotiations with China in ACFTA negotiations, implementing its Early Harvest Programme provisions on certain agri-products many months ahead of its fellow ASEAN member states (see Chapter 3). Bangkok hoped that negotiating an 'advance' bilateral deal with Beijing would further consolidate its sub-regional hub economy position in continental Southeast Asia. Thailand's FTA ambitions had spread further by 2003. On the eve of his visit to France, PM Thaksin announced in March that year his government's interest in an FTA with the EU.[115] By 2004, Thailand had concluded bilateral FTA negotiations with Australia and India, and Thai diplomats were furthermore engaged in negotiating FTAs with Japan, the US, New Zealand and Peru during this year. Deals with New Zealand, Peru and at the ASEAN level with South Korea were signed in 2005, while talks with Japan and the US continued into 2006. Overall, Thailand was party to six concluded FTA projects within the Asia-Pacific by December 2005 (Table 2.2) and had one of the most active FTA policies in the region.

Main determining factors

The three most important determining factors behind Thailand's bilateral FTA policy according to research interviewees are inter-linked. Explanations behind the highest rated factor, *strengthening diplomatic relations with key trading partners*, included "strengthening the regional network of bilateral relationships",[116] and that bilateral FTAs were "part of an region-centric foreign policy in which Prime Minister Thaksin is trying to position Thailand as ASEAN's new hegemonic power".[117] There was a consensual view that the government viewed the politico-diplomatic gains offered by FTAs more importantly than the potential economic gains. When asked, research interviewees concurred that the Thai Government were looking to eventually establish the aforementioned global spread of FTAs, starting first with a region-wide strategy. This was also strongly linked to Prime Minister Thaksin's own vision of using activist trade diplomacy, primarily through FTAs, to "project a dynamic image of Thailand, raise the country's international stature and impress the electorate."[118] Positioning this point in relation to the second highest rated determining factor, *instigating a new direction in Thailand's trade policy*, FTAs were part of the 'think new, act new' motto of the Thaksin Administration. Whilst the large number of FTA projects initiated by Thailand is indicative of policy-diplomacy activism, many research interviewees noted that the country's FTA policy was also reactively determined to a large degree, that is as a *response to the regional and global FTA trend*, the third highest rated factor.

Another highly rated determining factor behind Thailand's FTA policy was *helping consolidate domestic economic reforms*. Thailand's upstream producers (e.g. steel, chemicals) remain quite protected from foreign competition with help from relatively high import tariff rates and FDI restrictions in such sectors. Although the Thai Government 'sells' its FTA projects with trade partners as a means to restructure and open up the Thai economy, foreign investors have been confused in recent years by mixed signals sent out by the Thaksin Government on matters of trade and investment. At times it has stated its welcoming of foreign commercial interests and at other times it has appeared more cautious, stressing instead the prioritisation of economic nationalist objectives and building up Thailand's domestic market (Economist Intelligence Unit 2004). Certainly, the Thai Government wishes to maintain and develop strategic industry capacity in the economy's core sectors, such as steel, petrochemicals, food, textiles and autos, and FTAs offer an opportunity for the expansion of Thailand's exports in these industries.

Research interviewees afforded *WTO trade liberalisation inertia* the next highest rating, and Thailand's rating for this determining factor was one of the highest among the field researched country group (Table 2.1). Explanations for this primarily concerned Thailand's frustration with the pace of multilateral trade liberalisation in the agricultural and textile sectors, where it retains considerable competitive advantages. Some interviewees actually made a direct connection to the impatience of Prime Minister Thaksin himself with the WTO process. *Strengthen regional economic cohesion* was given the same significance rating, and interviewees pointed to the geoeconomic dimension of Thailand's FTA policy, especially in relation to the previously made point about Thailand's positioning itself as the national hub economy in Southeast and East Asia. Its 'advance' bilateral FTA negotiations with China as part of the ACFTA framework were particularly seen in such terms. *Towards wider regional trade arrangements*, although assigned a lower rating, was closely connected to the above factor, especially by government officials whereby Thailand's bilateral FTAs were viewed as a foundation on which future regional FTAs would be based, hence consistent with the lattice regionalism hypothesis.

2.8.2 The formation of Thailand's FTA policy

Thailand's prime trade policy-making agencies are the Ministry of Commerce (MOC), Ministry of Foreign Affairs (MFA) and Prime Minister's Office (PMO). As earlier indicated, the PMO has taken a more prominent role in trade policy formation since PM Thaksin took office in 2001. Furthermore, many research interviewees commented that Thailand's activist FTA policy derives much from Thaksin's results-oriented and so called 'economies of speed' leadership style. This has also created a more centralised, 'top down' system of economic policy formation in Thailand, with most FTA projects having originated from the PMO. It also has over-sight of FTA negotiating teams of MOC and MFA officials. Thailand's Trade Minister, Adisai Bodharamik, was renowned for being a somewhat reluctant trade liberaliser and for firing many neo-liberal technocrats within the MOC. While he has officially supported Thaksin's activist FTA policy, Adisai has been circumspect about opening up Thailand's sensitive industries to foreign competition in either bilateral or multilateral trade negotiations.[119]

Regarding stakeholder consultation, there was a general view that the Thai Government had largely failed to sufficiently consult with all groups in society. Civil society groups and academics have been the most vocal critics, claiming that the Thaksin Administration had not conformed to proper parliamentary process concerning FTA policy matters.[120] For example, Article 224 of Thailand's Constitution states that any agreement undertaken by the government that impacts on Thai sovereignty requires a two-thirds majority approval from Parliament. Aspects of Thailand's FTA negotiations with the US (e.g. on foreign investor rights) were deemed to invoke Article 224 but a parliamentary debate had not been accordingly activated. In February 2004, Thailand's Senate and opposition Democrat Party tabled a motion to discuss this issue but the government turned down the request. At a later point, Chairman of the Thai Senate Foreign Affairs Committee, Kraisak Choonhaven, had complained that, in relation to the Thailand–Australia FTA (TAFTA) project, "only occasionally were low-ranking officials sent to testify before Senate committees", and that, "the government never bothered to consult affected parties or parliament and only informed committees fleetingly. My committee, foreign affairs, had to get all its information from the Australian parliament website".[121] Political pressure mounted upon the government during 2004 to make its FTA policy more transparent and accountable. While chairing a special meeting of Thailand's International Economic Policy Committee in November that year, PM Thaksin announced the government would seek greater public involvement in the formation of its FTA policy and trade policy in general, and this would be part of the newly established Committee on FTA Negotiations remit.[122]

However, the Thaksin Administration came under criticism again on this issue during the third round of US–Thailand FTA negotiations in April 2005, when a campaign led by a civil society group called FTA Watch called for a public review of the FTA talks thus negotiated. FTA Watch argued that important issues of Thai sovereignty were at stake mainly because of US demands on IPR rights that affected the health concerns and food security of the Thai people.[123] In January 2006 came a more serious threat to the Thai Government's FTA policy when Kraisak Choonhavan, chair of

Thailand's Senate Foreign Affairs Committee, announced that TAFTA and other signed FTAs were unconstitutional because they had not been adequately debated in Parliament as required under Article 224.[124] More generally, there was a widely held view that the Thai Government had rushed the development of its bilateral FTA projects, leading as many analysts and stakeholders feared to a weakening of the country's bargaining position with trade partners. This related to both preliminary study work undertaken by the government and in the equipping of its FTA negotiator teams.[125] For example, the Thailand Textile Manufacturers Association expressed some concern over the lack of analysis conducted or sponsored by the government into the impact of the country's FTA with Australia, especially with respect to key domestic industries like textiles.[126]

2.8.3 Challenging areas and contentious issues

Table 2.1 shows that research interviewees rated *agriculture* and *opposition from Thailand's industry groups* as the two most important general hindrances. Agricultural issues cut both ways here, with Thailand's competitive advantages in key agri-sectors like rice being a concern for some FTA partners, and certain FTA partners in turn cite various Thai tariff and regulatory import barriers on agri-products. Thailand's FTA negotiations with Japan provide a good illustration of the former problematic for Thailand. Plans to initiate FTA negotiations in June 2003 were delayed by Japan owing to fierce opposition from its farm lobby.[127] In an attempt to appease Japan's farmers, PM Thaksin suggested that the Japan–Thailand Economic Partnership Agreement (JTEPA) could exclude agriculture, specifically commenting that, "concluding the FTA does not necessarily mean all sectors must be involved, so we believe it is better to start with sectors that would incur no problems."[128] However, even this could not assuage Japanese concerns and Thailand's farmers were not happy with Thaksin's apparent willingness to sacrifice their own interests for the sake of securing the 'result' of a JTEPA.

Planned JTEPA talks were subsequently postponed until February 2004. As it later transpired, Japan's Ministry of Agriculture, Forestry and Fisheries (MAFF) sought the inclusion of as many agricultural group representations as possible into the talks given the wide range of Thai agricultural exports into the country, and because it wished to bring as many farm product issues to the table as it could with the implicit intention of consolidating farmer resistance to the deal.[129] MAFF officials were particularly hoping to exclude rice in any final agreement. After five rounds of difficult negotiations over agriculture, Thailand agreed to this as part of a deal where Japan in return agreed to study eliminating or reducing tariffs on Thai chicken, sugar and starch. This deal was brokered between the PMs Thaksin and Koizumi on the sidelines of the October 2004 Asia-Europe Meeting (ASEM) summit held in Hanoi.[130] While this no doubt eased the path of JTEPA negotiations thereafter, it did mark a significant compromise to Thailand's rice industry, arguably its most important agri-sector. Both Thailand and Japan's main business associations, the Federation of Thai Industries and the *Keidanren*, have expressed disappointment over how negotiations have been in their view held hostage to agricultural issues.[131] Nevertheless, certain Thai industry groups have themselves opposed FTA-induced liberalisation of their sectors. In September 2004, JTEPA talks stalled after Thailand refused to fully open up its domestic market to Japan's car, auto part and steel exports.[132] Additional problematic protected sectors identified by other trade partners include Thailand's electronics and electrical products (particularly in relation to China and ACFTA), and the retail sector where Thai businesses were demanding greater protection, especially after the arrival of big foreign supermarket chains in the country.

Following on from an above point, Thailand's competitive advantages in certain agri-sectors explains most of the high ratings given to the *greater domestic problems confronting of FTA partner(s)* factor by research interviewees, especially Japan and South Korea. Thailand competitive textiles sector has also posed a challenge in FTA negotiations with developed countries like Australia, Japan and the US whose own textile industries have been in long-term decline. The long tariff liberalisation schedules Australia negotiated on textiles in TAFTA are indicative of this (see Chapter 3 case study on TAFTA and Appendix B). Australia and New Zealand also were reluctant to lower their strict quarantine standards to allow Thai imports into their domestic markets, and immigration control of Thai nationals was an issue in JTEPA negotiations as previously discussed in the Japan section.

Very mixed ratings were given to *lack of priority afforded by Thailand's trade partners*. On the whole this rating was low but specific high ratings were given in relation to the US's prioritisation of Thailand as a trade partner. Japan, China and Australia were thought by research interviewees to have afforded notable priority to Thailand in acknowledgement of its growing economic and political importance within ASEAN, and moreover the hub-linkage role an FTA with Thailand would serve in these countries' economic relations with Southeast Asia. Another higher rated hindrance factor worth commenting upon was *diplomatic over-reach/scarce diplomatic resources*. There are around 250 people working in the MOC's Trade Negotiation Department, and half of these are either trade negotiators or their support staff. The modal shift towards bilateral FTA negotiating has seriously over-stretched this Department. At the behest of the Thai Government, Ramkhamhaeng University was asked in early 2004 to design a curriculum to train up a new cadre of trade negotiators.[133] Up to then, the MOC were hiring international trade lawyers from foreign law firms, which was proving very costly – a predicament shared by many other Asia-Pacific states as discussed in Chapter 1.

Thailand's FTA negotiations with the US have too raised a number of contentious issues. The country's 1966 Treaty of Amity with the United States is particularly relevant because of the 'national treatment' advantages it confers to US firms in Thai markets over foreign rivals. According to the Treaty, American companies are the only foreign firms able to conduct business within the full legal framework of Thailand. Thus, US investors have the same rights as Thai firms in all but a few sectors, e.g. telecoms (where there exists a 25 percent foreign ownership limit), financial services and transportation.[134] Other FTA project partners – in particular Australia, Japan and New Zealand – sought parity treatment in their respective FTA negotiations with Thailand with varying degrees of success, partly due to US opposition to confer this parity. The Treaty itself was renewed in 2005, and Thailand pressed for various revisions. Thailand's FTA with the US has arguably proved the most contentious of all, based on both the significance of impact and the types of issues raised by the US in FTA negotiations. Of the latter, the US's demands on IPR, investment and government procurement regulations have been the most problematic. According to the USTR's 2003 Special 301 Report on Thailand,[135] IPR infringements in the country had led to an estimated annual trade loss to American firms of over US$160 million in 2002.[136] However, Thailand's firms and government were themselves concerned about US demands to fortify the intellectual property rights of American companies into sensitive areas, such as biotechnology where for example extended patents for living organisms would allow the US biotech firms to possibly dominate native plant species, including medicinal plants and cash crop species.[137] As the US section discusses further, Thailand was not the only trade partner to have been pressed by Washington on this matter. The Thai Government is also circumspect about further extending US investor rights beyond what American companies already enjoy over foreign rivals in the Thai–US Treaty of Amity. In response, Washington has taken Thailand to task over it being a non-signatory of the WTO Agreement on Government Procurement and the government's 'Buy Thai' public contract programme. Lastly, US business had complained about Thailand's complex tariff structure and high tariff rates generally, highlighting the fact that it has 46 different types of tariff and there is an average 24 percent tariff rate on US farm products. These contentious issues still beset Thai–US FTA talks during the sixth round of negotiations held in January 2006. Just after these talks came to a close, Thailand's chief negotiator, Nit Pibulsongkram, resigned his position, citing political pressures arising from both the lack of progress in the talks and mass public demonstrations in Thailand against the FTA.[138]

2.8.4 Impacts and consequences

Relations with bilateral FTA partners attained the highest rating and high ratings were given for *Thailand's influence in Southeast and East Asia* and *developing wider regional trade agreements.* Many research interviewees concurred with the view that Thailand's expanding FTA policy was strengthening its political position within the ASEAN group through extra-regional linkages formed with major powers in Asia-Pacific, i.e. Japan, China, the US. A few noted that a JTEPA would assist the development of the JACEP process, thus helping build a wider regional trade agreement in East Asia just as Thailand's 'advance' bilateral FTA with China was supposedly assisting ACFTA's development. Most research interviewees were positive in their assessment of how Thailand's FTA policy was impacting upon *international relations in the region.* The consequence of Thailand's FTA policy for *domestic economic restructuring* was deemed the second highest rated factor, and this applied in a broad sectoral sense to both agricultural and industrial products, especially transport equipment, mining, metals and chemicals. Many interviewees, whilst acknowledging the significant diplomatic impacts noted above, believed that the Thai Government had not fully considered the economic impacts that FTAs could bring.[139] The effects of free trade with China were particularly noted, and the early evidence from ACFTA's Early Harvest Programme supported such claims. In the first year of the agreement, Thailand's agricultural imports from China rose by 400 percent, while Thai agri-exports to China rose by 80 percent.[140] In a more specific example, Thailand's orange farmers complained that as a result of the country's FTAs with China and Australia they were not only facing a sharp increase in orange imports into the domestic market, but also continued difficulties in passing Chinese and Australian quarantine standards when exporting their products.[141] *Domestic economic policy reform* was quite highly rated mainly although opinion was divided as to whether FTAs would have a positive or negative effect overall here.

2.9   United States

2.9.1   The origins, determining factors and development of the US's FTA policy

The US: an international political economy overview

The US was the world's largest economy throughout the 20th century and remains so today with a GDP of US$11 trillion in 2004, well over double that of the next largest (Japan at US$4.5 trillion) and accounting for around half of the Asia-Pacific's GDP. In historic terms, American economic success has been mainly based on entrepreneurial dynamism, relatively abundant indigenous resources, and integration and development of a large domestic market that has provided US firms with the scale economy advantages and competitive springboard from which to dominate many world markets. Some would argue this success has also been founded on the US's exploiting its hegemonic position in the international economic system in particular ways, for example in using its power to open up foreign markets to American commercial interests. The US's financial and industrial might came to the fore in the post-1945 era, when it emerged as the undisputed global economic hegemon. It was the world leader in mass production industries, and product and process technologies. The internationalisation of American business accelerated during the early post-1945 years, riding on the back of the expanded international role of US capital in reconstructing Western Europe and parts of East Asia, especially Japan. With assistance from Britain and other European countries, the US was also instrumental in the construction of the 'new international economic order' based on the new multilateral institutions of the International Monetary Fund (IMF), International Bank for Reconstruction and Development (World Bank) and the General Agreement on Tariffs and Trade (GATT). It was from this time that the US became the primary standard bearer of market liberal capitalism and free trade. Yet as the post-war years wore on, America's hegemonic position succumbed to a series of mounting pressures. The US's involvement in the Vietnam War and its subsequent defeat coupled with the shock of the 1973/74 Oil Crisis and the withdrawal of the dollar from the Bretton Woods exchange rate system dealt severe blows to American societal and commercial confidence. This was further undermined by the gradual loss of US dominance in an increasing number of industries and world markets to European (especially German) and East Asian (especially Japanese) competitors.

The 1990s, however, saw a reversion to the American hegemonic position. The demise of the Soviet Union and the general retreat of communism worldwide left the United States as the sole military superpower, and moreover vindication that capitalism had proven the superior system. The economic malaise experienced by Japan's 'developmental' capitalism and a seemingly lacklustre Single European Market – based on 'social market' capitalism – only served to underline the apparent superiority of US championed 'market liberal' capitalism. It may appear somewhat incongruous that, according to certain analysts, the US is currently the world's most competitive economy[142] and yet has had world record-breaking trade deficits of late, approaching US$700 billion for 2005 with Japan and China together accounting for well over a third of this figure.[143] This trade deficit predicament has stirred reactionary protectionism from those industrial constituencies most affected by 'injurious' foreign competition. As we discuss later in more detail, US trade policy is significantly shaped by the interplay of competing vested interests, as clearly demonstrated by recent examples of US protectionism under the Bush Administration. These included the imposition of a 30 percent tariff increase on steel imports, countervailing duties on Canadian softwood lumber, and quotas on certain textile products imported from China. Thus, while US espouses the virtues of free trade and demand that its FTA partners offer comprehensive market access to American business in negotiations, at the same time it insists on protecting a range of domestic sectors from reciprocated liberalisation.

In addition to its considerable market power, the US utilises various other forms of power (e.g. technocratic) at its disposal to achieve its trade policy aims. Furthermore, at the time when the world is looking to the US as global economic hegemon to again demonstrate leadership and multilateral collegiality with regard to matters of international trade, finance and development, it has appeared of late to be more preoccupied with satisfying national interests and acting unilaterally in many cases. Acting bilaterally by pursuing FTAs with selected trade partners has also drawn criticism from multilateralists both inside and outside the US for further undermining the WTO system, although the EU is even more culpable in this respect as discussed in Chapter 1. Evidence from US negotiations on FTAs also supports the view that American foreign economic policy is perhaps more 'captured' now by domestic interests groups than at any time in the country's history (Bohara *et al* 2005; Feinberg 2003; Prusa 2005). It should too be noted that there remains a strong ideological orientation to US trade policy, especially since the 11 September 2001 terrorist attacks on the country. As then US Trade Representative, Robert Zoellick, remarked in a statement to a US Congress committee in February 2003, "America's trade agenda needs to be aligned with the values of our society. Trade promotes freedom by supporting the development of the private sector, encouraging the rule of law, spurring economic liberty, and increasing freedom of choice."[144] In an address made a couple of years earlier, Zoellick stated that, "we need to align the global trading system with our values (Zoellick 2001a)."

The origins and development of the US's FTA policy

The US joined the new Asia-Pacific FTA trend relatively late. Apart from NAFTA with Canada and Mexico (an extension of the 1988 Canada–US FTA), the US by 2000 had only concluded free trade agreements with Israel and Jordan. This compared to the EU's 27 concluded agreements at the time. Whilst the first-term Clinton Administration had proved quite energetic in pushing forward broad regional free trade projects such as APEC and the Free Trade Area of the Americas (FTAA) initiative, the record of Clinton's second-term was comparatively languid (Feinberg 2003; Schott 2001, 2004). An American Business Roundtable report published in February 2001 was highly critical of US Government inertia on trade activism during the latter 1990s, and moreover argued that the new Asia-Pacific FTA trend offered important new commercial opportunities for American companies.[145] Negotiations on two bilateral FTA projects were, however, initiated before the end of the Clinton Administration. The first of these projects, with Chile (USCFTA), actually dated back to the early 1990s (see Appendix A). Although formally proposed in January 1995, USCFTA negotiations did not commence until December 2000, around the same time as those for the second project in question, the US–Singapore FTA (USSFTA), which had only been formally proposed a month earlier.

After coming into office in January 2001, and leading up to the September 11 terrorist attacks on the United States, the Bush Administration did virtually nothing to develop its own FTA policy. To some extent it was preoccupied with trying to successfully launch a new round of global trade talks running up to the November 2001 WTO Ministerial Meeting at Doha. The continued lack of 'Fast Track' trade negotiation authority, to be later renamed 'Trade Promotion Authority' (TPA), was another key factor. 'Fast Track' enabled the executive arm of government to negotiate trade agreements without having to make regular consultations with the legislative arm (i.e. Congress) that then could demand amendments at every negotiating stage. This executive authority had been lost in 1994, and without 'Fast Track' the US's trade partners had little incentive to make concessions if Congress could demand post-negotiation amendments to any preliminary or final agreement brokered. Conversely, the US Trade Representative (USTR) office saw little point in initiating FTA projects if they were to be held so openly hostage to competing domestic political interests.

The Bush Administration succeeded in passing its TPA bill through Congress's House of Representatives in December 2001 by just one vote (215 to 214), and then was passed through to the US Senate in May 2002, which returned a far more convincing majority 66 to 30 vote in favour of TPA. The bill was then passed back to the House of Representatives in July 2002 for its final legislative passage, where it passed with a 215 to 212 majority.[146] Thereafter, the USTR started to develop a number of FTA projects, based on recommendations first submitted to a cabinet-level interagency group under the leadership of the National Security Council (NSC) and National Economic Council (NEC). Those with Australia, Malaysia and the Philippines were proposed from late 2002, the latter two as part of the US's Enterprise for ASEAN Initiative (EAI) towards Southeast Asia. A proposal for a Thailand–US FTA project later followed in July 2003. Earlier on that year, the US and the Central American Common Market group (CACM, comprising Costa Rica, El Salvador, Honduras, Guatemala and Nicaragua) formally announced their FTA proposal, the project being referred to as CAFTA. In June 2003, the US initiated an FTA project with Panama, and in November 2003 with the Andean Community (Peru, Colombia and Ecuador) countries. Projects with countries outside the Asia-Pacific region were also developed. The US–Morocco FTA was proposed in October 2002 and was signed in June 2004. A few months later the US signed an FTA with Bahrain. Negotiations for an FTA between the US and the South African Customs Union group commenced in June 2003. An FTA proposal between the US, the United Arab Emirates and Oman came in June 2004 as part of the Bush Administration's Middle East Free Trade Area Initiative, which envisioned a future FTA with the whole Middle East region. Within the Asia-Pacific specifically, the US had concluded six FTAs by the end of 2005 (Table 2.2).

The development of the US's FTA policy was very much shaped by the idea of 'competitive liberalisation', as articulated by Robert Zoellick, the US Trade Representative during the first Bush Administration (2001–2005). Competitive liberalisation concerns the pursuit of FTAs with certain trade partners in order to compel others to join in a gradually widening trade liberalisation process, whether at the bilateral, regional or multilateral level. The underlying principle of competitive liberalisation is that it becomes more imperative for reluctant trade liberalising countries to sign bigger trade deals that will help neutralise the trade diversionary effects of FTAs signed by 'pro-free trade' countries. Many observers believe, for example, that the US's development of bilateral FTAs with other Pacific American states (i.e. the CACM group, the Andean Community group and Panama) are a means to pressure Brazil into complying to Washington's demands in negotiations for establishing the Free Trade Area of the Americas (FTAA). This may be considered as a constituent part of the lattice regionalism dynamic, as Chapter 4 discusses this in some detail.

Main determining factors

Table 2.1 shows that a number of determining factors were thought similarly important in the development of the US's FTA policy. There was little difference in the assigned significance ratings given by research interviewees for these factors, and the US had the lowest top rating for the whole field-researched country group. This particular factor, *strengthening diplomatic relations with key trade partners*, was the highest rated for most within the group. In the US's case there are two main geopolitical dimensions to this. Firstly, the quite diversified spread of FTAs being pursued in terms of geography and development level is viewed by the USTR as "building a network coalition in different global regions", not least to "strengthen support for US foreign economic policy."[147] This connects with the USTR's 'competitive liberalisation' strategy from the more diplomatic perspective (rather than that of market access) in terms of Washington getting other countries to come on board with their general trade policy agenda. Secondly, FTAs are seen as part of the US's promotion of democracy, market-liberal economic development, and stability in the developing world. The belief that the US's FTA policy is driven more by political rather than economic objectives is especially held by the business community who as we later examine have been critical of the small market FTA partners selected by the Government.

Following on from these politico-diplomatic considerations, the extent to which FTA projects have formed part of *consolidating security alliances* in a post-9/11 context is a moot point. In February 2003, Robert Zoellick remarked that, "Trade is more than economic efficiency. It's about America's role in the world... The long-term war against terrorism has to include trade, openness and development."[148] However, many research interviewees made the point that the US should have prioritised FTAs with countries such as Indonesia and Malaysia if it wished to build a more effective coalition in its war on terror. These two countries had, though, opposed the US invasion of Iraq, and this leads us to the main connection that most research interviewees believed existed between the US's FTA policy and security, namely punishing certain current and prospective FTA partners that did not support this invasion. Chile and New Zealand are often cited examples here. In the Spring of 2003, the Bush Administration delayed the signing of the USCFTA after Chile had abstained from giving unqualified support of military intervention in Iraq on the UN Security Council.[149] The *Washington Post* made the point that the US Government's prioritisation of signing an FTA with Singapore (referred to as a "dictatorship") over Chile (a democratic country) sent "counterproductive signals" to the international community.[150] New Zealand's more overt opposition to the Iraq War significantly undermined its endeavours to commence FTA negotiations with the US, endeavours previously noted in this chapter that well pre-dated those made by Australia, perhaps the US's strong security ally in the Asia-Pacific.

Many research interviewed US Government officials believed that its FTA policy was not directly driven by security-related objectives, although the AUSFTA may be one exception to this rule in the Asia-Pacific context.[151] They pointed instead to the primacy of market access objectives, and a number of high-rated determining factors relate to this. It has already been noted in relation to *response to the regional/global FTA trend* that the US was particularly concerned about falling behind the EU. This had been expressed on numerous occasions in public statements made by USTR Zoellick and other government officials.[152] A study conducted by the National Association of Manufactures (NAM) in the early 2000s estimated that for example the US was losing US$1 billion a year in sales in Chile as a result of its FTAs with other countries, and this was naturally expected to increase once Chile's FTA with the EU was operationalised.[153] Many research interviewees noted that the 'FTA catch-up' imperative was a core argument made by those lobbying for the TPA bill in Congress.

This was closely linked to another high-rated factor – *WTO trade liberalisation inertia* – in that FTAs were more likely new market access gains than the multilateral trade system over the short to medium term. The WTO's Seattle Ministerial debacle was thought by many research interviewees to have been instrumental in the Clinton Administration's initial foray into FTA projects in 2000. During the first Bush Administration, the US signalled at both the Doha Ministerial of November 2001 and the Cancun Ministerial of September 2003 that it would take the bilateral and regional routes to free trade if the WTO failed to advance global trade talks. At the same time, and consistent with the competitive liberalisation approach, research interviewees also high-rated *helping achieve global free trade* as a determining factor of US FTA policy, especially how FTA partnerships helped the US form coalitions with 'like-minded' WTO members. Tied in with this was a plan unveiled by USTR Zoellick in November 2002 for the creation of global tariff-free trade in industrial products by 2015. There was a mixed response to this proposal, not least because with a relatively liberal industrial tariff regime the US would have to make relatively minor adjustments and sacrifices, which would not be the case for developing countries whose tariff levels were generally higher for various reasons. The US's attempts to catalyse agricultural trade liberalisation on a global level were also problematic. In 2002 and 2003, it proposed that all export subsidies be eliminated and that the average tariff rates on farm products be reduced from 62 percent to 15 percent. Washington also announced its willingness to cut its annual domestic agricultural subsidies by US$100 billion. Yet it was proposing these measures just two months after the May 2002 US Farm Bill sought to substantially raise many domestic agricultural subsidies, as is later detailed. The US's credibility problem on global trade liberalisation was compounded by a statement made around the same time by USTR Zoellick that, "the US will protect its national interests fully within WTO rules."[154]

Two other high-rated determining factors – *instigating a new trade policy direction* and *recent securing of Trade Promotion Authority* – are integral to each other. As previously noted, the securing of TPA enabled the US to substantially enhance its FTA policy. The majority of research interviewees contended that new FTA projects would not have been feasible without TPA being in place, and those foreign ambassadorial representatives stated that their country would not have commenced FTA negotiations without it. In this sense, it was seen more as an enabling factor than a determining factor, and was rated accordingly by research interviewees. The Bush Administration must seek renewal for TPA in July 2007, a crucial date for any bilateral FTA and global-multilateral trade negotiations in progress around this time.

One last high-rated determining factor behind the US's FTA policy was *strengthen regional economic cohesion*, and this too should be understood in the context of competitive liberalisation. A research interviewed Chilean Embassy official gave a useful illustration of one element of this strategy. In USCFTA negotiations, the US pushed for a chapter on telecoms liberalisation even though Chile had a highly liberalised market in this sector. Chilean trade diplomats realised that Washington wanted this to establish a precedent or template for when they came to negotiate the FTAA with countries such as Brazil, which has a highly protected telecoms sector.[155] However, the same did not apply to the APEC and hence wider Asia-Pacific context. Indeed, research interviewees were of the general view that *APEC trade liberalisation inertia* had given a relatively insignificant spur to the US's FTA policy, which is somewhat surprising given strong American advocacy for APEC's Bogor Goals on trade liberalisation during the 1990s. As documented in Chapter 1, the US's endeavours to advance APEC's trade liberalisation agenda through the Early Voluntary Sectoral Liberalisation (EVSL) scheme were blocked primarily by Japan in November 1998. Some may have expected a disappointed US to consider its bilateral FTA options at this point, just as the new Asia-Pacific FTA trend was emerging, yet it was another two years before the Clinton Administration did this. Research interviewees cited a number of reasons why the 'APEC failure' factor was largely irrelevant. The most important was that the US was fast losing faith in APEC from around 1996 onwards. One Department of Commerce official commented that the Individual Action Plan (IAP) scheme – APEC's first attempt at catalysing trade liberalisation – was producing results that "could not be more worthless."[156] Furthermore, very few US Government officials, especially trade professionals and diplomats, did not think that trade liberalisation in the Asia-Pacific could ever be achieved by the 2010/2020 deadlines.[157] A research interviewed USTR official was of the opinion that, "APEC's geography and economic disparity did not lend to unity, nor did its chosen operating modalities on trade liberalisation."[158]

2.9.2   The formation of the US's FTA policy

Of all the field-researched countries, the US has the most society-centric approach to trade policy formation. USTR officials themselves admit that while government strategic thinking (e.g. competitive liberalisation) provides some crucial backbone to US trade policy, it essentially acts in response to the lobbied demands of various domestic interest groups, be they from the business or civil society sectors.[159] Case studies of FTAs negotiated by the US examined in Chapter 3 testify to this, for example in USSFTA negotiations the lobbying of American Express in relation to financial services liberalisation and Wrigley concerning subsequent USTR pressures applied to Singapore to relinquish its chewing gum ban. The lobbying of American firm Pfizer to compel Australia to adjust its Pharmaceutical Benefits Scheme (PBS) in AUSFTA negotiations provides further illustration of this. This being said, the installation of TPA has brought a slight shift towards a more state-centric approach given that domestic interest groups have less numerous opportunities to lobby US Congress for amendments, or even to obstruct, a trade agreement in development.

The USTR is the country's prime trade policy agency and is under direct executive authority from the Presidential Office, or White House. In the USTR's own words, it is "responsible for developing and co-ordinating US international trade, commodity, and direct investment policy, and overseeing negotiations with other countries."[160] It consults and co-ordinates trade policy with other government agencies mainly through the Trade Policy Review Group (TPRG), the Trade Policy Staff Committee (TPSC), and the National Security Council/National Economic Council (NSC/NEC). The TPRG and TPSC are chaired and administered by the USTR and whose membership comprises 19 federal agencies and offices. Of these, the Department of State and the Department of Commerce are the most important. The Department of State used to be responsible for negotiating all trade agreements before the USTR's establishment in 1962, and today mainly plays a trade diplomacy role in the inter-agency division of labour. The Department of Commerce on the other hand works more on technical trade policy issues (e.g. patents enforcement, trade statistics) and offers a wide range of trade consultancies services for US business. Other key agencies include the Treasury Department, which also works on the technical policy side (e.g. customs) and trade-related financial matters, and also the International Trade Commission (ITC), which is an independent quasi-judicial federal agency that provides trade expertise to both the legislative and executive branches of government that can include FTA scoping studies. These agencies work especially closely with the USTR during FTA negotiations and in a generally supportive manner. There have been reports of inter-agency friction, such as between the USTR and the Treasury Department over the capital control issue in USSFTA talks (see Chapter 3) but these are generally rare.

The USTR also works in close consultation with US Congress, the legislative arm of federal government that consists of the House of Representatives (the 'Lower House') and the Senate (the 'Upper House'). Five members from each 'House' are appointed as official Congressional advisors on trade policy, and other members may be appointed as advisors on particular issues or trade negotiations. The Congressional committees with which the USTR most regularly consults on trade policy matters are the House Ways and Means Committee, the Senate Finance Committee, and the Leadership Offices of both Houses. Congress also maintains a system of private sector advisory committees to ensure that the government executive's trade policy and trade negotiation objectives are closely aligned with American commercial and economic interests. This is a key transmission mechanism for feeding domestic interests into the trade policy-making process. In addition, members of Congress are open to lobbying on an individual basis from domestic interest groups. Generally speaking, the US Senate is more pro-trade because members serve six-year terms and can think longer-term, whereas a House of Representatives member hold only a two-year term, thus having shorter-term perspectives and are more susceptible to local (protectionist) interests. After the US President selects an FTA partner, due notification is sent to Congress through the USTR at least 90 days before FTA negotiations are set to commence, with the USTR also making prior consultation with the Congressional Oversight Group.

In May 2003, the NSC advanced guidelines to improve the process by which potential FTA partners are assessed (General Accounting Office of the United States 2004). This both allowed for more involved inter-agency participation and also rationalised the criteria for FTA partner selection, this being to the following:

- *Country readiness*: involving the country's political will, trade capabilities, and rule of law systems.
- *Economic and commercial benefit*: assessing macroeconomic benefits (trade and investment potential) and the likely effects on specific products and sectors.
- *Benefits to the US's broader trade liberalisation strategy*: primarily relating to the prospective FTA partner's overall support for US trade goals.
- *Compatibility with US interests*: potential FTA partners are examined for their compatibility with broad US interests, including its support for US foreign policy (e.g. security) positions.
- *Congressional and private-sector support*: reviewing whether a particular FTA partner has sufficient support from US Congress, business groups, and civil society.
- *US government resource constraints*: mostly in relation to the USTR, and its ability to co-ordinate and delegate tasks with other trade policy related agencies.[161]

These criteria relate to various debates covered in this section. Table 2.1 shows that the US scores relatively highly on government–stakeholder workings in the formation of FTA policy. Agricultural groups attained the highest rating according to research interviewees. The US agriculture industry is generally competitive, and therefore market access is a key issue for American farmers in relation to FTAs, but there are also uncompetitive sectors like sugar whose representative associations ardently lobby the government to maintain high levels of protectionism. Consultative channels between the agricultural lobby and the government are extensive, as are those between business generally and the government. The latter can involve individual firms, industry associations like NAM and international-focused interest groups such as the US-ASEAN Business Council, which has played an instrumental role in developing FTA projects between the US and Southeast Asian countries, including advocacy lobbying in Congress and helping organise FTA scoping studies at the USTR's behest. These groups also comprise special coalitions formed between businesses operating in the FTA partners concerned, for instance the American–Australian Free Trade Agreement Coalition and the US–Singapore FTA Business Coalition, which is a derivative of the US-ASEAN Business Council. While America's civil society groups enjoy relatively high levels of contesting influence over trade policy formation compared to their counterparts from other Asia-Pacific states, this is significantly less than the agriculture and business lobbies. The US's proclivity to incorporate labour and environment clauses in its FTAs brings trade union and environmental groups into various forms of consultation with both the executive and legislative branches of government.[162] However, US civil society movements have been generally sceptical of FTAs, as is the general case across the Asia-Pacific and globally, and they have been quite effective at counter-lobbying pro-FTA business groups in Congress in certain cases. NGOs have also complained over the lack of transparency regarding FTA negotiations, and the USTR was criticised by the US's General Accounting Office for deficient use of its advisory committee mechanism during the development of the USSFTA project.[163]

The strong society-centric nature of the US's trade policy formation has lead to a particular duality in the technical policy approach to its FTAs. On one level, the USTR wishes to negotiate what it likes to refer to as a 'state-of-the-art' agreement. This relates to pioneering work in certain 'broad band' areas of commercial regulation that may serve as a template for wider regional and multilateral trade negotiations. Much of the pressure for this derives from the sophisticated demands of American firms in areas like IPR. At another level, the impingement of various domestic protectionist interests in the formation of US trade policy introduces numerous 'impurities' into more conventional areas of a free trade agreement in the form of exemptions, long tariff liberalisation phase-ins, and complex product-specific rules of origin (see Appendix B). This makes for an odd mix of technical policy innovation and old-fashioned protectionism, and relates to our debate in Chapter 4 on different FTA models emerging in the Asia-Pacific.

2.9.3   Challenging areas and contentious issues

As for most of the field-researched country group, agriculture was the highest significance rated hindrance factor to the development of FTA policy in the US's case (Table 2.1). However, this rating was not as high as in other countries and the US's 'hindrance factors' ratings were generally low. Nevertheless, agriculture has undoubtedly been a contentious issue in many FTAs the United States has negotiated. Many problems stem from the US's domestic agriculture policy, and in particular the 2002 Farm Bill, the signing of which is widely acknowledged to have been part of a wider political deal to ease the passage of TPA legislation through Congress.[164] In effect the Farm Bill was an advance side-payment to the country's farmers to compensate for intensified foreign competition brought on by future FTAs. The Bill consisted of a US$180 billion package of financial assistance to American farmers over a ten-year period, involving a substantial increase in price guarantees for crops such as corn and wheat, as well as introducing an 80 percent rise in new subsidies for others such as soybeans. Although Washington later signalled its willingness to relinquish certain agri-trade measures such as export subsidies, the Farm Bill further emboldened and even helped politically legitimise protectionist interests within the American farming lobby. The US sugar industry is probably the best illustrative case of this, with the American Sugar Alliance (ASA) fiercely lobbying for, and consequently securing a sectoral exemption on sugar in AUSFTA. In their defence, the ASA argued that the 2002 Farm Bill only helped restore certain levels of support that were previously withdrawn by the 1996 'Freedom to Farm' Bill (ASA 2003). Although a research interviewed ASA representative believed the 1996 Bill "unilaterally disarmed the US agriculture sector"[165] the sugar industry was one of the very few sectors largely unreformed by this legislation (Frydenlund 2002). In its second term, the Clinton Administration came back with a generous compensating price support system during late 1990s based on the justification that farmers deserved a share of the spoils borne from strong US economic growth over the decade. The 2002 Farm Bill took further significant steps in this direction, although American farmers remain let down over promises made by both the Clinton and Bush Administrations about opening up foreign markets more to US agricultural exports.[166]

The US's farmer groups have expressed dissatisfaction with the government's FTA policy generally. From a methodological perspective, they prefer multilateral over bilateral agri-trade negotiation because it is only from the former approach that trade partners like the Japan, South Korea and the EU are able to dismantle protectionist measures embedded in domestic systems of agriculture sector support. For example, if the US entered into FTA negotiations with South Korea, Seoul could only offer Washington concessions on international trade barriers (e.g. tariff and quota liberalisation) on a preferential basis. Any negotiated reductions made on levels of competitiveness-enhancing financial support (e.g. subsidies) awarded to Korean farmers would confer non-preferential benefits to all South Korea's trade partners, and hence trade negotiations on domestic agriculture support systems tend to be confined to the WTO multilateral forum (see Chapter 1). There is, though, an important linkage between bilateral FTAs and multilateral negotiations here. For example, in AUSFTA negotiations, the US's National Cattlemen's Beef Association (NCBA) argued that concessions first needed to be made at the WTO level by the EU, Japan and other countries on beef sector protectionism (especially on domestic support systems) before it would ease its opposition to opening up its own domestic market to Australian beef exporters.[167] Furthermore, in May 2003, NCBA economist Greg Doud stated in an address to a US Senate sub-committee that, "the NCBA firmly believes that any expansion of access to the US beef market must be part of an overall package that gains access for US beef exporters in Europe, Japan, Korea and other existing and emerging international beef markets. The NCBA will oppose any agreement that allows a net increase in access to the US beef market."[168] Agriculture was one of if not the most contentious issues in AUSFTA negotiations, where in return for Australia's complete and immediate elimination of its agri-product tariffs, the US insisted on tariff exemptions, long tariff liberalisation phase-ins for various products and other retained protectionist measures (see Chapter 3). Other FTA partners have experienced similar demands by the US for it to retain protectionist support in a number of sensitive agri-sectors. A little reported fact is that the US even insisted on numerous phase-in arrangements for the free trade entry of various agricultural imports from Singapore, which has virtually no agriculture sector to speak of (see Appendix B).

Textiles and steel were the two main sectors identified by research interviewees as the most problematic with respect to *opposition from (other) domestic industries*, although this hindrance factor was considerably less significance rated than agriculture. Textiles was certainly a sensitive area of negotiation in FTAs with most developing country partners, particularly with the CACM group. The second highest rated hindrance factor, and where the US scored highest across the field-research country group, was *diplomatic over-reach/scarce diplomatic resources*. In 2003, the USTR employed just over 200 personnel and sought to employ around 20 more, mainly in order to facilitate the development of FTA projects.[169] Inter-agency collaboration noted earlier allows for other government agency staff to be incorporated into the FTA negotiating division of labour, but is mitigated by certain budget constraints facing the USTR, as well as its much prized core role played within the government's inter-agency framework of trade policy formation.[170] The USTR's cadres has traditionally comprised trade professionals with very little political appointments made. USTR personnel are considered elite government corps, consisting of specialists in each sector (e.g. IPR, customs), and these work across different FTAs, often simultaneously. USTR research interviewees noted the main advantage of having a limited number of people was that knowledge and experience was more easily transposed across various FTA projects.

Nevertheless, other research interviewees generally held the view that USTR staff were overworked (one noted the relatively high turnover of USTR staff) and ultimately lacked the resources to negotiate many FTAs simultaneously, or take on relatively larger projects than had been thus far initiated. The General Accounting Office of the United States 2004 reported that 66 percent of USTR staff were deployed in six FTA projects in 2003 and that this was putting significant pressure upon available budgetary and personnel resources. Some have directly linked this problem to the competitive liberalisation strategy. Colvin (2004) highlights how this has spread already scarce USTR and other trade policy agency resources too thin across multiple and often minor FTA projects when more resources should be concentrated at the multilateral level. He observed for instance that under the Bush Administration the US has only filed an average of three cases a year to the WTO Dispute Settlement Body mechanism compared to an average of 11 annually under the Clinton Administration. In defence against such criticisms, USTR Robert Zoellick argued that the government's own selection criteria for FTA partners precluded certain big market countries (e.g. Japan, China, South Korea) because of foreseen problems in key areas such as agriculture.[171] While this may be a valid point, there remains the issue of how this strategy impacts upon international economic relations generally, a discussion taken up by Chapter 4. Returning to GAO study, it observed in relation to inter-agency co-ordination that, "Decisions about FTA partners are made with little systematic data or planning regarding trade-offs with other trade priorities, even though FTAs are resource intensive" (p. 2). One research interviewee observed the USTR's increased use of video-conferencing in FTA negotiations mostly to help reduce operating costs and staff jet-lag.[172] This being said, research interviewees rather contradictorily afforded a minor significance rating overall to FTAs being of *low foreign economic policy priority of government*, although we may distinguish between rhetorical priority – for example from speeches and other public statements made in relation to FTA policy development – and practical priority in terms of actual resources assigned to this task.

There was little comment ascribed to the next highest rated hindrance factor – *greater domestic problems of FTA partner(s)* – although special mention was given to agriculture and domestic political opposition to trade liberalisation in many Asia-Pacific countries, notably from Northeast Asia and Latin America. While *opposition from civil society groups/NGOs* within the US itself to FTA policy development was conferred a low significance rating generally, it did draw more commentary from research interviewees. Many thought the US's main trade union, the AFL-CIO (American Federation of Labor–Congress of Industrial Organisations), were highly organised and often very effective in their opposition to FTAs. One referred to the AFL-CIO as 'smart trade-bill killers', although many others commented that both the domination of Congress by pro-trade Republicans since the mid-1990s and the recent legislation of TPA has undermined their contesting influence over US trade policy. According to a research interviewed AFL-CIO official, "the post-9/11 political and international climate has also made it difficult for us to advance our interests and position on FTAs", this especially applying to agreements sought by the US with key security partners like Australia.[173] America's trade unions do, though, retain strong support from Democrat representatives in Congress, who are the main advocates of incorporating labour standards in FTAs and other types of trade agreement.

The common consensus view amongst research interviewees was the America's environmental groups enjoyed far less contesting influence over US trade policy than the country's trade unions. Both civil society groups have, though, been opposed to certain investment chapter measures normally included in FTAs negotiated by the US that provides a mechanism for American foreign investing firms to sue host governments for compensation in lieu of profit losses incurred by compliance to environmental, labour or other kinds of regulatory standards. A case often cited in relation to NAFTA's investment chapter provisions concerns the Ethyl Corporation's legal actions undertaken against the Canadian Government in 1997. Ethyl Corporation is a producer of MMT, a toxic fuel additive, and the Canadian Government's decision to ban the import and interstate transport trade of MMT on public health and environmental grounds led to the US firm threatening to sue for US$251 million in compensation. The firm argued the ban was an expropriation of its investments and was therefore illegal under the terms of NAFTA. The Canadian Government backed down, reversing the ban and paid Ethyl Corporation US$13 million in legal fees and compensation. Both the AFL-CIO and Friends of the Earth movement have contested the investment chapter provisions in FTAs the US has signed since NAFTA but with little effect. The approach taken by the US to investment rights in its FTAs does remain contentious, with critics making the general point that foreign investors should have access only to the same complaint mechanisms as domestic investors.

2.9.4   Impacts and consequences

According to research interviewees, the politico-diplomatic consequences of the US's FTA policy would be the most significant. Table 2.1 reveals that the highest rated factor here by far was the *relations with bilateral FTA partner countries*. The *US's influence in the Asia-Pacific region* was rated second and the impact of this policy upon *international relations in the region generally* was rated a close third. Connecting aspects cited by research interviewees included reasserting US hegemony and building coalitions of like-minded states, especially in terms of developing a global network of neo-liberal or free trade alliances with nations from different regions. In the Asia-Pacific context, one research interviewee believed that FTAs were an important bridge-building exercise after the souring of relations between the US and East Asian states during the 1997/98 financial crisis.[174] In line with previous discussions on the US's post-9/11 foreign economic policy, the impact of FTA policy on the '*war against terror*' was generally considered to be of limited politico-diplomatic significance. Some research interviewees made the point that many of the Asia-Pacific's predominately Muslim populated countries like Indonesia and Malaysia were not 'policy prepared' to initiate FTA negotiations, which relate to 'deficient capacity' issues discussed generally in Chapters 1 and 4.

The relatively high significance ratings generally assigned to politico-diplomatic consequences of the US's FTA policy is in some contrast to low ratings conferred to perceived economic impacts at home. Table 2.1 shows that this was a general pattern for the Anglo-Pacific economies from the group. One explanation for this is that these economies are already quite liberalised, hence the net effects of FTAs on further domestic liberalisation are comparatively marginal. Having said this, we have established that a number of US industry sectors remain protected, as more clearly exposed by the country's FTA negotiations with others. The impact on *domestic economic policy reform* and *domestic economic restructuring process* will remain limited as long as the executive and legislative branches of the US Government continue to appease various powerful domestic interest groups. FTAs were also thought to make little difference to US economic policy owing to the general openness (e.g. low average industrial tariff rate, liberalised FDI policy) and sophisticated regulation (e.g. in IPR enforcement) found in many if not most areas of the country's commercial regimes. Some research interviewees made the converse point that given the US's economic stature and neo-liberal demands in FTA negotiations that by far the most significant economic impacts are felt by FTA partners themselves, although theirs was a difference of opinion as to whether such impacts were negative or positive overall.[175] This issue is discussed further in Chapter 3's case studies on AUSFTA and USSFTA.

The consequences of the US's FTA policy *for the WTO* links closely to our debate on competitive liberalisation. Opinion was somewhat divided amongst research interviewees on this issue, although overall a feeling of positive rather than negative impact was apparent. On research interviewee even contended that without the US's promises of FTAs to certain developing countries from Latin America and Africa that DDR negotiations would never have progressed.[176] Another believed that those countries blocking a WTO agreement would have to eventually concede in order to offset the trade diversion effects of the US's FTAs.[177] However, a research interviewed National Association of Manufacturers official concurred with the argument that exporters from the US and its FTA partners may lose interest in the multilateral WTO route once they have secured free market access to big markets.[178] Furthermore, the trade diversionary effects of certain FTAs concluded by the US on third countries may be considerable, for example that of AUSFTA upon New Zealand as discussed earlier in this chapter.

2.10 Conclusion

This chapter has presented extensive country-specific detail on many of the key issues and arguments raised in Chapter 1 on the development of the new Asia-Pacific FTA trend, and has in addition laid important background context for arguments made in the concluding Chapter 4. The main observations that can be deduced from the country-specific analyses of this chapter are as follows. It is clear that the politico-diplomatic motives (especially *strengthening diplomatic relations with key trade partners*) behind the FTA policies of Asia-Pacific states are more significant than economistic motives. There are a variety of reasons for this, as Chapter 1 has previously discussed under the theme and different sub-categories of 'strategic diplomacy', e.g. co-operative diplomacy, security alliance diplomacy. Correspondingly, the main consequences of FTAs were also believed to be of a more politico-diplomatic than economic nature. Where economic motives do come into play, some FTA partners are chosen because they are big market countries (e.g. the United States, Japan and China), or because they are relatively easy economic partners to negotiate with, such as already well liberalised pro-trade countries like New Zealand, Singapore and Chile. There was also a general view amongst research interviewees that the economic consequences of FTAs upon the domestic economy depended on, as one may expect, the significance of the FTA partner and the comprehensiveness of the FTA signed.

Another high significance rated determining factor behind Asia-Pacific FTA policies was *response to regional/global FTA trend*, which relates back to the FTA 'catch-up' argument made in Chapter 1. For many Asia-Pacific countries, we could see a gestation of some kind of new FTA policy from the early 1990s onwards, at least in the thinking of trade policy strategisers. Moving from a multilateral to 'multi-track' diplomacy (i.e. incorporating FTAs) on market access issues was a recurrent theme for those states that had been multilateral purists (e.g. Australia, Japan, New Zealand) in the past. We also saw that for East Asian countries, the region's 1997/98 financial crisis helped catalyse FTA policy into actual proposed agreements by the late 1990s. Other high rated factors included *strengthen regional economic cohesion* and *WTO trade liberalisation inertia*. Regarding this latter point, many research interviewees across the Asia-Pacific particularly singled out the problems arising from the WTO's Seattle Ministerial Meeting in December 1999 as being an important spur to the region's new FTA trend. In terms of main hindrances to the development of FTA policies in the Asia-Pacific, agriculture was by far and away deemed to be the most obstructive factor. Other sensitive industry issues were also highly significant at times, as well as sensitive economic and social policy issues, especially those relating to health and culture. In Chapter 3 we continue to examine the issues covered here but from an individual FTA project perspective.

Notes

1 Some may contest the application of the term 'country' to Singapore (a city-state rather than a nation-state) and Taiwan (a contested state). This criticism is accepted but the term is useful for collective referent purposes.

2 Cairns Group membership comprises Argentina, Australia, Bolivia, Brazil, Canada, Chile, Colombia, Costa Rica, Guatemala, India, Indonesia, Malaysia, New Zealand, Paraguay, Philippines, South Africa, Thailand and Uruguay.

3 From the Cairns Group website: http://www.cairnsgroup.org/milestones.html.

4 Research interviews with various stakeholder representatives, Canberra, August 2003.

5 *Sydney Morning Herald*, 13.02.2003.

6 Confirmed in research interviews with two stakeholder representatives from different agencies, Canberra, August 2003.

7 Zoellick was addressing US Congress at the time. *New Zealand Herald*, 20.11.2002.

8   A view held by many research interviewees, Sydney and Canberra, July/August 2003.

9   Canberra, August 2003.

10 For example, the Queensland State Government made submissions urging DFAT to secure better market access to the US sugar market during AUSFTA talks.

11 According to a research interviewed DFAT official, this has especially occurred on issues of government procurement, services and investment regulations (Canberra, August 2003). An Australian Confederation of Trade Unions (ACTU) research interviewee claimed that the state governments were on the whole not happy with Canberra (Federal Govt) over lack of inclusion in FTA negotiations (Sydney, July 2003).

12 Research interviews conducted in Sydney (July 2003) and Canberra (August 2003).

13 Research interview with ACTU official, Sydney, July 2003.

14 *The Australian*, 17.11.2003.

15 *Japan Times*, 24.10.2000.

16 *Japan Times*, 30.09.2000.

17 *Japan Times*, 17.02.2004. By this time, MOFA had adopted a more positive view on FTAs generally but at times disagreed with METI over the choice of FTA partners. According to an interviewed research analyst, MOFA advocated projects with stable democratic states such as Australia and New Zealand for politico-diplomatic reasons whereas METI was mostly concerned with economic criteria in FTA partner selection.

18 Research interview with METI official, Tokyo, April 2002.

19 *Japan Times*, 04.05.2002.

20 Research interview with senior *Keidanren* official, Tokyo, April 2002.

21 Research interview with senior *Keizai Doyukai* official, Tokyo, April 2002.

22 *Asahi Shimbun*, 24.11.2003.

23 In 2003, Japan imported US$57 billion of farm imports and exported just US$2.6 billion.

24 In Japan's case from 60 percent in 1970 to 40 percent by 1999. In comparison, Britain's food self-sufficiency ration increased from 46 percent to 71 percent, and Switzerland's from 47 percent to 58 percent over the same period, while France and the US had become even greater net exporters of food during this time (MAFF 2002).

25 *Daily Yomiuri*, 28.10.2003.

26 Research interview with JA Zenchu official, Tokyo, April 2002.

27 In the words of a MAFF (2002) document, "products that are currently bound at zero under the WTO and products that are currently duty-free but are not bound at zero under the WTO under the Agreement between Japan and Singapore were subjected to tariff liberalisation" (p. 12). Hence the only contribution JSEPA made on agri-trade liberalisation was that Japan and Singapore agreed to keep agri-import tariff rates at zero in the extremely unlikely scenario where future WTO agreements led to the raising of their bound rates on these farm products.

28 Research interview with Rengo official, Tokyo, April 2002.

29 *Yomiuri Shimbun*, 26.08.2004. In Thailand's case this also applied to Thai chefs (where Thailand pressed for the minimum experience requirement to be lowered from ten years to five years or less) and masseurs whom at the time were not permitted work permit entry into Japan. The MHLW's reluctance to

lift this ban had reportedly stalled FTA talks with Thailand for a while (*Manila Times*, 14.02.2005).

30 Research interview with MOFA official, Tokyo, April 2002.
31 Research interview with EU trade official, Tokyo, April 2002.
32 Research interview with Canadian Embassy official, Tokyo, April 2002.
33 Research interview with MOFA official, Tokyo, April 2002.
34 *Stuff News*, 21.10.2003.
35 *Scoop News*, 04.05.2004.
36 Research interviews with MFAT officials, Wellington, August 2003.
37 Research interview with NZIER official, Wellington, August 2003.
38 *NZ Herald*, 26.04.2001.
39 That is products subject to such outward processing arrangements would be denied 'Hong Kong made' status, and thus incurring less favourable treatment, e.g. the generally higher tariffs applied to 'made in China' imports.
40 Australia and China had, though, made their official joint proposal for a bilateral FTA in October 2003, a few months before the official NZ–China FTA proposal made in April 2004.
41 'New Zealand's Approach to Free Trade Agreements/Closer Economic Partnerships/Strategic Economic Partnerships', accessed from MFAT's website (http://www.mfat.govt.nz/foreign/tnd/ceps/nzapproachtoftasjul05.html) accessed 04.01.2006.
42 Research interview with then New Zealand Trade Minister Lockwood Smith (Auckland, August 2003).
43 Research interview with trade policy analyst, Auckland, August 2003.
44 Research interview, Wellington, August 2003.
45 Research interviews with NZBR and AmCham NZ officials, Wellington and Auckland, August 2003.
46 Research interview, Wellington, August 2003.
47 *NZ Herald*, 23.11.2004.
48 Research interview, Auckland, August 2003.
49 *Stuff News*, 02.09.2004.
50 See www.converge.org.nz/pma/apsftsu1.htm.
51 See www.converge.org.nz/pma/apsingim.htm.
52 See www.converge.org.nz/pma/apsft.htm.
53 *New Zealand Herald*, 27.02.2001.
54 *New Zealand Herald*, 05.04.2002.
55 Research interview with trade policy analyst, Auckland, August 2003.
56 *ABC News*, 13.12.2002.
57 *The Star*, Malaysia, 15.11.2002.
58 Research interview with MFA official, Singapore, July 2002.
59 Research interview with key Singapore FTA negotiator, Singapore, July 2002.
60 Research interview with Singapore NGO representative, Singapore, July 2002.
61 Research interview with MTI official, Singapore, July 2002.
62 *Ibid*.
63 Research interview with International Enterprise Singapore (IES) official, Singapore, July 2002.
64 Research interview with MTI official, Singapore, July 2002.
65 Research interview, Singapore, July 2002.
66 Research interview with senior FTA negotiator, Singapore, July 2002.
67 Research interview, Singapore, July 2002.
68 As cited in *International Herald Tribune*, 26.01.2004.
69 *Reuters*, 20.10.2003.

70 *International Herald Tribune*, 26.01.2004.
71 *Korea Times*, 05.11.1998.
72 *Korea Times*, 12.01.1999.
73 Research interview with US Embassy official, Seoul, July 2002.
74 *Asahi News*, 01.11.2003.
75 *Korea Times*, 06.06.2003.
76 Research interview with MOFAT official, Seoul, July 2002.
77 Research interview with MOFAT officials, Seoul, July 2002.
78 Research interview with KITA official, Seoul, July 2002.
79 Research interviews with Korean Farmers Groups Association (KFGA) and MOFAT officials respectively, Seoul, July 2002.
80 *Joongang Ilbo*, 24.11.2002.
81 Research interview with senior FKTU official, Seoul, July 2002.
82 Research interview with senior GKU official, Seoul, July 2002.
83 Research interview with KIEP official, Seoul, July 2002.
84 The original quota level was set at 33 percent but this was raised in 1985 to 40 percent.
85 *International Herald Tribune*, 26.01.2006.
86 Research interview with KIEP official, Seoul, July 2002.
87 *Taiwan Economic News*, 14.11.2001.
88 *Taiwan News*, 15.11.2002.
89 *Taiwan Economic News*, 30.06.2003.
90 Some private sector feasibility studies on a Japan–Taiwan FTA have since been conducted but their activities have not generated much public interest.
91 One research interviewee estimated this to be between US$300,000 to US$600,000 for the Panama FTA project.
92 Low key talks with Japan, the Philippines and the US on FTA-related matters were apparently being conducted into early 2005 (Research interview with Taiwanese official, November 2004).
93 Research interview with MFA official, Taipei, April 2003.
94 Research interview with analyst from the Taiwan Institute of Economic Research (TIER), Taipei, April 2003.
95 *Taipei Times*, 14.10.2003.
96 *Ibid.*
97 *CAN News*, 13.12.2004.
98 *Taipei Times*, 18.01.2005.
99 Research interview, Taipei, April 2003.
100 Research interview with analyst from the Institute for National Policy Research (INPR), Taipei, April 2003.
101 *Taipei Times*, 26.09.2003.
102 Research interview, Taipei, April 2003.
103 Research interviews with foreign business office representatives, April 2003, Taipei.
104 Confirmed by research interviews, April 2003, Taipei.
105 Research interview, April 2003, Taipei.
106 Research interview with foreign representative office official, April 2003, Taipei.
107 *Taiwan News*, 22.11.2003.
108 Research interview with Ministry of Agriculture official, April 2003, Taipei.
109 Research interview with Ministry of Agriculture official, April 2003, Taipei.
110 Research interview with MOFA official, April 2003, Taipei.
111 *Taipei Times*, 14.11.2003.

112   *Taipei Times*, 12.05.2005.
113   Research interview with Thai FTA analyst and policy advisor, Bangkok, February 2003.
114   *Bangkok Post*, 04.12.1996.
115   *Bangkok Post*, 09.05.2003.
116   Research interview with Ministry of Foreign Affairs official, Bangkok, February 2003.
117   Research interview with foreign ambassadorial representative, Bangkok, February 2003.
118   *Ibid.*
119   As reported by many research interviewees, Bangkok, February 2003.
120   *The Nation*, 19.03.2004.
121   *Asia Times*, 07.07.2004.
122   *MCOT News*, 10.11.2004.
123   *Asia Times*, 14.04.2005.
124   *The Age*, 11.01.2006.
125   *The Nation*, 19.03.2004.
126   Research interview with senior TTMA official, Bangkok, February 2003.
127   *Japan Today*, 06.06.2003
128   *Japan Times*, 09.06.2003.
129   *Nihon Keizai Shimbun*, 31.05.2003.
130   *Channel News Asia*, 10.10.2004.
131   *Daily Yomiuri*, 30.05.2004.
132   *The Nation*, 03.09.2004.
133   *Miami Herald*, 13.04.2004.
134   Other exceptions included the exploitation of land and other natural resources, and domestic trade in indigenous agricultural products.
135   Thailand was placed on the USTR's Special 301 Watch List in 1994.
136   *Channel News Asia*, 05.05.2004. For example, pirated DVDs were found to make up 40 percent and pirated VCDs around 70 percent of the available movie product in Thailand.
137   *Bangkok Post*, 14.10.2003.
138   *The Nation*, 18.01.2006.
139   This view was especially held by foreign ambassadorial officials and FTA research analysts.
140   *Asia Times*, 07.07.2004.
141   *Asia Times*, 07.07.2004.
142   For example, see global competitiveness reports published by the World Economic Forum and the Economist Intelligence Unit.
143   *The Mainichi Daily*, 10.08.2005.
144   Robert Zoellick, statement made to the Committee of Ways and Means of the House of Representatives, 26 February 2003.
145   *International Herald Tribune*, 27.02.2001.
146   The Trade Promotion Authority Act of 2002 prevents US negotiators from concluding FTAs that: (i) reduce any rate of duty (other than a rate of duty that does not exceed five percent *ad valorem* on the date of the enactment of this Act) to a rate of duty which is less than 50 percent of the rate of such duty that applies on such date of enactment; and (ii) reduce the rate of duty below that applicable under the Uruguay Round Agreements, on any import sensitive agricultural product.
147   Research interview with USTR official, Washington DC, April 2003.
148   *New York Times*, 08.02.2003.

Asia-Pacific FTAs 149

149 Robert Zoellick himself commented at the time that 'people are disappointed' in Chile for having opposed the US's position during UN Security Council debates on the Iraq issue. According to his USTR office, the delay was owing to the time required to translate and legalise the FTA text into Spanish, and then back again into English but this excuse was much derided in the American media (*Washington Post*, 29.04.2003).
150 *Washington Post*, 19.03.2003.
151 Some research interviewees made the point that Morocco – seen by many as a key alliance state in the war on terror – was not chosen as an FTA partner for this reason but rather primarily because the US Ambassador stationed there, Margaret Tutwiler, was a close friend of the Bush family and USTR Robert Zoellick.
152 For example in an op-ed article in *New York Times*, 14.04.2002.
153 Research interview with NAM official, April 2003, Washington DC.
154 *Financial Times*, 26.07.2002.
155 Research interview with Chilean ambassadorial representative, Washington DC, April 2003.
156 Research interview, April 2003, Washington DC.
157 Confirmed by research interviews with Department of Commerce, Department of State and USTR representatives, as well as those from other stakeholding agencies, April 2003, Washington DC.
158 Research interview, April 2003, Washington DC.
159 Research interviews with USTR officials, April 2003, Washington DC.
160 From http://www.ustr.gov/Who_We_Are/Mission_of_the_USTR.html.
161 These six criteria were a rationalisation of thirteen wide-ranging points previously determined and used by the USTR.
162 For example, Friends of the Earth have representation on the USTR's Trade and Environment Policy Advisory Committee.
163 Research interview with CSIS representative, April 2003, Washington DC.
164 President Bush signatured the Farm Bill on the eve of the Senate vote on TPA legislation.
165 Research interview, April 2003, Washington DC.
166 Research interviews with farmer association representatives, April 2003, Washington DC.
167 Research interview with NCBA official, April 2003, Washington DC. The US beef industry itself does not receive any direct financial support from the government but only indirectly through the subsidisation of corn fed to cattle.
168 *High Plains Journal*, 30.05.2003.
169 Research interview with USTR official, April 2003, Washington DC.
170 Research interview with USTR official, April 2003, Washington DC.
171 *China Post*, 08.05.2004.
172 Research interview with Institute for International Economics (IIE) official, April 2003, Washington DC.
173 Research interview, April 2003, Washington DC.
174 Research interview with US–ASEAN Business Council representative, April 2003, Washington DC.
175 For example, an AFL-CIO official contended that NAFTA had led to lower median wages and a growing income divide in Mexico.
176 Research interview with IIE official, April 2003, Washington DC.
177 Research interview with Australian Embassy official, April 2003, Washington DC.
178 Research interview, April 2003, Washington DC.

3
FTA Project Case Studies

3.1 Introduction

This chapter presents eight case study analyses on some of most important free trade agreement (FTA) projects to have emerged within the Asia-Pacific in recent years. They have been selected as a representative sample of FTAs that have thus far emerged across the region as a whole. The FTA projects chosen are as follows:

- *Australia–US FTA (AUSFTA)*
- *ASEAN–China FTA (ACFTA)*
- *China's Closer Economic Partnership Agreements (CEPAs) with Hong Kong and Macao (HKCCEPA, MCCEPA)*
- *Thailand–Australia FTA (TAFTA)*
- *Japan–Mexico FTA (JMFTA)*
- *South Korea–Chile FTA (KCFTA)*
- *US–Singapore FTA (USSFTA)*
- *Trans-Pacific Strategic Economic Partnership Agreement (TPSEPA)*

These individual FTA case study analyses offer their own special perspectives on the political economic interactions between different sets of Asia-Pacific countries, and thereby insights into the heterogeneous nature of FTAs in the region.

3.2 Australia–US Free Trade Agreement (AUSFTA)

3.2.1 Origins and initial development

The idea of establishing an Australia–United States Free Trade Agreement (AUSFTA) had existed for some time. It was first proposed as long ago as 1934, and similar proposals followed in 1986, 1995 and 1997.[1] At these times, it was the US who approached Australia with a view to create an FTA link between the two countries. As detailed in Chapter 2, Australia was pursuing a staunch multilateralist, Asia-centric trade policy up until the mid-1990s under the Labour Party Government. It was not until the new John Howard Administration introduced a new trade diplomacy formula in the late 1990s that Australia's policy towards FTAs in general changed tack. By this time, Australia's trade with the US was booming owing to an economic resurgence in both countries. In October 2000, a decision was made at a Cabinet meeting of the Australian Government to pursue an FTA with the US. The following December Australia's Ambassador to the US, Michael Thawley, proposed an FTA between Australia and the US in a speech made in Washington DC. The announcement received a generally positive response from the US Government, which at the time was negotiating FTAs with Singapore and Chile. Australia and the US were both strong advocates of trade liberalisation, and there was at least an implicit alliance between them when it came to promoting freer trade within APEC (see Chapter 1). A transnational business lobby, AUSTA (the Australia–United States Free Trade Agreement Business Group) was established between Australian and American business interests that further advocated the AUSFTA cause. Both countries were also close security partners, and events after the September 2001 terrorist attacks on the United States strengthened their bilateral relationship further still. Chapter 2 discusses the importance of 'alliance politics' with respect to the AUSFTA project in some detail. Suffice to say here that the Australian Government's ardent support of the US-led 'war on terror' is generally regarded by most commentators to have played an important part in the Bush Administration's prioritisation of Australia as an FTA partner. As Australia's Trade Minister, Mark Vaile, was to later comment, "close friends are close friends, and anybody that has been in business knows that you'll do business with close friends because you trust them."[2] In early 2002, Vaile visited the US and pushed for the initiation of bilateral FTA talks. On a reciprocal trip made by US Trade Representative (USTR) Robert Zoellick to Canberra in November 2002, both sides announced plans to commence FTA negotiations in early 2003, with the initial aim of concluding an agreement by the end of 2004.

In the run up to the first AUSFTA talks, a controversy arose over two impact assessment studies. The report conducted by the Centre for International Economics (CIE), commissioned by Australia's Department of Foreign Affairs and Trade (DFAT), suggested that the implemented FTA would boost Australia's GDP by US$2 billion (Centre for International Economics 2001). However, another study report, undertaken by ACIL Consulting on behalf of the Rural Industries Research and Development Corporation, a government agency, concluded that AUSFTA would actually have an overall slight negative impact upon the Australian economy, a 0.02 percent GDP decrease by 2010 compared to the CIE's prediction of a 0.34 percent increase (ACIL Consulting 2003). Attempts were made by the Australian Government to suppress this second report given its pessimistic predictions, but this was leaked to the press in February 2003, forcing the Government into a defensive position whilst an intense public debate raged between the relative merits of the CIE and ACIL reports. Although both assumed full trade liberalisation under a final AUSFTA deal (which never transpired) and were based on a very similar econometric model structure, much of the contention between the two studies centred on two areas where their assumptions differed (Lloyd and MacLaren 2005). Firstly, the ACIL study did not assume an increase in service sector productivity from AUSFTA while the CIE report did. Secondly, the ACIL study assumed the standard values for Armington price elasticity effects (i.e. domestic consumers will prefer local over foreign products to some extent where their price and quality are very similar) whereas the CIE study doubled them. The ACIL study also concluded that the outcome for Australia would be strongly negative if politically sensitive agricultural sectors (sugar, dairy, beef) were not substantially liberalised, as actually occurred in AUSFTA negotiations. Further on in this case study we discuss how the controversy over AUSFTA's impact on the Australian economy later re-emerged. The first round of talks was held in March 2003 with a view to conclude negotiations by the end of the year.

3.2.2   Key areas of negotiation

Agriculture

Both countries were big competitive agriculture producers but what really mattered were their relative competitive positions. Australia's world-beating dairy, sugar and beef industries were of particular concern to US farmers. When Australia intensified its lobbying campaign for AUSFTA during the latter months of 2001, more than 40 US farm groups wrote to President Bush threatening to withhold support for Trade Promotion Authority (TPA) legislation (see Chapter 2) if the US Government agreed to start FTA talks with Australia. Around a year later, at the time the AUSFTA project was officially proposed, 20 American farmers groups sent a letter to USTR Zoellick and US Agriculture Secretary Ann Veneman stating their opposition to it. Sector-specific farmers groups organised their own 'campaigns of caution' regarding AUSFTA. In the dairy sector, the US's National Milk Producers Federation (NMPF) was opposed to the project, with NMPF President, Jerry Kozak, even going so far to state that, "this FTA will negatively impact our food security – and thus, also our national security. No homeland can be secure if the quantity and quality of its dairy supply is in doubt."[3] Although the NMPF were concerned about the competitive threat posed by Australian dairy farmers, it also acknowledged that the US dairy industry was eight times the size of its Australian equivalent. One could therefore argue that anticipated 'competitive displacement' (i.e. trade creation) effects from AUSFTA in this sector could have been far greater if the relative industry size differential been not so large. The US dairy industry is highly protected with tariff rates approaching 100 percent on certain products. The country's sugar industry was even more protected, and the American Sugar Alliance (ASA) succeeded in getting sugar completely excluded from AUSFTA.

The other key agri-sector where the US sought significant exemption was the beef industry. Like its dairy industry counterpart, the National Cattleman's Beef Association (NCBA) contended that any bilateral concessions made in AUSFTA negotiations in their sector should be offset by market access gains at the multilateral level in WTO negotiations. Thus, before the US opened up their beef market to Australia, American farmers should secure much improved market access themselves to the most protected beef markets (e.g. the EU and Japan) worldwide. The NCBA felt there was much scope for this given that the US only exports ten percent of its beef production. From Australia's perspective, former Labour Party Trade Minister, Peter Cook, made the point that AUSFTA was limited in what it could deliver to Australian farmers because bilateral agreements are not able to address the domestic farm support system issue: unsubsidised Australian farmers would still have to compete with significantly subsidised American farmers after a concluded FTA.[4]

The only Australian agri-sector targeted for particular attention by the US was wheat. Australia's Wheat Board (AWB) was established as a statutory agency and a legislated monopoly to manage both the domestic marketing of wheat and export marketing of wheat and flour. American negotiators raised the pressure upon Australia to dismantle the AWB during the fourth round of negotiations held in December 2003, stating that they needed some sort of 'trophy' to present to the US farming community to offset concessions granted to Australia in the aforementioned agri-sectors. This was a difficult area for Australia's ruling National Party as it had just beforehand passed a motion in parliament insisting that the AWB remained intact. Moreover, the AWB argued in its defence that unlike similar large US operations it was not subsidised, and therefore enjoyed less of a competitive advantage over American wheat producers than was commonly perceived.[5] The US also addressed Australia's rigorous quarantine regime in FTA negotiations, claiming that this system was costing US farmers between US$100 million to US$500 million a year.[6]

Pharmaceutical benefits scheme (PBS), entertainment industry and other issues

Australia's quarantine regime was not the only what may be usually deemed 'domestically embedded' policy realm to be targeted by US negotiators in AUSFTA talks. As Chapter 2 details, the Pharmaceutical Benefits Scheme (PBS) was a mechanism designed to maintain the price of medicines at affordable prices for the Australian public. American pharmaceutical companies were, however, complaining that these lower prices were costing them around US$1 billion a year in lost profits, and were pressing the USTR to negotiate hard on this matter. These firms were amongst the biggest donors to the US Republican Party, and moreover they looked to AUSFTA as setting a precedent for tackling similar schemes elsewhere in the world. Nevertheless, the Australian Government strongly resisted any pressure to dismantle the PBS, not least because a then recently published a report by the Australia Institute estimated that prices for medicines would double if the demands of American pharmaceutical firms in AUSFTA negotiations were met.[7]

Another of Australia's 'domestically embedded' sectors up for AUSFTA negotiation was the nation's entertainment industry. Like many other countries, Australia maintained local content regulations in television broadcasting and also offered subsidy support for domestic television and film production.[8] The US pressed for further opening up these markets even though American television and film dominated the Australian market to the extent of 70 to 90 percent penetration. As with the PBS issue, there was huge public support in Australia for the Government to resist American demands in this area. After the second round of FTA talks in May 2003, the chief AUSFTA negotiators from both sides (Mark Vaile and Ralf Ives) offered assurances that neither media local content rules nor the PBS were at threat under a future FTA deal, although Assistant USTR Ralf Ives did indicate at this time that the US might press Australia on the transparency of processes by which new drugs are tested under PBS arrangements.[9] High profile Australian actors, such as Bryan Brown and Toni Colette, entered into the public debate, arguing that 'culture' should be omitted from AUSFTA talks. However, some representatives from Australia's farming community were angered over the general opposition taken by the media industry to AUSFTA. For example, Noel Campbell, Chairman of Bonlac Foods, stated that it was disappointing to hear Australia's actors talking about not trading culture "for a few lamb chops".[10] Such inter-sectoral tensions and trade-offs have been a recurrent theme in FTA negotiations in the Asia-Pacific region, as we shall see in other FTA case studies in this chapter.

Other key issues were foreign investment, telecommunication sector privatisation, rules of origin and fast ferries. The US wanted Australia to remove certain regulations on foreign investment (e.g. on foreign takeovers) that were deemed to restrict the commercial operations of American firms. American companies were also lobbying for a NAFTA-style investment chapter to be incorporated into AUSFTA that would allow investing firms the right to sue the Australian Government for any policy actions that seriously compromised their business activities. The US also requested that the Australia Government sold its majority stake in Telstra, the country's biggest telecommunications company, in order to open up the telecoms sector more to foreign competition. Washington had demanded the same from Singapore in its FTA negotiations and Singapore duly complied (see USSFTA case study). During the second round of FTA negotiations, the US pushed for strict product-specific rules of origin (RoO) to be included into the AUSFTA text, whereas Australia wanted to keep these as simple as possible.[11] Earlier bilateral FTAs negotiated by both countries with Singapore revealed this difference in approach, with the USSFTA containing 284 pages of documentation on RoOs while SAFTA the rules of origin section only took up 15 pages. Regarding fast ferries, Australia is the world's leading producer in this sector but the US's Jones Act of 1920 required vessels used for the US domestic cargo trade to be built at American yards. Australia wanted the US to at least to grant an exemption from the Jones Act to open up the American market to its fast ferry exports.

3.2.3   Negotiation process and outcomes

The December 2003 deadline to conclude AUSFTA negotiations was missed. At the fifth round of talks held that month, a number of unresolved issues still existed between both sides, mostly relating to agriculture. A sixth round was soon convened in January 2004 but FTA talks also stalled owing to US objections to include sugar in the final deal. The Bush Administration had around this time been heavily criticised by domestic lobby groups for agreeing to even modest increases in sugar quotas during different FTA negotiations with four Central American countries (from the CACM group), and therefore making additional concessions in this highly protected sector to Australia was deemed too politically difficult by the US Government. Partly to compensate, the US did though soften its demands for changes to Australia's PBS and television local content rules. At this stage of the talks, the US was insisting on phasing in liberalisation on beef and dairy imports from Australia for at least 20 years while Australia was proposing this period be halved to ten years.[12]

A final agreement on these outstanding issues was reached in the seventh round of AUSFTA talks held a few weeks later in February 2004. Most controversially, Australia agreed to the US's demand to completely exempt sugar from the FTA, and US negotiators also secured 18-year phased-in liberalisation on beef, dairy, horticulture and cotton. Other key sectors of Australian agriculture faced long liberalisation phase-in periods, e.g. wool ten years and wine 11 years (see Appendix B). This was a great disappointment to Australia's farmers who were hoping for a generally comprehensive free trade arrangement across all agri-sectors. This indeed was what the Australian Government were indicatively promising at the onset of AUSFTA talks almost a year earlier. The country's main agricultural lobby, the National Federation of Farmers (NFF), had at first threatened to pull its support for any agreement that contained significant exemptions on farm products but later accepted that some improved market access to the US was better than none (NFF 2004).

At the close of the AUSFTA deal, Prime Minister John Howard commented that, "I came to the conclusion that it would have been against the national interest to give up a deal that is going to be of enormous benefit to the rest of the economy because we couldn't get something on sugar."[13] The US thus maintained its quota limits on Australian sugar imports at 87,000 tonnes per annum, which represented around an eight percent allocation of its total import quota for all countries. In a side-payment arrangement with Australia's sugar farmers, the Howard Administration offered them a new A\$440 million support package, which was in addition to a levy Australian consumers already paid to fund a sugar industry restructuring programme. Similarities can be made here with the even more generous side-payment made by the South Korean Government to the country's farmers as part of the Korea–Chile FTA (see later case study on this). In addition, the US's negotiated retention of safeguard mechanisms that would trigger the implementation of emergency trade barriers on evidence of injurious foreign competition deemed to harm American producers of certain farm products, such as flour, tomatoes, asparagus, pears, apricots, peaches, oranges and grapes. On its part of the AUSFTA deal on agriculture, Australia offered US farmers immediate duty-free entry into its own markets.

The US eventually dropped its demands for Australia to scrap the AWB and also many of its demands on Australia to adjust its quarantine regime. However, the US did secure the concession that a bilateral judicial review and appeal process be established to look at quarantine law rulings that affected US imports into Australia. According to Weiss *et al* (2004) the exact judicial authority of this process in relation to Australia's own national laws remains unclear, and hence a cause for concern if these laws can be effectively challenged by the US by this means. Similar bilateral judicial review and appeal processes were created in relation to PBS drug pricing and listing decisions. An Australian Senate Committee report published in 2004 raised concerns about how new patent provisions introduced by AUSFTA could delay the introduction of generic pharmaceutical products to the Australian market, potentially leading to increased prices.[14] Regarding the entertainment industry, Australia's 55 percent local content rule remained intact, although as a consequence of AUSFTA the Government could no longer raise the rate above this. With respect to new emerging media products, such as pay TV and multi-channelling, this rate was negotiated at a 20 percent maximum.

On foreign investment, AUSFTA now allowed American firms to make investments worth up to A\$800 million without first requiring clearance from Australia's Foreign Investment Review Board, compared to the A\$50 million limit applied to all other countries. However, the Japanese Government expressed concern over the implications this had for the long-standing agreement between Australia and Japan – the 1976 Nara Treaty – in which companies from either country will not be treated in a discriminatory manner, relative to companies from any third country. In response, Canberra stated that it would look into extending similar treatment to Japanese investing firms in Australia.[15] This element of AUSFTA demonstrated how bilateral FTAs could both cut across existing economic agreements of one of the FTA partners with a third country, and also extend discriminatory treatment beyond the trade policy domain. The latter would especially apply to certain 'broad band' FTAs where one FTA partner is seeking deeper market access with regard to the other, and this relates closely to the US 'asymmetric neo-liberal' FTA model discussed in Chapter 4.

On telecoms sector privatisation, the Australian Government held out against US demands for it to sell its majority shareholding in Telstra. However, in a side letter written to the USTR Robert Zoellick, Australian Trade Minister Mark Vaile confirmed the negotiated understanding that his government remained committed to the eventual privatisation of Telstra. The AUSFTA text also contained a 46-page annex listing the different product-specific applications of rules of origin. Just as with the phase-in liberalisation schedules, the high level of differentiation across different product sectors could be mostly attributed to the interplay of various domestic interests in US trade policy formation (see US section in Chapter 2). Manufacturing groups from both Australia and the US were generally content with AUSFTA outcomes, although the US made no concessions on the fast ferry issue. Both sides agreed to immediately eliminate tariffs on the vast majority of their bilateral trade, and barriers were retained on only a handful of low-tech products, such as textiles, clothing and footwear (see Appendix B).

3.2.4 The AUSFTA impact studies controversy continued

As AUSFTA negotiations were drawing to a close in early 2004, the controversy over the estimated impact of the agreement upon the Australian economy re-emerged. Some commentators had noted at this time that the Australian dollar's 13.4 percent appreciation against the US dollar since the release of the CIE (2001) study had significantly reduced its estimated benefits.[16] Moreover, the CIE model was based on the assumption of comprehensive liberalisation across all sectors, including agriculture. By this time it was apparent in the final FTA negotiating stage that this was not likely. In an article written for *The Australian* newspaper in February 2004, former trade policy adviser and critic of the current Australian Government's bilateral FTA policy, Professor Ross Garnaut, contended that, "the part of the 'less than A\$3 billion' that comes from America's own liberalisation derives overwhelmingly from two products only: dairy and sugar."[17]

Only two months later in April 2004, the CIE published another study report on AUSFTA's impact, this time asserting that the anticipated gains for the Australian economy were even greater than its first study was suggesting (Centre for International Economics 2004a). The new study, once more commissioned by DFAT, now estimated that there would be annual boosts to Australia's GNP of A$6.1 billion by 2014 as a consequence of AUSFTA. The higher estimates were primarily derived from new assumptions concerning investment liberalisation and dynamic productivity gains stemming from 'broad band' FTA elements in the agreement. In a further twist to the tale, a study undertaken by Philippa Dee, a highly respected trade economist, on behalf of the Australian Senate Select Committee on AUSFTA and published in June 2004 came up with very different estimates (Dee 2004). This report predicted that AUSFTA would add a mere A$53 million annually to Australia's economy, and moreover it questioned the assumptions of the recently published CIE study. For example, it contended that double counting had occurred when assessing particular gains from the FTA and prior commitments on liberalisation made by both countries through the WTO. More importantly, according to the Dee report, the compliance costs incurred from adhering to AUSFTA's stricter rules on intellectual property rights (IPR), whereby net royalty payments were expected to increase by around 25 percent a year as a result, which would eventually convert into an annual A$700 million a year in additional costs to Australian firms. In final conclusion, the Dee report stated that the net A$53 million annual increase in Australia's GNP was, "a tiny harvest from a major political and bureaucratic endeavour" (p. 35). In the first ten months of AUSFTA entering into force, Australia's trade position with the US deteriorated quite significantly. Trade figures for October 2004 to October 2005 showed that Australia's exports to the US had fallen by 4.7 percent while US imports had risen by 5.7 percent.[18] It was obviously too early at this time to make a long-term assessment regarding AUSFTA's trade impact but these figures did mean the Australian Government had to defend the deal, with Mark Vaile citing the increase in bilateral investment activity from AUSFTA.

Drawing one's own conclusions about which of the studies on AUSFTA's impact is most valid largely rests how realistic are the underlying assumptions used in the economic modelling. To some extent, vested interests also must be taken into account. The fact that DFAT was charged with realising the successful conclusion of AUSFTA negotiations, and more importantly had earlier tried to conceal the somewhat downbeat findings of ACIL's study on AUSFTA, meant that its commissioning of further impact studies – as was the case with the second CIE report – was likely to elicit public suspicion. Not only was the Dee report requested by a cross-party parliamentary committee, and thus less susceptible to captured political interests, but the organisation itself was renowned for its technical expertise in studying the impact of 'broad band' FTAs.

3.3   ASEAN–China Free Trade Agreement (ACFTA)

3.3.1   Origins and initial development

The ASEAN–China FTA (ACFTA) project has had one of most profound impacts on the whole Asia-Pacific FTA trend. There are various reasons for this. Perhaps the most important was that it marked China's initial foray into FTAs, and therein the country's intent to take some form of lead in the regional integration process (De Santis 2005). The ACFTA project is widely acknowledged to have spurred Japan into seeking a similar FTA 'coalition' with the ASEAN group, motivated partly by any regional hegemonic aspirations behind this initiative of China's (Tongzon 2005; Wong and Chan 2003). Other trading partners of Southeast Asia also in time sought a similar FTA link with ASEAN, including South Korea, Taiwan, Australia, New Zealand, the EU and the US. Another reason behind ACFTA's significance concerns its creation of the world's most populous free trade zone, incorporating around 1.7 billion people and representing a collective GDP of almost US$2 trillion. It also makes a substantial *de facto* contribution to the East Asian regional integration process by incorporating the majority of the region's countries into a singular FTA arrangement. Whether or not ACFTA will provide the foundation of a wider unified East Asia FTA depends on both the implemented substance of the agreement and its 'competition' with other FTA models to emerge in the region, e.g. ASEAN–Japan, Japan–South Korea. For China, the launching of ACFTA negotiations was the country's most important trade diplomacy initiative after gaining accession to the WTO, and marked China's more proactive engagement in the international trading system generally.

The penetration of the Chinese Diaspora in Southeast Asia may also have figured in Beijing's prioritisation of ASEAN as an early FTA partner. Southeast Asia's ethnic Chinese communities had made significant contributions to the region's economic development and their business network linkages with China based companies were extensive (Crawford 2000). The origins of ACFTA also lay in progressively developing relations generally between ASEAN and China (Cheng 2001; Holst and Weiss 2004; Tongzon 2005). Both sides were meeting in various regional and multilateral fora by the end of the 1990s. The ASEAN Regional Forum was helping promote closer security ties while the ASEAN Plus Three (APT) framework was fostering closer economic and financial co-operation between Southeast Asia and China. From 1995 to 2004, average trade growth between China and ASEAN exceeded 15 percent annually. By 2005, ASEAN was China's fifth largest trade partner, and China was the sixth largest trade partner of ASEAN.

On the sidelines of the 2000 APT summit, then Thai Trade Minister Supachai Panitchpakdi (who later became WTO Secretary-General) proposed the creation of a regional mechanism through which China and

ASEAN could negotiate mutual tariff concessions to assist less developed countries in Southeast Asia.[19] The first formal proposal for ACFTA came in November 2000 (see Appendix A). In October 2001, the ASEAN–China Experts Group published its ACFTA study report, entitled 'Forging Closer ASEAN Economic Relations in the 21st Century', in advance of the November 2001 APT summit. At the event, China and ASEAN agreed on the broad negotiating framework for ACFTA, and announced their intention to implement the agreement by 2010. An ASEAN–China Trade Negotiating Committee was established in May 2002, which held its first round of ACFTA negotiations at this time. A deadline of 30 June 2004 was set to finalise negotiations on the manufactured goods trade component of ACFTA. The talks proceeded very quickly and at the November 2002 APT summit held in Phnom Penh the 'Framework Agreement on Comprehensive Economic Cooperation between ASEAN and China' (in which the FTA arrangement was embedded) was signed. The Agreement laid out the basic objectives and timeframes of establishing ACFTA between China and ASEAN member states. The ACFTA was negotiated in a rather unique way by starting with an agreed commitment in the November 2002 Framework Agreement to establish an free trade zone between China and ASEAN by 2010, and thereafter actually negotiating how this was to be done over the following two or three years. As we see below, it began with a partial implementation arrangement on selected farm products under the so called Early Harvest Programme (EHP). In most FTAs, signatory partners would first conclude a complete deal and then start implementing it after it enters into force. However, the approach adopted by ASEAN and China was at least consistent with a key point stressed in this book, that of FTA heterogeneity.

3.3.2   The content and negotiation of ACFTA

The Early Harvest Programme was the initial focus of the ACFTA project after the November 2002 Framework Agreement had been signed. It entailed a series of tariff cuts to be implemented within three years on selected agricultural and forestry products. Thailand took the initiative of concluding an EHP agreement with China bilaterally in June 2003 – a few months ahead of other ASEAN member states, most of which signed the special EHP protocol agreement at the November 2003 APT summit. The Thai–China EHP agreement came into effect in October that year, and the EHP protocol agreement on 1 January 2004. Thailand's proactive approach was indicative of its 'pathfinding' bilateral economic diplomacy, in which bilateral initiatives such as this were intended to catalyse Southeast Asian economic integration, on both an intra-regional and extra-regional basis (Dent 2006a). Singapore was a fellow partner to Thailand in this respect, and indeed had made frequent signals to Beijing of its desire to negotiate a full FTA with China on an accelerated, bilateral basis, and hence in advance of other ASEAN member states.[20]

Under the EHP, certain tariff lines across Chapters 1 to 8 of the Harmonised System of Tariffs code were to be gradually eliminated, thus covering live animal, meat, fish, dairy, forestry, vegetable, fruit and nut products. This comprised around 600 agricultural goods in total across both sides, and their tariff-rates were to be reduced down to a maximum of ten percent by 1 January 2004, then to five percent by 1 January 2005, and finally to zero percent by 1 January 2006. Newer ASEAN members – Cambodia, Laos, Myanmar and Vietnam, or the CLMV group – were permitted exclusions from the EHP product list as well as extended periods of implementation depending on current tariff levels and the country. Vietnam was obliged to completely eliminate tariffs on all EHP products by 1 January 2008, while Laos and Myanmar had until the beginning of 2009 and Cambodia until the beginning of 2010. This was in keeping with the 'adjustment' flexibility granted them by other ACFTA partners. More generally, the CLMV group was allowed to implement ACFTA arrangements (e.g. on full industrial tariff liberalisation) by 2015, five years longer than the more developed ASEAN-6 group, i.e. Brunei, Indonesia, Malaysia, the Philippines, Singapore and Thailand.

Only one ASEAN-6 member state – the Philippines – was not able to finalise its position regarding the EHP agreement in time for its entry into force in January 2004. The November 2003 protocol stated that the Philippines had to declare whether or not it sought product exclusions from EHP imports from China. The Philippines had wanted processed foods included in the EHP, where it held a competitive advantage, but China had opposed this. Manila argued that such a concession would have allowed it to offset the expected worsening of its trade balance on unprocessed foods as a consequence of ACFTA. All ASEAN member states were supposed to have submitted their exclusion list requests by March 2003, but it took until September 2004 for Manila and Beijing to finally reach a deal on the EHP, whereby the Philippines agreed to liberalise over 200 out of the 417 EHP tariff lines under Chapters 1 to 8 the ASEAN group had agreed to open up. Most of the other core ASEAN states had agreed to about 90 percent of that total.[21]

Overall, though, China was offering the greater concessions under the EHP – which Beijing had originally proposed – as it was willing to liberalise ahead of its ASEAN partners, open up more tariff lines (around 560) and moreover its average tariff rates on agricultural imports were generally higher than ASEAN countries. While China negotiated for rice and palm oil be excluded from ACFTA all together, it agreed to extend concessions on 130 specific manufactured products across various sectors to those ASEAN member states that felt they had not benefited sufficiently from the EHP. This particularly applied to Singapore and Brunei, both of which had very small agriculture sectors. Malaysia, Thailand and Indonesia also agreed to concede manufacture EHP concessions to the two micro-states.

Negotiations on eliminating tariffs on industrial products overshot their June 2004 deadline but an agreement was signed later that year in November at the 10th ASEAN Summit held in Vientiane, Laos. Under the ACFTA Trade in Goods Agreement, which entered into force in July 2005, the ASEAN-6 members and China would remove tariffs on 90 percent of their industrial product lines by 2010, whereas the CLMV group had until 2015 to achieve this. The remaining ten percent were placed in the 'sensitive' category and were to be liberalised even more gradually. Negotiations on ACFTA's services and investment chapters were still ongoing in 2006. Both sides agreed to use the ASEAN Investment Agreement as the template for investment chapter negotiations. Negotiations on ACFTA's rules of origin were completed by December 2003, these being based on the AFTA model, i.e. 40 percent regional cumulative value (see Appendix E).

Under ACFTA, China and ASEAN agreed also to extend their economic co-operation in various areas. Both sides signed a memorandum of understanding on agricultural co-operation in November 2002 that covers forestry, livestock production, fisheries, biotechnology, post harvest technology and standard conformity of farm products. A similar side agreement was signed on information and communication technology (ICT) in June 2003 covering: information infrastructure development; ICT application development, compatibility, integrity and security of ICT systems; e-ASEAN project implementation; and the establishment of an ASEAN–China Seminar framework. Other areas of co-operation targeted by the ACFTA Framework Agreement include human resource development (HRD), transport, investment facilitation, science and technology collaboration, mass media, environment and SMEs. In addition to these generic areas of co-operation a number of specific collaborative projects have been proposed, most notably the Mekong River Basin development and the Singapore-Kunming Railway Project.[22] This could be viewed as part of a wider co-operation diplomacy that had been fast developing between China and ASEAN as earlier indicated (Yang 2004). As Chapter 4 discusses, the inclusion of these elements within ACFTA was in line with an emerging East Asian model on FTA formation that combined trade liberalisation with complementary economic co-operation measures.

3.3.3 Impacts from ACFTA

Economic modelling conducted by the ASEAN Secretariat estimated that ACFTA should increase ASEAN's exports to China by 48 percent and China's exports to ASEAN by 55 percent, leading to a subsequent 0.9 percent increase in ASEAN's GDP and 0.3 percent increase in China's GDP (Yang 2004). Expectations surrounding the implementation of the EHP may have played some part in boosting bilateral trade generally between ASEAN and China, reaching US$78.3 billion in 2003, an increase of 42.8 percent from 2002. More specifically, China's imports from

ASEAN increased by 51.7 percent to US$47.3 billion while China's exports to ASEAN rose by 31.1 percent to US$30.9 billion dollars, hence leaving China with a US$16.4 billion trade deficit with Southeast Asia in 2003. However, at the micro-level, Thai farmers and government officials were complaining about the flood of cheap Chinese agri-product imports into the country after the Thai–China EHP agreement entered into force in October 2003. The political fall-out from this development led to the stalling of Thai–China talks on the industrial goods agreement of ACFTA for a few months in early 2004.[23] Thai authorities were also complaining that its farm product exporters were experiencing difficulties with China's customs procedures, claiming that Chinese officials were demanding second inspections of Thai products for chemicals and diseases, even though these had been certified by Thai authorities before being despatched for export. In addition, Thailand was getting frustrated by the length of time taken by China's customs procedures over granting import licences and other registration documentation required by Thai agri-exporters. These problems and difficulties faced by Thailand seemed to be reflected in the trade statistics: in the first year of the agreement, Thailand's agricultural imports from China rose by 400 percent, while Thai agri-exports to China rose by 80 percent.[24] Although the situation was later to turn more in Thailand's favour a year or so later, this presented a good illustration of how crucial impediments to free trade may still persist after an FTA enters into force. In most FTAs, these kinds of problems can be addressed if effective review mechanisms have been incorporated into the agreement.

The ASEAN group had enjoyed a significant trade surplus with China for some time leading up to the ACFTA project. Many elements of Southeast Asia's business community were, however, concerned that ACFTA trade liberalisation would intensify industrial competition from China and eventually tilt the trade balance more in China's favour (Wong and Chan 2003; Tongzon 2005). Over recent years there had been significant growth in intra-industry trade between both sides with the expansion of increasingly higher-tech and differentiated industrial product trade. This contrasted with the past where commodity and raw material trade made up a more significant proportion of bilateral flows (Wong and Chan 2003). ASEAN and China particularly competed in wide range of labour-intensive manufacturing activities such as textiles, lower-tech electronic and electrical goods, plastics and basic engineering products (Holst and Weiss 2004). This increase in competitive contact between ASEAN and China offered broad scope for trade creation (see Chapter 1). At the same time, China was fast improving its techno-industrial capacities whilst remaining cost competitive owing to its seemingly inexhaustible supply of both low-cost skilled and unskilled labour, and consequently out-competing Southeast Asian rival producers in various sectors.

There was further concern in Southeast Asia that ACFTA trade liberalisation could induce further investment diversion from ASEAN to China. China had already overtaken Southeast Asia as a favoured location for inward foreign direct investment (FDI) some years beforehand. Wong and Chan (2003) neatly summarise ASEAN's fundamental predicament on this issue: "Compared to ASEAN, which generally lacks an adequate base of supporting industries, China has a huge integrated industrial base and is strongly capable of providing auxiliary items like processing equipment, intermediate parts, and electronic components needed for manufacturing. Given its moderately well-developed basic technology industries such as machinery, China has the potential to develop an extensive network, or clusters, of supporting industries. Foreign companies could find it conducive to locate in China and benefit from agglomeration economies generated from being close to those supporting industries (p. 510)." On the other hand, ACFTA trade liberalisation means that many Southeast Asia based producers may decide to remain located within ASEAN rather than move operations to China because of new tariff free advantages of exporting to the Chinese market from the region. The net balance of trade–investment effects from ACFTA will only be known after a few years of the agreement being in force as these are the kind of dynamic, longer-term effects borne from FTAs. Chapter 4 discusses the broader international political economy impact of ACFTA with particular regard to East Asia's regional integration.

3.4 China's Closer Economic Partnership Agreements (CEPAs) with Hong Kong and Macao (HKCCEPA, MCCEPA)

3.4.1 Origins and initial development

Historic key events provide the background to China's FTA or Closer Economic Partnership Agreement (CEPA) projects with Hong Kong and Macao. Although both ex-colonies retained their own economic, legal and political systems under Special Administrative Region (SAR) status, their reversion of sovereignty to China in 1997 and 1999 respectively intensified debate about the coalescence of a Greater China economy. Economic integration between Hong Kong and China was particularly well developed by this time with many Hong Kong based firms gradually extending and relocating their commercial operation into the mainland. Macao was also involved in a similar but less extensive integrative process with China. Free trade agreements would help reduce the transaction costs of cross-border business activities within the Greater China economy, as well as further cement the mainland's political integration with Hong Kong and Macao.

China's accession to the WTO in November 2001 was also a crucial factor. Now that China was obliged to adhere to the same international trade rules as other WTO members, its trade partners could sign up FTAs with her with due confidence, including Hong Kong and Macao who remained separate WTO member states after the transition of sovereignty. When China announced the launch of FTA negotiations with ASEAN in the same month, Beijing made it clear that Hong Kong and Macao would not be included in the ACFTA deal.[25] A few days after this announcement, Hong Kong SAR Chief Executive, Tung Chee Hwa, approached Beijing with a proposal of creating a free trade zone between Hong Kong, China and Macao. The moribund state of the Hong Kong economy was no doubt another instrumental factor behind the proposal. Unemployment had risen to around eight percent and the Hong Kong Government were looking for new policy initiatives to boost economic growth.

The Hong Kong–China CEPA (HKCCEPA) was formally launched in December 2001 after a meeting between Chinese President Jiang Zemin, Chinese Premier Zhu Rongji and Tung Chee Hwa. A first round of FTA negotiations was convened soon afterwards in January 2002. Just before the second round of FTA talks held in late March, Beijing had raised the idea of establishing a CEPA first between Hong Kong and the border-zone city of Shenzhen, and then possibly extend the arrangement to Guangdong province and Macao.[26] Essentially, then, Beijing was making a case for a full CEPA involving the whole of China should be preceded by some kind of zonal experimentation in the Pearl Delta area. Yu Xiaosong, Chairman of the China Council for the Promotion of International Trade, neatly summed up the position of the Chinese Government at this juncture: "There will be no problem with mainland's exports to Hong Kong as the SAR has been a free-trade territory. But it will be difficult for the mainland to give tax-free treatment to all imports from Hong Kong because the territory, as an entrepot centre, has few locally-manufactured products." He further commented that, "We have to be careful and cautious so that we do not give others an excuse to accuse us of violating the principle of equal treatment enshrined in the WTO rules."[27] However, the zonal experimentation proposal never came to fruition.

3.4.2 Key areas of negotiation

Aside from discussions over the geographic scope of the proposed Agreement, the initial key problems in the HKCCEPA talks concerned matters of the standard of market entry, the definition of a Hong Kong company and, closely related to this, the rules of origin issue.[28] These last two items in particular stalled the second round of negotiations in March 2002. With Hong Kong registered firms operating so integratively with mainland China it was often difficult to determine what constituted Hong Kongese business activity and what did not. Interestingly, Hong Kong's FTA negotiations with New Zealand were at the same time running into the ground over the same issue, as the Hong Kong Government could not give sufficient assurances to New Zealand that imports from the entrepot economy would not originate from China, at least to a certain local value content threshold. During this stage of the talks, China reportedly proposed a 25 percent value content criterion. This was a low ratio by comparison to Asia-Pacific and general international FTA norms (see Appendix E), yet Hong Kong's business associations argued that 25 percent was too high, and were hoping for looser rules of origin in order to attract more foreign manufacturers to establish assembly factories into their economy.[29] Conversely, Beijing was concerned about how Hong Kong could be used as an entrepot conduit by third countries to procure free market access to mainland China, and hence wanted assurances that Hong Kong's general rules of origin regime was sufficiently robust. There were also some in the Hong Kong government who wanted a slightly higher RoO ratio to give firms greater incentive to source locally for inputs fed into export production for the China market.

By the third round of HKCCEPA negotiations, held in June 2002, the main issues for discussion apart from rules of origin were market access in certain service sectors, the proposal for a common currency, and whether Macao should be included in the CEPA arrangement. Little progress was achieved, however, in these areas and no further negotiations were convened for the remainder of the year. When both sides reinitiated CEPA talks in January 2003, Hong Kong and China announced their intention to conclude an agreement by June that year.[30] A fourth round soon followed in February 2003. This new momentum was, however, stalled somewhat by the deepening SARS health crisis. The next talks did not take place until June 2003, the deadline month set earlier in the year.

Given that Hong Kong's entrepot economy was already very open to foreign commerce there was greater onus on China to make concessions. Services now made up around 86 percent of the economy, and hence it was in this industry sector that Hong Kong sought improved access to the Chinese market. Although China offered quite broad access to its shipping, logistics and film industries for companies incorporated in Hong Kong, access remained limited in finance sector activities, especially insurance, securities trading and banking. One of Beijing's long held concerns in the CEPA talks was that opening up its service sector to Hong Kong would allow foreign banks based there to infiltrate mainland China's financial markets. Although China was obliged to open up these markets, and also the telecommunications sector, after 2006 in accordance to its WTO accession commitments, limitations would be retained on foreign firm operations in the country.

The hard fought HKCCEPA negotiations on service sector market access in the June 2003 round of talks was closely bound to the issue of business incorporation. Hong Kong's commercial laws treated all incorporated business the same, regardless of whether it was locally owned or a subsidiary of a larger company with headquarters and owners abroad. The critical issue of negotiation was whether the local subsidiaries of multinational enterprises (MNE) would be allowed greater access to the Chinese market under HKCCEPA rules. China, on the other hand, had extensive regulations that distinguished between domestic-owned business operations and those deemed to be at least partly foreign-owned. During the negotiations, foreign governments (including the US) and foreign business associations made a plea to Hong Kong and China to avoid an agreement that would end Hong Kong's tradition of treating all businesses equally.[31] Yet Beijing was wary of allowing too many Hong Kong-based foreign companies to qualify for CEPA benefits. This especially applied to Hong Kong's powerful finance sector, which was dominated by foreign firms. A compromise position that arose in the June 2003 talks was that Hong Kong based firms that were already well established in the mainland would qualify for CEPA treatment.

3.4.3   The final agreement

As the end of June approached, Hong Kong and Chinese government negotiators intensified their efforts to resolve all outstanding issues. The CEPA talks came to a rushed conclusion on 29 June 2003, with a deal signed but which lacked details in a number of key areas. Both sides reportedly wanted at least a framework agreement signed in advance of a mass civil protest planned in Hong Kong on 1 July, this being the sixth anniversary of the territory's reversion to Chinese sovereignty. Even though further HKCCEPA details were released a few months later in October, several matters relating to the agreement's implementation remained unclear according to media sources, for example on how firms were supposed to apply for CEPA privileges.[32]

In the final deal signed in June 2003, China agreed to immediately lift tariffs on 273 products from Hong Kong on the CEPA's entry into force, which was 1 January 2004, and to lift all remaining tariffs from two years later in 2006 (see Appendix B). Under China's WTO accession agreement, it had promised to reduce the overall average tariff rate on imports to nine percent by 2007, thus Hong Kong's benefits secured under the CEPA relative to China's other trade partners extended beyond this date. Hong Kong firms also secured immediate open access in 18 service industries including accounting, advertising, construction, film production, health care, insurance, legal counselling, logistics, real estate, telecoms, tourism and transportation. On the matter of business incorporation, the CEPA carried provisions designed to prevent MNEs not already active in the mainland from opening shell companies as a means to circumvent China's aforementioned regulations on domestic and foreign owned business. The required minimum assets for Hong Kong banks that establish branches in China was lowered from US$20 billion to US$6 billion. Most of the concessions on service industries required Hong Kong based companies to have been operating in China for at least three to five years, depending on the industry. Regarding rules of origin, a 30 percent value content minimum was finally agreed upon, based on the product's export value (see Appendix E). While it was agreed to omit the creation of a common currency as part of the HKCCEPA, both sides agreed to hold further discussions in the future.

3.4.4   Expected and actual impacts

Although Hong Kong's economic activity seemed to pick up almost immediately the Agreement was signed, the main effects of the HKCCEPA were believed to be much longer-term. Yet there was much dispute over whether the net balance of effects would be positive or negative. While Hong Kong's Commerce and Industry Secretary, Henry Tang, was generally optimistic about the CEPA's general macroeconomic impact upon the Hong Kong economy, he was also aware of concerns over how the Agreement's benefits would be distributed amongst Hong Kong society.[33] More than a quarter of the territory's four million workforce had only a basic secondary level education, and it was recognised that these could lack the skills and income to adjust to CEPA-induced structural shifts in the Hong Kong economy. As Tang remarked on the issue, "It would be very difficult to retrain them to be fit for work in the knowledge-based economy."[34] The CEPA was also expected to further accelerate the flow of Hong Kong investments to the mainland, and further skew investment to the service sector instead of manufacturing (Antkiewicz and Whalley 2005). This could potentially exacerbate the territory's structural unemployment problem and low productivity rate. Moreover, there was a belief amongst Hong Kong economists that the CEPA's zero tariffs would not attract much additional foreign manufacturing investment, which was believed by many to be key to restoring Hong Kong's economic fortunes.[35] Soon after the signing of the HKCCEPA, several MNEs based in Hong Kong had reportedly relocated their regional headquarters and research centres to mainland China.[36]

However, studies made nine months after HKCCEPA entering into force revealed disappointing results. According to Hong Kong's Trade and Industry Department, the total value of Hong Kong-made goods exported tariff-free to China during January–August 2004 was about HK$660 million, a very small share of its total domestic exports to the mainland, which exceeded HK$20 billion over the same period. Tariff savings deriving from HKCCEPA were calculated at HK$30 million over this time, well short of the anticipated HK$750 million a year savings previously estimated in the FTA's scoping studies. Numbers on expected applications from Hong Kong firms to service sector access to China were also well down. Furthermore, many Hong Kong based firms continued to complain that the finally agreed 30 percent rules of origin ratio was too restrictive as nearly all their imports of raw materials or components were sourced over the border in

China. Those complaining most vehemently were Hong Kong watchmakers, who are lobbying for their products to qualify for zero tariff as long as assembly took place in Hong Kong, which effectively amounted to an exemption from HKCCEPA's rules of origin regime altogether.[37]

3.4.5 Macao–China CEPA (MCCEPA)

As previously noted, Hong Kong had originally proposed a trilateral CEPA agreement between itself, China and Macao. However, Beijing preferred to initially proceed on a bilateral basis with Hong Kong. As HKCCEPA talks neared a conclusion, though, a first round of negotiations on a Macao–China CEPA (MCCEPA) took place on 20th June 2003. By this time, a basic template from the HKCCEPA model had been established and could be simply transposed into a Macao–China agreement. Indeed, there is much symmetry between the two CEPAs in terms of principles and content. The same 273 product tariffs were to be immediately eliminated when the MCCEPA came into force on 1 January 2004, with complete tariff elimination by the beginning of 2006, and China agreed to open up 18 service sectors to Macao-based businesses, just as it had for their Hong Kong counterparts. Similar arrangements on rules of origin, customs procedures and 'FTA-plus' aspects (e.g. investment promotion, e-commerce, industrial co-operation, tourism) were factored into the Agreement. The Macao–China CEPA project also set a record for the quickest conclusion of FTA negotiations in the Asia-Pacific (and possibly in the world), taking just five months for a final deal to be signed, which occurred in October 2003. With both CEPAs in place, it was hoped that the agreements would expedite the greater economic integration of the Pearl River Delta region.

3.5 Thailand–Australia Free Trade Agreement (TAFTA)

3.5.1 Origins and initial development

Certain geo-strategic factors were relevant in the initiation of the Thailand–Australia Free Trade Agreement (TAFTA) project. Both countries were members of the Cairns Group, the coalition of major agricultural producer nations. Australia had lent strong support for Supachai Panichpakdi, Thailand's candidate for the position of WTO Director-General, who took office in 2002. Australia had also been looking to establish an FTA link with the whole ASEAN group during 1999 and 2000. However, Malaysia's Asia-Centric Prime Minister, Mahathir Mohamad, vetoed the proposal for an ASEAN–CER free trade agreement in October 2000 (see Chapter 2). The following month at the 2000 APEC summit, Singapore and Australia had announced their intention to initiate bilateral FTA negotiations. Thailand and Australia too sought to circumvent the Malaysian veto through bilateral means. In April 2001, Australia signalled its interest in negotiating a bilateral FTA with Thailand, and in July that year both sides agreed to initiate a joint scoping study. The study report, published in May 2002, estimated that TAFTA would boost Thailand's GDP by US$25.2 billion and Australia's by US$6.6 billion over 20 years. The first round of TAFTA negotiations took place in August 2002, and a second round the following October, with both sides soon afterwards announcing their intention to sign a concluded FTA by June 2004. By the third round of talks, held in January 2003, the broad parameters of TAFTA had been established. An 'Early Harvest' action plan was also agreed on at this point, whereby certain areas of negotiation were prioritised for accelerated development on cross-sectoral issues, including investment protection and promotion, mutual recognition arrangements, and competition policy.

3.5.2   Key areas of negotiation

A fourth round of TAFTA negotiations took place in April 2003 and a fifth round in June 2003, when both sides stated that they would try to conclude talks by the time of the October 2003 APEC summit, hosted by Thailand in Bangkok. The fifth round of TAFTA negotiations coincided with that year's APEC Trade Ministers meeting, also held in Bangkok. It was here that Australia's Trade Minister, Mark Vaile, announced that in the conclusion of a TAFTA deal, Australia expected Thailand to grant the same, if not better, treatment in commercial relations as enjoyed by the US under the terms of the Thailand–US Treaty of Amity.[38] The Treaty, signed in 1966, afforded American nationals and companies incorporated in the US or Thailand that are majority-owned and controlled by US citizens the ability to conduct business in Thailand on par with the rights of Thai nationals (see Chapter 2). This conferred significant advantages to US investors over foreign competitors. For example, US nationals were largely exempt from the business licensing requirements of Thailand's Foreign Business Act, which imposes a wide range of restrictions on foreign investment activities, and licences could be extremely difficult to obtain.[39] In return, Thai nationals enjoyed certain special visa privileges with the US. The Treaty was subject to re-negotiation every ten years, and Thailand faced pressure from other countries to terminate the Treaty, or at least extend the concessions therein to all Thailand's trade partners. This was based largely on the argument of establishing consistency with Thailand's commitment to WTO accords, especially the GATS that upheld the principle of universal national treatment and non-discrimination on services trade, and the exceptions under GATS – negotiated in the 1994 Uruguay Round agreement – were supposed to be phased out by January 2005.

Thailand at least accepted the principle of Australia's arguments on the Treaty of Amity as both sides went into the sixth round of TAFTA negotiations, convened in August 2003. Other key unresolved issues of negotiation, with the October 2003 deadline for concluding talks looming, were import tariff liberalisation in certain agricultural and industrial sectors, rules of origin, quarantine regulations, IPR, professional services and investment. Negotiating the finer points of differentiated tariff elimination schedules had proved very time-consuming, and Appendix B's section on TAFTA shows how it has amongst the most extensively differentiated schedules on tariff liberalisation of any Asia-Pacific FTA. Because this was also an agreement between a developed country and a developing one there were hard negotiations on many of TAFTA's 'broad band' elements noted above, e.g. investment, IPR. Thailand was concerned that it lacked sufficient institutional and industrial capacity to cope with many of the demands Australia was making in these areas[40] (the developing countries and 'deficient capacity' issue is discussed more generally in Chapter 4). Furthermore, Thailand expressed significant concern over Australia's stringent quarantine regime, with Thai Commerce Minister, Adisai Bodharamik, commenting that, "We want to make sure that when it is done the FTA must be a real one, that it can be implemented. If it cannot be implemented because of quarantine regulations getting in the way, then we have to start from the beginning."[41] Because of these and other difficulties, such as over rules of origin, he believed that only a "framework" of a deal on TAFTA could be agreed by deadline.[42] In the event, special talks were scheduled on unresolved issues after Adisai Bodharamik and Mark Vaile officially signed the basic framework of a TAFTA deal at the October 2003 APEC summit.

On trade liberalisation, Australia agreed to immediately eliminate 83.2 percent of its tariffs on entry into force of the Agreement (January 2005), while Thailand agreed to eliminate 49.4 percent of its tariffs, this covering 77.9 percent of its imports by value from Australia. For Australia, a further 12.9 percent of tariffs were to be phased down to zero by 1 January 2010, and another 3.9 percent of tariff lines to zero rates by 2015. Meanwhile, Thailand agreed to phase another 43.7 percent of its tariffs down to zero by 2010, and a further 6.9 percent to zero rates in the period 2015–2020. Thailand was also conceded a special exception for certain dairy products (skimmed milk powder, liquid milk and cream), the import tariffs on which would not be fully eliminated until 2025. This was quite a concession made by Australia given the importance of its dairy industry and the commensurate political clout of its dairy producers lobby. Thailand's insistence of special treatment for its dairy industry was due partly to its long-standing sponsorship of the Thai royal family. As a special Royal project, it continued to enjoy significant financial support and trade protection. Although the industry was comparatively inefficient, with an average herd size of around ten cattle, it had nevertheless become relatively large, employing over 200,000 people and accounting for roughly 60 percent of Thailand's total dairy product consumption. While it appears that Australia made more concessions on tariff liberalisation in terms of sectoral coverage, it should be remembered that Thailand was making the much bigger adjustment owing to its relatively much higher existing tariff rates. Australia's average MFN tariff rate was 3.9 percent in 2004 while Thailand's was 15.0 percent (Centre for International Economics 2004b).

Other sectors deserving particular mention include Australia's securing of a ten-year phase-in for tariff elimination on textile, clothing and footwear (TCF) imports from Thailand, although it agreed to immediately halve its then existing rate of 25 percent down to 12.5 percent. In addition to dairy, Thailand was permitted phase-ins of between ten to 15 years to liberalise trade barriers on other sensitive farm products such as oranges, sugar, asparagus, beef, pork and lamb. Regarding service sector issues, and linking back to the US–Thai Treaty of Amity issue, Thailand agreed under TAFTA to allow Australian companies to own 60 percent of companies in many service sectors (up from the previous limit of 49.9 percent), although with exclusions applied to telecommunications, financial services, engineering and accounting. In return, Australia would allow Thai nationals to invest in legal advisory services, architecture, auto-repair shops, telecommunications, education, mining and all types of manufacturing. However, Australia was not willing to give much ground on quarantine related issues. Special negotiations on the matter continued after TAFTA's 'framework' deal was signed at the October 2003 APEC summit. Talks here centred on the delays Thai food exporters were experiencing with Australian customs authorities owing to an apparent relative lack of quarantine inspectors. In the final side agreement reached in April 2004, Australia agreed to find the extra resources to accelerate the quarantine inspection of its Thai imports. Other residual issues left over from October 2003, such as on anti-dumping duties and TAFTA's dispute settlement mechanism, were also resolved by this time. The Agreement was officially signed by Thai Prime Minister Thaksin and Australian Prime Minister Howard in May 2004 and entered into force in January 2005.

The final text of TAFTA comprised 19 chapters and ran to more than 120 pages. From Australia's perspective, the Agreement offered wider market access to a number of important sectors where Thailand's tariff levels had been comparatively high, such as lamb (32 percent), fruit and vegetables (up to 42 percent), processed foods and fisheries (both around 30 percent), automobiles (up to 80 percent) and steel (10 percent). According to Australia's Senior Trade Commissioner to Bangkok, Cameron Macmillan, Australian service sectors that would particularly benefit from TAFTA included legal services, architecture and engineering services.[43] For Thailand, its automobile sector especially anticipated to benefit from TAFTA, with an expected 30 percent rise in export sales to Australia. Thailand's tropical fruit and vegetable producers were also expecting to see their share of the Australian market increase significantly as a consequence of TAFTA.[44] Overall, Thailand was expected to gain more from TAFTA than

Australia in terms of boosted export sales (Centre for International Economics 2004b). However, during January to November 2005, Thailand's exports to Australia rose by 31 percent (totalling US$2.9 billion) compared to the same period of 2004, yet Australia's exports to Thailand grew faster at 59 percent (totalling US$3.0 billion). The main reasons given for these figures were a sharp rise in Thailand's gold and oil imports from Australia,[45] and the extent to which this may be attributable to TAFTA is not clear. A study report published by Australia's Centre for International Economics also estimated that Thailand's GDP would rise by 0.16 percent as a result of TAFTA in 2005 and would be 0.45 percent higher from 2020 onwards. Meanwhile, Australia's GDP would rise by 0.01 percent in 2005 from TAFTA related effects and by around 0.03 percent in 2010 (Centre for International Economics 2004b).

3.5.3   Subsequent developments

The politically sensitive issue of Thailand's dairy farming surfaced again a couple of months after TAFTA's signing. In July 2004, the Thai Holstein-Friesian Association, representing Thai dairy farmers, called again for milk products to be exempted from the agreement and had petitioned Thailand's King to open talks with the government on the matter. The previous year, the Association had presented a petition to the government, making the same demand. However, just as then, the government did not capitulate, stating in its defence that the gradual removal of the existent five percent tariff on Australian milk imports would not lead to injurious competition faced by Thai dairy producers.[46] One month into TAFTA being in force, the Thai media also made the observation that many Australian automobile retailers had not passed on TAFTA's five percent tariff cut on imported Thai vehicles in their prices.[47] For example, only five out of nine light trucks and SUV models eligible for TAFTA treatment had their prices reduced as a result. While some importers had opted to add extra specification to their models, many simply used TAFTA tariff savings to boost profit margins. Although price-setting decisions take into account a range of criteria, such as market demand cycles, this matter does raise the issue of how the benefits of FTAs are distributed between relevant stakeholders. For instance, multinational enterprises *per se* are prominent FTA advocates for good reason, as they are generally best positioned to extract substantial benefits from the agreements.

3.6   Japan–Mexico Free Trade Agreement (JMFTA)

3.6.1   Origins and initial development

The Japan–Mexico FTA (JMFTA) project was one of the earliest of the new wave of Asia-Pacific FTA projects to be launched, being first proposed at the September 1999 APEC summit. Just prior to this, a Japan–Mexico Closer

Economic Relations Committee had held in first meeting in February 1999, and Japan's largest business association, the *Keidanren*, published its 'Report on the Possible Effects of a Japan–Mexico Free Trade Agreement on Japanese Industry' in April 1999 (Keidanren 1999). According to an interviewed official in Japan Ministry of Economy, Trade and Industry (METI), Japan's motives behind this project lay primarily in redressing the commercial disadvantages facing Japanese firms in Mexico.[48] In November 2000, the Mexican Government terminated its *maquiladora* system, whereby companies manufacturing in Mexico and exporting finished goods were conferred preferential tax treatments on parts used in the manufacturing process. Many Japanese auto companies had based their production in Mexico to produce for the North American market. After Mexico had signed an FTA with the European Union (EU), these companies were further disadvantaged in relation to their European and American rivals.[49] Mexico maintained very high tariffs (around 50 percent in 2004) on automobile imports. Studies from METI suggested that Japanese auto producers and other manufacturers were losing around 400 billion yen (US$4 billion) annually from Japan's lack of an FTA with Mexico.[50] Although Mexico had by this time was a signatory party to FTAs with around 30 trade partners, it had no such agreement with an Asian country. An FTA with Japan would provide Mexican firms with significant commercial opportunities and Mexico more generally an important new geopolitical link with the East Asia region (Yoshimatsu 2005).

In April 2000, the Japan External Trade Organisation and Mexico's Ministry of Commerce and Industrial Development published a joint study report on bilateral economic relations between the two countries, and more specifically on a prospective bilateral FTA project. No further progress was made over 2000. Japan was preoccupied with preparations for its first 'test case' FTA with Singapore, and Mexico was also engaged in formal FTA negotiations with Singapore, although these broke off in December 2000 after Mexico's new President, Vicente Fox, took office. Under Fox, Mexico switched priority to Japan, calling for an early start of JMFTA negotiations on a bilateral FTA. It is likely that this arose from new questions raised amongst Mexico's policy-makers and business community concerning the relative commercial benefits of securing an FTA with Japan before Singapore. As Appendix D indicates, Mexico's bilateral trade with Japan was five times greater than its trade with Singapore. In June 2001, Japan and Mexico agreed to set up a Joint Study Group (JSG) on their bilateral FTA project, which comprised of policy-makers, business leaders and academics from the two countries. The JSG's report was published in July 2002 after five meetings, and which recommended an early start to FTA negotiations. Plans to do so were formally announced at the October 2002 APEC summit with the aim of concluding talks by the time of the following APEC summit due to be held in October 2003. The first round of FTA negotiations was held in November 2002 at Tokyo. By August 2003 four rounds of negotiations had been conducted. Until then, the talks had attracted relatively little media attention, but this changed as the October 2003 deadline approached and negotiators from both sides came under greater pressure to resolve key disputes between them.

3.6.2 Key areas of negotiation

Given that Mexico is a relatively large exporter of agricultural products and Japan maintains a highly protected agriculture sector, it was always anticipated that agriculture would be the most difficult area of JMFTA negotiations. This especially related to pork, on which Japan applied a 50 percent import tariff and accounted for nearly half of Japan's farm imports from Mexico, as well as ten percent of Mexico's total exports to Japan.[51] Another difficult product sector was orange juice, a major export item for Mexico and one on which Japan applied a 25.5 percent import tariff. Japan was generally resistant to making concessions in the agriculture sector. At the fourth round of FTA negotiations in August 2003, Tokyo tabled an offer to liberalise tariffs on some 300 farm products but with pork excluded on the list. Mexico had, though, been asking for tariff elimination on 485 farm products, including pork, and refused to concede ground.[52] A lower-house parliamentary election approached in Japan at the time of the fifth round of JMFTA negotiations held in October 2003, and the country's trade negotiators were told to stand firm in its position on agriculture.[53] In the days running up to hosting the WTO's Ministerial Meeting at Cancun in September 2003, the Mexican Government announced that it might postpone indefinitely the development of all its FTA projects.[54] Hence, both sides were in no mood to make compromises as the October 2003 deadline to conclude JMFTA negotiations loomed. Yet the stakes were high, especially for Japan, which was trying to establish itself as a credible FTA partner. As Toshihiro Iwatake, Director-General of the Japan Automobile Manufacturers Association's international department commented at this time, "If the negotiators fail to reach an agreement this time, [Japan's] whole FTA momentum would subside."[55] This was confirmed by a senior METI official who, under anonymity, remarked to the media that, "If we can't cut a deal with Mexico, we won't be able to cut a deal with any."[56] Mexico had also at this time started to exclude companies from nations with which it has no FTA from participating in bids for government procurement contracts.[57]

At this juncture, Japan and Mexico's positions were as follows. Regarding pork products, Mexico wanted Japan to reduce tariffs to zero but accepted import quota limits. In the October 2003 negotiations, Japan offered to reduce pork import tariffs down to 2.2 percent (an improvement on its previous offer of 4.3 percent) and apply an annual quota of between 70,000 to 80,000 tonnes, which was around twice the quantity of Mexican pork at that time Japan imported from the country. However, Mexico still insisted on a zero-tariff regime and a quota limit of around 250,000 tonnes. Japan in turn rejected this demand. With its dwindled number of pig farmers distributed across all 47 prefectures of Japan, such a compromise was deemed politically difficult for the ruling LDP Government, especially given the country's imminent elections. An impasse also existed over orange juice, where Mexico initially wanted Japan to phase out tariffs on imports of the product over ten years, but Japan rejected this idea and later proposed creating a tariff-free quota arrangement. Mexico agreed to this in principle and demanded a higher level quota of 6,500 tonnes a year, which Japan in turn rejected.[58] Given that Mexico exported only around 1,500 tonnes of orange juice annually, Mexican negotiators were probably using this tactic as a means to link a compromise agreement on pork. On other matters of agriculture, Mexico was pressing Japan to open up its markets for chicken and beef. Japanese negotiators counter-argued that its powerful farm lobbies would particularly resist liberalisation here, and moreover injurious foreign competition could undermine already fragile political support for the Japanese Government's ongoing reforms in these sectors. Japan did, though, offer to eliminate its tariffs on various Mexican farm imports, including avocados, pumpkins, watermelons and asparagus.[59]

The disputes over agricultural products dominated the October 2003 negotiations. In addition, Japan had made demands regarding Mexico's steel import barriers. Mexico offered to open its market in this sector but under certain rules of origin that would make it impossible for Japanese steel producers to export effectively to the market. These rules stipulated that the iron ore used to make the steel products had to be from Japan, and as the natural resource poor country imported virtually all of its ore this made compliance extremely difficult.[60] Japanese negotiators argued that most of its steel exports to Mexico were surface-treated sheets used for automobiles that were not in competition with Mexican products, but Mexico refused to concede movement on the issue and claimed it needed about 15 years to scrap steel import tariffs to help its general-purpose steel producers adjust to new Japanese import competition. Mexico was likewise resisting Japanese demands to completely scrap its 50 percent tariffs on automobile imports from Japan, or increase its tariff-free quota of around 30,000 units of year.

Despite these differences on both agriculture and industry products, both sides had by this time reached agreement on around 90 percent of the areas covered by the JMFTA negotiations. Japanese officials themselves partly admitted that one possible reason why talks did not progress at this time was due to their relative inexperience at FTAs negotiations in comparison to their Mexican counterparts, whose negotiating tactics reportedly baffled them, as noted above on the demand linkage made by Mexico on pork and orange juice.[61] Another reason for the lack of progress concerned inter-ministerial conflicts within Japan's negotiating team, whereby representatives from METI and the Ministry of Agriculture, Forestry and Fisheries (MAFF) came to blows owing to their resistance to make concessions to each other in their respective sectors of interest.[62] Prime Minister Koizumi, himself frustrated by Japan's failure to meet the October deadline to conclude JMFTA talks, decided in November 2003 to take greater charge of the negotiating, with his Office thereafter taking on the central managerial role in subsequent negotiations with Mexico and other FTA partners (see Chapter 2). Both METI and MAFF also established their own FTA task forces soon after the failed JMFTA negotiations with a view to reflecting on how and why the talks broke down as well as strategising on Japan's FTA policy in general.

3.6.3   Final outcomes

Further rounds of negotiations were held over the next few months. During vice-ministerial level talks held over November and December 2003, Mexico again asked that Japan completely lift its tariffs on orange juice and citrus fruit, and set duty-free import quotas for pork at 120,000 tonnes a year (down from the previous request of 250,000), chicken at 30,000 tonnes and beef at 40,000 tonnes. Again Japan refused to concede.[63] Running up to the eighth round of JMFTA negotiations held in January 2004, Mexican Economy Minister, Fernando Canales, threatened to abandon JMFTA negotiations if a deal was not reached by the end of March, much to the dismay of Japanese officials. However, the January 2004 talks achieved no breakthrough and it was agreed to convene further rounds in late February and early March. A deal was finally brokered during this period. Final points of agreement were reached by video-conferencing between Ministers from both countries, ending 16 months of hard fought negotiations. On pork and orange juice, Japan agreed to apply low-tariffs on annual import quotas of 85,000 tons and 6,500 tons, respectively. It also agreed to open up its market to various other Mexican agricultural products, including tomatoes, mangos, squash, eggs, wine and tobacco. On steel and automobiles, Mexico agreed to eliminate tariffs within ten years and seven years respectively, as well as establish a tariff-free import quota for Japanese automobile exports, equivalent to five percent of Mexico's domestic market, from year one of the JMFTA's entry into force.[64]

The JMFTA will phase out tariffs on 90 percent of bilateral trade between Japan and Mexico over a ten-year period, corresponding to 98 percent of Japanese exports and 87 percent of Mexican imports. The final text was also generally consistent with Japan's 'economic partnership' approach to FTAs, comprising 15 chapters that included themes on promoting bilateral co-operation in nine fields, including assistance for small and medium-sized enterprises, tourism, the environment, and human resource development (see Appendix C). As Mexican Economy Minister Fernando Canales commented, "The FTA is not merely about abolishing tariffs; it develops markets and further cooperation between the two countries."[65] In terms of expected benefits, Mexico anticipated a US$12 billion increase in inward Japanese direct investment during the initial ten years of the JMFTA, and an annual growth of ten percent in Mexican exports to Japan.[66] Japan meanwhile expected its exports to Mexico to could eventually grow by up to 400 billion yen (US$4 billion) per annum. This was a considerable increase: in 2004 Japan's exports to Mexico were valued at US$5.2 billion.[67] Both sides signed the agreement in September 2004 and the JMFTA came into force in April 2005.

3.7   South Korea–Chile Free Trade Agreement (KCFTA)

3.7.1   Origins and initial development

The KCFTA was first proposed at the November 1998 APEC summit, making it one of the very earliest of the Asia-Pacific's new wave of bilateral FTA projects. It was also amongst South Korea's first ever FTA projects to be initiated, the other being with Japan, which was launched in the same month (see Appendix A). Chile, on the other hand, had already negotiated a number of FTAs by this time, mostly with fellow Western Hemisphere states. In many ways, the two countries made an odd FTA pairing, and South Korea's choice of Chile as an initial FTA partner surprised many.[68] The relative geographic positions of the two countries are virtually antipodean, and neither was a particularly important trade partner to the other. In 2004, their total bilateral trade was US$2,571 million (Appendix D). This made Chile around the 30th most important national trade partner for South Korea, and South Korea around the 15th most important trade partner for Chile. Nor were there obviously close political, diplomatic and strategic ties between the two nations on which an FTA would be founded.

One of the most cited specific reasons why South Korea prioritised Chile as an early FTA partner was attributed to the different agricultural season cycles between the two countries. According to this reasoning, the potential competitive tensions between Korean and Chilean farmers under FTA conditions would be minimal. Although economic links between the two countries had not been that significant, both sides believed an FTA would confer important new commercial opportunities. A Korea Institute for International Economic Policy (KIEP) report estimated that it would provide a US$660 million boost to South Korea's exports to Chile and a US$220 million increase in Chilean imports (Cheong 2002). More specially, South Korea's Ministry of Foreign Affairs and Trade (MOFAT) believed the FTA would enable South Korea to overtake Japan in Chile's imports of automobiles imports.[69] South Korea already had 26 percent of the Chilean market in 2002. However, this share was shrinking, largely attributed by Korean analysts to the implementation of the Chile–Argentina–Brazil automobile free trade pact in the same year, and also the EU–Chile FTA that came into effect in February 2003.[70] Furthermore, South Korea needed a bridgehead into a fast integrating and emerging Latin American market, just as Chile needed the same strategic advantage in East Asia for similar reasons.[71]

Domestic political reasons were also relevant. Chilean President Eduardo Frei was coming to the end of his political term and had not secured an FTA with the US by this time. Frei sought to make political capital from the KCFTA project with an eye on Chile's 1999 elections. Over in South Korea, Kim Dae-jung had begun his term in office from 1998 and wanted to demonstrate his 'open trading nation' credentials from an early stage. The KCFTA provided such an opportunity. At the outset of the KCFTA project in late 1998, the South Korean Government believed the different agricultural season cycle factor would help expedite negotiations to a relatively speedy conclusion.[72] A very quick KCFTA scoping study soon followed, conducted over just a few weeks from March 1999 onwards. The scoping study for the Japan–Chile FTA took two years to complete by comparison. There was a general consensus amongst all FTA stakeholders in retrospect that the scoping study was rushed and consequently limited in providing accurate assessments of the likely economic impacts of an implemented KCFTA, as well as in anticipating any possible backlash from certain interest groups, especially the farming lobby.[73]

The first round of KCFTA negotiations was held in December 1999, and the expectation at the time of the conclusion of negotiations within a year was no doubt based on the limited and optimistic analysis of the scoping study. By the fourth round of negotiations, held in December 2000, a stalemate arose between the two sides over agriculture. South Korea felt unable to concede to Chilean demands on the liberalisation of certain sensitive agri-products owing to the fervent opposition from Korean farmers. During 2001, negotiations were suspended while the South Korean Government attempted to broker a compromise at the domestic level with the farming lobby on agricultural trade issues. In the meantime, Seoul sent a special envoy to Chile to explain the difficulties South Korea faced with liberalising its agriculture trade sector. The Chilean Government responded in a letter sent to MOFAT stating that it would wait until South Korea was ready to resume FTA negotiations. Special high-level talks on the KCFTA were held at Los Angeles in February 2002 in an attempt to break the deadlock over agriculture, but these failed.

3.7.2 Key areas of negotiation

Agriculture

Why, then, had KCFTA talks floundered so comprehensively over 2001 and much of 2002 on agricultural issues? Much blame may be apportioned to the rushed scoping study that led to the South Korean Government underestimating Chile's agriculture sector competitiveness. Chile exported US$1.12 billion worth of fruit in 2001, with grapes accounting for around half this amount (taking a 20 percent global market share) and apples a fifth. Before the FTA was concluded, South Korea only imported grapes and kiwi fruit from Chile, with a 47.5 percent tariff rate applied. Furthermore, those making the different seasonal cycle argument forgot to factor in an increasing number of Korean Jeju Island farmers who were producing all year round using hot houses in the winter months, and were investing large sums in this relatively expensive method of production. Chapter 2 details the reasons behind South Korea's uncompetitive and highly protected agricultural sector, as well as the political sensitivity associated with it. Like their Japanese counterparts, South Korean farmers were not just concerned about injurious competition from Chilean farmers arising from the KCFTA but perhaps more importantly about the precedents it set for future FTAs the government wanted to pursue.

South Korea's farmers were pitched against the country's business lobby, which argued that farm and forestry products accounted for less than five percent of imports from Chile, with the remaining 95 percent consisting of minerals and manufactured good imports. They made the further point that South Korea stood to gain a US$400 million improvement to its trade balance from the KCFTA deal according to their estimates. Relations between South Korea's farmers and the government were also difficult throughout the whole negotiation process. Initiating a constructive dialogue between the government and the farmers on KCFTA matters was not helped by the very different figures each side presented on anticipated income losses. South Korea's Ministry of Agriculture and Forestry (MAF) contended that its own study estimated this to be 30 billion won (US$20 million) for fruit farmers, whereas a study presented by the farmer's suggested a figure of 2,800 billion won (US$1.9 billion). A study by the Korea Rural Economic Institute calculated income loss to fruit farmers to be around 280 billion won (US$190 million).[74] We later discuss how a deal between the government and the farmers on income loss compensation proved to be essential in South Korea's attempts to ratify the KCFTA. Trade negotiations over agriculture have always involved some degree of intense domestic negotiations, but in the KCFTA's case it almost completely overshadowed international-level negotiations.

In the final KCFTA deal, South Korea secured tariff reduction phase-ins of between five to ten years on almost all agricultural product sectors. More specifically, grapes were subject to a special ten-year 'seasonal' tariff reduction schedule, and a 16-year tariff reduction schedule was applied to imports of certain Chilean dried milk, prepared food and fruit juice products. Phased-in liberalisation under various tariff quota schedules was applied to particular beef, poultry and dairy products, as well as mandarins, olives and plums. There were also tariff liberalisation exemptions on 21 agri-imports from Chile, including rice, apples and pears, which would thus continue to attract very high tariff-rates from South Korea. Chile itself negotiated a significantly smaller range of liberalisation phase-ins and exemptions, and both sides agreed to consider liberalising a further number of agri-products after the completion of the WTO's Doha Development Round (see Appendix B).

Industry

South Korea's premier business association, the Federation of Korean Industry (FKI) was somewhat disappointed about the government's choice of Chile as South Korea's first FTA partner given it was a relatively insignificant trade partner. Moreover, according to the FKI, the government failed to sufficiently consult with them at the outset of the KCFTA project.[75] However, the FKI did lend its full support to the government's position as negotiations on industry sector issues with Chile gathered pace. South Korea's leading exports to Chile were transport equipment, automobiles, petroleum oils, washing machines and other electrical and electronic products. Chile's top export to Korea was copper, with other key exports being other metals and minerals, wood, cement, chemicals, processed foods, transport equipment and textiles. Whereas South Korea front-loaded almost all of its negotiated liberalisation phase-ins and opt-outs in agriculture and some raw material products, Chile chose to do the same across a wide range of industrial products (see Appendix B). Given that industrial products accounted for a substantial majority of trade flows between the two countries, Chile would thus appear to have secured a significantly wider range of concessions. In the final KCFTA deal, Chile was obliged to immediately eliminate tariffs on only 2,439 products (42 percent of total products, and only 30 percent of total industry products) originating from South Korea, compared to South Korea's obligation to immediately eliminate tariffs on 9,740 products (87 percent of total) originating from Chile. Furthermore, Chile negotiated three to 13 year phase-ins across most industry product sectors, with liberalisation exemptions also applied to a number of industrial products, including refrigerators and washing machines. South Korea meanwhile negotiated for a tariff reduction schedule on only one industry product sector (copper cathodes). This relative imbalance in industrial trade concessions was the price South Korea had to pay for protecting its farmers.[76] Moreover, with each side deciding to leave protectionist measures in place in sectors where they lacked relative competitive advantage, they minimised the KCFTA's potential to generate trade creation gains, which was already quite limited given the essentially inter-industry nature of South Korea–Chile bilateral trade (see Chapter 1).

3.7.3 South Korea's KCFTA ratification debacle

A deal on the KCFTA was reached in October 2002 after six rounds of negotiations, and the leaders of both countries signed the Agreement in

February 2003. However, it took another year for the KCFTA to be ratified owing to strong and effective political resistance mounted by South Korea's farming lobby, with support from miscellaneous civil society groups (many of which were linked to the country's 'Anti-WTO' movement) and the large number of legislative representatives that supported the farmers' position. In June 2003, around 140 members of South Korean parliament – the National Assembly – signed a petition opposing the KCFTA's ratification.[77] As a consequence, the recently elected Roh Moo-hyun Administration decided to postpone the submission of the KCFTA bill to the National Assembly for a few weeks until certain supplementary measures had been added, these primarily relating to a compensation programme for farmers adversely affected by injurious competition from Chilean agricultural imports. The South Korean Government had already been working on such a programme well before KCFTA talks had been concluded.[78] When the FTA bill was first submitted for ratification on 8 July 2003, it was accompanied by a special relief measures bill that offered the farmers 1 trillion won (US$850 million) over seven years.[79] However, this proved insufficient to placate the demands and concerns of farmers groups, many of which were opposing the KCFTA outright no matter what compensation was being offered.

Strong opposition to the KCFTA bill, both inside and outside the National Assembly, persisted to November 2003, when the Roh Administration made a second attempt at ratification. In the run-up to this, the South Korean Government announced a programme of 119 trillion won (US$100 billion) worth of measures over ten years to help the farm sector cope with wider domestic market opening in general, and hence was also linked to agri-trade talks in the WTO's Doha Round.[80] The support programme included direct subsidies, debt write-offs, rural development projects, preferential loan rates and tax breaks for farmers, and so on. Specifically concerning the KCFTA, the Government also raised its special relief measures offer to 1.2 trillion won, as part of an FTA Special Fund.[81] Yet, this was not enough to persuade most farmers groups, which took to the streets again in thousands during November and December to protest against the second attempt at ratifying the KCFTA. On the day of the vote, about 20 National Assembly representatives supporting the farmers' cause blocked the floor proceedings during the plenary session when voting was due to take place, consequently leading to another postponement.[82]

With the KCFTA still not ratified by the end of 2003, South Korea was at serious risk of losing its credibility as an FTA partner. An announcement from MOFAT stated that a vote against ratification of the KCFTA would negatively influence current negotiations for FTAs with Japan, Singapore, and ASEAN, and harm international confidence in the country.[83] End of year South Korea–Chile trade figures were further causes for concern. Imports from Chile had jumped from US$754 million in 2002 to US$1,058 million in 2003, which made Korean farmers even more agitated over cheap Chilean food products entering the South Korean market.[84] Meanwhile, South Korea's exports to Chile had risen by a much smaller degree, from US$454 million in 2002 to US$517 million for 2003.[85] Many South Korean firms were particularly concerned about the drop in sales for some of their key products in the Chilean market, such as automobiles, mobile phones and steel. For example, South Korean car producers saw their market share drop by 19 percent in Chile over the year, falling from second position to fifth overall.

The South Korean Government made another attempt at ratifying the KCFTA bill in January 2004, but was again thwarted by the actions of farmer supporting lawmakers in the National Assembly, who surrounded the seat of National Assembly speaker Park Kwan-Yong and blocked the presentation of the bill to a plenary session.[86] Outside, around 3,000 protesting farmers clashed with riot police, who had erected a barricade of some 100 buses to block the farmers from marching near to the parliament building. Earlier that month in Santiago, the Chilean parliament had ratified the KCFTA after a long period of waiting upon political developments in South Korea. Further political wrangling ensued, and the remaining National Assembly representatives who supported the farmer's opposition to the KCFTA came under increasing pressure to relent. Around this time, National Assembly Speaker Park Kwan-yong had also met with the heads of major South Korean political parties and called for their cooperation on the bill. Another vote was planned for 16 February 2004. This time there was no blocking of the floor: the farmer-supporting legislators claimed that they had done enough to express their opposition to the Agreement.[87] The results of the vote on the KCFTA bill were 162 in favour, 71 against and one abstention, and the KCFTA was finally ratified. South Korea's first FTA subsequently came into force on 1 April 2004.

3.7.4 Early impact assessments

Trade data for 2004 showed significant increases in the value of bilateral trade between South Korea and Chile. In this year, and nine months into the KCFTA coming into force, South Korea's exports to Chile increased by 33 percent to reach US$690 million (up from US$517 million in 2003), and Chile's exports increased by 80 percent to reach US$1.9 billion, although the rising world market price for copper accounted for a notable element of this. South Korea's imports of agricultural imports from Chile increased by 24 percent in 2004, slightly higher than the 20 percent increase in its total agricultural imports. However, MAF announced that over 12,000 peach, kiwi and grape farms across the country had decided to end production since the KCFTA's ratification.[88] Like many FTAs recently signed in the Asia-Pacific, it will take some time before the fuller impact of KCFTA upon both the South Korean and Chilean economies can be comprehensively assessed.

3.8   US–Singapore Free Trade Agreement (USSFTA)

3.8.1   Origins and initial development

The USSFTA has been one of the highest profile FTA projects in the Asia-Pacific. Much was made of the fact by both parties that this was the first FTA signed between East Asia and the United States. The origin of the project had various roots. Both Singapore and the US were at one time party to the Pacific-5 FTA project proposal of the late 1990s. Although this plan was aborted, as Chapter 1 notes it did help the five countries concerned (others being Australia, New Zealand and Chile) identify potential bilateral FTA partners. Towards the end of 2000, then US Ambassador to Singapore, Stephen Green, spent much time promoting the idea of a USSFTA in the United States, with allegedly strong encouragement from the Singapore Government.[89] Events moved very quickly, not least helped by the fact that Green had close links with Bill Clinton. The actual proposal for USSFTA came from discussions between Singapore Prime Minister Goh Chok Tong and US President Bill Clinton on 16 November 2000 in Brunei during a round of golf.[90] Both leaders were at the time attending that year's APEC summit in Brunei. Their mutual agreement to initiate an FTA was soon converted into action, and the first round of negotiations commenced around two weeks later on 4 December, thus forgoing any formal FTA study phase.

President Clinton pushed for brisk conclusion of the FTA before the end of his term of office by December 2000. The Singapore Government were open to this idea,[91] but it would have been unprecedented to conclude an FTA in just one month of negotiations, and without any official prior scoping study. Moreover, after the second round of negotiations held in January 2001, a far greater number of negotiating issues arose than was first thought. When the new Bush Administration took office the same month the whole process had to virtually start from scratch.[92] For instance, the views and interests of US industry sectors were more thoroughly surveyed, leading to more negotiating demands from the American side.[93] The establishment of the US-Singapore FTA Business Coalition – a transnational lobby group previously noted in Chapter 2 – lent further support to the USSFTA project, as well as shape the initial negotiating agenda to some extent, especially from the US's perspective. By March 2001, the Singapore Government was confident that the USSFTA deal would be concluded by the end of that year. The third round of negotiations was held in May 2001, with two more convened that year in July and October. The October meeting came just a month after the September 11 terrorist attacks on the United States, adding a new strategic dimension to the USSFTA project. The Singapore Government had always tried to sell the project to its Southeast Asian neighbour countries as further anchoring American interests in their region. Prime Minister Goh had done this from the start, especially after Malaysia's criticism of Singapore seeking bilateral trade deals outside the

ASEAN group instead of adhering more closely to the cause of Southeast Asia regional solidarity. Singapore has also been a long-standing security ally of the United States, and some observers believed that Singapore's strong support of the Bush Adminstration's stance on terrorism and the Iraq war helped prioritise the USSFTA project over other FTAs the US was involved with, though this was denied by George Yeo in a media interview given in May 2003.[94]

3.8.2 Key areas of negotiation

Manufacturing

Textiles proved a difficult issue in the USSFTA negotiations. The US wanted to maintain a strong degree of protection in this sector, even though Singapore no longer had a real competitive advantage in this industry. Such was the resistance from their American counterparts that Singapore's trade negotiators almost gave up all their demands in the textiles sector.[95] Before the FTA, Singapore's textile exporters faced US import duties of between 17 to 33 percent. In the end, the US relented and offered concessions. While textiles is deemed an old fading industry in Singapore, it still employed around 10,000 people in the city-state.[96] Most American manufacture exports to Singapore already enjoyed tariff-free entry, and Singapore agreed to reduce all remaining tariffs on US imports to zero percent. The US, however, choose to use tariff liberalisation phase-in schedules of up to ten years on a number of industrial product imports from Singapore, a number that was notably greater than that requested by Japan in its FTA with Singapore (see Appendix B).

Services

Given that Singapore offers virtual tariff-free entry on most goods, what the city-state can offer on services market access is what especially interests its FTA partners. It was the services sector where the US felt it had the most to gain from an USSFTA deal, particularly in banking and finance, telecoms, insurance, courier services, and legal services. In the banking sector, Citibank was the only US bank in Singapore with a Qualifying Full Bank (QFB) licence before the FTA was signed, which gave it unlimited rights to open new branches, relocate existing ones and install off-site automated teller machines (ATMs). With the USSFTA, the quota on US banking licences lifted, as was the limit on the number of service locations after two years. American Express lobbied the US Government especially hard on pressuring Singapore to open up retail access (e.g. ATMs per branch, number of branches, etc.) in this sector. Singapore is also a major regional communications hub for transmitting and receiving flows of important financial information, therefore making the IPR of data transmission highly relevant to US trade negotiators in the finance sector generally.[97]

In the telecoms sector, American firms had complained to Singapore's telecom regulating body (Infocomm Development Authority) that the price of locally leased circuits from fixed line provider SingTel was well above international market rates, although SingTel denied this. In addition, there were claims of predatory monopolistic behaviour and price-fixing in SingTel's marketing of international services, which for example made international mobile phone charges extremely expensive on both outgoing and incoming calls. Not only did the Singapore Government agree to open up its telecoms sector, but it also agreed to sell its remaining 67.6 percent shareholding in SingTel and ST Telemedia as part of the USSFTA deal.[98] As we saw earlier in this chapter, the US had similarly pressed Australia in AUSFTA negotiations to privatise its telecoms sector. In legal services, the US managed to secure recognition for graduates with more prominent US law degrees for admission to Singapore's Bar Council. Talks over legal services liberalisation were particularly difficult as this concerned a key function of state autonomy for Singapore, and it managed to persuade the US that this aspect of the agreement would not be subject to the USSFTA's dispute settlement mechanisms.

Miscellaneous issues

Regarding *rules of origin*, Singapore introduced two special aspects to its RoO regime that were incorporated into the USSFTA. The first of these was the outward processing (OP) scheme that enabled firms based in the city-state to outsource part of their production process to neighbouring countries, and would normally apply to lower value-added or the labour-intensive production of semi-manufactured products. Any Singapore-based value added activities undertaken prior to the outsourcing activity would also qualify for 'local content' under OP conditions, which is not conventional RoO practice. Outward processing rules have been deployed in Singapore's other FTAs (see Appendix E). The second special aspect of Singapore's RoO regime was the Integrated Sourcing Initiative (ISI), and this operates only in the USSFTA. Under the ISI scheme, firms based in Indonesia's Batam and Bintan Islands industrial parks (which were originally established and still managed with the help of Singaporean quasi-government agencies) could dispatch components to Singapore for final production under RoO exempt terms. There are around 700 foreign companies operating in the Batam Island industrial park, 70 percent of which are Singapore-based, and mostly involved in information technology and electronics production as part of wider regional production networks operating in Southeast and East Asia.

In *agriculture*, the US did not agree to immediately open up its market to Singapore's agricultural exports, minor though they were, but rather applied its usual range of tariff reduction schedules based on phased-in liberalisation of up to ten-year periods. As Appendix B details, the US also agreed only to raise its quota limits on certain farm products on a gradual basis. Singapore's agriculture sector is tiny, accounting for less than 0.1 percent of its GDP. Moreover, it exports virtually no raw agricultural produce, although it does export processed foods to some extent. There was much criticism of Japan's protectionist stance on agriculture in the JSEPA, but strangely there was virtually no mention in the media of the US's resistance to immediate liberalisation in the agriculture sector during USSFTA negotiations.

Concerning *intellectual property rights*, Singapore offered to further strengthen its IPR regime, especially with regard to strengthening protections against the illegal copying of copyrighted materials such as music, films, books and software. The city-state faced around 70 US demands on its IPR laws, including 'soundmarks' and 'smellmarks', these being types of trademark governing the sounds (such as the distinctive revving sound of a Harley Davison motorbike) and smells of products e.g. cosmetics.[99] Singapore was largely compliant on IPR issues as it wished to attract higher value-added and high tech FDI, especially in biotechnology.

On *labour* issues, Singapore resisted the inclusion of any significant labour provisions in the USSFTA, although a labour clause was incorporated. The Singapore state maintained various controls in the labour market and over labour organisation, and did not wish these controls to be compromised. Singapore took a similar defensive position on *environmental* clauses, raising concerns in US Congress over the city-state's alleged noncompliance to international agreements on the control and use of chlorofluorocarbons (CFCs), in particular in failure to phase out the production and recovery of all used CFCs, and the re-export of newly-produced CFCs through trans-shipment arrangements. Singapore denied the charges and stated on the latter account that the chemicals do not technically enter the city-state. More generally, Howard Shaw, SEC Executive Director, stated with regards to USSFTA that, "there was a missed opportunity to push corporations in both countries to be more responsible in their environmental practices".[100] In May 2003, the Environmental Investigation Agency (EIA), an international non-profit environmental group, alleged that Singapore plays a major role in the smuggling of illegally cut timber. The specific timber in question was ramin, a tropical hardwood tree species protected under the Convention on International Trade in Endangered Species, or CITIES. The EIA reported that Singapore was responsible for exporting millions of dollars of ramin without CITIES permits over a ten-month period from 2001 and 2002, and feared that the USSFTA could exacerbate the situation.[101] However, in June 2003, the US and Singapore signed a Memorandum of Intent on Environmental Co-operation as an extension of the USSFTA's environmental provisions, which committed both sides to meet at least every two years to set up a plan of action for boosting bilateral and regional environmental projects.[102]

Final hurdles and sticking points

Capital controls. The USSFTA negotiations had almost wound up by November 2002 until the US Treasury weighed in with its last minute demand for Singapore to relinquish its use of *capital controls* as part of the FTA deal. The US Treasury had noted an interest in this issue from the very beginning, arguing it should be considered part of the financial services liberalisation talks, but it was put in the 'too difficult box' to start with and thereafter forgotten about until this final gasp intervention by the US Treasury.[103] However, the Singapore Government was highly defensive on this issue, relating the maintenance of such controls to part of Singapore's national economic security. Furthermore, the USTR was allegedly furious with the Treasury for taking this course of action, seeing that it could jeopardise the whole FTA deal at the very last moment.[104] The Singapore Government resisted the hard line taken by the US Treasury, calling its bluff in effect. Singapore Trade Minister, George Yeo, stated at the time that his government "were not comfortable" with these demands.[105] During the 1997/98 financial crisis, the Monetary Authority of Singapore (MAS) had used capital controls with effect, helping the city-state to largely avoid the financial and economic turbulence that engulfed much of the Southeast Asian region. On the one hand, Singapore is an advocate of transnational economic liberalism and sought to attract investment funds to develop its position as a regional financial centre. On the other hand, the maintenance of 'financial-credit' security remains a priority objective in Singapore's foreign economic policy (Dent 2002).

At least three of the four countries that had previously signed FTAs with the US had agreed to cede their rights to emergency capital controls, so this demand from the US Treasury followed a pattern.[106] There were no capital control provisions in other bilateral FTAs Singapore had negotiated up to this point, these being with Japan, New Zealand and Australia. In the US, Democratic Senators Sander Levin (Michigan), Robert Matsui (California) and Barney Frank (Massachusetts) wrote to USTR Robert Zoellick stating their support for the Singapore position, proclaiming that countries should be able to "curb hot money, which can have a destabilizing effect on the global financial system."[107] Extended negotiations over capital controls prolonged the full conclusion of USSFTA talks well into January 2003, a compromise deal being struck after a final round of telephone negotiations between US Treasury Undersecretary John Taylor and the MAS Managing Director Koh Yong Guan (Koh and Lin 2004). In the end, the USSFTA included a special provision under which the MAS would not be liable for claims by US investors if its capital controls lasted for less than a year and did not "substantially impede transfers".[108] This only applied to capital transactions such as portfolio investments and inter-bank loans, but not to repatriated profits, dividend payments or proceeds from direct investments. These provisions were very similar to the compromise Chile struck with the US when it concluded its FTA negotiations some weeks earlier.

The US Treasury and American investor firms had initially demanded the complete elimination of capital controls in both the Singapore and Chile FTA negotiations. It was hence generally acknowledged that it was the US that made more of the compromise rather than Singapore.[109] As an MAS official stated after the final agreement on capital controls was struck, "in an extreme balance of payments crisis that threatens to severely destabilise the economy, Singapore needs the flexibility to take all appropriate measures, including, where absolutely unavoidable, restrictions on capital flows".[110] Writing for the *Financial Times* just after the agreement was struck, the renowned free trade advocating economists Jagdish Bhagwati and Daniel Tarullo made an impassioned case for small developing countries like Singapore and Chile to retain such regulatory options in an era when financial crises where occurring with increasing regularity. They also noted that since the 1997/98 East Asian financial crisis, the IMF has "changed its thinking and acknowledged the need for careful policies that monitor and, in some cases, regulate capital flows."[111]

Chewing gum. Singapore had famously imposed its ban on the production, sale and advertising of chewing gum in 1992. The government was particularly concerned about how certain gum chewing offenders were deliberately jamming up the doors of subway trains in city-state's impressive Mass Rapid Transport system. The chewing gum ban became a USSFTA issue after the American firm Wrigley lobbied the USTR to make it a negotiating agenda item early on in the talks. According to some observers, Wrigley – the world's largest chewing gum producer – were more concerned about the future China market, in that Beijing still looks to Singapore as how a future Chinese-based society and economy could be, i.e. economic prosperity combined with social control. Wrigley's alleged concern was that if Singaporeans continued to not chew gum it could transpire to be a future norm for China's citizens.[112] There may be some truth in this given that Singapore was such a small market, and therefore wider motives lay behind Wrigley's extensive lobbying efforts.

After USTR negotiators proposed that Singapore should completely lift its chewing gum ban, Trade Minister George Yeo reportedly sent an article on medicinal chewing gum to his Singapore Cabinet colleagues for discussion. He then instructed his chief USSFTA negotiator, Tommy Koh, to offer a compromise of permitting the sale of medicinal chewing gum only.[113] This was generally accepted by the US, and the USSFTA deal subsequently allowed for Singapore's importation of chewing gum "with the therapeutic value for sale and supply subject to the rules and regulations on health products." However, Wrigley was somewhat concerned that this wording inferred the need to acquire a medical prescription to procure their products, which in turn would be sold only in pharmacies. Moreover, whereas Pfizer's Nicorette brand (a no-smoking aid) was sure to qualify, Wrigley was uncertain whether their two sugar-free brands, Extra and Orbit, would meet the 'therapeutic value' criteria. In support of Wrigley's cause, Senator Phil Crane, Chairman of the Trade Subcommittee on the House Ways and Means panel, argued when the USSFTA bill was being discussed in US Congress over the summer of 2003 that, "if they retain the language that requires a prescription to buy chewing gum, then we have not succeeded."[114] Crane represented the state of Illinois, where Wrigley is based with its headquarters in Chicago. He was joined by his fellow Illinois Senator, Dick Durbin, who stated that the "proposal must sound completely bizarre, that a dentist can prescribe chewing gum as long as it is sugarless."[115]

Singapore's Ministry of Trade and Industry (MTI) made an announcement in July 2003 in response to Wrigley's requests. It agreed that, "Orbit and Orbit White [teeth whitener version] can be sold by pharmacists over the counter, subject to the condition that buyers' particulars are recorded", and further stipulated that, "other regulations applicable to medicinal products approved for sale by pharmacists over the counter would also apply to Orbit and Orbit White. In particular, the packaging and advertising for both products must pertain only to therapeutic, not recreational use, and must match the approved claims. Advertisements will require a permit from health regulatory authorities."[116] The same statement made it clear that the ban will continue on other types of chewing gum, and that stiffer penalties will be introduced for littering involving the indiscriminate disposal of used gum. At this time, the penalty for smuggling gum into the city-state was already one year in jail and an S$10,000 fine (approx US$5,500). The MTI would also continue to assess requests from chewing gum firms on a case-by-case basis. In March 2004, Singapore began the partial lifting of its chewing gum ban, starting with the permitted sale of Pfizer's Nicorette brand, and this could be sold over the counter after an initial consultation with a pharmacist.[117] However, 'patients' needed to get a doctor's prescription to obtain Biotene gum – an oral health product produced by US firm Laclede – that was launched in the city-state later that month.[118] In May 2004, Wrigley's Orbit chewing gum went on sale over the counter in Singapore's pharmacies. At the same time, the government controlled Straits Times newspaper published an article highlighting the problems caused by chewing gum litter and the costs incurred for government contracted cleaning companies.[119] This episode in the USSFTA project demonstrated how Singapore was again able to resist US pressure to comply with its demands when negotiations encroached on matters of political and social control. The US underestimated Singapore's defensive reaction concerning these matters, as noted above. Nevertheless, under the USSFTA, American firms now enjoyed a number of preferential market access advantages over their foreign rivals in Singapore's services sector.

3.9 Trans-Pacific Strategic Economic Partnership Agreement (TPSEPA)

3.9.1 Origins and initial development

The TPSEPA is in many respects the most vital FTA to observe and analyse from the perspective of the 'lattice regionalism' hypothesis because it is the only Asia-Pacific FTA to date that has progressed from bilateral-to-plurilateral evolution. Somewhat ironically, though, the founding bilateral FTA in question – that between Singapore and New Zealand – itself was a residual diminished outcome from an originally proposed Pacific-5 FTA first discussed in the late 1990s between these two countries plus the United States, Australia and Chile. The idea to create a Pacific-5 FTA apparently came from then USTR Charlene Barchevsky. In the run up to the 1998 APEC summit in Kuala Lumpur, she approached New Zealand's Trade Minister, Lockwood Smith, and suggested that he should make the proposal for a Pacific-5 FTA for political reasons, the US being mindful of appearing too dominant over the APEC trade agenda.[120] As noted in Chapter 1, the motives at play here were to catalyse trade liberalisation movement within APEC at a time when the Early Voluntary Sectoral Liberalisation (EVSL) scheme seemed to running into a brick wall over agriculture. The Pacific-5 FTA project was thus conceived as a pan-Pacific alliance of states that wished to stir other APEC members into action on trade liberalisation, especially its Asian members, who may feel compelled under a 'competitive liberalisation' dynamic to initiate their own new FTA projects in order to secure similar market access benefits and preferences, with the US or any other Pacific-5 FTA member.

The Pacific-5 FTA proposal, however, did not get sufficient backing from US President Bill Clinton, mainly because his administration did not possess 'Fast Track' negotiating authority at the time. Australia's own FTA policy was still at a formative stage at this time and were not ready to commit either to the proposal. Although Chile has discussed the possibility of a bilateral FTA with New Zealand back in 1995, its efforts were concentrated on securing a separate FTA deal with the US. This left only Singapore and New Zealand as willing FTA partners within the Pacific-5 group, who announced at the 1999 APEC summit their decision to proceed with a bilateral FTA of their own, officially referred to as the Agreement on a New Zealand–Singapore Closer Economic Partnership, or ANZSCEP. Although Singapore and New Zealand were relatively small trading economies, the ANZSCEP – signed just over a year later in November 2000 – did have important demonstration effects for other Asia-Pacific states. It was the Asia-Pacific's first cross-region FTA (in this case between an East Asian and Oceanic state), and showed that free trade deals could be done between different and distant countries in the region.

Indeed, even as the ANZSCEP was being signed on the sidelines of the 2000 APEC summit in Brunei, the leaders of New Zealand, Chile and Singapore discussed and endorsed the idea of extending the agreement to include Chile in a Pacific-3 FTA (P3FTA) arrangement. At this point, though, it appeared that the intention was not to achieve this through trilateral negotiations but rather through parallel bilateral talks. Singapore and Chile had already announced plans to negotiate a separate bilateral FTA in September 1999 at the Auckland APEC summit, and this was reconfirmed in October 2001 at the APEC summit convened in Shanghai.[121] At the 2000 Brunei summit, New Zealand and Chile had also announced that they would embark on bilateral FTA negotiations. The idea to conclude a P3FTA arrangement by co-ordinated bilateral means prevailed into 2002. It was also still unclear at this stage whether Australia had completely ruled itself out of joining the plurilateral FTA project. The idea to attract Australia into the FTA project was partly motivated by the need to maintain Chile's own interest in it. Chile's President Ricardo Lagos was allegedly not as enthusiastic about the P3FTA compared to New Zealand's Prime Minister Helen Clark and Singapore's Prime Minister Goh Chok Tong because he did not believe it would have much of an economic impact. However, scoping studies conducted between the three countries that were published just before the October 2002 APEC summit recommended the commencement of negotiations, either bilaterally or trilaterally.[122] While Chile, New Zealand and Singapore all had very open and reasonably similar commercial policy regimes, the advice from the technocracies of each country was that there were sufficient differences between them that only trilateral negotiations could effectively address. As Chapter 1 discussed, every FTA is essentially shaped by, or is the creation of interactions between the political economies of the negotiating parties. A decision to proceed bilaterally would mean that the FTA terms and conditions agreed upon by Singapore and Chile would not only have to prove consistent with the prior agreed and implemented ANZSCEP but also with concomitant bilateral negotiations between Chile and New Zealand. While special protocols, exemptions or other particularities of technical policy (e.g. product-specific tariff liberalisation schedules or RoO) agreed upon bilaterally could be accommodated in a trilateral FTA arrangement, separate bilateral negotiating tracks were less likely to minimise these deviations than 'all in' trilateral negotiations.

The P3FTA project was officially proposed at 2002 APEC summit where the three countries' leaders announced that the first round of trilateral negotiations would commence in July 2003, which they duly did, with the aim then of concluding an agreement by APEC's October 2004 summit. In September 2003, intermediate talks between P3FTA officials were held in Singapore on certain technical matters. Plans to conduct the second official round of talks in November 2003 were, though, postponed as the Chilean Government wished to undertake further domestic consultations with the country's dairy farmers, who were anxious over FTA liberalised competition from their New Zealand counterparts. It was not until August 2004 that a second round took place, where the main issues of negotiation were trade in goods, rules of origin, technical barriers to trade, trade in services, financial services, investment, and intellectual property. Discussions were also held between labour and environment officials during this round.[123] A third round soon followed in December 2004 in which the talks mostly concentrated on market access, services and investment schedules. The original deadline for concluding negotiations was pushed back to mid-2005. Fourth and fifth rounds occurred in March and April 2005 respectively. By this time, Brunei – which had participated in FTA negotiations as an observer since the second round – had become a full negotiating party. The change from a trilateral to a quadrilateral arrangement required a renaming of the P3FTA, this being to the Trans-Pacific Strategic Economic Partnership Agreement, or TPSEPA. A sixth and final round of negotiations took place in May that year, and the TPSEPA was initialled by representatives from all four countries on the sidelines of the APEC Trade Ministers Meeting at Jeju Island, South Korea in June 2005. Accompanying agreements on labour co-operation and environment co-operation were signed a month later in July 2005.[124] The TPSEPA entered into force on 1 January 2006, making it the first operational multi-party trans-Pacific FTA.

3.9.2   Key areas of negotiation and other issues

ANZSCEP–TPSEPA linkages

An important starting point in the TPSEPA negotiations was to what extent could the already in force ANZSCEP between New Zealand and Singapore provide a template for this wider quadrilateral agreement. Singapore declared at the beginning that it wished to follow the ANZSCEP model, with one research interviewed Singaporean official commenting on the matter, "why re-invent the wheel?"[125] Having succeeded in persuading New Zealand to exclude labour and environment standards from the ANZSCEP text, Singapore was particularly keen for TPSEPA to follow suit. The city-state's labour movement was strictly controlled by the government, and its per capita pollution levels remained quite high, not least because it has one of the world's fastest expanding petrochemical industries. However, New Zealand and Chile wanted labour and environment provisions in the text and a compromise ensued. On the sides of the agreement, TPSEPA parties signed a Labour Co-operation Memorandum of Understanding, thus not a binding agreement on trade-related labour policy commitments, whereas the Environmental Co-operation Agreement did entail firmer commitments not to relax or weaken environmental laws and standards to gain a competitive trade advantages. There was a broader issue at stake here too. As one research interviewed TPSEPA negotiator remarked, "one of the interesting issues that arose in the early stages of negotiations was the weight that we should have put on making the Agreement attractive for expansion to future partners – for example through an 'open architecture' and/or excluding potentially unpalatable features such as provisions on labour and environment – versus making the Agreement an ambitious, high quality agreement."[126] This highlighted the lowest common denominator problem, similar to that which has beset APEC in recent years in that multiple or expanding group membership entails degree of compromise that lead to gradually diluted outcomes. In the TPSEPA's case, Singapore was at least persuaded to sign some form agreement on labour and environment.

Other differences between the ANZSCEP and TPSEPA are apparent (see Appendix C). In addition to labour and environmental provisions, the TPSEPA included additional thematic elements not covered the ANZSCEP, namely on agriculture and primary industry co-operation, education co-operation, scientific and technological co-operation, and IPR provisions that went beyond the ANZSCEP simply deference to the TRIPS agreement under the WTO. Singapore had pressed for human resource development co-operation and science and technology co-operation to be incorporated during the second round of talks, with Prime Minister Goh Chok Tong commenting that, "FTAs are too narrow. We want to extend FTAs out into capacity building, co-operation in science and technology."[127] There were conversely some ANZSCEP thematic elements not covered by the TPSEPA, such as e-commerce and investment. The omission of an investment chapter in the original TPSEPA text was especially significant, although all four parties had agreed to start commence negotiations on investment by no later than 2008. Rule of origin (RoO) provisions in the two agreements were also different. In the TPSEPA, a combination of 45 and 50 percent regional value content (RVC) and change of tariff classification (CTC) rules were agreed upon. This was seen as an improvement on the ANZSCEP, which was based solely on a 40 percent RVC rule. As discussed in Chapter 4, the CTC model has become increasingly common internationally, this RoO modality believed to have the advantages of being simpler for business to comply to and easier for governments to manage. Moreover, New Zealand and Singapore based firms could use the RoO provisions of either the TPSEPA or ANZSCEP, depending on their preference. This was one technical policy solution that is relevant to the bilateral-to-plurilateral FTA evolution debate on lattice regionalism, in that exporting firms had the choice between either agreement on RoO compliance. On the one hand, this option of choice could be seen as advantage to business, but on the other hand confusion may easily arise where there exists choice between provisions from the multiple bilateral FTAs and their superseding plurilateral FTA.

Net economic benefits in question?

Of greater importance was what net economic benefits could the TPSEPA offer to its signatory parties. The trade liberalisation gains were very small as the commercial regimes of the TPSEPA partners were already very open to each other before negotiations commenced. Singapore–New Zealand bilateral trade was duty-free under the terms of the ANZSCEP. Before the TPSEPA, New Zealand also conferred duty-free entry on 67 percent of imports from Chile and 99 percent of imports from Brunei. What the Agreement had to offer on tariff liberalisation arrangements, over and above those already provided by the ANZSCEP, could be summarised as follows:

- Brunei to immediately eliminate duties on 92 percent of product lines with remaining tariffs eliminated by 2015.
- Chile to immediately eliminate duties on 89 percent of product lines with remaining tariffs eliminated by 2017.
- New Zealand to immediately eliminate duties on 96 percent of product lines with remaining tariffs eliminated by 2015 (steel and iron, cosmetics, hair care and jewellery by 2008, plasterboard and white ware goods (e.g. refrigerators) by 2010, TCF products by 2015).
- Singapore to immediately eliminate all duties on the TPSEPA entering into force.

Moreover, trade flows within the TPSEPA zone were relatively small, further diminishing the scope for net trade liberalisation benefits. For instance, Singapore–Chile bilateral trade in 2004 was just US$98 million while New Zealand's bilateral trade with Chile and Brunei amounted to only US$56 million and US$142 million respectively, and Brunei–Chile bilateral trade that year was a mere US$1 million (Appendix D).[128] The combined tariff savings for New Zealand exporters from TPSEPA tariff liberalisation was estimated at little more than US$1.5 million, though by the same token the cost of lost import tariff revenue was correspondingly low.[129] When, however, the trade gains from an FTA are minimal, the actual costs of first negotiating and then operationalising the agreement comes under closer scrutiny, as has especially been the case in audits on the US's FTA policy (see Chapter 2). The negotiating costs for TPSEPA in US dollar terms was likely to have been a good seven-figure sum, and New Zealand had estimated that the ongoing operational costs of its compliance with the Agreement was around US$100,000 annually (MFAT 2005).

In other areas of commercial regulation, a negative list was agreed upon for services sector liberalisation in relation to national treatment and market access obligations, which was seen by the negotiating parties as an advance on the ANZSCEP that took a positive list approach to listing service sector commitments. The TPSEPA also went further than the ANZSCEP on national treatment obligations in various sectors, including tax-related services, real estate, and miscellaneous civil aviation services. In addition, an MFN clause was incorporated into the Agreement whereby service suppliers from each party would be automatically conferred the same level of benefits any party made in future FTAs that were higher than those already provided by TPSEPA. In the TPSEPA negotiations, New Zealand was able to secure parity market access benefits with American firms in the Chilean and Singaporean markets in relation to the terms of the bilateral FTAs both countries had signed with the US in 2003 (MFAT 2005).

Given that TPSEPA's net trade liberalisation gains were so marginal, the 'broad band' nature of the Agreement was afforded some considerable emphasis in how it was promoted or 'sold' to stakeholders. This was of course reflected in the Agreement's actual title. While much was then made of the strategic and economic co-operation dimension, in reality there was little substance on how TPSEPA parties were going to achieve the loftily stated aims in these respects. The Agreement committed the signatory parties to engage in commercial policy co-operation that further assisted trade and investment facilitation amongst them, for example on minimising the impact of regulations and on attaining greater transparency in areas such as customs procedures, government procurement, SPS measures and other standards and conformance measures. Various sectors of economic co-operation were identified – namely research, science and technology, education, culture, and primary industry – but as with commercial policy co-operation, the text was somewhat vague on how this co-operation was going to be actualised. For example, on education TPSEPA parties would focus on, *inter alia*, "the possibility of mutual recognition of qualifications" (Chapter 16, Article 16.6 of the TPSEPA text). The main mechanism that would ensure that co-operation in these fields progressed was regular discussions at the TPSEPA Commission, a body established to oversee the implementation of the Agreement generally. In essence, the TPSEPA sought to engender further the spirit of economic co-operation between the four parties, building on existing bilateral ties and programmes but committing no party to any specific projects of co-operative venture.

Sector-specific issues

Amidst the importance afforded to advanced commercial regulation and co-operation in TPSEPA, primary sector issues were prominent in the negotiations. Primary industry trade and services trade was important for all TPSEPA parties with the exception of Singapore. For Brunei this mostly related to oil, and for Chile and New Zealand various mineral and agricultural products. For example, coal was New Zealand's single biggest export to Chile, accounting for about a quarter of total exports to the country, but various dairy products together still accounted for around half of that total. Although Chile's own dairy industry had become increasingly competitive, moving recently into a net exporting position, it was still wary of opening up its dairy market to New Zealand exporters, insisting on a special safeguard mechanism to be included in the TPSEPA whereby a six percent duty would be applied on the judgement of injurious competition from NZ dairy imports.[130] Similarly, Chile insisted that tariff liberalisation of its sugar import tariffs would only occur if another party had an exportable surplus in this sector. This may seem counter-intuitive – one party agreeing to open up its market if another had become more (and not less) of a competitive threat to the former's domestic producers – but the logic here was that Chile should not bother liberalising its sugar product sector if there were no TPSEPA partner that had any sugar to export to it in the first place, which was the reality. What Chile really wanted to avoid was setting a precedent that could be latched onto my future FTA partners, so similarities can be made here with Japan's reluctance to liberalise its farm product trade with non-agricultural Singapore in the JSEPA. Chile's tariff liberalisation phase-in schedules on dairy and other agricultural products were amongst the longest in the Agreement.

The TPSEPA partners also sought to co-operate more closely on primary industry activities. New Zealand had already bought into various Chilean concerns in the agriculture and forestry sectors. Fonterra, New Zealand's biggest dairy company, had a 51 percent majority holding in Soprole, one of Chile's big four dairy producers that had a 25 percent share of the local market in 2004, and by this time was exporting more Chilean products than it was importing from New Zealand.[131] Another New Zealand firm, Carter Holt and Fletcher, had also played a major role in the development of Chile's forestry industry (Murray and Challies 2004). Suggested areas of co-operation in primary industries would allow New Zealand to share or export its expertise in agricultural technology and machinery, and allow Singapore to do the same in the biotechnology sector, which had been recently prioritised for development.

3.10 Conclusion

Chapter 1 presented a macro perspective on the new Asia-Pacific trend, then Chapter 2 offered a more micro perspective by examining the FTA policies of key countries in the region. This chapter has taken a further micro perspective by focusing on individual FTA projects, and a number of important observations can be made from the analysis made here. We have seen how FTA project development often entails intricate bargaining processes of concession and compromise in edging forward towards a deal. From this we saw the use of different negotiating tactics in FTA talks, both when governments were dealing with their foreign counterparts or with their own domestic constituencies. Transnational coalitions can also emerge between stakeholders operating in or across FTA partner countries, especially involving business and mainly with the purpose of advocating the agreement. In some FTA projects it was noted how countries seek parity or similar preferential market access advantages as secured by others with

the same FTA partner. Understanding the interface between domestic politics and international economic relations in FTA negotiations is particularly
crucial. In this chapter, special attention was paid to the interplay of
domestic actors and their varying levels of contesting influence through
the phases of an FTA project's development. Tensions frequently arise
between domestic stakeholder groups, as we especially saw between the
business community and farmers groups, with each seeking different outcomes from FTA negotiations. The influence of key individuals in catalysing certain FTA projects was also noted in certain cases, this tending to
apply to smaller countries with their relatively small policy-making elites,
although this situation can too arise in large countries like the United
States.

For most FTA projects analysed in this chapter it was shown that negotiations on tariff liberalisation could be very time-consuming and complicated
but that bargaining on 'behind the border' market access and rights issues
(e.g. investment, IPR) could be even more so owing to the political sensitivities stirred by the perceived 'foreign meddling' of FTA partners in the
domestic affairs of the nation. This particularly was the case in the AUSFTA
and USSFTA projects. 'Broad band' FTAs have an impact that extend beyond
the economic and politico-diplomatic to include the social, cultural, environmental and other domains. As with globalisation, they can penetrate
various elements of the national political economy, thus broadening the
range of domestic stakeholders with an interest in the FTA's negotiation and
outcomes. It was noted how these outcomes can be very different, and that
there is often contestation between stakeholders and analysts regarding the
anticipated impacts of FTAs. This chapter further confirmed that agriculture
is by far the most sensitive industry sector issue in FTA negotiations within
the Asia-Pacific, and in certain cases it almost completely dominated the
talks, e.g. the JMFTA and KCFTA. Furthermore, some countries have to make
bigger adjustments and concessions than others in FTA deals. This generally
depends on the relative politico-economic power differentials between trade
partners (e.g. Singapore and the United States in USSFTA) or on economic
development levels (e.g. Thailand and Australia in TAFTA). Issues of 'asymmetry' arising from bilateral FTAs are discussed in some detail in Chapter 4,
and this next chapter will more generally examine the relationship between
bilateral FTAs and Asia-Pacific regionalism, and therein present the main
conclusions of this book's study and analysis.

Notes

1 Research interviews with foreign ambassadorial staff and research analysts, Canberra, August 2003.
2 *ABC Online* (Australia), 16.03.2003.
3 *ABC News*, 14.01.2004.
4 *Herald Sun*, 14.04.2003. The 'unnegotiability' of domestic agricultural subsidies in bilateral FTA talks has been previously discussed in Chapters 1 and 2.

5   *The Age*, 14.11.2003.
6   *EU Business*, 15.04.2003.
7   *The Age*, 14.01.2004.
8   At the time around 55 percent of commercial television primetime viewing must be Australian made.
9   *The Australian*, 30.05.2003.
10 *The Age*, 27.11.2003.
11 *Australian Financial Review*, 03.06.2003.
12 *The Age*, 23.01.2004.
13 *Reuters*, 08.02.2004.
14 *Herald Sun*, 14.06.2004.
15 *The Australian*, 22.04.2004.
16 *The Age*, 26.01.2004.
17 *The Australian*, 10.02.2004.
18 *ABC News*, 04.01.2006.
19 *International Herald Tribune*, 09.10.2000.
20 Singapore had proposed this idea at both the 2002 and 2003 APT summits (*Business Times*, 14.11.2002; *Channel News Asia*, 13.11.2003).
21 *ABS-CBN News*, 12.09.2004.
22 In ACFTA's economic co-operation framework, five priority sectors have been chosen, namely agriculture, ICT, HRD, investment and the Mekong River Basin development.
23 *The Nation*, 19.02.2004.
24 *Asia Times*, 07.07.2004.
25 *Straits Times*, 07.11.2001.
26 *China Daily*, 12.03.2002.
27 *Ibid.*
28 *China Daily*, 01.02.2002.
29 *China Daily*, 21.05.2002.
30 *China Daily [Hong Kong Edition]*, 09.01.2003.
31 *New York Times*, 13.06.2003.
32 *Straits Times*, 13.10.2003.
33 *International Herald Tribune*, 30.06.2003.
34 *Straits Times*, 13.10.2003.
35 *Straits Times*, 13.10.2003.
36 *Ibid.*
37 *Straits Times*, 10.09.2004.
38 *The Nation*, 06.06.2003.
39 Research interview with US official, Bangkok, February 2003.
40 Research interviews with Thai Government officials, Bangkok, February 2003.
41 *The Australian*, 02.10.2003.
42 *Ibid.*
43 *The Australian*, 22.04.2004.
44 *The Nation*, 22.04.2004.
45 *The Nation*, 05.01.2006.
46 *The Nation*, 21.07.2004.
47 *The Australian*, 26.01.2005.
48 Research interview, Tokyo, March 2002.
49 Negotiations on the EU–Mexico FTA were concluded in November 1999, and the Agreement came into force in July 2000.
50 *Japan Times*, 08.10.2003.

51   Pork was one of Japan's most protected agri-products overall, and a sector in significant decline with production falling by a quarter since the early 1990s, and the number of pig farmers from 30,000 to just 10,000 by 2003.
52   *Japan Times*, 28.08.2003.
53   Japan's governing Liberal Democratic Party naturally did not want to lose public support from rural voters at this time. Owing to the country's 'districting' system, a rural vote can carry twice as much weight as an urban vote. See Japan section in Chapter 2.
54   *Japan Times*, 11.09.2003. President Fox's National Action Party had also lost seats in its lower-house election for Congress the previous July, and his public support has declined amid a struggling domestic economy (*International Herald Tribune*, 19.10.2003).
55   *Japan Times*, 08.10.2003.
56   *Ibid.*
57   *International Herald Tribune*, 19.10.2003.
58   *International Herald Tribune*, 19.10.2003.
59   *Japan Times*, 08.10.2003.
60   *International Herald Tribune*, 19.10.2003.
61   *Financial Times*, 17.10.2003.
62   During the October 2003 talks, Mexican Economy Minister, Fernando Canales, found himself negotiating with three Japanese ministers – Foreign Minister Yoriko Kawaguchi, Trade Minister Shoichi Nakagawa and Agriculture Minister Yoshiyuki Kamei. Canales later told his aides that he did not want to go through similar negotiations again (*Japan Times*, 31.12.2003).
63   *Japan Times*, 16.12.2003.
64   *The Asahi Shimbun*, 11.03.2004.
65   *Japan Times*, 02.04.2005.
66   *Epoch Times* (Vietnam), 15.03.2004.
67   *Japan Times*, 02.04.2005.
68   Research interviews, Seoul, July 2002.
69   *New York Times*, 17.02.2003.
70   *Korea Herald*, 18.06.2003. The Korea Trade Promotion Agency (KOTRA) in particular had made these arguments.
71   Research interviews with South Korean Government officials, Seoul, July 2002.
72   From various research interviews, Seoul, July 2002.
73   From various research interviews, Seoul, July 2002.
74   Research interview with Korea Rural Economic Institute official, Seoul, July 2002.
75   Research interview with FKI officials, Seoul, July 2002.
76   In addition, Chile's financial market liberalisation was not extended to South Korean firms under the terms of the KCFTA. The Chilean Government also insisted at the last moment in KCFTA talks that financial market liberalisation was off limits to Korean firms. South Korea conceded this point and both sides agreed to revisit the issue in 2006.
77   *Korea Herald*, 17.06.2003.
78   Research interview with MAF official, Seoul, July 2002.
79   *Korea Herald*, 16.07.2003.
80   *Chosun Ilbo*, 13.11.2003.
81   *Korea Times*, 26.12.2003.
82   *Korea Herald*, 31.12.2003.

83   *Chosun Ilbo*, 07.01.2004.
84   In immediate preceding years, Chile's exports to South Korea were US$815 million in 1999, US$905 million in 2000, and US$696 million in 2001.
85   Previously to this, South Korea's exports to Chile had been US$455 million in 1999, US$593 million in 2000, and US$573 million in 2001.
86   *Business Day News*, 08.01.2004.
87   *Chosun Ilbo*, 17.02.2004.
88   *Chosun Ilbo*, 15.03.2005.
89   From research interview in Singapore, July 2002.
90   It was Goh who asked Clinton for a game. Their match started around midnight and was almost called off because of rain.
91   *Straits Times*, 07.12.2000.
92   Confirmed from research interviews in Singapore (July 2002) and the US (April 2003).
93   For example, American Express requested that the USTR negotiate for the opening up of Singapore's retail banking sector to American firms.
94   *Straits Times*, 02.05.2003.
95   *Straits Times*, 25.11.2002.
96   *Straits Times*, 09.05.2003.
97   A point particularly stressed by a Citibank research interviewee, New York City, April 2003.
98   This divestment was contained in a side letter signed between Singapore's Trade and Industry Minister, George Yeo, and USTR Robert Zoellick.
99   *Straits Times*, 25.11.2002.
100   *Straits Times*, 16.05.2003.
101   *Asia Times*, 07.05.2003.
102   *Straits Times*, 16.06.2003.
103   Research interview, Washington DC, April 2003.
104   Research interview, Washington DC, April 2003.
105   *Reuters*, 19.11.2002.
106   Canada and Mexico complied with this in NAFTA, and Jordan in its bilateral FTA with the US according to Singapore's *Straits Times*. We may infer Israel did not in its FTA with the US (*Straits Times*, 25.11.2002). The US also demanded that Thailand relinquish similar controls during their bilateral FTA negotiations in 2005 (*Bangkok Post*, 22.11.2005).
107   *New York Times*, 12.12.2002.
108   *Reuters*, 17.01.2003.
109   Research interviews, Washington D.C. and New York, April 2003.
110   *Straits Times*, 17.01.2003.
111   *Financial Times*, 17.03.2003. Bhagwati and Tarullo made the further point that, "Imagine that a government imposes short-term capital controls in order to manage financial problems. Compensation will ensue, but only for American investors. The citizens of the developing country will then see a rich US corporation or individual being indemnified while everyone else in the country suffers from the crisis. One would be hard-pressed to think of a better prescription for anti-American outrage."
112   Research interviews, Washington D.C. and New York, April 2003.
113   *Channel News Asia*, 27.11.2002.
114   *The Hill*, 18.06.2003.
115   *Chicago Sun Times*, 21.01.2003.

116 MTI Press Release, *Importation And Sale Of Chewing Gum With Therapeutic Value Under The US–Singapore Free Trade Agreement,* 12 July 2003.
117 *Reuters,* 17.03.2004.
118 *Channel News Asia,* 31.03.2004.
119 *Straits Times,* 24.05.2004.
120 Research interview with APEC member state ex-trade minister.
121 *Straits Times,* 19.10.2001.
122 *Channel News Asia,* 27.10.2002.
123 *Channel News Asia,* 21.08.2004.
124 Brunei signed these in August 2005. Brunei also had two years thereafter to negotiate with other TPSEPA parties on its service sector commitments.
125 Research interview, Wellington, August 2003.
126 Research interview with MFAT official, Wellington, August 2003.
127 *Business Day* (South Africa), 04.05.2004.
128 Chile was ranked 51st in New Zealand's export destinations and 47th in source of imports, while Brunei was ranked 115th and 20th respectively.
129 Estimated to be around US$230,000 annually for New Zealand (MFAT 2005).
130 Chile then applied a six percent flat tariff rate on virtually all imports.
131 *New Zealand Herald,* 18.08.2004.

4
New FTAs in the Asia-Pacific: Towards Lattice Regionalism?

4.1 Introduction

Chapter 1 presented an overview of the new FTA trend in the Asia-Pacific, which has been a predominantly bilateral FTA trend. Chapter 2 then examined the FTA policies of various Asia-Pacific countries, and this was followed in Chapter 3 by case studies on individual FTA projects. Together, these chapters provided wide-ranging macro and micro perspectives on the region's FTA trend. In this chapter, we discuss the broader international political economy implications of this new trade bilateralism, particularly regarding its impact upon economic regionalism in the Asia-Pacific. The relationship between economic bilateralism and regionalism has become an increasingly important to understand given the intensification of both forms of international association and linkage not just in the Asia-Pacific but also in other regions. We first analyse the nature and development of economic bilateralism and regionalism before presenting the 'lattice regionalism' hypothesis, which posits that an increasingly dense pattern of bilateral FTA activity positively contributes to regionalism processes and to regional community-building generally. The analytical framework for the lattice regionalism hypothesis is set out based on the two counter-perspectives of 'region-convergent' bilateralism and 'region-divergent' bilateralism. This framework is then applied to the evidence arising under various key issues relating to the new Asia-Pacific FTA trend, these being previously noted or discussed to some extent in earlier chapters, such as the 'spaghetti bowl' problem, competitive liberalisation and hub-and-spoke patterns of FTA formation.

4.2 Economic bilateralism and regionalism in perspective

4.2.1 Historic overview of economic bilateralism

Bilateral trade agreements have been a contentious issue in the economics and international political economy literature for some time (Cadot *et al*

2001; Collie 1997; Deardorff and Stern 1994; Freund 2000; Goyal and Joshi 1999; Krugman 1991; Riezman 1999; Westhoff *et al* 1994). Bilateral economic alliances between states have a generally longer history than their regional-level counterparts (notwithstanding imperial or commonwealth-based multi-nation arrangements), mainly because they have been much easier to arrange owing to various political, geographic, economic and socio-cultural factors. For some time, these were invariably embedded within bilateral security alliances, although there was a growth of 'non-embedded' bilateral trade agreements after the Second World War (Irwin 1993; Kennedy 1988; Powers 2004).

Bilateral trade agreements (BTAs) can be dated back to ancient history. In modern historic terms, the 1703 Methuen Treaty between England and Portugal is often cited as a landmark agreement, not just due to its longevity but also because it was in many ways a precursor to modern commercial agreements. The Methuen Treaty conferred preferential access to Portuguese wines in the English market and English woollens to the Portuguese market, thus allowing each country to expand specialisation through trade in industries where each had particular competitive advantages. It was not, though, until the mid-19th century that BTAs began to proliferate, and as with regionalism it was Europe where this activity was primarily concentrated. The Anglo-French commercial treaty of 1860 spurred other nations to sign similar trade agreements to counter the expected trade diversion from the integration of Europe's two largest economies. Under the 1860 Treaty's provisions, Britain agreed to make its own tariff reductions universally applicable to all nations (i.e. 'most favoured nation', or MFN, treatment), while France lowered its duties on British imports only, adopting a dual system of relatively lower tariff rates for MFN-selected countries and higher rates for others. A cascade of bilateral trade agreements subsequently followed as third countries sought equal market access rights in the French market.

Between 1861 and 1866, France concluded separate bilateral agreements with Austria, Belgium, Italy, Netherlands, Norway, Spain, Sweden, Switzerland and the German *Zollverein* states. These were not full FTAs but the tariff reductions involved were significant. Moreover they contained unconditional MFN clauses whereby any future reduction in tariff rates to other MFN trade partners would be applied between all bilateral signatories. Irwin (1993) observed that this treaty network "extended the coverage of low tariffs to virtually all of Europe" (p. 97) during the latter 19th century. As most countries in the continent sought MFN treatment with others, this helped advance trade liberalisation in a region that accounted for a huge share of global trade, not least because European colonial trade was generally incorporated into this MFN trade network. Irwin concluded that, "a single bilateral agreement to reduce tariffs blossomed into dozens of bilateral accords, resulting in an effectively multilateral arrangement under which international trade entered an unprecedented liberal era" (1993: 97). While these bilateral agreements were subject to periodic review, there was in practice a limited commitment to progress toward further lowering of tariff levels, and moreover many agreements were open to expire after a time.

At the beginning of the 20th century, Britain had concluded BTAs with 46 states, Germany with 30 states, and France with more than 20 states. According to Irwin (1993), this 'progressive bilateralism' as he called it made a significant contribution to the development of European regional integration during the late 19th and early 20th centuries. Furthermore, he argues these agreements helped create a relatively open global commercial environment in which average tariff levels were gradually reduced over the period, partly through this MFN-based bilateralism that acted as a surrogate multilateral system. Indeed, the 1860–1914 international trade system has strong similarities with the post-1947 General Agreement on Tariffs and Trade (GATT) system in that unconditional MFN treatment prevailed – amongst 'treaty signatories' rather than 'member states' – and that MFN coverage was in the former case, as Irwin put it, "effectively multilateral via bilateral agreements" (p. 99). Today, the WTO is, of course, the custodian of MFN trade and separate bilateral agreements are no substitute for a global multilateral system of trade rules. Moreover, today's bilateral FTAs, whether in the Asia-Pacific or elsewhere, are non-MFN agreements, being essentially preferential in nature by not extending the trade liberalisation agreed between bilateral trade partners to others.

Returning to the historic path of trade bilateralism, the First World War disrupted the growth of both bilateral and regional trade agreements only for a few years. When the trend resumed in the early 1920s, new agreements emerged in a more adversarial trading environment marked by protectionist inter-bloc competition. Attempts were made during the mid-1920s to restore the MFN-based liberal trading environment, culminating at the 1927 World Economic Conference where delegates called for the reduction of trade barriers and the restoration of effective MFN trade. The revised Franco-German trade agreement signed in the same year readopted the MFN clause, and there was also a sharp increase in the number of countries linked by commercial treaties by the following year, rising from 30 in 1927 to 42 by 1928. At the same time, average tariff levels between the major trading powers began to fall again. However, the onset of economic depression abruptly reversed this trend as countries sought to safeguard their domestic markets with protectionist measures. Tariff rate hikes ensued across Europe in the latter half of 1929. In addition, the US's introduction of the Smoot-Hawley tariff in June 1930 led to another round of retaliatory tariff rises, with the agriculture sector particularly protected against foreign imports.

The great powers concluded trade agreements with certain security allies and other nations in their sphere of influence e.g. colonies. At the same time they raised their trade barriers against non-signatories, thus leading to significant trade diversion. Examples of these trade agreements included the French imperial customs union established in 1928, the British Commonwealth system of preferences formed in 1932, various bilateral treaties signed by Germany, the 20 or so bilateral commercial agreements signed by the US with mostly Latin American countries, and Japan's expanding Greater East Asia Co-Prosperity Sphere. Irwin (1993) referred to this phase of trade agreements as 'pernicious bilateralism', characterised by the application of various quantitative restrictions and other discriminatory trade barriers on third country imports. The volume of world trade declined 40 percent over 1929 to 1932, and world output by 20 percent. The debate over whether these trade agreements deepened the global economic depression of the era and exacerbated the political tensions that culminated in the Second World War continues (Oye 1992; Winham 1992). A strong postwar consensus emerged for creating a multilateral trade system that would prevent the emergence of rival trade blocs, whether founded on bilateral or regional alliances. The then newly formed GATT framework was charged with this responsibility, and codified rules that aimed to minimise a bilateral or regional trade agreement's discriminatory side-effects (see Chapter 1).[1] Chapter 1 also discusses how one of the key challenges confronting the WTO today has been the proliferation of bilateral FTAs, especially since the mid-1990s. There are more bilateral FTAs now than there has ever been, and the Asia-Pacific region is responsible for much of this recent growth in trade bilateralism.

4.2.2   Regionalism in perspective

There are various contesting discourses on regionalism and an expanding range of regionalism typologies have arisen therein. One explanation for this is that different forms of regionalism have evolved over time in response to changing conditions and developments within the international system, e.g. globalising processes. In general terms, regionalism may be generally viewed as the structures, processes and arrangements that are working towards greater coherence within a specific international or global region in terms of economic, political, security, sociocultural and other such linkages (Fawcett and Hurrell 1995; Gamble and Payne 1996; Hettne *et al* 1999). More specifically, economic regionalism can arise either: (i) as a result of public policy initiatives, such as an FTA or other state-led projects of economic co-operation and integration that originate from inter-governmental dialogues and treaties; or (ii) from more micro-level processes that stem from a regional concentration of private or civil sector activities, such as intensifying international trade between firms within a particular regional zone, which may be more distinctly referred to as 'regionalisation'. In this context, economic bilateralism (rather than 'bilateralisation') may be viewed in similar terms to the type (i) definition of regionalism above, but where just two trade partners are involved.

Regionalism has been a defining feature of the international system for some time. Putting aside examples of coercive imperial regionalism, integrational arrangements that emerged in 19th century Europe, such as the *Zollverein* customs union between 18 different German states, are often cited as the historic antecedents of regionalism.[2] However, imperialism remained the main norm or determinant of regional or trans-regional integration up until World War Two. In the early post-war period, Europe was again the global focal point of regionalism, embarking on new ambitious regionalist projects, the most important being the European Economic Community (EEC) founded by the 1957 Treaty of Rome.

Chapter 1 has already noted the progressive stages of economic integration that can occur from *free trade agreements* to *customs unions* to *common markets*. This draws originally upon the work of Viner (1950), later refined and built upon by Meade (1955), Gehrels (1956), Lipsey (1957), Balassa (1961) and Michaely (1965). *Economic and monetary union* is considered the fourth progressive stage of regional integration whereby a common currency and finance policy is established to optimise the workings of the common market. The European Union (EU) remains the only regional group that has substantively implemented this stage of regional integration. Moreover, the EU remains the world's most comprehensive and sophisticated form of regionalism by far. During much of the Cold War period, Euro-centric theories (e.g. functionalism, neo-functionalism, neo-federalism, inter-governmentalism) and empirics on regionalism dominated the field. Other regions invariably looked to Europe as the model on which to develop their own regionalist projects. This usually focused on the progressive linear stages of integration noted above that concomitantly entailed a gradual institution-building process, such as establishing supranational agencies (e.g. the European Commission) charged with overseeing integrational projects.[3] The European model of regionalism was thus a technocratically constructed, treaty-driven process of inter-state regional co-operation and integration.

Towards the end of the 1980s, other regions with markedly different politico-economic traditions, such as East Asia and the Asia-Pacific, began to question the usefulness of emulating the European model of regionalism (Katzenstein 2000; Poon 2001). This was based on the argument that the development of regionalism was always embedded in a specific set of economic, socio-cultural, political and historic path dependent factors, which therefore did not lend to uniformity of experience (Hettne and Soderbaum 2000; Wallace 1994). Furthermore, major structural transformations in the international system, primarily arising from the end of the Cold War from the early 1990s onwards, presented opportunities for new innovative forms of regionalism to emerge (Milner 1992). The 'open regionalism' principles on which the Asia-Pacific Economic Co-operation (APEC) forum was originally established is a case in point and discussed later in the chapter. In addition to the EU and APEC, other prominent regional economic groupings to have emerged by the 1990s included the North American Free Trade Agreement (NAFTA), Mercosur (Southern Common Market), the Central American Common Market (CACM), the Gulf Cooperation Council (GCC), the Caribbean Community and Common Market (CARICOM), the South African Development Community (SADC), the South Asian Association for Regional Co-operation (SAARC), and ASEAN, the Association of South East Asian Nations.

Ideas that challenged the Euro-centric dominance in regional integration studies became collectively known as 'new regionalism' theory (NRT). Amongst NRT's foremost theorists and works were Fawcett and Hurrell (1995), Gamble and Payne (1996), Hettne and Inotai (1994), Hettne *et al* (1999), Mansfield and Milner (1998), Marchand *et al* (1999) and Stroper (1997). Globalisation provides an important context to the development of new regionalism. The past emphasis on introverted, defensive regional blocs during the Cold War bipolarity period has given way to more outward-looking and flexible forms of regional co-operation and integration in a world where trade and other economic barriers between global regions (e.g. Europe, East Asia, Latin America) are diminishing whilst global systems of connectivity between them are strengthening. Moreover, (new) regionalism, regionalisation and globalisation are all seen as part of the same broad process of increasing integration, interdependence and connectivity between internationally dispersed economic activities, agents and material aspects of the world economy.

Various disciplinary fields have contributed to NRT's development, most importantly from international political economy, political science, international relations, sociology and economic geography. This more multi-disciplinary approach marked a shift away from the more narrow economistic approach and its limitations in understanding both the fuller political, social and other causes and consequences of economic regionalism (Mansfield and Milner 1999). Furthermore, new regionalism theorists have sought to broaden our understanding of what we mean by 'region'. Rafael (1999) for instance suggests that a region may be defined as "that which can be alternately or simultaneously appear in various guises: politically as an administrative unit, culturally as an ethnic enclave or linguistic community, economically as zones of production and exchange" (p. 1208). Economic geographers have particularly highlighted how the transnational business activities and systems are creating new regional (or sub-regional) economic spaces that cut across national economies (Olds *et al* 1999; Borrus *et al* 2000). The business or market-led driving forces behind this trend is perhaps better characterised as regionalisation rather than regionalism, although governments do invariably foster the development of these so called 'growth triangles' or 'growth polygons' (e.g. the Indonesia-Malaysia-Singapore Growth Triangle, Tumen River Area Development Project, Greater Mekong Sub-region project) that are notably prevalent in East Asia. The key point made by economic geographers is we need to think about regional or sub-regional economic coalescence in different spatial terms than before in which regionalist projects comprised a collection of whole national economies with neatly defined borders. Furthermore, the increasing irrelevance of distance in a globalising world economy has led to countries from different regions to sign a growing number of trans-regional economic agreements, such as the Trans-Pacific Strategic Economic Partnership Agreement (TPSEPA) and Bangkok Agreement discussed later in this chapter. Moreover, some Asia-Pacific bilateral FTA partners (e.g. South Korea and Chile) are virtually antipodean in their relative geographic position. Advances in transportation and communication technologies are diminishing the cost and logistical constraints on developing trans-regional trade alliances. This is highly relevant to Asia-Pacific given its hemispheric proportions.

The social construction of regions, and therein regionalism itself, is another distinctive strand to new regionalism theory, although sociological perspectives on regional group development date back a while. For example, during the time of the EEC's emergence, Deutsch (1957) contended that increased communication amongst states can help create a sense of community amongst them by developing trust, establishing mutual interests and an appropriation of 'we-ness'. Wendt (1992), Hurrell (1995) and others have brought new social constructivist ideas and perspectives to the study of regionalism. According to Wendt (1992), growing interdependences within a globalising world are creating new transnational communities of common interest, and a sense of 'region-ness' derives from this process where patterns of economic and political transactions and social communications are concentrated within particular regional spaces, that may in turn be differentiated from other regionalised communities. In a similar vein, Jayasuriya (1994) argued that, "regionalism is a set of cognitive practices shaped by language and political discourse, which through the creation of concepts, metaphors, analogies, determine how the region is defined; these serve to define the actors who are included (and excluded) within the region and thereby enable the emergence of a regional entity and identity" (p. 412). An ideational dimension or foundation to any regionalist project is thus essential (Breslin and Higgott 2000). For Hurrell (1995) the study of regionalism entails the method of "conceptualising the interaction between material incentives, inter-subjective structures, and the identity and interests of the actors" (p. 72) with regard to the region concerned and conceptualised four different phases of 'regionness', namely:

- *regional space*: the spatial or territorial dimension in which a group of people live within a geographically bounded community, rooting regionness in territory.
- *regional complex*: increased social contacts and transactions within a specified regional space, but these can be both positive and negative. The emergence of a regional complex leads to ever widening trans-local relations.
- *regional society*: as regionalisation intensifies, so do different actors from the region associate with each other in a transcendence of national space. A regional society emerges from the intensified communication and interaction between multiple actors within the specified regional space.
- *regional community*: the development of the region "into an active subject with a distinct identity, institutionalised or informal actor capability, legitimacy and structure of decision-making in relation with a more or less responsive regional civil society, transcending old state borders" (Hurrell 1995: 466).

Following on from the last and most developed of these categories, we may posit that common identity and common interest formation are central to the idea of *regional community-building*, and that region-wide phenomena such as the new Asia-Pacific FTA trend must bring coherence to these processes if they are adjudged to be making a positive contribution to regional community-building *per se*. More generally, whereas traditional regionalism theory is primarily focused on state actors, NRT stresses the importance of non-state actors and multilateral institutions in the development of regionalism, in its various guises. There is hence corresponding plurality in both the different forms of regionalism and the different stakeholder influences that can shape its nature and direction. In sum, *new regionalism* may be contrasted with its more traditional Euro-centric counterpart by its particular emphasis on: multiple and co-existent levels and forms of regional co-operation and integration (e.g. state-driven, market-driven; sub-regional, trans-regional); a less technocratically determined and more socially constructed or ideational view to understanding regional community-building; the connections between regionalism and extra-regional processes and structures at the global and multilateral levels. New regionalism theory has thus helped open up a wider scholarly debate on different ideas and kinds of regionalism that are emerging in the contemporary world order. Our discussion on the lattice regionalism hypothesis, which examines the relationship between economic bilateralism and regionalism, forms part of that debate.

4.2.3 Regionalism in East Asia and the Asia-Pacific: an introductory overview

As with bilateralism, the development of regionalism has been quite mixed across the Asia-Pacific region. Regionalist projects in Pacific America – especially involving Latin American states – have existed for some time and are quite pervasive, e.g. CACM, NAFTA. In East Asia, it is deepening regionalisation rather than regionalism that has primarily bound together the region's economies more closely together over recent decades, driven first by the regional production networks established by Japanese MNEs (the so called 'flying geese' model of regionalisation) and then by other forms of transnationalised business activities, such as the aforementioned sub-regional 'growth triangles' or 'growth polygons' (Ng and Yeats 2003). Trade statistics indicate the extent to which East Asia's regionalisation and economic interdependence have deepened in recent years. Since the 1980s, East Asia's intra-regional trade ratio has nearly doubled, from 23 percent in 1980 to 41 percent by 2004.[4] In absolute terms, East Asia's intra-regional trade volume had increased almost eightfold from 1985 to 2004, and stood at over US$300 billion in 2004 (IMF 2005).

Only in Southeast Asia is there orthodox trade regionalism – the ASEAN Free Trade Area (AFTA) project – whereas Northeast Asia remains the world's most significant region without such a project. The ASEAN Plus Three (APT) framework – created in the wake of the 1997/98 financial crisis and comprising the ASEAN group plus Japan, China and South Korea – has provided a much stronger basis for deepening economic regionalism in East Asia. To date, though, the APT framework has concentrated more on enhancing regional financial integration (i.e. financial regionalism) rather than specifically trade integration, with Japan taking an initial lead through the 1998 New Miyazawa Initiative and other co-operative diplomacy measures (Dieter and Higgott 2003; Hughes 2000; Hund 2003; Kikuchi 2002; Stubbs 2002; Terada 2003).[5] There is also the continuing debate over whether supposedly shared 'Asian values' may be considered a foundation on which Hurrell's (1995) previously noted forms of 'regional society' or 'regional community' could emerge (Nabers 2003; Terada 2003). We should also note how APEC represents an ambitious attempt to bind all Asia-Pacific states together in the world's largest trans-regional grouping, and through its founding principles of 'open regionalism' has sought to explicitly highlight the linkages between regionalism, multilateralism and globalisation – this being that regionalist projects can, at least in theory, make positive contributions to the development of the multilateral trade system and wider globalising processes (see introductions to AFTA and APEC in Chapter 1).

With the above in mind, East Asian and Asia-Pacific experiences of regionalism have probably offered more empirical substance for new regionalism theory than any other region. New economic geography and social constructivist approaches are especially useful when analysing new developments in East Asian regionalism. At the same time, the complex diversity of East Asia and the Asia-Pacific, in terms of economic, political and socio-cultural heterogeneity, does place particular constraints on advancing regional economic co-operation and integration (Dent 2003b; Jayasuriya 2004; Katzenstein 1997; Krumm and Kharas 2004; Petri 1993; Ravenhill 2002). As Petri (1993) has commented, "the development of regional institutions [in East Asia] is complicated by both the diversity of the region's countries and by the preferences of many of the region's countries for informal, negotiated (as opposed to legalistic) approaches to policy" (p. 43). This complex diversity explains to some extent why FTA bilateralism maybe preferred to pan-regional economic projects, such as an East Asia Free Trade Area (EAFTA), because bilateral FTAs offer paths of least resistance by comparison with regard to forging integrative links amongst the region's economies.

Interestingly, bilateralism has also been the preferred route of choice regarding the APT framework's first centrepiece project, the Chiang Mai Initiative (CMI), which consists of a series of bilateral currency swap agreements between APT member states. A currency swap is an agreement to exchange one currency for another and to reverse the transaction at some later date. Under the CMI, those East Asian countries with large amounts of foreign currency reserves are thus willing to 'swap' some of their hard (i.e. more stable) currency (e.g. dollars, yen) for weaker local currencies (e.g. Indonesian rupiah) when under attack from market speculators. The aim here is to restore some stability in the financial system and position of these weaker currency economies and thus try to head off a full-blown crisis. Although the amounts of foreign exchange committed to the CMI system are relatively low, at just over US$40 billion by 2005, it does mark an important step forward in cultivating regional financial co-operation in East Asia. Thus, the relationship between economic bilateralism and economic regionalism in East Asia has both trade and finance dimensions through bilateral FTAs and the CMI's bilateral currency swap agreements respectively. Further discussion on different aspects of East Asian and Asia-Pacific regionalism is made throughout the remainder of this chapter.

4.2.4 Bilateralism and regionalism in other regions: Europe and Latin America

In this section we examine the relationship between bilateral FTAs and regional trade integration in two other regions – Europe and Latin America – where both activities have been prominent. The main purpose of this comparative analysis is to consider whether some form of lattice regionalism has emerged elsewhere in the international economic system. This serves as a reference point for our discussion on the Asia-Pacific and the lattice regionalism hypothesis.

Europe

As previously noted in Chapter 1, Europe remains the world's main hub for FTA activity, centred on the European Union. The EU is itself the world's most sophisticated form of regional economic integration, and its bilateral FTAs with prospective member states on its periphery (mostly in East Europe) are essentially part of a pre-accession conditioning process that help these countries assimilate into the EU's various commercial regimes, which includes rules on trade, investment, competition policy, intellectual property rights, industrial standards, and so on. The EU has even promoted sets of pre-accession countries forming regional FTAs between themselves (e.g. the Central Europe Free Trade Area, or CEFTA, and the Baltic Free Trade Area, or BAFTA) as practice for joining the larger EU regional trade arrangement. The EU broadly determines the terms and conditions of its pre-accession bilateral FTAs, with for example very similar modalities on rules of origin (RoO) and commercial liberalisation applied to all agreements.[6] Thus, a hub-and-spokes pattern of FTA activity is clearly evident in Europe (Wonnacott 1996).[7] The number of spokes will of course diminish as EU enlargement progresses, as occurred most recently in May 2004 when ten East European states joined the EU, consequently subsuming 31 bilateral FTAs into an expanded Single European Market.

Europe's hub-spoke pattern of FTA activity does comply to the lattice regionalism hypothesis to some degree in that the bilateral FTAs concerned are formed with a view to enhancing regional economic integration and regional community-building generally. Moreover, the pre-accession process has also entailed a profusion of bilateral FTA links between different candidate countries, such as between CEFTA and BAFTA countries, as part of laying a wider foundation for the Single European Market's expansion into East Europe (see Chapter 1). As the EU enlarges further, so most likely will new FTA spoke linkages with new periphery states, for example with ex-Soviet republics like Moldova and Ukraine. Whether this process is best characterised by 'expanding hub regionalism' or 'lattice regionalism' is a debateable point. The Asia-Pacific does have 'hub' powers (the US, Japan and China) but no singular dominate hub power that lies at the determining centre of the regional economic integration process, and this is what makes the EU unique globally. A more polycentric pattern of hub-and-spoke FTA activity is apparent in the Asia-Pacific region as we later discuss.

Latin America

The concentration of FTA activity in Latin America (i.e. South and Central America) is second only to Europe amongst the world's regions, not including the Asia-Pacific 'trans-region'. As Chapter 1 details, it has been host to a relatively large number of well established regional and bilateral FTAs. Regional FTAs comprise Mercosur, the Andean Community, CACM and CARICOM. Ill fated attempts had been made previously to create a pan-regional FTA, including the Latin American Free Trade Association (LAFTA), established by the Montevideo Agreement of February 1960 between Mexico and the Spanish and Portuguese speaking nations of South America. The envisaged free trade area never materialised and LAFTA subsequently folded. This was superseded by the less ambitious Latin American Integration Association (LAIA/Aladi) in 1980 that still binds together the ex-LAFTA countries in its membership, but whose organisational apparatus wields limited power amongst them. The LAIA exists as an umbrella organisation whose main function is to act as a forum for bilateral and sub-regional sectoral negotiations and agreements between members. Many so called bilateral Economic Complementary Agreements (ECAs) were signed between Latin American countries as part of the LAIA framework. ECAs are sub-FTA arrangements in terms of both their scope and depth of trade liberalisation, thus being 'partial scope' agreements, and these were later superseded by more comprehensive FTAs that were aligned more with NAFTA norms and modalities than those from the LAIA framework. Indeed, NAFTA has had a particularly notable influence on FTA activity in Latin America, with many of the region's countries seeking new NAFTA-consistent or compatible FTAs in order to themselves follow Mexico's lead in securing a free trade pact with the US (Estevadeordal 2002; Salazar-Xirinachs 2001).

Table 1.4 in Chapter 1 shows that various bilateral FTAs between Latin American countries operate on a country-to-country (e.g. Chile–Mexico) and country-to-regional group (Costa Rica–CARICOM, Panama–CACM) basis. While some degree of consistency with the aforementioned NAFTA norms and modalities prevails amongst these agreements, Estevadeordal (2002) notes that there exists significant heterogeneity in terms of tariff liberalisation phase-in schedules, RoOs and other technical policy aspects. This is particularly relevant to plans to create a Free Trade Area of the Americas (FTAA) across the whole Western Hemisphere, which was first proposed at the All-Americas summit of December 1994 in Miami between 34 American nations with the initial aim of establishing the FTAA by the end of 2005. The United States has strongly advocated NAFTA as the benchmark for the FTAA, including the incorporation of environmental and social clauses that many Latin American countries remain unenthusiastic about. However, Brazil in looking to play a sub-regional leadership role in South America has challenged the US's assumed hegemonic position in FTAA negotiations, championing the simpler Mercosur model as an alternative to NAFTA. As Phillips (2004) argued, "While it would not do to overstate [Brazil's] opposition to the idea of an FTAA itself, Brazilian engagement in the hemispheric process is premised on the construction of sub-regional leadership as a means of steering the hemispheric process away from unilateral US dominance" (p. 12).

At the Fourth Summit of the Americas held in November 2005, 29 of the 34 American nations agreed to proceed with FTAA negotiations, with the four Mercosur nations (Brazil, Argentina, Paraguay, Uruguay) plus Venezuela opting to re-examine their position after the WTO Ministerial Meeting the following month in Hong Kong. The failure to conclude a Doha Round agreement at Hong Kong in December 2005 led to the five nations further prolonging their decision on the FTAA talks. There was solidarity amongst Mercosur nations to maintain the salience of their sub-regional grouping and the principles of mutual co-operation on which the region integration arrangement was based, in preference to a US-led regional trade liberalisation project that was believed would primarily serve US commercial interests and further bind Latin America into the US sphere of influence.[8]

To conclude, it was Pacific America where FTA activity was already quite well established before the new Asia-Pacific FTA trend took off, and there are grounds for arguing that a lattice regionalism dynamic has played out in Latin America to some extent, with the LAIA framework and NAFTA's norms and modalities setting certain parameters for FTA practice conducive to bilateral-to-regional FTA evolution arising within the region. However, the problems with advancing the pan-regional FTAA project have been noted, especially in relation to the Mercosur nations' resistance to subsuming their trade block into a more NAFTA-oriented arrangement. This relates to the key issue of FTA hub or FTA model competition that is discussed later in the chapter.

4.3 The lattice regionalism hypothesis

4.3.1 Introduction

The simultaneous intensification of economic bilateralism and regionalism in recent years is constituent to the broader integrational trend of globalisation. Moreover, given their rising prominence in the global political economy, the interface between economic bilateralism and regionalism has become critically important to understand with primary regard to their compatibility, and also how this in turn affects the new multi-layered economic relationships and governance structures being forged by these twin processes. A core objective of this book's study is to consider whether bilateral FTAs are making positive contributions towards regional community-building in the Asia-Pacific. This in essence is the lattice regionalism hypothesis: to what extent in this FTA bilateralism precursory to the development of East Asian or Asia-Pacific's economic regionalism. The analytical framework that will examine this hypothesis is based on the two counter-perspectives of 'region-convergent' bilateralism and 'region-divergent' bilateralism. Taking these in turn, *region-convergent bilateralism* broadly posits that intensifying bilateralism can make positive contributions to the development of regionalism, and hence this supports the lattice regionalism hypothesis. In contrast, *region-divergent bilateralism* posits that that intensifying bilateralism within a region undermines the development of regionalism. This, then, rejects the lattice regionalism hypothesis and questions the contributions that bilateral FTAs are supposedly making to regional community-building within the Asia-Pacific. Theorisation on these two counter-perspective concepts is presented that centre on specified 'points of contention'. These are quite general in nature and relate to the politico-diplomatic, economic, technical policy, regional organisation and development-related dimensions of regionalism.

4.3.2   Region-convergent bilateralism

Sub-structural foundation for regionalism

The first region-convergent point of contention posits that intensifying bilateralism may provide a sub-structural foundation for regionalism to develop. This is primarily founded on the argument that a gradual evolutionary process of bilateral-to-plurilateral rationalisation may eventually lead to regional-level agreements and forms of co-operation arising, and this should be particularly expected where a dense and overlapping spread of bilateral agreements is evident. There are two main dimensions to this, the first being the technical policy dimension. For example, if three or four states have separate bilateral FTA links with each other, significant technical policy and commercial benefits can be realised by rationalising these into one unified plurilateral or sub-regional FTA arrangement. Having one set of unified rules would help negate the so called 'spaghetti bowl' problem discussed later of having different sets of trade rules for each separate bilateral FTA. The politico-diplomatic dimension concerns how dense FTA bilateralism can create a networked community of political leaders, policy-makers and other FTA-advocating stakeholders within a region from which comes the consensus and political will to create enlarged or regional FTAs. In both technical policy and politico-diplomatic terms, the perceived benefits of this 'rationalised bilateralism' become greater as the number of bilaterally linked states increases.

Congruent processes and objectives

The second region-convergent point of contention posits that bilateralism and regionalism are engaged in congruent processes and objectives. In other words, bilateralism and regionalism may be involved in serving similar ends, and even working in concert with the other. This is particularly relevant to regional organisations such as APEC, APT and ASEAN. Hence for this to apply, bilateral FTAs must enhance existing forms of regionalism and contribute to their further development, not undermining their coherence. Each regional community-building project sets itself objectives and a *modus operandi* of processes by which these objectives are to be achieved. The Bogor Goals project of APEC, in which a free trade and investment zone is to be created in the Asia-Pacific by 2020 in accordance with the 'open regionalism' process, is an example of this, and a key issue we discuss later in the chapter. Whereas, then, the first point of contention is primarily concerned with *structure*, this point is more concerned with *process*. Of course, there is a significant degree of co-determinacy at work: structure and process advance interactively.

Preliminary conditioning to regional economic liberalisation and integration

The third region-convergent point of contention relates to how bilateral FTAs help economic agents (e.g. firms, consumers) become more conditioned to foreign competition through market opening effects. This is an important preliminary stage of gradualised adjustment to economic liberalisation and integration at the regional level, whether this is entailed in membership of existing regional organisations (e.g. AFTA and ASEAN, the Bogor Goals and APEC) or in the development of new regional projects, such as the idea of an East Asia Free Trade Area discussed in the APT framework. Domestic firms (especially protected ones) may resist proposals to suddenly open up home markets to all their regional competitors without the preliminary conditioning stages provided by bilateral FTA liberalisation and integration. Bilateral FTAs may also help build public support amongst consumer groups for wider regional FTAs if bilateral arrangements first demonstrate price reduction effects through the lowering of trade barriers.

4.3.3 Region-divergent bilateralism

Undermining or capturing effects

The first region-divergent point of contention posits that intensified bilateralism may undermine the integrity or capture key aspects of regional organisations. This may arise from the objectives and actions of bilateral partnerships being essentially inconsistent with those of the regional organisation to which both parties belong, or by a certain bilateral partnership dominating the organisation's agenda at the expense of other member state interests. There may be politico-diplomatic and technical policy aspects to this, as we later examine. Furthermore, this takes the counter-view to the second region-convergent point of contention on *congruent objectives and processes* and is also particularly relevant to the relationship between bilateral FTAs and APEC-led economic regionalism in the Asia-Pacific. In addition, a profusion of bilateral economic agreements, like FTAs, can create a complex set of preference-based rules that fracture a region's commercial regulatory environment, consequently undermining attempts at harmonising the technical policy aspects required to foster economic regionalism.

Intensifying bilateralism and inter-state rivalry

The second region-divergent point of contention posits that deepening bilateralism within a region can create increasingly convoluted patterns of reactive counter-balancing manoeuvres amongst the region's constituent states, leading to potentially hazardous inter-state rivalry. There is a switch of emphasis here in relation to dense bilateralism, from the 'co-operative' international relations view normally associated with neo-liberal institutionalism – that would suggest the creation of further interdependent conditions from which we should expect regionalism to flourish – to the 'competitive' inter-state behaviour perspective offered by neo-realist analysis. According to this point, competitive bilateralism makes it difficult to cultivate regional partnerships through the more adversarial environment of international economic relations that bilateral FTAs create.

Reinforced power asymmetries

The third region-divergent point of contention posits that unchecked bilateralism serves to further exaggerate or reinforce power asymmetries within a region, which in turn may work against regional community-building. This follows on from the second region-divergent point of contention in that bilateralism often works in favour of *realpolitik* as it allows stronger and more resourceful partners to broker better deals, which in turn are not cushioned by the checks and balances otherwise provided by regional or multilateral organisations, where the power of big trade partners is to some extent circumscribed by the collective membership of that organisation.

Exacerbating the development divide

The fourth region-divergent point of contention concerns how economic bilateralism may exacerbate the existing development divide within a region or regional organisation. This may particularly arise where the bilateral partners concerned explicitly or implicitly prescribe to economic Darwinism, whereby those states in a region with stronger technocratic, institutional and industrial capacities are able to run much further ahead of 'weak capacity' states by actually being able to sign bilateral FTAs in the first place. While this approach may be deemed pragmatic given extant development asymmetry within the regional group, it risks making that asymmetry even more pronounced, thus making regional community-building more difficult to achieve.

4.4   Key issues of debate

In this section we cover the key issues of debate relating to the FTA bilateralism–regionalism relationship, and therein evaluation of the lattice regionalism hypothesis. Different points of contention under region-convergent and region-divergent bilateralism earlier outlined will brought to bear according to their relevance in each debate. The key issues debated are: the 'spaghetti bowl' problem; the politico-diplomatic discourse on lattice regionalism; competitive liberalisation; hubs, spokes and contesting FTA models; APEC and FTAs; developing countries and FTAs.

4.4.1 The 'spaghetti bowl' problem

The problem outlined

The so called 'spaghetti bowl' problem was first coined by Bhagwati (1995), and essentially relates to technical policy dimension of FTAs. Previous chapters have discussed the matter of FTA heterogeneity and how significant technical policy variance exists between different agreements in terms of rules of origin, scope and implementation schedules of liberalisation, customs procedures, and 'FTA plus' or 'broad band' elements. Complying with different bilateral FTA rules can impose significant managerial and transaction costs on firms, incurred by having to first identify which specific rules apply to what trading activity and then take differentiated actions (e.g. in production, distribution, customs compliance, etc.) in accordance to those rules. Different product-specific phase-in schedules adds a temporal dimension to this, that is these rules may change over time and therefore need to be tracked, often up to 20 or 25 years.

The spaghetti bowl problem may be more closely aligned with the region-divergent bilateralism perspective (*undermining and capturing effects*) in that bilateral FTAs cause a convoluted pattern of trade rules within a region that are not easily harmonised into a unified plurilateral or regional agreement. On the other hand, the fact that different economies in the region are at least signing the same broadly similar level of integrational agreement (i.e. FTAs) does to some extent support the argument that intensifying FTA bilateralism can provide the *sub-structural foundation for regionalism* to develop from a technical policy perspective. One could argue that the very same asymmetry and inconsistency of bilateral FTA rules and schedules creates an imperative to rationalise them into wider plurilateral agreements, or at least establish agreed codes of FTA practice between the region's states. The WTO has itself noted that dense patterns of bilateral FTAs within a region "should lead to the consolidation of RTAs and rationalisation among participants who may be forced to align themselves with one or other regional grouping", and that, "harmonisation in the granting of tariff concessions and in the rules of origin can reduce significantly the administrative burden associated with membership in multiple RTAs" (WTO 2002a: 11). Moreover, Lloyd (2002) has argued that 'state-of-the-art' FTAs can have positive demonstration effects for others, forming technical policy templates on which other agreements can base themselves, therefore leading to a greater international alignment in FTA practice. Contributions made by the US–Canada FTA (the precursor to NAFTA) and ANZCER (Australia–New Zealand Closer Economic Relations) regarding to the multilateral General Agreement on Trade in Services (GATS) are instances of this, and have been acknowledged by the WTO.[9]

Chapter 3's case study on the Trans-Pacific Strategic Economic Partnership Agreement (TPSEPA) – a quadrilateral FTA between Brunei, Chile,

New Zealand and Singapore – presents the only real case of bilateral-to-plurilateral FTA evolution entirely within the Asia-Pacific, but this was essentially an extension of the pre-existing bilateral FTA between New Zealand and Singapore and therefore not a harmonisation of two or more agreements. There is also the Bangkok Agreement, first signed in 1975 and upgraded in November 2005, which is a partial scope agreement between three Asia-Pacific countries (China, Laos, South Korea) and three South Asian countries (Bangladesh, India and Sri Lanka).[10] The six countries agreed to reduce tariffs from 1 July 2006 between them by an average of 30 percent, from 22 percent previously, and extend the agreement from 1,800 to 4,800 products, mostly in agricultural, textile and petrochemical sectors.[11] This new accord was renamed the Asia Pacific Free Trade Area, which somewhat overstated its scope both in geographic and trade liberalisation terms. Moreover, the region's bilateral FTA trend only marginally impacted on this enhancement of the Bangkok Agreement: none of its Asia-Pacific signatories were party to a signed bilateral FTA at the time; South Korea and India were exploring a bilateral FTA project, as was China and South Korea but only at a very basic study level; Bangladesh, India and Sri Lanka had signed an accord in January 2004 that committed them to operationalise a South Asia Free Trade Agreement by 2006, the other members being Bhutan, the Maldives, Nepal and Pakistan.

Another plurilateral FTA project involving Asia-Pacific and South Asian states is the BIMSTEC (Bay of Bengal Initiative for Multi-Sectoral Technical and Economic Cooperation) arrangement, first established in 1997 between Bangladesh, Bhutan, India, Nepal, Myanmar, Sri Lanka and Thailand. In 2004, four BIMSTEC members – Bangladesh, India, Sri Lanka and Thailand – committed to abolish tariffs between them by 2012, with the other, less developed members given until 2017 to join the tariff-free arrangement.[12] Again, the influence of the Asia-Pacific bilateral FTA trend was relatively marginal here at best. Thailand had concluded negotiations on a basic free trade agreement with India in October 2003, but interestedly its implementation was long delayed because of unresolved disagreements over rules of origin provisions. This will most likely be a difficult area of negotiation in both the BIMSTEC and Bangkok Agreement FTA projects as India in particular prefers a different approach on rules of origin (change of tariff classification and value content modalities) than ASEAN states generally, which prefer a simpler value content based approach. Indeed, this was a contentious issue in the ASEAN–India FTA negotiations during 2004 and 2005,[13] and further highlighted the problem of harmonising different FTA modalities once countries have established their own particular approaches.

APEC and the spaghetti bowl problem

Since 2003 efforts have been made within APEC to create a code for FTA 'best practice' amongst its member states. The Trade Forum section of the

Pacific Economic Co-operation Council (PECC), an APEC associated entity that conducts policy study analyses on its behalf, has played an important role here. PECC submitted its Best Practice FTA recommendations (PECC 2003b) to the 2004 APEC Ministerial Meeting that were duly endorsed and come under 12 headings (APEC 2004), namely:

- *Consistency with APEC principles and goals*: that APEC members' pursuit of FTAs should not distract from the realisation of the Bogor Goals, these being to establish complete trade and investment liberalisation by 2010 (by developed country members) and 2020 (by developing country members). Reconciling FTAs with APEC's core principle of 'open regionalism' (i.e. liberalisation by unilateral, non-discriminatory means) is discussed later in the chapter, but the main implication here was that the concessions granted between FTA parties should be multilateralised to all other APEC members by these target dates.
- *Consistency with the WTO*: in relation to disciplines of the WTO, especially those contained within Article XXIV of the GATT and Article V of the GATS (see Chapter 1).
- *Going beyond WTO commitments*: to build upon existing WTO obligations and explore new areas of trade and investment liberalisation not yet reached by WTO consensus.
- *Comprehensiveness*: APEC members should strive to make the scope of liberalisation as comprehensive as possible, across all sectors. Phase-in schedules for trade barrier elimination should be kept to a minimum, but also take into account the different levels of development among the FTA parties.
- *Transparency*: FTA texts should be made readily available as soon as the agreement has been signed.
- *Trade facilitation*: FTAs should include practical measures and co-operative efforts to facilitate trade and reduce transaction costs for business.
- *Dispute settlement mechanisms*: should be included in the FTA.
- *Simple rules of origin*: that are easy to understand and comply with, and must recognise the increasingly globalised nature of production, as well as the efforts of APEC to promote regional economic integration by adopting RoO that maximise trade creation and minimise trade distortion.
- *Co-operation*: FTAs should include commitments on economic and technical co-operation that ensure agreements have maximum utility and benefit all parties.
- *Sustainable development*: FTAs must not be environmentally harmful.
- *Accession of third parties*: whereby FTAs should have an accession clause that allow third parties to join the agreement on negotiated terms and conditions.
- *Periodic review provisions*: that ensure full implementation of the FTA's terms and provisions, and that can identify further areas for development within the agreement, e.g. on liberalisation and co-operation.

The above are perhaps better described as 'best principles' rather than 'best practice' because there are no specifics on actual technical policy practice (e.g. maximum time periods on tariff liberalisation phase-in schedules, particular RoO modalities to be adopted). As one APEC paper commented, a 'constructive ambiguity' was required in order that all 21 member-states found these principles on FTA conduct acceptable (APEC 2005a: p. 1), and this lowest common denominator problem has limited APEC's ability to realise its ambitions generally (see Chapter 1). Moreover, many APEC member states have not complied even in principle to these recommended guidelines on FTA practice. For example, the RoO 'best practice' implicitly suggests that product-specific RoO should be avoided but this has already become a well established norm in the FTA policies of many Asia-Pacific states, most prominently the US and Japan. Furthermore, many of the region's FTAs do not have an accession clause or provisions on economic co-operation (Appendix C). In relation to the first 'best practice' code listed, most bilateral FTAs thus far signed amongst APEC member states include trade liberalisation schedules that extend beyond the Bogor Goals' 2010/2020 deadlines. For instance, in the tariff liberalisation schedules of the Australia–US FTA (AUSFTA), signed in 2004, run well beyond the 2010 target date set for developed member states, into which category Australia and the United States both fall. In some cases, AUSFTA's schedules run up to 18 years (see Chapter 3). This pattern is replicated in many other new Asia-Pacific FTAs,[14] and moreover many 'sensitive' sectors have been completely exempted from any liberalisation. Establishing FTA conformity with the Bogor Goals' deadlines would therefore require 'liberalisation upgrades' in many FTA arrangements that would usually come through agreement-wide periodic review processes.

There is also the issue of whether the 'best practice FTA' recommendations can be applied retrospectively to the now large number of FTAs already in force. However, retrospective application was not being explicitly recommended. Instead, the 2005 APEC Leaders Declaration called for "the development of model measures for as many commonly accepted FTA chapters as possible by 2008."[15] If APEC had responded more quickly, establishing conformity guidelines at the onset of the new Asia-Pacific FTA trend, then the spaghetti bowl problem may have been more effectively addressed. As it now stands, there exists considerable FTA heterogeneity in the Asia-Pacific both in terms of politico-economic approach and technical policy aspects. One problem is that countries can take very different views on certain technical areas of FTA practice. For example, Australia and New Zealand argue that the strict quarantine regulations they insist upon in their FTAs – primarily because of the importance of their agri-sectors – are essentially welfare-enhancing trade policy mechanisms, whereas others may view these regulations as a form of protectionism.

The Asia-Pacific business community has become increasingly concerned about the FTA heterogeneity issue. In November 2003, Mexico, one of the most FTA active countries not only in the Asia-Pacific but also the world, announced a moratorium on its FTA policy at the behest of the country's business sector, who had informed the government of their inability to exploit the benefits of existing agreements Mexico had with over 30 countries. The President of the Mexican Foreign Trade Council, Carlos Rojas, remarked at the time that, "the whole point of these efforts is to boost Mexican exports, not to collect agreements."[16] A year earlier, Calman Cohen, the head of the free trade advocating Emergency Committee for American Trade, stated that, "Bilateral FTAs are a two-edged weapon. They offer the prospect of expanded trade and investment. But if their provisions are mutually inconsistent, they create a more difficult trading environment."[17] In October 2004, the APEC Business Advisory Council also raised concerns about the potential of bilateral FTAs to impose additional transaction costs on business, and specifically cited the spaghetti bowl problematic of differentiated trading rules and regulations. In the run up to the 2005 APEC summit, Hyun Jae-hyun, Chair of the APEC Chief Executive Officer Summit, held in parallel to the summit in Busan, commented that, "bilateral FTAs vary from one case to another at the risk of creating great confusion", and called upon APEC to apply stricter guidelines on FTA practice.[18]

Rules of origin revisited

Chapter 1 introduced the issue of rules of origin (RoO) in its discussion of preferential RoO and WTO level negotiations on the subject. Rules of origin are an integral element of FTAs as they aim to establish the location of value-adding production, and thus whether goods qualify for FTA treatment. They are often cited as the most important element of the spaghetti bowl problem because RoO regimes vary considerably from one FTA to another, and because they can significantly impact upon regional and global production networks, as acknowledged in the APEC Best Practice FTA recommendations discussed earlier. There is also a consensus in PECC that "RoO can be at least as important as tariff elimination in determining the degree of market access conferred by an FTA" (APEC 2005b: p. 1). As noted in Chapter 1, compliance to an FTA's rules of origin not only incurs an administrative cost to business (proportionately higher for small and medium-sized enterprises, or SMEs) but also additional production costs to final goods producer firms in particular by their having to purchase inputs from within the FTA area when extra-FTA sources elsewhere in the firm's regional production network are cheaper. These complications increase where countries have entered into a number of FTAs with varying RoO regimes, and are compounded where product-specific rules apply. This is a particularly crucial issue for East Asia as its exports have the highest import content ratios of any region in the world as a consequence of extensively operating regional production networks (Kimura and Ando 2004; World Bank 2005).

Product-specific RoO.   Many countries have a predilection for product-specific RoO, leading to free trade agreements devoting literally hundreds of pages to incorporating such rules. For example, the US–Singapore Free Trade Agreement (USSFTA) contained 284 pages of product-specific RoO documentation while the Japan–Singapore Economic Partnership Agreement (JSEPA) had 203 pages. Appendix E shows the RoO regimes for various Asia-Pacific FTAs in comparison to each other and other FTAs around the world. The Kyoto Convention is an instrument adopted by the World Customs Organisation in its efforts to standardise and harmonise customs procedures and policies, such as on RoO. It uses two basic criteria to determine the origin of an internationally traded product, these being: (i) *wholly obtained or produced*, when the product has either been extracted or processed only in one FTA partner; (ii) *substantial transformation*, which is more complex and involves three main components, these in turn being:

- *Change in tariff classification (CTC)*, between the manufactured good and the inputs from extra-FTA parties used in the productive process. The CTC may require the product to alter its chapter (two digits under the Harmonised System of Tariffs), heading (four digits), sub-heading (six digits) or item (8–10 digits) from the country of export. Under CTC rules, a finished export good is eligible for FTA treatment if it is classified in a different tariff category from all its input materials and components sourced from third countries. These rules may sometimes be combined with those on value content (see below), as for example found in the Trans-Pacific Strategic Economic Partnership Agreement (TPSEPA). The CTC modality has become increasingly common internationally because it is believed to be: (i) cheaper and simpler for businesses to apply; (ii) easier for governments to administer; (iii) inherently more predictable and consistent in terms of origin outcomes, i.e. once qualified, always qualified (MFAT 2005).
- *Value content (VC)*, which stipulates that a product must acquire a minimum local value in the exporting country. This can be expressed as a minimum percentage of value (domestic or regional value content, RVC), or as the difference between the value of the final good and the costs of the imported inputs (import content, IC), or as the value of parts (VP) that ascertains the minimum percentage of originating parts out of the total. The IC rule tends to be expressed as a maximum percentage of value originating from non-member economies. Value content criterion can be applied to all products (e.g. a general 40 percent RVC rule, as used in AFTA) as well as on a product-specific basis.
- *Technical requirement*, which requires the product to undergo certain processing operations in the originating country. This could be, for example, to meet particular health and safety or environmental standards or the importing country.

The more product-specific RoO are incorporated into an FTA, the more complex and costly it becomes for firms to adhere to its provisions. Research conducted by Estevadeordal and Suominen (2005) suggested that the RoO regimes of NAFTA, the JSEPA, the Korea–Chile FTA and the US–Chile FTA were the most trade restrictive of Asia-Pacific FTAs surveyed, primarily because of their extensive product-specific RoO provisions. In addition, a 2004 report published by Australia's Productivity Commission concluded that the country's bilateral FTAs with the US and Thailand had amongst the world's most restrictive RoO regimes, mainly because of product-specific provisions, and estimated that the annual costs of complying with RoO ranged between 1.5 percent to 6.0 percent of the total cost of the good (Productivity Commission 2004). Regime-wide RoO, however, tend to add greater flexibility to rules compliance and are more trade facilitative.

Regime-wide RoO.   While some FTAs do not have product-specific RoO, all have regime-wide rules. Most FTAs carry a *de minimis* rule (also known as tolerance) that permits a specified maximum percentage of non-originating materials to be used without affecting origin. There may also be a roll-up or absorption principle applied, which allows materials that have acquired origin by meeting specific processing requirements to be considered originating when used as inputs in a subsequent transformation. Finally, cumulation provisions enables producers from an FTA party to use non-originating materials from another FTA party (or parties) without forfeiting preferential status. Bilateral cumulation provisions permit materials and components originating in the two FTA parties concerned to be considered 'domestic' in origin. Diagonal cumulation allows for FTA parties tied by the same RoO regime to use materials originating in any part of that RoO domain to be considered as 'domestic' also. This is particularly found in a situation where, for example, Country A has FTAs with Countries B and C (that may or may not have an FTA between themselves), and subsequently Country A permits materials and components from Country C to be 'domestically counted' in the relevant processed exports sent from Country B that enter Country A. Finally, full cumulation represents an extension of the diagonal cumulation provision principle by allowing goods produced in the same RoO domain to be considered 'domestic' in origin, even if these were not originating products.[19] Whereas *de minimis*, roll-up and cumulation provisions permit leniency in the application of RoO, duty drawback precludes the refunding of tariffs on non-originating inputs that are subsequently included in the final product exported to the FTA partner. Duty drawback is often used by developing countries as a means to encourage exports and attract inward foreign investment, and it also confers a cost advantage to the FTA-based producers who gear their final goods to export over producers selling their final good in the domestic market (Estevadeordal and Suominen 2003, 2005).

RoO and lattice regionalism. The cumulation provisions on RoO would seem to offer scope for addressing the spaghetti bowl problem. The EU's Pan-European System of Cumulation (PESC) model of RoO has allowed for widespread diagonal cumulation in its FTAs signed with neighbouring European countries in order to promote the development of regional production networks, and a close alignment between these cumulation rules has been established (Augier *et al* 2005). This has helped develop a regional domain of common RoO in Europe, a principle that if applied to East Asia and the Asia-Pacific would similarly help foster the regionalisation of business activity. Such a development would be consistent with region-convergent bilateralism, especially concerning how a dense pattern of bilateral FTAs may provide a *sub-structural foundation for regionalism* to develop. For example, if Japan were to establish bilateral FTAs with a number of East Asian trade partners – that may in turn have FTAs with each other – a similar diagonal cumulation arrangement could emerge. However, this implies some degree of rules of origin compatibility being established between the bilateral FTAs. In addition, this RoO 'family' (a term often used by WTO officials) may compete with China-centred or US-centred counterparts, and similar difficulties arise in an East Asian or Asia-Pacific regional setting where these overlap, e.g. JSEPA, USSFTA, China–Singapore FTA as part of ASEAN–China (ACFTA). There would need to be alignment, therefore, between the different hubs or 'heads' of these RoO families.

In Pacific America, it remains unclear whether NAFTA rules or origin regime will shape that of the FTAA's as some countries in the region follow LAIA or Mercosur templates on RoO. For example, the Andean Community and CARICOM draw upon LAIA rules (across the board chapter heading CTC or VC), while Mercosur and its FTAs with Chile and Bolivia mainly use chapter heading CTC rules as well as VC and technical requirement rules. Furthermore, the US's bilateral FTAs with Jordan and Israel diverge significantly from the NAFTA model, working on VC provisions alone. In general, the RoO regimes of East Asian and Oceanic FTAs are less product-specific in nature compared to the PESC and NAFTA approaches. Relatively simple VC provisions are often used, when defined as domestic content, typically ranging from 30 percent to 50 percent. For example, AFTA and ACFTA are both set at 40 percent, the Hong Kong–China Closer Economic Partnership Agreement (HKCCEPA) at 30 percent, the Pacific Island Countries Trade Agreement (PICTA) at 40 percent and ANZCER at 50 percent, (Appendix E). While we noted earlier that JSEPA has over 200 pages of product-specific RoO protocol, its rules are far less complex than its PESC and NAFTA counterparts. However, a common East Asian RoO model is unlikely to arise in the foreseeable future, rather instead competition between Japan or China determined RoO regimes. This relates to our later discussion on FTA model contestation in the Asia-Pacific. In sum, there appears to be a clear case that the technical policy aspects of FTA heterogeneity, as exemplified by differentiated RoO regimes, presents a significant challenge to the idea that inter-linked bilateral FTAs can provide a sub-structural basis on which to found sub-regional or regional free trade agreements.

4.4.2 The politico-diplomatic discourse on lattice regionalism

Overcoming the spaghetti bowl problem is not just a technical policy challenge but also a political one. Technical policy variance between different FTAs may be overcome if sufficient political will and technocratic capacity and resources exist to realise wider sub-regional or regional FTAs. From the region-convergent bilateralism perspective, the recent profusion of Asia-Pacific FTAs may be considered as a sub-system or sub-structure of trade arrangements with no regional 'nerve centre', yet possessing the potential to network together the region's states at both the micro and macro-levels. This latter aspect can relate to Asia-Pacific FTAs representing a collective of states that have converged in their approach to the regional trade agenda. While this in itself does not constitute institutionalised regionalism, the Asia-Pacific FTA pattern does mark an important development in regional economic culture by such a growing region-wide convergence around a particular trade diplomacy practice or norm.

Indeed, there has been much rhetoric from certain Asia-Pacific governments concerning the ultimate objective of knitting together separate bilateral agreements into an East Asia or Asia-Pacific Free Trade Agreement. Singapore has perhaps been the most regular and ardent proponent of this idea from the earliest stages of its FTA policy (Daquila and Huy 2003; Dent 2005b; Desker 2004). In January 2001, then Prime Minister Goh Chok Tong stated, "our FTAs actually will pave the way for [the] APEC-wide trade area", and that it was "Singapore's intention to spin a web of interlocking free trade agreements between APEC members, which could help move the organisation toward achieving free trade in the Asia-Pacific."[20] His Trade Minister, George Yeo, followed this up in March 2001 with this statement in the context of the USSFTA project: "if others also make similar moves, in the end there'll be a number of overlapping FTAs in the Pacific and we might well decide that one day, why not have a Pacific-wide FTA."[21] In acknowledging that the proliferation of bilateral FTAs risked creating a chaotic system of trade rules, Goh later remarked in October 2003 that, "this is where, after some time, we must sit down to see how we can link up all the FTAs to create a larger, regional or cross-regional agreement."[22]

Political leaders from many other Asia-Pacific countries – most notably Japan, China, South Korea, Chile and Australia – have expressed similar views. For example, soon after Japan and South Korea announced their FTA project in 1999, government officials from both sides raised the idea of an eventual extension to a trilateral FTA that would include China (Cai 2001; Dent and Huang 2002), although interestingly Tokyo and Seoul later went cool on the idea when Beijing suggested the creation of a Northeast Asia FTA in 2002. The previous year, Beijing had also proposed the creation of a Greater China FTA, incorporating Hong Kong, Macao and Taiwan, the latter's participation being dependent on the resolution of various Cross-Strait issues (see Chapter 2).[23] On a more ambitious regional scale, Chile's President Lagos, as host of APEC's 2004 summit, stated in May 2004, "What happens if you put together all the agreements that already exist among the different APEC economies? If you put all those agreements together, then it may emerge probably – a general kind of agreement among the different countries."[24] Just before the inaugural East Asia Summit, held in December 2005, Australia's Foreign Minister, Alexander Downer, proposed the creation of an Asia-Pacific free trade zone founded on the existing "regional architecture" of FTAs.[25]

While the politico-diplomatic discourse on bilateral-to-regional evolution of FTA development (i.e. lattice regionalism) remains strongly subscribed to by many Asia-Pacific leaders, little has been done to articulate the idea of beyond the political rhetoric. However, it does reveal that the new FTA trend has made Asia-Pacific states more predisposed to this idea of networking their economies together. This is likely to have an initial sub-regional focus (e.g. Northeast Asia), from which wider regional arrangements (e.g. East Asia) can be conceived. The idea of creating an East Asia Free Trade Area (EAFTA) that could emerge from a sub-structural foundation of bilateral FTAs has been mooted, through the APT framework and other regional fora (Terada 2003; Stubbs 2002). Chapter 1 examined that a main reason for East Asia's predilection for FTAs *per se* arose out the new co-operative diplomacy in the aftermath of the 1997/98 East Asian financial crisis, whereby FTAs would help better manage region-wide economic interdependence. Furthermore, and with special regard to social constructivist perspectives from new regionalism theory discussed earlier, East Asia's new 'FTA culture' may be contrived as a new norm of common trade policy behaviour that has forged new associative and ideational links between different stakeholder groups, i.e. from government, business and certain elements of civil society. Research fieldwork for this book suggests that the FTA negotiation process has deepened micro-networking links between government trade policy officials in particular (and to some extent business representatives) that could facilitate the longer run development of economic co-operation in East Asia, whether on a bilateral or regional basis. This also relates closely to Wendt's (1992) earlier noted idea concerning the creation of transnational communities of common interest and the sense of 'regionness' derived therein from such kinds of socialisation processes and frameworks.

However, Ravenhill (2003) questions whether the new FTA trend may be viewed as a new means of projecting a collective East Asian identity as many of the bilateral FTAs partners chosen are outside the region. In another work, Ravenhill (2002) argues that inter-state rivalries and suspicions remain a salient feature of East Asia's international relations. Indeed, relations between the region's two most powerful states – Japan and China – must be both strong and harmonious if East Asian regionalism is to be cultivated. History shows that bilateral alliances between leading states often provide the cornerstone of regionalist projects. Perhaps the most well known is the Franco-German bilateral relationship on which contemporary developments in European regional integration have been principally founded. From this alliance has come both the political vision and will to drive forward the integration process. In South America, the Brazil–Argentina bilateral relationship became even more predominant within Mercosur when Presidents Lula and Kirshner took up their respective offices (Phillips 2004). Although many regional integration projects have been politically and technocratically driven by a hegemonic state at the centre (e.g. the US in NAFTA, India in SAARC, South Africa in SADC), bilateral alliances can also perform the same function. In East Asia's case, however, the various antagonisms that continue to beset Sino-Japanese relations would seem to make this a rather distant prospect.

4.4.3 Competitive liberalisation

Competitive liberalisation is closely associated with the US's FTA policy, especially under the United States Trade Representative (USTR) Robert Zoellick, who served this office from 2001 to 2005. It's principles and philosophy have been adopted by other pro-free trade Asia-Pacific countries, especially when defending the use of FTAs in the face of criticism from those advocating a multilateral approach only in advancing trade liberalisation. Chapter 2 has previously introduced competitive liberalisation in its study of the US's FTA policy. To restate, it concerns how the pursuit of FTAs with certain trade partners can compel others to join in a gradually widening trade liberalisation process, whether at the bilateral, regional or multilateral level (Zoellick 2001a; 2001b). Competitive liberalisation works on the principle that it becomes more imperative for recalcitrant trade liberalisers to sign bigger trade deals that will help neutralise the trade diversionary effects of FTAs signed by 'pro-free trade' countries. A number of academics have articulated or supported this argument (Andriamananjara 2003; Bergsten 1994; Dobson 2001; Goyal and Joshi 1999; Lloyd 2002). An often cited example of competitive liberalisation in action was the US's support for enhancing APEC's trade liberalisation objectives (i.e. the Bogor Goals project) during the late months of 1993 that was allegedly designed to pressure the EU into coming to a final agreement on agriculture during a critical phase in finalising Uruguay Round negotiations. The specific rationale here was that, for non-APEC members, new multilateral free trade agreements would help offset the negative externalities generated by the creation of a Pacific free trade zone. The competitive liberalisation dynamic thus connects to the *congruent objectives and processes* point of contention under region-convergent bilateralism in that an increasingly dense pattern of bilateral FTAs could bring similar pressures to bear in creating pan-regional FTA arrangements. Competitive liberalisation also relates to the third region-convergent point of contention, this being *preliminary conditioning to regional economic liberalisation and integration* and based on the argument that bilateral FTA deals offer initial gradual adjustment stages for domestic firms in the lead up to bigger regional and multilateral agreements on trade liberalisation.

There are, however, certain caveats to consider. Andriamananjara (1999, 2000, 2003), Bond and Syropoulos (1996), and Yi (1996) accept that while the intensification of FTA activity can induce excluded countries to press for accession to existing FTAs, as well as promote both region-wide and multilateral trade liberalisation processes, they also contend that incumbent FTA members may not have the same incentives to do so. This is because the improvements in market access benefits afforded exclusively to FTA members can mitigate their willingness to undertake or support wider regional and multilateral trade liberalisation deals as this will reduce the FTA margins of preference enjoyed by the incumbents concerned. Andriamananjara (2003) analyses this using a Cournot oligopoly model of identical countries whereby the external tariff (i.e. on outsider countries) is assumed fixed and profit level considerations primarily determine decisions on FTA expansion. According to these assumptions, if the FTA were allowed to expand, profits accruing to insider firms (i.e. FTA-based) first increase to an optimum point and then decline. The optimum profit point for insiders is therefore reached before the FTA embraces all countries. Meanwhile, profit levels for outsider firms only decline in line with FTA expansion. So, while the incentive for outsiders to accede to the FTA increases, insiders can have motive to limit membership, hence suggesting that constraints exist on how far the competitive liberalisation dynamic may catalyse a broader trade liberalisation process, including the formation of pan-regional FTAs. The economistic argument, based on arguably narrow assumptions, may appear too reductionist in approach to many, and therefore limited in explanatory power, but the general principle of the argument is a valid one: that is once countries have gained virtually free access to large country markets through bilateral FTAs, their incentives to support regional and multilateral trade liberalisation agreements may diminish (Krueger 1997; Ravenhill 2003).

Similar unintended negative outcomes from 'competitive liberalisation' may arise at the regional level. For example, once individual ASEAN member states have secured free market access through bilateral FTAs with 'great power' trade partners they may be less inclined to fulfil their AFTA commitments as exploiting the opportunities arising from regional free trade becomes comparatively less important. Southeast Asia's intra-regional trade ratio is only just over 20 percent, meaning that the region only accounts for around a fifth of the ASEAN group's total international trade. A fundamental objective of the AFTA project is to expand intra-regional trade in Southeast Asia as part of fostering regional community-building. Bilateral FTAs with those outside the region, whilst a pragmatic risk-averse trade strategy in post-crisis Southeast Asia, could serve as distractions to realising this objective.

From a different but related perspective, Baldwin (1997, 1999) has argued that regional FTA expansion may arise based on a large 'hub' FTA in which more and more outsider countries accede through bilateral 'spoke' FTA links. He refers to this process as the 'domino theory' of regionalism, and draws extensively upon the EU enlargement experience discussed earlier in this chapter. According to Baldwin, the main motive for EU trade partners was to seek parity market and foreign investment access to the Single Market with respect to each other. As more countries become insiders so the economic costs of remaining an outsider increases, thus leading to intensifying FTA activity. The core incumbent state or states within the 'hub' has or have an incentive to enlarge the regional FTA because they are in a position of power to set the terms and conditions of third country accession, in alignment with the core incumbents' interests. There is hence a competitive liberalisation dynamic of sorts working here in that outsider countries are competing to liberalise their trade regimes with an FTA hub power as early as possible. Yet as noted earlier, the EU experience is rather unique, and moreover the hub-and-spoke FTA issue maybe considered distinctly different from that of competitive liberalisation because there are other politico-economic factors to consider, such as the interaction between competing FTA models based around hub powers.

There are also inherent risks in pursuing a competitive liberalisation strategy in that it may *intensify inter-state rivalry within a region*, a region-divergent point of contention. Propagating a trade diplomacy culture whereby a critical mass of FTAs is designed to beget more FTAs, based on the defensive and reactive motive of mitigating the negative impacts of other agreements, is more likely to breed a form of competitive bilateralism where each country seeks a preferential market access advantage over others. This may lead to more antagonist trade relations between states within the same region rather than the co-operative economic diplomacy required to forge regional and multilateral trade deals (Gordon 2003). The scramble between Japan and China to sign FTAs with other East Asian countries, and particularly with the ASEAN group, has for example heightened tensions in the Sino-Japanese relationship. Competition between ASEAN member states to sign the best bilateral FTA deals with key trade partners outside Southeast Asia has also raised tensions within the regional group (Dent 2006a). Singapore, and to a lesser extent Thailand, have prescribed to the competitive liberalisation approach as politically articulated in their 'pathfinding' bilateral FTAs with the US, Japan, Australia, New Zealand and others as a means to catalyse Southeast Asia's trade liberalisation both within the region and with extra-regional FTA partners. Malaysia, Indonesia and the Philippines have been somewhat critical of this approach, stating that Singapore and Thailand were putting their own national interests ahead of ASEAN led regional community-building,[26] although subsequently initiated bilateral FTA policies of their own to seek the same market access preferences enjoyed by Singapore and Thailand.

We can draw upon further evidence from Southeast Asia concerning how competitive liberalisation may have adverse politico-diplomatic effects. After the launch of the ACFTA project in November 2001, Thai Prime Minister, Thaksin Shinawata, reportedly informed his Chinese hosts at the inaugural Boao Forum held in April 2002 of Thailand's willingness to conclude a bilateral FTA with China without waiting for other ASEAN member states.[27] With regard to ASEAN-level 'region-to-country' FTA projects with extra-regional trade partners, individual ASEAN member states have scope to compete with each for relative market access gains where negotiations are arranged on a separate bilateral basis, e.g. Japan–Indonesia. This is indeed the norm with only the ACFTA project as the exception where ASEAN negotiates collectively. Intra-regional competition for trade preferences in the same extra-regional trade partner's market causes suspicion and potential animosity, especially where one ASEAN member state appears to have secured a significant market access advantage over another. Certain member states are indeed closely observing and monitoring the progress and details of other member states FTA projects. For example, the day after Singapore concluded its FTA negotiations with the US, Malaysian Government officials called their American contacts to probe what strategic advantages Singapore would now have over Malaysia, and a proposal for a US–Malaysia FTA came soon afterwards from Kuala Lumpur.[28] Moreover, both Malaysia and the Philippines will want to ascertain in their respective bilateral FTA negotiations with Japan whether the concessions they obtain from Tokyo are inferior or not to concessions offered to Thailand in its own bilateral negotiations with Japan, and to Singapore in the already concluded JSEPA. Thus, while competitive liberalisation may lead to a cascade of FTA activity, it can also cause significant politico-diplomatic tensions that are not conducive to regional community-building.

4.4.4 Hubs, spokes and contesting FTA models

Introduction

We have already discussed the significance of hub-and-spoke patterns of FTA formation and linkage in the world trade system. In this section, we consider the emerging FTA 'hub' models in the Asia-Pacific, and how these may contest for influence and supremacy in the region's international political economy. This issue is especially pertinent to both region-convergent and region-divergent bilateralism. The consolidation of FTA hubs may on the one hand bring about a certain degree of trade policy convergence within a region, as noted earlier. This is consistent with the *congruent processes and objectives* aspect of region-convergent bilateralism, and thus supports the lattice regionalism hypothesis. On the other hand, the development of different FTA models may *reinforce power asymmetries* within a region – a region-divergent bilateralism aspect – through allowing powerful trading nations to exert their interests over weaker nations with greater effect, for example through pressure to comply with particular commercial policy practices determined by the hub power, e.g. on RoO, IPR, etc. Competition between FTA hub models may also arise as each hub power seeks to advance their own FTA model both within the region and in the multilateral trading system, for example by seeking to get their norms accepted within the ambit of the WTO. Moreover, as Scollay (2003) argued, "the unequal distribution of gains between 'hubs' and 'spokes' may also be a source of tension and conflict" (p. 7). At both 'hub–hub' and 'hub–spoke' levels, bilateral FTA activity may lead to *intensified inter-state rivalry with the region*, another region-divergent point of contention.

Emerging FTA models in the Asia-Pacific

Four FTA models now seem apparent in the Asia-Pacific region, and this may be discerned from the technical policy content of each model and the politico-economic fundaments underlying it, as will be made clear. The four FTA models in question are the US's 'asymmetric neo-liberal' model, Japan's 'developmental–industrial' model, China's 'emerging developing country' model, and Australia and New Zealand's 'closer economic relations' model. Competition between FTA models (i.e. the holistic approach to FTA formation) and modalities (i.e. particular aspects of that approach, such as its preferred RoO regime) can be expected amongst major trade powers because FTAs help determine the regulatory framework in which international trade and business occurs. As USTR Robert Zoellick commented when urging US Senate approval of Trade Promotion Authority (a.k.a. 'fast track') legislation, "each [FTA] agreement made without us may set new rules for intellectual property, emerging high-tech sectors, agriculture standards, customs procedures or countless other areas of the modern, integrated global economy – rules that will be made without taking account of American interests."[29] Let us first consider the US's own FTA model.

The US's 'asymmetric neo-liberal' FTA model. Chapters 2 and 3 present studies on the reasons behind and the outcomes of the US's 'asymmetric neo-liberal' approach to its FTA policy. This concerns how the United States applies considerable diplomatic pressure upon its FTA partners to comprehensively open up its markets to American commercial interests while at the same time insisting on protecting a range of domestic sectors from reciprocated liberalisation (Feinberg 2003). Thus, in addition to seeking tariff-free entry for its exporters, the US typically demands wide-ranging, 'behind the border' access to its FTA partner's markets that can include infrastructural sectors (e.g. telecommunications), financial services, media and entertainment sectors, and others. This often entails the deregulation of certain sectors, many of which may concern sensitive areas of public policy, such as health, culture and national security. In addition, the US usually presses its FTA partners to adopt core elements of its own national IPR regime (e.g. the 1998 Digital Millennium Copyright and Copyright Term Extension Acts) that go well beyond the WTO's Trade-Related Aspects of Intellectual Property (TRIPS) agreement.[30] Investment rights that extend beyond usual provisions on national treatment to include provisions that allow American companies to take legal recourse against the policies or actions of host country governments that infringe upon their invested business interests are another typical feature of this model. The privatisation of certain nationalised industries can also be demanded by the US in its FTA negotiations, as was the case with both Australia and Singapore concerning their telecoms sectors (see Chapter 3). Of all Asia-Pacific countries, the US is the most insistent on using 'negative list' modalities in various aspects of sector and services liberalisation, which as Chapter 1 notes restricts the options of one FTA partner limiting market access concessions to another over the long-term.

Furthermore, labour and environment clauses are often included that oblige FTA partners to meet higher standards of commercial and policy practice in these areas when trading with the US. In return, the US offers highly differentiated access provisions to its own markets, entailing complex sets of liberalisation schedules and rules of origin stipulations relating to various sensitive industry sectors and product lines (see Appendix B). The US can push for this asymmetric liberalisation – that is, for the FTA partner to comprehensively open up its own market while the US itself retains various protectionist derogations – because it argues it has the much bigger market to offer in the balance of FTA preferences. However, the flaw in this argument is that there is a much larger number of American and foreign firms competing in this market than in any other national market, thus bringing into question any real advantage conferred in terms of proportionate market access.

The US's FTA model is also primarily concerned with market access issues with very few or no provisions on economic co-operation or development assistance incorporated into the FTA text. Sometimes a package of trade capacity assistance measures are offered to developing country FTA partners as a side agreement to the deal. For example, during the US's FTA negotiations with the CACM group, National Action Plans were put together for Costa Rica, El Salvador, Guatemala, Honduras and Nicaragua to identify each country's trade capacity building needs. According to the USTR, these plans served as "a tool for mobilizing and managing trade capacity building assistance – both from public and private sources – to support participation in the negotiations, implementation of the negotiated agreements, and help make the transition and changes necessary to realise the linkage between trade and development."[31] A similar package was put together for the US's FTA negotiations with the SACU group. The US trade capacity assistance budget has risen quite significantly in recent years, from US$504.5 million in 2000 to US$1,342 million by 2005, yet this was still a rather modest figure in GDP per capita terms by international comparison. Moreover, the trade capacity assistance packages that accompany bilateral FTAs have been the exception rather than the rule: by 2005 only CACM and SACU partners had been offered them.[32] Furthermore, much of the assistance conferred here over and above that already provided by previously initiated USAID programmes is directed to ultimately helping implement market opening to US business interests. One could also argue that the assistance directed to training negotiators of developing country FTA partners also enabled the US to capture the negotiating process to some extent through possibly biasing the negotiators in question and making them somewhat compliant or beholden to their American 'tutors'.

In addition, the US's penchant for comprehensive 'behind the borders' market opening of an FTA partner's economy to American firms requires that partner to have robust enough technocratic and institutional capacities in the first place to implement the kind of agreement and its constituent economic reforms preferred by Washington. This, then, potentially if not actually precludes a large number of developing countries candidates for FTA partnership with the US, and makes the US the most selective FTA partner amongst the Asia-Pacific countries studied based on this criteria. The issue of whether FTA partner candidates have sufficient technocratic and institutional capacity to implement agreements with the US is a crucial issue for the American business community, who have lobbied Washington hard on the matter.[33] The US's preferences on FTA content are also reflected within NAFTA, and these have also shaped the provisions and modalities (e.g. on RoO) of other Asia-Pacific FTAs, even those not involving the US itself, such as the Taiwan–Panama FTA.

Japan's 'developmental–industrial' FTA model. Japan's own FTA model has some similarities with the US model but the differences are more striking. Both Japan and the US have wide-ranging vested industrial interests to protect (e.g. agricultural and labour-intensive sectors in structural decline) and this is reflected in the product-specific RoO regimes and various derogations on liberalisation (e.g. long phase-in schedules) found in their respective FTAs. As advanced industrial economies, Japan and the US also have an interest in signing sophisticated 'broad band' FTAs that incorporate provisions in areas such as intellectual property rights, mutual recognition agreements, investment, and e-commerce. However, the philosophy underpinning Japan's approach to FTA is fundamentally different to that of the United States. Indeed, Tokyo has a preference for the term 'economic partnership agreement' (EPA) rather than 'free trade agreement' (METI 2001, 2005b). As discussed in Chapter 2, the EPA approach derives partly from Japan's developmental political economy, which concerns the pivotal role of the state in realising transformative economic development objectives in partnership with business and societal groups (Aoki 2004; Ogita 2003). But perhaps a more important derivative of the EPA approach is Japan's large-scale development assistance programme that has made an especially significant impact on developing East Asian countries over time. While the US has advocated freer markets as the prime tool for development, Japan has traditionally placed greater emphasis on foreign aid and economic co-operation.

The confluence between Japan's trade and aid policies can be seen in the constituent elements of its FTAs, or EPAs. Thus, economic and technical co-operation, or ecotech, is conferred the same priority as trade liberalisation or market access more generally. This is particularly evident in Japan's FTAs/EPAs with Southeast Asia, which has received 30 percent of Japan's overseas development assistance since the 1990s. At the signing of the Tokyo Declaration in December 2003, Japan and ASEAN announced plans to incorporate various co-operative measures covering economic, political, security and social areas into the Japan–ASEAN Comprehensive Economic Partnership (JACEP), the framework that would later include an FTA element. The JACEP commits Japan to reinforce integration within ASEAN by narrowing economic gaps among the ten ASEAN states, enhancing the competitiveness of ASEAN countries and strengthening co-operation between Japan and ASEAN on issues such as institutional and human capacity. Japan has dedicated a fund of around US$4 billion to realising these objectives.

The equal status afforded to development co-operation provisions may also be considered a projection of Japan's developmental statist model onto its trade policy canvas insofar as these provisions entail proactive state involvement in realising transformative development objectives, e.g. in the fields of science and technology, human resource development (HRD), e-commerce and other areas of economic co-operation (Appendix C). This may be viewed as a kind of 'developmental inter-statism' in that priority is conferred to strengthen politico-diplomatic ties and cultivating new frameworks of economic development co-operation through this type of FTA approach. There are commercial motives at play here. For example, as part of its FTA negotiations with Thailand, Japan offered a package of economic co-operation programmes to assist the development of the Thai automobile sector.[34] In doing so, it was hoped to further improve the supply chain capacity of local Thai firms employed in the regional production networks of Japanese automobile manufacturers operating in the country (Yoshimatsu 2003; Miller *et al* 2004).

Hence, the 'broad band' nature of Japan's FTA model is skewed more towards enhancing economic co-operation rather than the behind-the-border market access bias found in the US model, and these differences in thematic content are clearly revealed in Appendix C. Yet Japan's insistence that trade liberalisation cover primarily *industrial* sectors, with an aversion to include agriculture, can run counter to the aforementioned developmental objectives, especially where the FTA partner is a developing country and hence its current development is still significantly dependent on agricultural exports. This is the main problematic with Japan's 'developmental–industrial' FTA model. Furthermore, Japan's FTAs partners have been on the whole sceptical about the actual level of economic co-operation they expect to be forthcoming from Japan as a result of their economic partnership agreements.[35] Finally, and just as with any FTA hub power, Japan's EPA approach could be viewed as bringing other East Asian states more closely into the country's sphere of commercial, regulatory and diplomatic influence, with it sitting in the regional centre. However, China's dramatic economic ascendancy presents a significant challenge to any regional hegemonic aspirations held by Japan (De Santis 2005; Rose 2004).

China's 'emerging developing country' FTA model. China's FTA model is not as well defined as the US's or Japan's, yet it can similarly be understood as a derivative of its national political economy. Whilst China's economy is fast advancing in terms of its techno-industrial and commercial sophistication, it should still be considered as essentially an emerging developing country. Its regulatory, legal and corporate governance structures are approaching the norms of a modern capitalist economy but there remain significant gaps in these areas. Given this, China has a penchant for relatively simple FTA frameworks with a narrow policy and regulatory focus (Antkiewicz and Whalley 2005). 'Broad band' elements, where they are included, tend to focus on like Japan's EPA model on development co-operation, rather than on elements such as IPR and investment (see Appendix C). Indeed, China's FTAs with Hong Kong and Macao are officially known as Closer Economic Partnership Agreements (CEPAs), thus with similar co-operative connotations as Japan's EPA approach. Yang (2004) notes that co-operation diplomacy is also a prominent feature of China's relations with ASEAN, as reflected in the ACFTA project (see Chapter 3).

Unlike Japan and the US, China has a preference for simple, regime-wide only rules of origin normally based on a value content modality. Trade liberalisation is primarily concerned with goods trade although services trade liberalisation is also included to varying degrees. Hong Kong's FTA negotiators fought a tough battle with Beijing over services liberalisation in its CEPA negotiations, as Chapter 3's case study on the agreement details. China also is particularly sensitive in areas deemed to infringe on national sovereignty, such as liberalisation of infrastructural, culture-related or strategic industry sectors. Relatively simple liberalisation phase-in schedules tend to be used, as in the CEPAs with Hong Kong and Macao in which 273 product lines were selected for first phase immediate tariff elimination with complete liberalisation for all products scheduled two years into the agreement coming into force. An 'Early Harvest Programme' of initial phase liberalisation in mostly agricultural products has been another feature of China's FTAs, as in ACFTA. In addition, China likes its FTA partners to agree to provisions on anti-dumping duties and countervailing duties to be incorporated that commit that partner to strictly adhering to WTO rules on this commercial policy practice. These types of duties have been applied extensively on competitively priced Chinese exports, which is typical for an emerging competitive developing country exporter. Finally, there are similarities between China's 'emerging developing country' model and FTAs signed amongst other developing countries, such as AFTA (Southeast Asia) and PICTA (Pacific Island countries).

Australia and New Zealand's 'closer economic relations' FTA model.   Australia and New Zealand are signatories to the longest standing bilateral FTA in the Asia-Pacific. Their 1983 ANZCER agreement is the bedrock of both countries' preferred FTA model, and is founded on the principle of comprehensive dynamic liberalisation. In this model, the scope of liberalisation tends to be complete both in terms of conventional trade liberalisation (e.g. tariff elimination) offered to FTA partners and in the covering of many 'behind the border' areas of commercial activity where the FTA partner is a developed country. This latter aspect thus has similarities with the US approach, which is not surprising given the 'market liberal' economy connection between these Anglo-Pacific countries. In the Closer Economic Relations (CER) model, marginally greater market access benefits may be conferred to developing country FTA partners, as in the Thailand–Australia FTA, although this does not mean the developing country partner has to make less of a commercial regime adjustment given their tariff levels are invariably much higher than developed countries. 'Dynamic' liberalisation comes from further broadening, deepening or accelerating of the FTA's liberalisation elements with comprehensive review and upgrading processes, as most evidently advanced in the ANZCER and Singapore's bilateral FTAs with Australia and New Zealand. These latter two agreements entailed the immediate and universal elimination of all tariffs between both signatory countries, making them amongst the world's 'purest' FTAs (see Appendix B). Australia also agreed to unilaterally liberalise its agricultural product tariffs in AUSFTA.

Contesting FTA models

One of the key debates about the emergence of different FTA models in the Asia-Pacific is to what extent we may expect contestation between them in terms of establishing regional norms of commercial policy and regulatory practice. There is also the question of whether an East Asian FTA model could arise based on a converged Japanese and Chinese approach to FTA formation. If this occurred, it could rival the US's own FTA model on which NAFTA and many other free trade agreements in the Western Hemisphere are founded or influenced by. We have already noted that both the Japanese and Chinese FTA models tend to embed trade liberalisation in a broader economic co-operation agreement. This is not only evident in agreements signed by Japan and China themselves but in those signed between other Asian countries. For example, the ASEAN–Korea, ASEAN–India, ASEAN–Australia/New Zealand, and Korea–India agreements are referred to as either 'Comprehensive' or 'Closer' Economic Partnership agreements. It is clear that economic and technical co-operation aspects will figure prominently in the negotiated final text of each agreement, thus consistent with the core 'economic co-operation' principles on which the Japanese and Chinese FTA approaches are founded. Furthermore, although the Korea–Singapore agreement is referred to as a Free Trade Agreement, it is very closely modelled on the Japan–Korea FTA project (still in negotiation by early 2006) and the JSEPA, whereby economic co-operation is afforded the same thematic priority as trade liberalisation. The TPSEPA is another case in point, where Singapore played a key role in advocating the economic co-operation dimension of the agreement (see Chapter 3) to its fellow parties, namely New Zealand, Chile and Brunei.

The basis for an East Asian FTA model, and hence a possible future EAFTA itself, is likely to rest, then, on this twinning of economic co-operation and trade liberalisation. However, significant levels of development asymmetry exist in East Asia, implying that the region's more developed countries have quite different economic co-operation interests compared to its less developed countries. Japan, South Korea, Singapore and Taiwan – advanced economies with robust trade policy capacities and the region's strongest developmental states – will wish to advance economic co-operation into relatively sophisticated industry sectors, such as broadcasting and e-commerce, whereas China and most ASEAN member states will press for co-operation in more basic, labour or resource-intensive sectors like agriculture and mining. Yet as Appendix B indicates there are many cross-sectional (as opposed to industry-specific) areas of economic co-operation commonality amongst East Asian FTAs, including science and technology, energy, education and SME development. Different East Asian states may have different preferences on the specific type or form of co-operation to be advanced in these areas but at least there is some convergence of interest in terms of the areas chosen for co-operation. What then becomes important is whether substantive economic co-operation arises from any agreement signed and thus what contribution it will make to regional community-building in East Asia. It is not clear from evidence of already in force bilateral FTAs that carry economic co-operation provisions (e.g. JSEPA) whether there should be cause for optimism here.

Notwithstanding the broad philosophical consensus amongst East Asian states on twinning economic co-operation with trade liberalisation, there still remains the challenge discussed earlier of achieving convergence on the technical policy aspects of FTAs, especially regarding trade liberalisation and regulation. For instance, Japan and South Korea prefer product-specific RoO (for industry protection reasons) whilst China and the ASEAN group do not. For similar motives, Japan and South Korea have pressed for multi-scheduled programmes of phased-in liberalisation across various product lines whereas China and ASEAN have preferred much simpler arrangements by comparison. Japan and other more advanced East Asian economies have an interest in fortifying IPR enforcement within FTAs whilst China and the ASEAN group do not, preferring to stress intellectual property *co-operation* (see Appendix B). East Asian countries will thus have to agree on lowest common denominators across various technical policy fields – both regarding basic trade liberalisation and 'broad band' elements – for a regional FTA to be realised, and this may be widely understood as a process of reconciling the needs and interests of developing and developed countries. If this cannot be achieved, then the prospect of competing FTA hubs in East Asia becomes more likely (Baldwin 2004).

When considering whose needs and interests will most prevail in both the formation of a regional hub FTA model (e.g. East Asia), and the contestation between hub FTA models themselves (e.g. Japan and US), certain aspects of international power relations must be taken into account. It is not being suggested that FTA hub competition between the Asia-Pacific's major trade powers will necessarily become a defining feature of the regional political economy but this is more likely to transpire if hub-and-spoke FTA bilateralism and regionalism continues to intensify. This may become a self-fulfilling prophecy as hub powers compete amongst themselves to acquire FTA partners as part of extending their spheres of commercial policy and regulatory influence across the Asia-Pacific, or counteract the influence of other hub powers by also signing an agreement with the same third country partner or partners.

A hub-and-spokes FTA pattern may be conducive to an eventual regional FTA being realised if the separate spoke FTAs may be made compatible with each other in this coalesced arrangement, as with the EU's pre-accession FTA process noted earlier. This would be consistent with region-convergent bilateralism under the *sub-structural foundation* and *congruent objectives and processes* points of contention. However, the hub power will want to differentiate the terms of conditions of each spoke FTA to some extent, depending on the politico-economic interaction with the spoke FTA partner. For example, the hub power may wish retain complex trade protection in sectors where the spoke partner poses a significant competitive threat, or decide to press for incorporating certain 'broad band' elements with those partners where deemed appropriate (e.g. on competition policy) and moreover to the hub's advantage. We have already discussed the problems of achieving technical policy convergence amongst a set of heterogeneous FTAs. Continuing in the context of region-divergent bilateralism, there is the further problem of *reinforced power asymmetries* arising from FTA hub powers using their relational power advantage over weaker trade partners to secure agreements more skewed to the hub power's interests generally. This power asymmetric problem does not arise to the same degree in multilateral arrangements as the influence of strong countries is more effectively circumscribed by collective membership power effects within the multilateral organisation or arrangement. Weaker countries may form coalitions within the multilateral fora to counterbalance hub power influence, and multilateral institutions are supposed to deliver agreements that represent the interests all members in an equitable manner (Narlikar 2003). Regional organisations such as APEC and APT can serve a similar purpose but are also susceptible to the same structural power dilemma as multilateral organisations in that powerful countries may be in a position to shape the rules and norms of the organisation by which all other member must comply. Significant power asymmetries will always exist in an international system where hub powers prevail. With regard to the Asia-Pacific's new FTA trend, it is a question of how best do non-hub powers deal the emergence of FTA hubs, and what are the systemic implications arising from a situation of contesting FTA hub models.

4.4.5   The Asia-Pacific Economic Co-operation (APEC) forum and FTAs

Introduction

An overview of APEC's organisational development, aims and attempts to advance trade liberalisation in the Asia-Pacific was previously made in Chapter 1. In this chapter, we have already discussed recent endeavours within APEC to establish codes of best FTA practice, and noted the importance of this given that the new FTA trend in the region has significant ramifications for APEC as an organisation. From the region-convergent perspective, some have argued that the proliferation of FTAs in the region is *congruent with the objectives of processes* of APEC as they help realise the aforementioned 'Bogor Goals' of establishing a free trade and investment zone across the Asia-Pacific by the 2010/2020 deadlines (Bergsten 2000, 2001). Thus, FTA bilateralism is serving similar ends as the regional organisation, and hence helping to bed down Asia-Pacific regionalism by this APEC-supporting process. Furthermore, bilateral FTAs offer *preliminary conditioning to the regional economic liberalisation and integration* in accordance to the APEC agenda generally. From a region-divergent bilateralism perspective, it could be argued that FTAs have *undermined* APEC's viability by subverting its founding principle of non-discriminatory 'open regionalism' and essentially *capturing* its objectives on trade liberalisation.

Open regionalism and reciprocity choice

It is widely acknowledged that the bilateral FTA trend has effectively supplanted APEC led initiatives on trade liberalisation in the Asia-Pacific. In addition to laying down terms of guidance on 'best FTA practice', arguments have been made for APEC to somehow adopt bilateral and plurilateral FTAs. For instance, Bergsten (2000, 2001) even suggested that FTAs constituted APEC latest strategy on trade liberalisation. However, unlike the previous failed Individual Action Plan (IAP) and Early Voluntary Sectoral Liberalisation (EVSL) strategies, FTAs have not evolved from any formal APEC process at all, nor can they be unless a switch in reciprocity choice is made regarding the method by which APEC-led trade liberalisation is supposed to be achieved. By this we mean the choice between specific reciprocity and diffuse reciprocity. As Keohane (1990) noted, successful developments in multilateralism have been partly founded on the mutual expectations of diffuse reciprocity, whereby signed up member states profit over time from the aggregated benefits expected in total from a multilateral agreement, such as the 1994 GATT Uruguay Round. Diffuse reciprocity is the underlying basis of APEC's open regionalism, and hence the *modus operandi* for realising the Bogor Goals.

In contrast, bilateralism is motivated by specific reciprocity: that is "the simultaneous balancing of specific *quid pro quos* by each party with every other at all times" (Ruggie 1993: 11). Not only, then, do FTAs run counter to the MFN principle of trade liberalisation but they also work on a specific rather than a diffuse reciprocity basis. The shift in preference amongst APEC's membership from 'concerted unilateral liberalisation', as embodied in the IAP and EVSL schemes first discussed in Chapter 1, to the 'concerted bilateral liberalisation' approach of FTAs clearly marks this switch in reciprocity choice by Asia-Pacific states. While, for instance, APEC members played a wait-and-see game on IAPs, proving reluctant to voluntarily jump first on unilateral trade liberalisation, bilateral FTAs were based on negotiated and firm understandings on reciprocated gains, committing trade partner in a mutually binding agreement to reduce trade barriers between them. The FTA route to trade liberalisation is thus completely incommensurate with APEC's still prescribed to principle of 'open regionalism'. Although the continued profusion of FTAs may well help achieve trade liberalisation in the Asia-Pacific, it is the *means* by which this goal is realised that runs counter to what APEC is supposed to uphold.

Coming to terms with the FTA issue

In addition to undermining the basis of APEC open regionalism, FTAs have also become the prime focus of regional trade diplomacy in the Asia-Pacific, making APEC look increasingly redundant on trade liberalisation issues. As the region's FTA trend has intensified, so has the organisation had to afford greater priority to addressing the FTA issue. To set the broader context of these twin endeavours, the development of APEC statements on the FTA trend should be examined. In November 2000, then Chairman of APEC's Economic Committee, Mitsuru Tanuichi, stated that, "pushing WTO and pushing RTAs should and will go together."[36] Tanuichi, then Deputy Director-General of Japan's Economic Planning Agency, made this announcement around of time of JSEPA's launch. At the 2000 APEC Brunei Summit, the Leaders Declaration noted that, "We note the recent developments in regional trading arrangements in the Asia Pacific. We agree that regional and bilateral trade agreements should serve as building blocks for multilateral liberalisation in the WTO. We therefore affirm that the existing and emerging regional trading agreements should be consistent with WTO rules and disciplines. We also believe that these arrangements should be in line with APEC architecture and supportive of APEC's goals and principles."[37] Very similar statements could be found in the APEC Leaders Declarations of the following five summits, and encompassing the region's FTA activity more into APEC's organisational ambit was ascribed increasing importance with each new Declaration. By the time of the 2002 summit, held in Los Cabos, Mexico, the Asia-Pacific FTA trend has proliferated to such a degree that in the eyes of many it was beginning to supplant APEC's functions for trade liberalisation diplomacy. Hence the Leader's Declaration reflected attempts to embrace bilateral FTAs into the Bogor Goals project. The statement also hinted of concern over the variance of trade rules generated by FTA proliferation in the region, and the need to establish some consistency between them. The 2002 Leader's Declaration stated that, "We called for an exchange of views in APEC on regional and bilateral trade agreements, noting that these agreements need to be consistent with WTO rules and disciplines and APEC's goals and principles."[38]

In response to the region's new FTA trend, and hence to make the organisation itself appear more relevant, APEC has tried to both enhance its own trade policy initiatives, or as earlier noted sought to adopt or rein in FTA activity within the Asia-Pacific, e.g. through 'best practice' guidelines. In 2001, APEC came up with the *'pathfinder'* concept whereby subsets of members may pilot new initiatives designed to spearhead APEC's work in certain areas, with other members joining at a later stage (MacDuff 2002). Notwithstanding their incompatibility with APEC's open regionalism principles, bilateral FTA projects were seen as consistent with this pathfinder approach, although it required them to have open accession clauses, which many did not (see Appendix C). Also in 2001, APEC member states endorsed a proposal to strengthen the IAP peer review process that included the establishment of IAP Peer Review Teams to conduct studies of economies under review. However, Findlay *et al* (2003) contends that within IAP peer review processes there has been apparently very little debate or analysis of the impact of the new FTA trend. Moreover, IAPs remained just as weak an instrument by the mid-2000s for advancing trade liberalisation as they did a decade earlier when they were first launched.

To compensate for continued failures on the trade liberalisation front, APEC summits have turned more to trade facilitation initiatives where there is stronger group-wide consensus and where far greater progress has been achieved. At the 2001 summit, APEC leaders signed up for the *Shanghai Goal on Trade Facilitation* with its aim of reducing trade transaction costs by five percent by 2006 (APEC 2002). A similar proposal followed at the 2004 summit, the *Santiago Initiative for Expanded Trade*, in which APEC member states pledged to continue efforts to reduce business transaction costs "by cutting red tape, embracing automation, harmonizing standards and eliminating unnecessary barriers to trade."[39] Trade ministers were also to make yet further recommendations to their leaders on how to boost trade liberalisation in a mid-term review on the Bogor Goals to be presented at the following year's summit in Busan. However, no substantive new measures were proposed in this review. Instead, it noted how trade and investment flows had increased in the region and implicitly ascribed credit to APEC for the reduction in the average tariff rate amongst its membership from about 17 percent in 1989 to 5.5 percent in 2004. Rather, this could be almost entirely attributed to the GATT Uruguay Round tariff liberalisation commitments of APEC members, and more lately the effects of bilateral FTAs themselves. The review also reminded APEC members again to sign 'high-quality' FTAs that were consistent with APEC 'best practice' guidelines as part of the *Busan Roadmap* (to the Bogor Goals).

Somewhat frustrated by both APEC's lack of substantive progress on catalysing trade liberalisation, and the 'spaghetti bowl' problem caused by proliferating bilateral FTAs, the APEC Business Advisory Council discussed at their May 2004 meeting in Taipei a proposal for creating a Free Trade Area of the Asia-Pacific (FTAAP). This was essentially a regional FTA that would encompass APEC's entire membership, and was forwarded to the 2004 Santiago Summit for consideration. It was implicitly argued that the bilateral FTAs were in some way providing the region-convergent basis (i.e. a *sub-structural foundation, congruent processes and objectives*) on which an FTAAP would be constructed (Scollay 2004). Fred Bergsten, who as Chapter 1 noted had advocated a very similar approach within APEC a decade or so earlier, lent his support to the FTAAP proposal, remarking that, "The only decisive way to restart the momentum of both APEC and global trade liberalisation, with all its political and security as well as economic benefits, is to launch the FTAAP process at Santiago," and further commented in the context of competitive liberalisation that non-APEC members like the EU, Brazil and India "could simply not afford to accept the discrimination that an FTAAP would imply for them. Hence they would have to 'sue for peace' by insisting on a rapid and substantively ambitious conclusion to the Doha Round."[40] At the summit, the proposal received backing from the hosts,

Chile, as well as the US, Canada, Australia, New Zealand, Singapore and Taiwan. The first five of these are the Asia-Pacific's most prominent free trade advocating nations. It was also no surprise that Taiwan supported the idea of an FTAAP given that it would circumvent the politico-diplomatic constraints on advancing its bilateral FTA policy arising from ardent and effective opposition from China (see Chapter 2). However, China, Japan, Malaysia and Indonesia expressed their opposition to the FTAAP proposal, stressing instead the core East Asian preference for advancing APEC's ecotech agenda. With no APEC-wide consensus, the FTAAP proposal was consequently ditched.

What serves what?

Our analysis in this chapter has shown that there are various problematic areas in APEC's relationship with FTAs. While APEC has sought to adopt the Asia-Pacific FTA trend as being integral to its own trade liberalisation agenda, it is APEC that is subservient to the FTA trend and not vice versa. By the mid-1990s, the APEC process had helped socialise Asia-Pacific trade ministers to the point where bilateral FTA deals were at least talked about, and this was an important origin of the earlier discussed politico-diplomatic discourse on FTAs and lattice regionalism. Thereafter, APEC ministers meetings and summits have provided showcase opportunities for announcing progressive developments of different FTA projects (e.g. the launch of negotiations or feasibility studies) or the actual signing of free trade agreements, as documented in Appendix A. We may expect APEC to further facilitate bilateral FTA development, and this deepening bilateralism based on preferential, specific reciprocity trade relations will thus to continue to undermine or capture at least the principles by which APEC promotes the advance of trade liberalisation and regional community-building *per se*. Region-divergent bilateralism has thus prevailed in this respect.

Jibes about the perceived redundancy of APEC – such as being 'four adjectives in search of a noun', or standing for 'Ageing Politicians Enjoying Cocktails', or 'a perfect excuse to chat' and not much else – partly stem from FTAs usurping a core aspect of APEC's work and purpose. The organisation is still perhaps the best forum for Asia-Pacific trade issues to be discussed, even if its functional capacity for actualising trans-regional trade liberalisation seems to have significantly diminished. As Otto (2000) argued, many of APEC's problems arise from it being essentially a 'declaratory regime' rather than a fully fledged regime, in that while its norms and procedures help reduce the transaction costs of concerted action, the organisation lacks the capacity to prescribe specific policies, generate sanctionable rules, binding decision-making procedures and other institutionalised mechanisms that are often necessary to help address particular types of problems (e.g. the EVSL programme debacle), or realise relatively ambitious objectives, such as the Bogor Goals. In sum, APEC has lacked the capacity to either resist the proliferation of bilateral FTAs in the Asia-Pacific or effectively adopt them into its ambit.

4.4.6   FTAs and developing countries

Development enhancing aspects of FTAs

Our last key issue of debate concerns the relationship between FTAs and developing countries. The case for region-convergent bilateralism here primarily rests upon the development enhancing aspects of FTAs, and hence how bilateral FTAs may build support amongst economic actors for more ambitious regional integration projects. Regional integration has been long viewed as an important development strategy option for developing countries (Bhagwati 1968; Cooper and Massell 1965; Gamble and Payne 1996; Johnson 1965; Schiff and Winters 2003; World Bank 2005). The urge amongst them to form stronger regional economic groupings must be generally viewed in the context of various integrational forces at work in today's globalising world economy. An essential function of an RTA is to create a larger unified, and hence more 'rationalised', market space for transnational commercial activities to operate within, yielding benefits of economies of scale, greater product and sourcing choices, and so on. Bilateral FTAs can perform these kinds of functions amongst developing countries on a smaller scale, but those signed with large developed countries may offer similar or even greater economic benefits. Southeast Asia is a useful illustrative example with regard to AFTA and the various bilateral FTA projects initiated by certain ASEAN member states (especially Singapore and Thailand) with the US, China and Japan.

Free trade agreements can lead to a wider development interaction between signatory countries. Coe *et al* (1997) found that trading partners obtain access to a country's stock of technological knowledge in proportion to their imports from that country. Thus by assisting the expansion of trade, and also foreign investment flows, FTAs can assist in the technology transfer process. Agreements that foster shared experiences in trade capacity-building can perform important development functions. This, then, will depend on the kind of 'broad band' FTA that developing countries sign with more advanced trade partners. Any emerging East Asian FTA model, with its emphasis on economic co-operation to complement trade liberalisation, is hence more likely to make contributions to trade capacity-building than other Asia-Pacific FTA models previously discussed. It also follows that FTAs that do seek to advance economic co-operation and free trade hand-in-hand offer greater opportunities for developing countries to catch up with developed countries in their region. More generally, FTAs can enhance regional economic interdependence between developed and developing countries where a pattern of agreements involving both country types is evident. We may therefore expect region-convergent outcomes from the strengthening of such ties and a closing of a region's development divide. Regional economic co-operation and integration is more difficult to accomplish however when asymmetry in development levels prevails.

The deficient capacity problem and the development divide

The above points rest on the assumption that developing countries have sufficient 'capacity' to effectively engage in bilateral FTA projects, meaning to initially study their prospective costs and benefits, negotiate them, implement signed agreements, and maximise their net welfare effects. By 'capacity' we are referring to the various development-related functions of the nation concerned, primarily comprising:

- *Technocratic capacity*: the quality and quantity of the nation's technocrats, either directly employed by or seconded to the government, that can be drawn upon to develop FTA projects (e.g. as negotiators or study analysts) and a robust FTA policy generally.
- *Industrial capacity*: the ability of the economy's industrial sectors to expand operations in newly created FTA markets, and therein undertake necessary structural adjustments required to compete effectively within those markets.
- *Institutional capacity*: the ability of the nation's institutional frameworks (e.g. legal, socio-cultural) to accommodate the various policy-related commitments incorporated into the FTA, such as on intellectual property rights and competition policy. Examples of 'institutions' in this sense mainly relate to agencies (e.g. anti-trust regulators, patent regulators) and associated laws and rules devised to enforce legislation once enacted.

As Chapter 1 first discussed, developing countries often lack these forms of capacity and it can pose fundamental constraints on and problems with entering into certain kinds of FTA project, especially those with developed countries that wish to negotiate on broad and sophisticated market access issues. Here, technocratic and institutional capacity deficiencies are particularly relevant, and Chapter 1 noted the cross-sectional linkages between the two, e.g. policy coherence. In this chapter, we are more specifically concerned with how the deficient capacity problem may *exacerbate the development divide within a region*, a region-divergent point of contention. Those developing countries with relatively strong capacity functions stand a better chance of being selected by developed country partners because they are more likely to accommodate developed country demands to incorporate market access 'broad band' measures (e.g. on competition policy, financial services liberalisation) into the FTA. For instance, Japan, the US and Australia all choose Singapore and Thailand as their first Southeast Asian FTA partners. More advanced developing countries such as these tend to have stronger export industry capacities than their less advanced coun-terparts. Thus, FTA conferred preferential access to developed country markets will spur the export-led growth rate of the former yet further ahead of the latter, thus prospectively leading to greater divergence in income levels between the region's states generally. Although very poor developing countries are conferred trade concessions in 'generalised systems of prefer-ence' schemes and non-reciprocal trade agreements, more advanced devel-oping countries are also often beneficiaries of the same schemes and agreements.

A number of Asia-Pacific developing countries remain more or less mar-ginalised in the region's new FTA trend. In East Asia, this especially includes the lesser developed members of ASEAN, namely Cambodia, Laos, Myanmar and Vietnam. While they are all participants in the AFTA regional project, as well as signatories to 'region-to-country' agreements that ASEAN has brokered with China and South Korea, none of these member states had launched 'country-to-country' bilateral FTA projects of their own by the end of 2005, whereas Singapore had initiated nine (ten including the TPSEPA) just within the Asia-Pacific region alone and Thailand six (see Chapter 1). Throughout 2003, Vietnam made several attempts to convince Japan to become its first bilateral FTA partner but was told by Tokyo that it must first accede to the WTO and demonstrate its capacity to accommodate certain 'broad band' FTA measures of interest to Japan. Even Southeast Asia's middle-order developing countries have faced significant capacity constraints in their attempts to develop their bilateral FTA policies as their comparatively low number of bilateral FTA projects thus far initiated suggests: by December 2005, two for the Philippines and one for Indonesia.[41] In Northeast Asia, Mongolia remains the only WTO member not party to any kind of FTA. In Oceania, the Pacific Island Country (PIC) group have their own regional trade agreement, PICTA, and a non-reciprocal trade agreement (PACER, the Pacific Agreement on Closer Economic Relations – see Appendix A) with Australia and New Zealand (Tabaiwalu 2005). In Pacific America, the Andean Community countries of Columbia, Ecuador and Peru are well behind the more advanced economies of Mexico and Chile in the number of bilateral FTAs signed with other countries (see Chapter 1). It is not just the lack of FTA-conferred preferen-tial access to developed country markets owing to capacity constraint issues facing weaker developing countries that is a problem. When developing countries do enter into bilateral FTA, their relatively weak capacity position places them at a relative disadvantage in negotiating with developed country partners. This relates again to the *reinforced power asymmetries* aspect of region-divergent bilateralism. Let us examine the broader perspec-tive on region-divergent outcomes in relation to each capacity area.

Technocratic capacity.   Even when developing countries do have ade-quately trained numbers of technocrats at hand to negotiate and implement FTAs, entering into a number of bilateral projects can place significant pressure upon these scarce resources, moreover diverting them from negotiating regional and multilateral trade agreements. Furthermore, governments must have the technocratic capacity to develop coherent policy frameworks that take into account the social, economic and other outcomes from signing FTAs. Developing countries have particular interests to consider in constructing this framework, such as: (i) the nation's trade balance and debt position, which are often precarious; (ii) infant industries and the agri-sector; (iii) FTA-induced reductions in import tariff revenue, which can be a significant source of tax income for developing countries; (iv) how broad market access demands of developed country FTA partners may compromise certain economic and social aspects of the nation's development policies. Without such a framework, developing countries may find themselves disadvantaged in FTA negotiations, as they are not able to properly assess the expected cost-benefit impacts of the agreement, not just upon industries but also other sectors such as health, food security, etc. This makes it important to involve related stakeholders in the impact assessment process, and ideally in wider consultative processes when formulating FTA policy, which presents another technocratic challenge for developing countries (Khor 2005). An UNCTAD (2004) report on developing countries and FTAs/RTAs furthermore noted that, "The effective management of the interface between national development objectives, regional initiatives and the overall trading environment demands the synchronising of domestic developmental requirements and objectives with external commitments in different layers of integration [e.g. FTAs]. This in turn requires the development of a development-oriented trade policy, and that there be a clear picture of the developmental implications of norms and disciplines being developed in the different layers of integration" (p. 15). Achieving this policy coherence with respect to FTAs thus presents a particular technocratic challenge for poorly resourced developing countries.

Industrial capacity.   The stronger a developing country's industrial capacity, the better positioned it is to optimise the new market opportunities presented by an FTA. WTO rules permit developing countries under certain terms and conditions to protect infant industries from injurious foreign competition (Amsden and Hikino 2000). As Wade (2003) notes, all fast developing countries in history experienced similar stages of protectionism before the capabilities of their firms were deemed to be robust enough to compete in international markets. This applied to Britain when it tried to catch up with Holland in the 17th and 18th centuries, to Germany and the United States when attempting to catch up with Britain in the 19th century, and to Japan and other newly industrialising economies from East Asia and elsewhere in the 20th century when endeavouring to close the techno-industrial gap with the West. Although adapting to the competitive disciplines of more liberalised market conditions can strengthen industrial capacity, intensified foreign competition arising from an FTA can also cause terminal damage to certain industry sectors. Developing countries may have sufficient restructuring capacity to address this problem but promising infant industries may fall victim to this injurious competition from developed countries that have pressured developing countries in FTA negotiations to abolish protection of these industries. For example, Thailand argued the case for protecting its nascent e-banking sector in FTA negotiations with the US, which was insisting that Thailand comprehensively liberalise its financial sector.[42] Furthermore, if under FTA liberalisation import growth runs significantly faster than export growth owing to a developing country's poor restructuring capacity then this may create balance of payments problems and subsequently other forms of macroeconomic disequilibria, e.g. inflation, rising foreign debt levels (Santos-Paulino 2005). Under WTO rules, developing countries are allowed longer transition periods for implementing trade liberalisation for this main reason (WTO 2003b). The Asia-Pacific region's most developed countries (Japan, the US, Canada, Australia and New Zealand) have also generally agreed to their developing country FTA partners to adopt multiple phase-in schedules on tariff elimination, thus allowing scope for gradualised industrial restructuring adjustment, but not without some reciprocation on their part. This especially applied to developed countries seeking the same gradualised liberalisation of their own industry sectors in structural decline, such as textiles.

Institutional capacity.   Following on from the above point made on adapting to the competitive disciplines brought on by FTAs, Das (2001) highlights a further related advantage arising from FTAs in that they commit developing countries to undertake structural economic reforms, such as eliminating restrictive trade practices and licensing procedures, streamlining customs procedures and regulations, integrating financial markets, and simplifying transfers and payments procedures. An implicit argument here is that this will strengthen the institutional capacity of developing countries to accommodate new areas of commercial regulation, including IPR, e-commerce, foreign investor rights, competition policy and rules on government procurement. As previously noted, the US in particular has a penchant for FTAs that incorporate 'WTO-plus' measures in these areas – often referred to as 'Singapore Issues', after the 1996 WTO Ministerial Meeting held at Singapore where they were tabled for discussion – that commit FTA partners to go beyond agreements or proposed measures at the WTO level. Discussions on the 'Singapore issues' had, though, been shelved at the WTO on the insistence of developing countries as part of the 'July 2004 package' agreement. Developing country resistance to linking Singapore Issues to trade agreements, whether multilateral or bilateral, relates to their weaker institutional capacity in comparison to developed countries to both accommodate the regulatory demands involved and exploit the commercial opportunities that may arise from such types of agreement. For example, regarding IPR, former head of the World Bank's trade research department, Michael Finger, estimated that the cost to developing countries of implementing their TRIPS obligations amount to US$60 billion annually (Finger 2002). For the Asia-Pacific's developed countries, IPR constitutes a key element in any FTA they negotiate, and have sought to advance intellectual property right protection beyond the TRIPS agreement, including patents and access to medicines, data exclusivity, and the protection of plant varieties. This point was raised earlier under the US 'asymmetric neo-liberal' approach to FTAs. Not only may the developing country FTA partner lack the institutional capacity to implement and therefore enforce such IPR legislation but compliance may incur certain competitive disadvantages and compromise certain industrial capacities, e.g. in the agro-business or pharmaceuticals sectors.[43] A similar unequal capacity disadvantage arises in government procurement rules, where developed countries have pressed their developing country FTA partners to include provisions that permit foreign companies to bid on the same terms with local companies for government contracts. Khor (2005) argued that, "This would drastically limit or eliminate policy space for the developing-country government to give preferential treatment to local companies and persons, and remove a crucial instrument for boosting the domestic economy" (p. 5).

Philippines case study.   The Philippines presents a useful case study on the deficient capacity issue. In their report published by the Philippine Institute for Development Studies, Medalla and Lazaro (2004) argued that the country had a weak technocratic and institutional framework for developing and negotiating FTA projects, and that the Philippines had appeared more of a passive negotiator or participant in its FTA projects. Not only did the country suffer from having only a small pool of sufficiently skilled and technically trained FTA negotiators but also public regulations on issues such as IPR and quarantine lacked the robustness demanded by more developed FTA partner countries, like the US, Japan and Australia. These kinds of regulatory gaps had led developed countries to afford low FTA project priority to the Philippines and other 'weaker' developing countries. In the meantime, the Philippines was recommended to rectify its deficient capacity problems by devoting considerably more resources to developing much higher level standards in these regulatory areas. Medalla and Lazaro (2004) also noted that the government has no concrete strategies or well defined policies toward FTAs. It was their view that the government had not sufficiently mapped out industry-by-industry adjustment and competitiveness strategies with industry leaders so as to maximise the potential commercial benefits of FTAs for the economy. The government's failure to properly identify what were the key sensitive industry issues from the onset was also highlighted to enable the classification of what products are negotiable and non-negotiable. They furthermore stated that, "institutional mechanisms, such as trade remedies and dispute-settlement mechanisms, should put emphasis on mutually agreed solutions and take into consideration other existing mechanisms like that of the WTO and other FTAs which may have proper concurrent jurisdiction" (p. 3). In addition, they recommended that the government should not only focus on what type of preferential treatment to give, but also have an established set of criteria in choosing an FTA partner. Their report thus highlighted typical capacity deficiency challenges facing developing countries in developing their FTA policies. More generally, if such challenges are not met it could exacerbate the development divide, thus leaving a significant obstacle in the path to regional community-building in the Asia-Pacific.

The reinforced power asymmetry problem revisited

Developing countries entering into FTAs with developed countries may find themselves disadvantaged by undue pressures placed upon their technocratic, industrial and institutional capacities. This will offset the earlier noted preferential market access gains of the more advanced developing countries being better able to sign FTAs in the first instance, hence to some extent mitigating the diverging income gap between FTA active and non-FTA active developing countries. Nevertheless, the income gap between developed and developing countries *per se* may diverge as a result of the latter group's general deficient capacity problems. Developing countries in the Asia-Pacific and elsewhere have greater scope to negotiate for non-reciprocal outcomes on trade liberalisation and other obligations in the WTO than in bilateral FTAs. This is mainly because certain 'development principles' are encoded in particular WTO rules but not always in bilateral agreements. Our discussions on different FTA models within the Asia-Pacific is relevant here as the 'economic co-operation' dimension found in East Asian FTAs are more aligned to the WTO in this respect. Khor (2005) makes the more general point that the, "equal treatment of parties that are unequal in capacity is likely to result in unequal outcomes. Whilst an advanced developing country that is already highly liberalised may be able to bear the pressures of faster liberalisation, other developing countries may not be able to compete with the faster opening of their markets or with other demands of the developed country" (p. 6). In a similar vein, Malaysian Prime Minister Mahathir Mohamad wryly commented in relation to developing countries and bilateral FTAs that, "We are ready to be exploited but (we) must be fairly exploited."[44]

Developing country groups within the Asia-Pacific (ASEAN, Pacific Island Countries, Andean Community, CACM) should where possible pool the group's technocratic capacities when dealing with any powerful trade partner to avoid that partner exploiting their relational power advantages, and moreover insist on negotiating on a 'group-to-country' basis. This, however, has often proved difficult. Taking ASEAN as an example, it has only managed to secure 'group-to-country' only FTA negotiations with China and Korea. Japan, Australia, New Zealand and the US have expressed their preference for parallel 'country-to-country' bilateral negotiations alongside 'group-to-country' talks. This potentially allows for individual ASEAN member states to be played off against others, thus leading to sub-optimal outcomes for each state as well as undermining ASEAN regional cohesion on economic and trade policy matters. This appeared to be the case emerging in the JACEP project during 2005, where there seemed to be no clear standard framework or format agreed between ASEAN states for separately negotiating bilateral FTAs with Japan, or how Japan's separately negotiated bilateral FTAs with Singapore, Thailand, the Philippines, Malaysia and Indonesia would be harmonised within the overall JACEP framework.[45] To counter this, ASEAN could insist on an MFN approach whereby market access concessions offered by an extra-regional partner to any ASEAN member state is then offered to all member states. This could be naturally applied to other developing country groups in the Asia-Pacific, to some extent therefore helping avert further region-divergent outcomes from developing countries' engagement in the region's new FTA trend.

4.5 Conclusion

This book has made a comprehensive study of the new Asia-Pacific FTA trend. In this concluding chapter, we have examined the critical relationship between FTA bilateralism and economic regionalism. It was argued that understanding the different aspects of this relationship is of great importance when considering the region's current and future international political economy. The emergence of FTA bilateralism in the Asia-Pacific was first put in historic perspective by looking at the earlier phases of trade bilateralism around the world. That experienced by Europe and the United States in the latter half of the 19th century and early half of the 20th century was particularly instructive. The 1860–1914 system of MFN-based trade bilateralism operated on the principle of minimised preferentialism but was then supplanted by the overtly preferential bilateralism and defensive protectionism that characterised international economic relations during the inter-war period. Whilst in recent times Asia-Pacific states have continued to liberalise their trade barriers generally, the increasing number of bilateral FTAs they are signing are inherently preferential in nature and hence creating structures of discriminatory trade relations in the region. Notwithstanding the potential risks this poses to the WTO and the multilateral trading system, there are grounds to justify the deepening bilateral FTA trend in the Asia-Pacific if it was making positive contributions to regional community-building, which is the essence of the lattice regionalism hypothesis.

The analytical framework developed in this chapter for examining the lattice regionalism hypothesis rests on two counter-perspectives, these being region-convergent bilateralism that supports the hypothesis, and region-divergent bilateralism, which rejects it. Under each counter-perspective are certain 'points of contention' that constituted the main substantive basis of the framework, these being deployed to critically assess the lattice regionalism hypothesis with regard to key issues in the FTA bilateralism–economic regionalism relationship in the Asia-Pacific. The first key issue addressed was the so called 'spaghetti bowl' problem, which particularly concerned the technical policy aspects of FTA heterogeneity. It was noted that a strong rationale exists for harmonising the different trade rules and regulations created by proliferating bilateral FTAs into coalesced sub-regional or regional arrangements. However, actually achieving such harmonisation is both in technical policy and political terms very difficult to achieve as each bilateral FTA is a bespoke product of the political economic interaction between different pairs of trade partners. We then considered the extent to which the politico-diplomatic discourse on bilateral FTAs and regionalism thus far developed amongst the Asia-Pacific political elite has advanced the prospects of lattice regionalism. Here, it is the power of commonly held ideas and beliefs by this political elite that is important because from this can come the political impetus to forge wider regional trade agreements from foundational bilateral FTAs. Yet there has been no real substance beyond the rhetoric from the Asia-Pacific's political leaders as to how the bilateral-to-regional evolution of economic integration is to be realised. Moreover, Asia-Pacific states have maintained a clear preference for bilateral rather than regional FTAs since the new bilateral FTA trend began in the late 1990s. Only a handful of relatively small sub-regional trade agreements (e.g. TPSEPA, PICTA, BIMSTEC) have been developed involving Asia-Pacific countries since this time, and moreover these agreements have not emerged from an overlapping set of bilateral FTAs amongst the countries concerned. Hence the links to a lattice regionalism dynamic here are tenuous at best.

The next key issue discussed was 'competitive liberalisation', which is based on the agglomeration principle that a growing critical mass of lower level (e.g. bilateral) FTAs creates politico-economic pressures upon recalcitrant trade liberalisers to sign bigger (e.g. regional or global-multilateral) trade deals. Connections here could be made to the 'domino theory' of trade integration in that one set of FTAs can lead to a cascade of others being signed as outsider countries seek to neutralise the trade diversionary effects of existing agreements in force. This is a dynamic process because as more countries become insiders so the economic costs of remaining an outsider increases, thus further intensifying FTA activity. It was argued, though, that there are inherent risks in pursuing a competitive liberalisation strategy. For example, after countries have gained free trade access to large country markets like the US through bilateral FTAs, the marginal market access benefits of then supporting regional and multilateral trade liberalisation agreements diminish accordingly. Competitive liberalisation also risks intensifying inter-state rivalry within a region by propagating a trade diplomacy culture based on the defensive and reactive motives of mitigating the negative impacts of other agreements. 'Competitive bilateralism' perhaps better describes the current reality of Asia-Pacific trade diplomacy whereby countries are seeking preferential market access advantages over others through bilateral FTAs, giving rise to politico-diplomatic tensions that are not conducive to regional community-building.

Closely linked to this was our debate on hubs, spokes and contesting FTA models. Here, we identified four different FTA models – the US's 'asymmetric neo-liberal' model, Japan's 'developmental–industrial' model, China's 'emerging developing country' model, and Australia and New Zealand's 'closer economic relations' model – and considered issues of alignment and contestation between them. These could provide hubs from which regional FTAs or other forms of economic regionalism could develop, such as an alignment between Japan and China's FTA model in East Asia founded on their similar priority afforded to advancing economic co-operation as well as trade liberalisation in their free trade agreements. At the same time, we may expect competition between FTA models and their constituent modalities (e.g. a preferred RoO or IPR regime) amongst major trade powers owing to the importance that FTAs now have in shaping the regulatory environment of the international trade system. Such a contestation could further intensify inter-state rivalry between the Asia-Pacific's major trading countries, as well as reinforcing power asymmetries within the region by these countries using their relational power advantage over weaker trade partners to secure agreements more skewed to the former's interests.

The relationship between APEC and FTAs was then considered. The idea that the new Asia-Pacific FTA trend was helping APEC realise its Bogor Goals of establishing a free trade and investment zone in the Asia-Pacific by 2020 was critically evaluated. Although FTAs may well help advance trade liberalisation in the region, and hence help reach this objective, it is the means by which the Bogor Goals are supposed to be achieved that is the crucial issue. Notwithstanding the continued ambiguity over the exact meaning of 'open regionalism', APEC still officially subscribes to its emphasis on the non-discriminatory and MFN-based path to establishing free trade. This is underpinned by the diffuse reciprocity principle whereby member states benefit over time from the aggregated benefits expected in total from a regional or multilateral agreement. Bilateral FTAs are, in contrast, based on specific reciprocity whereby pairs of countries agree to confer trade preferences and other commercial advantages on a *quid pro quo* basis and thus to the exclusion of other trade partners. It is this switch in reciprocity choice brought on by bilateral FTAs that subverts APEC's *modus operandi* on trade liberalisation, and in doing so has made the regional organisation look increasingly redundant given that the Bogor Goals represent its centrepiece project. We saw how attempts made by APEC to adopt or rein in the bilateral FTA trend have largely failed, although APEC meetings and dialogues have contributed to the socialisation of the Asia-Pacific's trade policy elite and subsequently helped foster the politico-diplomatic discourse on FTAs and lattice regionalism.

Finally, we discussed the key issue of FTAs and developing issues. The long-standing view that regional trade agreements form an important element in the economic development strategies of many developing countries was acknowledged. It was however argued that the ability of developing countries to effectively engage in any FTA project depended on their possessing sufficient levels of technocratic, institutional and industrial capacity. Evidence from the Asia-Pacific FTA trend indicated that many developing countries lacked such capacity to initiate a bilateral FTA policy, and those developing countries that had managed to instigate bilateral FTA projects were often at a capacity disadvantage when negotiating with developed countries. There potential negative economic and social impacts upon a developing country that could result from this capacity imbalance in FTA negotiations were discussed. Furthermore, bilateral FTAs were in the case of ASEAN – the Asia-Pacific's largest developing country regional organisation – potentially undermining its regional community-building endeavours within Southeast Asia. Another crucial point made was that more advanced developing countries have stronger export industry capacities than their less advanced counterparts, and therefore the FTA conferred preferential access to developed country markets will spur the export-led growth rate of these more advanced developing countries further ahead of non-signatory weaker developing countries. Thus, in sum an intensifying bilateral FTA trend can exacerbate the development divide within a region owing to these various deficient capacity factors, and it was noted that regional or multilateral trade agreements offer better options for these factors to be addressed.

In final conclusion, there appears to be more convincing evidence and arguments to expect more region-divergent than region-convergent outcomes from the FTA bilateralism in the Asia-Pacific. This study thus rejects the lattice regionalism hypothesis. To generalise, it is contended that the new bilateral FTA trend will mostly work against regional community-building in the Asia-Pacific through undermining the coherence and viability of existing regional organisations, intensifying inter-state rivalries, reinforcing power asymmetries and exacerbating the development divide in the region. The main recommendation from this book's study is that the risks and dangers associated with the new Asia-Pacific FTA trend need to be taken very seriously indeed. Moreover, it is time for economic diplomacy efforts to be diverted away from bilateral FTAs towards realising more critical international political economy challenges, especially securing a new multilateral trade agreement at the WTO that is primarily designed to boost the sustainable economic prospects of developing countries.

Notes

1 However, Yanai (2001) notes how the legacy of bilateralism persisted, observing that, "early GATT tariff negotiations were multilateral only in name. In reality, they were bilaterally negotiated between principal supplier states and principal consumer states based on reciprocity. The results of such negotiations were given to all contracting parties of the GATT on an unconditional MFN basis" (p. 8).

2 The *Zollverein* arrangement was formed over 1818 to 1834 and preceded the unification of the German state a few decades later. Elsewhere in Europe, the Swiss Confederation was established in 1848 as an economic union, and the Italian states created a customs union between them during 1860–1866, again preceding unification of their respective nation-states.

3 *Neo-functionalists* for example asserted that the emergence of a politico-economic community of nations came about when functional linkages in policy areas are accompanied by regional institution-building (Corbey 1995).

4 This compared to Europe's 62 percent and North America's 46 percent.

5 The APT framework was established in December 1997 at its inaugural summit convened in Kuala Lumpur.

6 'Commercial liberalisation' refers to the liberalisation of trade and investment regimes.

7 Even the long-standing European Free Trade Association (EFTA) group is bound in the EU's orbit to a significant extent by its party to the EU determined European Economic Area arrangement.

8 Regarding technical policy issues, Brazil and the other Mercosur nations opposed the US's demand to including investment, competition and government procurement in the FTAA negotiations.

9 Research interview with WTO officials, Geneva, September 2002.

10 The Bangkok Agreement was originally an initiative of the Economic and Social Commission for Asia and the Pacific (ESCAP), and is Asia's oldest preferential trade agreement. India, Bangladesh, South Korea, Laos and Sri Lanka were the Bangkok Agreement's founding members, with China acceding in 2001.

11 *Bloomberg News*, 02.11.2005. More specifically, China offered tariff reductions on 1,697 product lines, India on 570, South Korea on 1,367, Sri Lanka on 427 and Bangladesh on 209.

12 Tariffs began to be reduced in mid-2006, with products designated for 'fast track' treatment to be traded on a zero-tariff basis by mid-2009 for the three developed members and by mid-2011 for the poorer members.

13 *Financial Express* (India), 02.07.2005.

14 The Thailand–Australia FTA (TAFTA) has tariff liberalisation schedules on certain agricultural products that run up to 2025, although this is an arrangement between a developed and developing country.

15 APEC 2005 Leaders Declaration, or Busan Declaration, 18–19 November, p. 2.
16 *Associated Press*, 14.11.2003.
17 *Financial Times*, 18.11.2002.
18 *Korea Times*, 02.11.2005.
19 In a survey on the RoO regimes within RTAs, the WTO (2002b) found that 58 out of the 87 FTAs surveyed carried diagonal cumulation provisions, although most of these 58 were accounted for by European FTA linkages. The same survey found that only eight FTAs possessed full cumulation provisions. Meanwhile, 85 carried *de minimis* provisions and 81 adhered to the roll-up principle.
20 *Straits Times*, 26.01.2001.
21 *Straits Times*, 17.03.2001.
22 *Reuters*, 19.10.2003.
23 *Commercial Times* (Taiwan), 30.11.2001.
24 *Straits Times*, 25.05.2004.
25 *The Age*, 05.12.2005.
26 Research interviews conducted in Singapore and Malaysia (December 2004), and Thailand and Indonesia (July 2005).
27 *The Nation*, 20.04.2002.
28 Research interview conducted by the author with US–ASEAN Business Council representative, February 2003.
29 *New York Times*, 14.04.2002.
30 For example, the US were reportedly wanted to incorporate a 25-year period rule for enforcing drug patents in its FTA negotiations with Thailand during 2005, thus looking to extend beyond the 20-year period norm under TRIPS. *Asia Times*, 14.04.2005.
31 From USTR website: http://www.ustr.gov/Trade_Agreements/Bilateral/%20CAFTA-DR/Trade_Capacity_Building/Section_Index.html (accessed August 2005).
32 The CACM countries received US$47 million in trade capacity-building funds from the US in 2003. The US had also pledged a US$140 million capacity-building programme for FTAA participants.
33 Research interview with (US) National Association of Manufacturers representative, Washington DC, April 2003.
34 In introducing the scheme, Japan's Minister for Economy, Trade and Industry, Shoichi Nakagawa, remarked that, "we will meet their requests by providing know-how and technological assistance for industrialisation efforts, including personnel training at small and medium-sized enterprises." *Kyodo News*, 17.06.2005.
35 Research interviews with government officials and research analysts in Singapore, Thailand, Indonesia and Malaysia (December 2004, July 2005).
36 *Straits Times*, 13.11.2000.
37 Leader's Declaration of the 2000 APEC Economic Leaders Summit.
38 Leader's Declaration of the 2002 APEC Economic Leaders Summit.
39 Leader's Declaration of the 2004 APEC Economic Leaders Summit.
40 *AFP Press*, 10.11.2004. Bergsten also claims that in the early 1990s, APEC once considered sub-regional trade agreements as a viable way forward on Asia-Pacific trade liberalisation, primarily based on extensions of NAFTA. He cites the last report of APEC's Eminent Persons Group, which Bergsten chaired, which suggested a set of principles for 'open sub-regionalism' in the Asia-Pacific (Eminent Persons Group 1995).

41 This relates to 'country-to-country' bilateral FTA projects (e.g. Japan–Philippines) and not 'country-to-region' FTA projects such as ACFTA.
42 *The Nation*, 22.09.2005.
43 During US–Thailand FTA negotiations in 2005, for example, American pharmaceutical companies were lobbying US trade negotiators to restrict Thailand use of 'compulsory licensing' that allowed governments to circumvent laws protecting patented drugs so that cheaper generic versions could be produced, especially to tackle Thailand's AIDS problem. *Asia Times*, 14.04.2005.
44 *SBS News*, 21.10.2003.
45 Research interviews with government officials and research analysts in Singapore, Thailand, Indonesia and Malaysia (December 2004, July 2005).

Appendix A: The Chronological Development of Asia-Pacific FTA Projects

Notes

The sequential order of the FTA projects listed in this appendix corresponds to Table 1.2 in Chapter 1. The codes for development phase levels reached by FTA projects over time are given below.

[P] *Proposal for FTA made*: When either leaders or high government officials (e.g. Trade Ministers) from each FTA partner have mutually agreed to proceed at some point to FTA negotiations. This may have occurred after a commissioned FTA feasibility or scoping study, i.e. a pre-proposal study.

[S] *Study phase of FTA project*: When feasibility or scoping studies have been initiated, either separate or on a joint basis. The study phase usually comes after an FTA project has been formally proposed but in some cases governments will undertake or commission feasibility studies before proceeding to a formal proposal, such as the Australia–US FTA. In certain cases there may appear to have been no official study phase (e.g. Singapore–Canada FTA, Taiwan–Panama FTA), and sometimes only one FTA partner government appears to have initiated an official feasibility study, such as New Zealand in its FTA project with Hong Kong, or Australia's FTA project with Singapore.

[N] *Negotiating phase of FTA*: Noted from the first round of official FTA negotiations between FTA partners.

[C] *FTA negotiations concluded.*

[F] *FTA enters into force.*

Concluded or proposed before 1998

1.   *Australia–New Zealand Closer Economic Relationship (CER) Agreement*

The first full FTA to be established in the Asia-Pacific, entered into force on 1 January 1983. Built on a series of preferential trade agreements that had previously removed tariffs and quantitative restrictions on 80 percent of Australia–New Zealand trade. The CER concept was first introduced in March 1980 by a joint Ministerial communiqué. The first general review of the CER occurred in 1988, resulting in the signing of three protocols that accelerated the process of tariff liberalisation, brought services trade under the CER Agreement (the world's first bilateral FTA to do so), and established 'best practice' quarantine procedures. The 1992 general review updated the list of services exempt from the 1988 CER Protocol and clarified the CER's rules of origin. The 1995 general review focused on advancing trade facilitation issues, including the removal of residual regulatory barriers to trade. In March 2004, Australia and New Zealand discussed the idea of developing a trans-Tasman single economic market at a summit meeting between Prime Ministers John Howard and Helen Clark.

2.   *Chile–Mexico FTA*

Signed in September 1991 and into force January 1992. Tariffs on nearly all products were gradually reduced or eliminated by January 1996. Those on 181 other products were reduced from six to four percent in that month and subsequently abolished in 1998. Around 100 products are excluded from the agreed tariff cuts, including tobacco, sugar and petroleum. Partial liberalisation of investment, services and intellectual property also began in 1998.

3.   *Central America Common Market (CACM)*

CACM member states comprise Costa Rica, El Salvador, Honduras, Guatemala and Nicaragua. In 1993 they signed the Central American Economic Integration Protocol (or Protocol of Guatemala) to the General Treaty on Central American Economic Integration of 1960, a former agreement that had some success at liberalising intra-regional trade for a decade but then broke down owing to conflicts between certain CACM members (especially El Salvador and Honduras) and other factors, such as the impact of the 1970s oil crises. The 1993 Protocol established a regional FTA arrangement that operates bar region-wide or single country exemptions in key product sectors, e.g. coffee, sugar, certain petroleum derived products, tobacco, alcohol. Elements of a customs union also operate and there exist aspirations to realise other integrative objectives, including the eventual free movement of labour and capital and establishing monetary union.

4.   *North American Free Trade Agreement (NAFTA)*

A trilateral FTA between the US, Canada and Mexico, entered into force on 1 January 1994. Based on the *Canada–US* FTA, signed in 1988. Negotiations with Mexico began in June 1990, and an 'in-principle' agreement was signed in December 1992. A series of stringent compatibility measures were implemented running up to NAFTA's launch. The NAFTA stipulated the removal of most intra-group tariffs by January 2003. Tariff and non-tariff restrictions on certain sensitive goods are to be finally eliminated by January 2008. Additional measures include the liberalisation of services trade and investment restrictions and enhanced intellectual property protection.

5.   *Mexico–Costa Rica FTA*

Signed in April 1994 and into force January 1995 with a tariff liberalisation schedule of ten years.

6.   *Chile–Panama FTA*

First proposed in 1996 and negotiations commenced this year. Talks broke down in October 1998 after disagreement how to proceed on financial services. Negotiations were re-initiated in July 2004 and a free trade agreement agreed upon in February 2006 after the 15th round of talks.

7.   *Chile–Canada FTA*

Signed in November 1996 and into force July 1997. It specifies the immediate elimination of tariffs on almost 80 percent of traded items, and tariffs on remaining tariff lines are to be phased out over a period of up to 18 years. The liberalisation of certain services trade sectors is also included in the Agreement. On 1 January 2000, the schedule of tariff elimination on a number of goods was brought forward by between two to seven years.

8.   Mexico–Nicaragua FTA

Signed in December 1997 and into force July 1998 with a tariff liberalisation schedule of ten years.

9.   Chile–Peru FTA

Signed in June 1998 and into force July 1998. The agreement establishes five different tariff reduction schedules (i.e. immediate zero duties upon entry into force of the agreement, five, ten, 15, or 18 years) that are differentiated by the type of product and cover almost the entire universe of goods traded between the two countries. The sensitive textile industry has its own special tariff reduction schedule that will be phased in over the next three to eight years to culminate in zero duties for all items by 2006. In the agreement, Chile specifically managed to retain the right to maintain a price band mechanism on a select group of basic agricultural commodities, while Peru retained its special surcharge system for similar products.

10.   Chile–CACM FTA

Chile signed an FTA with the CACM group in October 1999, which entered into force with Costa Rica in February 2002, and with El Salvador in June 2002. Other CACM countries had yet to enact the agreement by 2005.

11.   Association of Southeast Asian Nations (ASEAN) Free Trade Agreement (AFTA)

A sub-regional FTA between the ten ASEAN states of Brunei, Cambodia, Indonesia, Laos, Malaysia, Myanmar, the Philippines, Singapore, Thailand and Vietnam. The core of AFTA was concluded by 31 December 2002 between the original ASEAN-6 members (Brunei, Indonesia, Malaysia, the Philippines, Singapore and Thailand) in industrial goods trade. Thailand and Malaysia were still negotiating up until September 2002 on Malaysia's decision to delay the liberalisation of its auto sector until 2005. Tariff elimination and reductions are made via the Common Effective Preferential Tariff (CEPT) mechanism, with allowances for fast-track tariff cuts and temporary and permanent exclusions. Newer ASEAN members have up to 2006 (Vietnam), 2008 (Laos and Myanmar) and 2010 (Cambodia) to meet the AFTA deadline on industrial goods trade. Thereafter, the original ASEAN-6 are working towards the total elimination of all import duties (including those on agriculture) by 2015, while for newer ASEAN members this deadline is 2018.

12.   US–Chile FTA

1991: Chile approached the US and proposed a FTA, but was asked to wait until after the introduction of NAFTA. Change of US government (Clinton) and loss of 'fast track' negotiating authority caused further delay.
December 1994: Chile asks again at the All-Americas Summit convened at Miami.
January 1995: Formally proposed. [P]
December 2000: First round of FTA negotiations. [N]
December 2002: FTA negotiations concluded after 14 rounds of talks. [C]
June 2003: FTA signed.
January 2004: FTA enters into force. [F]

13.   Mexico–Northern Triangle (El Salvador–Guatemala–Honduras) FTA

June 1997: Formally proposed. [P]

October 1998: FTA negotiations commence [N]
June 2000: FTA signed. [C]
March 2001: FTA enters into force with El Salvador and Guatemala. [F]
June 2001: FTA enters into force with Honduras. [F]

Proposed in 1998

14. South Korea–Chile FTA

November 1998: Formally proposed at the APEC Kuala Lumpur summit. [P]
December 1998: Korea–Chile FTA steering committee established.
March 1999: The first high-level working group meeting was held in, which began to conduct a feasibility study on the project. [S]
September 1999: Both sides announce plans at the Auckland APEC summit to launch FTA negotiations at the end of the year.
December 1999: First round of FTA negotiations. [N]
February/March 2000: Second round.
May 2000: Third round.
December 2000: Fourth round. FTA talks stall over agriculture issues.
February 2002: High-level talks held in Los Angeles fail to break the deadlock over agriculture.
August 2002: Fifth round.
October 2002: FTA negotiations concluded after six rounds of talks. [C]
February 2003: FTA signed.
July 2003: South Korean Government submits the FTA bill for ratification in the National Assembly.
August 2003: Chilean lower house of parliament ratifies FTA.
December 2003: South Korea's National Assembly delays voting on the FTA bill.
January 2004: Chilean upper house of parliament ratifies the FTA. South Korea's National Assembly delays voting on the FTA bill again.
February 2004: South Korea's National Assembly finally ratifies the FTA.
April 2004: FTA enters into force. [F]

15. Japan–South Korea FTA

November 1998: Formally proposed at the inaugural gathering of Japan–South Korea Cabinet Ministers Meeting. [P]
December 1998: The Korea Institute for International Economic Policy (KIEP) and Japan's Institute of Developing Economies (IDE) at JETRO established the '21st Century Japan–Korea Economic Relations Study Team', and commence their joint study on a bilateral FTA project. [S]
March 1999: Leaders from both countries announce the Japan–Korea Economic Agenda 21 for enhancing bilateral economic relations in which an FTA would play a central role.
May 2000: KIEP-IDE Joint Study, *Towards Closer Japan–Korea Economic Relations: Proposal for Formulating a 21st Century Partnership*, is published.
September 2000: Both sides agree to establish their own FTA Business Forums, consisting of selected business executives.
December 2000: Korea–Japan FTA Business Forum meet in Seoul for their inaugural meeting.
May 2001: Japan–Korea FTA Business Forum meet in Tokyo for their inaugural meeting.

September 2001: First Joint FTA Business Forum meeting held in Seoul.

January 2002: Second Joint FTA Business Forum meeting held in Tokyo, from which was released a Joint Communiqué that stated a Japan–South Korea FTA should be actively promoted.

March 2002: At their summit meeting, Korea President Kim Dae-jung and Japan Prime Minister Junichiro Koizumi agree to establish a Japan–Korea FTA Joint Study Group, consisting of policy-makers, business leaders and academics from the two countries. Japan and South Korea also sign a bilateral investment treaty at this summit.

February 2003: Three rounds of Japan–Korea FTA Joint Study Group discussions held by this time.

October 2003: At the 2003 APEC summit, both sides announce their intention to conclude an FTA by the end of 2005, and to start FTA negotiations by the end of 2003.

December 2003: First round of FTA negotiations. [N]

March/April 2005: Seventh round. Talks stalled over agricultural issues and by the flaring up of a decades-old territorial dispute over the Takeshima (Japan)/Dokdo (Korea) islands.

16.   *South Korea–Thailand FTA*

November 1998: Formally proposed. [P]

November 1999: Agreement reached on a joint feasibility study to be conducted by KIEP on the Korean side, and the Department of Business Economics under Thailand's Ministry of Commerce and Chulalongkorn University on the Thai side. [S]

March 2001: Joint feasibility study completed but not published because the findings were deemed too sensitive, especially with regard to South Korea's agriculture industry.

October 2003: South Korean President Roh Moo-hyun announces that his country cannot rush into an FTA with Thailand, stating that South Korea must first come to terms with agricultural reform.

Proposed in 1999

17.   *South Korea–New Zealand FTA*

July 1999: proposal for a bilateral FTA first made at a summit in Seoul. [P]

September 1999: At a summit meeting in Wellington, South Korean President Kim Dae-jung and New Zealand Prime Minister Jenny Shipley agree to initiate studies on a bilateral FTA, to be undertaken by the Korea Institute of International Economic Policy (KIEP) and New Zealand Institute of Economic Research (NZIER).

October 1999: FTA study phase begins. [S]

April 2001: Study report produced by NZIER.

August 2001: Review meeting of the findings of the first joint study held in New Zealand.

October 2003: The New Zealand–Korea Business Council, further promotes the idea of a bilateral FTA.

18.   *New Zealand–Singapore Closer Economic Partnership (ANZSCEP)*

September 1999: Formally proposed at the APEC Auckland summit. [P]

October 1999: Scoping study of proposed FTA initiated. [S]

January 2000: First round of FTA negotiations. **[N]**
August 2000: FTA negotiations concluded after six rounds of talks. **[C]**
November 2000: FTA signed.
January 2001: FTA enters into force. Both sides agreed to meet by January 2008 to review those services trade sectors that remained to be fully liberalised by 2010. **[F]**

19.   *Japan–Singapore Economic Partnership Agreement (JSEPA)*

September 1999: Formally proposed at the APEC Auckland summit. **[P]**
December 1999: Leaders from both sides agree to establish a Joint Study Group (JSG) consisting of business leaders, government officials and academics to look at a bilateral FTA project.
March–September 2000: JSG meets five times. **[S]**
October 2000: Agreement to initiate negotiations in January 2001.
February 2001: First round of FTA negotiations. **[N]**
October 2001: FTA negotiations concluded after four round of talks. **[C]**
January 2002: FTA signed.
November 2002: JSEPA enters into force. **[F]**

20.   *Singapore–Mexico FTA*

September 1999: Formally proposed at the APEC Auckland summit. **[P]**
July 2000: First round of negotiations. **[N]**
November 2000: Four rounds of negotiations conducted by this time.
December 2000: New Mexican President Vincente Fox de-prioritises Singapore–Mexico FTA project. Negotiations are postponed indefinitely.

21.   *Japan–Mexico FTA*

September 1999: Formally proposed at the APEC Auckland summit. **[P]**
April 2000: Japan's JETRO and Mexico's Ministry of Commerce and Industrial Development (SECOFI) published a study report on a bilateral FTA project as part of looking at ways to strengthen economic relations between the two countries generally. **[S]**
June 2001: Both sides agreed to set up a Joint Study Group (JSG), consisting of policy-makers, business leaders and academics from the two countries.
September 2001: First JSG meeting held.
July 2002: JSG report is published after five JSG meetings.
October 2002: At the 2002 APEC summit, both sides announce their intention to conclude a bilateral FTA by the 2003 APEC summit.
November 2002: First round of FTA negotiations. **[N]**
October 2003: Fifth round of FTA negotiations conducted in Tokyo. The aim to conclude FTA talks by this month fails owing to disagreements on agriculture liberalisation, especially pork and orange juice.
March 2004: FTA negotiations concluded after 14 rounds of talks. **[C]**
September 2004: FTA signed.
April 2005: FTA enters into force. **[F]**

22.   *Canada–Costa Rica FTA*

November 1999: Formally proposed. **[P]**
February 2000: Scoping study on FTA initiated. **[S]**
June 2000: First round of FTA negotiations. **[N]**

April 2001: FTA negotiations concluded after seven rounds of talks. The agreement is also signed in this same month. [C]
November 2002: FTA enters into force. [F]

23.   *Pacific Island Countries Trade Agreement (PICTA)*

October 1999: Leaders of the Forum Islands group (Pacific Island Countries plus Australia and New Zealand) agree to initiate negotiations on two parallel trade agreements, these being a Pacific Island Countries Trade Agreement (PICTA) and a Pacific Agreement on Closer Economic Relations (PACER). PICTA is an FTA between the 14 Pacific Island Countries (PICs). PACER provides Australia and New Zealand an assurance that they will not be disadvantaged in PIC markets as a result of any arrangements the PICs may conclude with the EU and other developed country trade partners. In return, Australia and New Zealand provide trade facilitation and financial and technical assistance to the PIC group under the PACER arrangement. Imports from the PIC group had previously been granted duty free access on a non-reciprocal basis to the New Zealand and Australian markets under the South Pacific Regional Trade and Economic Agreement (SPARTECA). The PIC group comprises the Cook Islands, Federated States of Micronesia, Fiji, Kiribati, Nauru, Niue, Palau, Papua New Guinea, Marshall Islands, Samoa, Solomon Islands, Tonga, Tuvalu and Vanuatu. [P]
April 2000: First round of negotiations on both Agreements. [N]
June 2001: Negotiations concluded. PIC Trade Ministers endorse PICTA at a meeting in the Samoan capital Apia. They agree to exempt a number of products (most notably alcohol and tobacco) from trade liberalisation for the first two years (different excepted imports lists for different PIC states), to allow a study into what impact liberalisation may have. These products will be completely liberalised by the end of 2015. Some countries subsequently look to develop new sources of tax revenue. The larger PIC economies are scheduled to abolish most tariffs by the end of 2009 and the smaller ones by the end of 2011. [C]
August 2001: Leaders of most PIC members sign PICTA and PACER. It is agreed that PICTA will enter into force after six countries have ratified it, and PACER after seven countries have done so.
October 2002: PACER enters into force between Australia, Cook Islands, Fiji, New Zealand, Niue, Samoa, and Tonga after these countries ratify the agreement.
April 2003: PICTA enters into force between the Cook Islands, Fiji, Nauru, Niue, Samoa, and Tonga after these countries ratify the agreement. [F]
June 2003: Solomon Islands and Kiribati both ratify PICTA and PACER.
August 2003: Papua New Guinea ratifies PICTA.
June 2005: Vanuatu ratifies PICTA. PICTA now in force between ten PIC economies.

24.   *Japan–Chile FTA*

November 1999: Formally proposed. [P]
May 2000: JETRO and the Chile's Directorate General of International Economic Relations (DIRECON) establish a bilateral FTA study group. [S]
June 2001: Study group releases its report, recommending the commencement of FTA negotiations as soon as possible.
November 2002: Chilean Foreign Minister, Soledad Alvear, visits Japan and conveys her government's interest in starting FTA talks as soon as possible.
February 2003: Both sides agree to discuss the feasibility of a bilateral FTA at talks planned for the end of this year.

November 2004: In the run up to the 2004 APEC summit, both sides announce their continued commitment to the FTA project with the hope of commencing talks in the new year.
October 2005: Announcement made that both sides plan to commence FTA negotiations in early 2006.

Proposed in 2000

25. *Panama–CACM FTA*

June 2000: Formally proposed. [P]
October 2000: FTA negotiations commence. [N]
February 2002: FTA signed. [C]

26. *Singapore–Australia FTA*

November 2000: Formally proposed at the APEC Summit. The Australian Government commission a study report around this time. [P] [S]
February 2001: First round of FTA negotiations. [N]
November 2002: FTA negotiations concluded after ten rounds of talks. [C]
February 2003: FTA signed.
July 2003: FTA enters into force.

27. *ASEAN–China FTA (ACFTA), or Framework Agreement*

November 2000: Formally proposed. A scoping study is also initiated. [P] [S]
March 2001: ASEAN–China Experts Group on Economic Co-operation created, with one of its tasks being to study the feasibility of an ACFTA project.
November 2001: Both sides agree on the broad negotiating framework for ACFTA, with the announced intention to implement the agreement by 2010.
October 2001: Scoping study report, 'Forging Closer ASEAN Economic Relations in the 21st Century', is published.
May 2002: First round of FTA negotiations. [N]
November 2002: First phase FTA negotiations concluded. ASEAN and China sign their 'Framework Agreement' at the 2002 ASEAN Plus Three (APT) summit in Phnom Penh that commit both sides to liberalise bilateral trade by 2010. Cambodia, Laos, Myanmar and Vietnam (CLMV group) to meet this target by 2015. ASEAN and China also agree to an 'Early Harvest' programme (EHP) of immediate tariff cuts to be implemented within three years on selected agricultural and forestry products. [C – agricultural]
June 2003: Thailand and China conclude negotiations on a bilateral EHP agreement ahead of other ASEAN member states.
October 2003: Thai–China EHP agreement enters into force, covering 188 agricultural products.
November 2003: All ASEAN member states and China sign an EHP protocol agreement at that year's APT summit covering Harmonised System of Tariffs (HST) chapters 1 to 8, as well as 130 specific manufactured goods.
January 2004: EHP protocol agreement enters into force, although the Philippines and China have yet to negotiate the former's proposed EHP exclusion list. [F]
June 2004: The 30th June 2004 deadline for concluding negotiations on tariff elimination for all remaining manufacturing sector products is missed.
September 2004: The Philippines and China finally reach a conclusion on their EHP arrangement.

November 2004: Second phase FTA negotiations concluded. At the APT Summit held in Vientiane, both sides reach an agreement on the elimination of tariffs for all products, with sensitive list exemptions and phase-ins. Some inclusion of services trade liberalisation also agreed upon. [C – **industrial**]
December 2004: Tariff levels on EHP products to be reduced to a ten percent maximum by the end of the month.
January 2005: Tariff elimination on non-EHP manufactured products to commence implementation.
June 2005: China and ASEAN agree to eliminate tariffs for 7,445 categories of goods, or a total of 95 percent of overall goods, by 2010.
December 2005: Tariff levels on EHP products to be reduced to a five percent maximum by the end of the month.
December 2006: Tariff levels on EHP products to be reduced to zero percent maximum by the end of the month.

28.   US–Singapore FTA

November 2000: Formally proposed at the APEC summit. [P]
December 2000: First round of negotiations. [N]
November 2002: Eleventh formal round of negotiations. Attempts to finalising an agreement are hindered by unresolved issues over Singapore's right to use capital controls.
January 2003: Final FTA negotiations concluded through video-conferencing and telephone conferencing. [C]
May 2003: FTA signed.
January 2004: FTA enters into force. [F]

Proposed in 2001

29.   Thailand–New Zealand FTA

March 2001: Formally proposed. [P]
June 2003: At the 2003 APEC Trade Ministers' meeting in Khon Kaen, both sides agree to undertake a joint scoping study into a bilateral FTA.
October 2003: At the 2003 APEC summit in Bangkok, both sides announce their plans to commence FTA negotiations as soon as their scoping study is complete with a view to signing an FTA by the 2004 APEC summit.
December 2003: Joint scoping study initiated between the Thai Ministry of Commerce and the New Zealand Ministry of Foreign Affairs and Trade. [S]
April 2004: Joint scoping study completed.
June 2004: First round of FTA negotiations. [N]
November 2004: FTA negotiations concluded after four rounds of talks. [C]
April 2005: FTA signed.
July 2005: FTA enters into force. [F]

30.   Hong Kong–New Zealand FTA

November 2000: Both sides discuss in Wellington the idea of initiating a bilateral FTA project.
April 2001: Formally proposed. The New Zealand Government publishes a bilateral FTA discussion paper, and also initiates a consultation study. [P] [S]
May 2001: First round of FTA negotiations. [N]
January/February 2002: Fifth round of FTA negotiations.
March 2002: Talks stalled over the disagreements on rules of origin issues.

31. *South Korea–Mexico FTA*

June 2001: Formally proposed. [P]
July 2002: Agreement to initiate a scoping studies on a bilateral FTA at the end of the year. However, this deadline is missed.
November 2003: Scoping studies initiated. [S]
October 2004: First meeting of the Korea–Mexico Joint Experts Group on bilateral economic relations discusses the progress of FTA scoping studies.
December 2004: Second meeting of the Korea–Mexico Joint Experts Group.
September 2005: Planned start for FTA negotiations are stalled owing to unresolved matters regarding auto sector investment issues. Both sides instead agree to sign a Strategic Economic Complementation Agreement (SECA) as soon as possible, which will include: customs-free trade for selected items; efforts to increase service trade and investment; and expanded cooperation in a range of other fields including technology, human resources, tourism and fisheries and small and medium-sized business.

32. *Canada–CACM FTA*

September 2001: Formally proposed. [P]
November 2001: First round of FTA negotiations. [N]
February 2004: Tenth round of FTA negotiations. Talks stalled over the disagreements on issues such as textiles and agriculture.

33. *Thailand–Australia FTA*

April 2001: Australia sends signals to Thailand that it may be interested in a bilateral FTA project after Malaysia vetoes an AFTA-CER FTA proposal.
July 2001: Formally proposed. [P]
November 2001: At the WTO Doha Ministerial Meeting, Australian and Thai Trade Ministers agree terms of reference for their bilateral FTA scoping study. [S]
May 2002: Joint study on FTA published.
August 2002: First round of FTA negotiations. [N]
October 2002: Second round of FTA negotiations.
November 2002: Both sides make a joint statement announcing their intention to conclude FTA negotiations by June 2004.
January 2003: Third round of FTA negotiations.
April 2003: Fourth round of FTA negotiations.
June 2003: Fifth round of FTA negotiations. Both sides also announce their intentions for an earlier conclusion of FTA negotiations by October 2003, in time for the APEC summit hosted by Thailand.
April 2004: FTA negotiations concluded after eight rounds of talks. [C]
July 2004: FTA signed.
January 2005: FTA enters into force. [F]

34. *Singapore–Canada FTA*

October 2001: Formally proposed at the APEC Shanghai summit. [P]
January 2002: First round of negotiations. [N]
October 2003: Sixth round of negotiations. Talks stall for undeclared reasons.

35. *Hong Kong–China Closer Economic Partnership Agreement (HKCCEPA)*

December 2001: Formally proposed. [P]
January 2002: First round of FTA negotiations. [N]

June 2003: FTA negotiations concluded after five rounds of talks. Agreement signed at the end of the month. [C]
January 2004: FTA enters into force. [F]

36.   *Japan–Thailand Economic Partnership Agreement (JTEPA)*

November 2001: Formally proposed. [P]
February 2002: Joint study group created to examine ways of enhancing bilateral economic ties, including an FTA. [S]
January 2003: Both sides announce plans to commence FTA talks in mid-2003.
June 2003: Launch of FTA negotiations postponed owing to Japan's inability to secure a domestic consensus on agricultural trade issues.
February 2004: First round of FTA negotiations. [N]
February 2005: Ninth round of FTA negotiations. Disagreements arise on steel, automotive and agriculture sector issues.
August 2005: Basic agreement reached after ten rounds of talks.

Proposed in 2002

37.   *Taiwan–Panama FTA*

February 2002: Formally proposed. [P]
October 2002: First round of FTA negotiations. [N]
August 2003: FTA negotiations concluded after six rounds of talks. [C]
September 2003: FTA signed.
January 2004: FTA enters into force. [F]

38.   *Australia–US FTA*

December 2000: Australia's Ambassador to the US, Michael Thawley, proposes an FTA between Australia and the US in a speech made in Washington DC.
January 2001: Australia's DFAT commission two study reports on the impact of AUSFTA. [S]
November 2002: Formally proposed. [P]
March 2003: First round of FTA negotiations. [N]
February 2004: FTA negotiations concluded after seven rounds of talks. [C]
May 2004: FTA signed between the trade ministers of both countries.
January 2005: FTA comes into force. [F]

39.   *Malaysia–US FTA*

October 2002: Formally proposed at the 2002 APEC Los Cabos summit. [P]
November 2002: Feasibility studies initiated. [S]
May 2004: Both sides sign a Trade and Investment Framework Agreement (TIFA), a pre-requisite for the US before FTA negotiations can commence.
May 2005: A second round of TIFA consultations are held and both sides reconfirm their commitment to work towards commencing FTA negotiations.
October 2005: The US announces that it would like to conclude an FTA with Malaysia by June 2007, the month when the US President's current Trade Promotion Authority expired.

40. *Philippines–US FTA*

October 2002: Formally proposed at the 2002 APEC Los Cabos summit. **[P]**
May 2003: The US announces that Thailand, Indonesia and the Philippines are at the top of its list of future potential FTA partners in Asia.
August 2004: The Philippines' Department of Trade and Industry (DTI) commissions the Philippine Institute for Development Studies to undertake a cost-benefit study on the proposed FTA between the Philippines and the US. **[S]**
March 2005: The US urges the Philippines to proceed with preparations towards launching FTA negotiations, subject to the country first signing a TIFA.

41. *South Korea–Singapore FTA*

November 2002: Formally proposed. **[P]**
March 2003: First meeting of Joint Study Group (JSG) conducting the FTA feasibility study. **[S]**
October 2003: Joint Study Group report published, recommending the start of FTA negotiations as soon as possible. Leaders from both sides agree to commence negotiations in early 2004.
January 2004: First round of FTA negotiations. Both sides announce their intention to conclude negotiations by the end of the year. **[N]**
November 2004: FTA negotiations concluded after seven rounds of talks, held on the sidelines of the 2004 APT summit in Vientiane. **[C]**
August 2005: FTA signed.
January 2006: FTA enters into force. **[F]**

42. *Trans-Pacific Strategic Economic Partnership Agreement (TPSEPA) – Singapore, New Zealand, Chile and Brunei*

1995: New Zealand and Chile discuss the possibility of a bilateral FTA but no agreement to initiate negotiations was reached.
September 1999: Singapore–Chile bilateral FTA formally proposed at the APEC Auckland summit.
October 2000: New Zealand–Chile bilateral FTA formally proposed at the APEC Brunei summit.
November 2000: The idea of a 'Pacific-3' FTA (P3FTA) involving New Zealand, Chile and Singapore raised during the APEC Brunei Summit.
October 2001: The P3FTA issue discussed again during the APEC Shanghai Summit.
November 2001: New Zealand and Chile agree to initiate parallel feasibility studies on a P3FTA project. **[S]**
October 2002: Parallel feasibility studies published, recommending the commencement of negotiations, either bilaterally between New Zealand and Chile, or trilaterally with Singapore. The latter approach is formally proposed at the 2002 APEC Los Cabos Summit, with the aim of concluding negotiations by APEC's October 2004 summit. **[P]**
July 2003: First round of FTA negotiations. **[N]**
April 2005: Fifth round of FTA negotiations. Brunei, which had participated in preceding rounds of FTA negotiations as an observer, took part in this round as a full negotiating party.
May 2005: FTA negotiations concluded after six rounds of talks. **[C]**
June 2005: FTA signed at the APEC Trade Ministers Meeting in Jeju, South Korea.

July 2005: Accompanying agreements on labour co-operation and environment co-operation signed.
January 2006: FTA enters into force. [F]

43.   *Japan–Philippines Economic Partnership Agreement (JPEPA)*

May 2002: Both sides commit to initiating feasibility studies on a bilateral FTA.
October 2002: JPEPA Working Group initiates its feasibility study on the FTA. [S]
November 2002: Formally proposed at the 2002 APEC summit. [P]
December 2003: Working Group feasibility study published.
February 2004: First round of FTA negotiations. [N]
July 2004: During the third round a stalemate arises over the Philippines' requests concerning the entry of Filipino nurses, health workers and lawyers into Japan.
November 2004: Basic agreement reached after six rounds of talks.
November 2005: Both sides hope to sign a full agreement after resolving certain trade and immigration issues.
December 2005: Final negotiating held up by a case filed by civic groups with the Philippines Supreme Court that placed a temporary restraining order on the Philippine government from concluding a bilateral Free Trade Agreement (FTA) with Japan.

44.   *Taiwan–Costa Rica FTA*

October 2002: Formally proposed in a joint communiqué signed at a summit held in Taipei. An agreement signed on IPR protection was also signed at this summit, seen as paving the way for the FTA project. [P]

45.   *Japan–Malaysia Economic Partnership Agreement (JMEPA)*

December 2002: Formally proposed. [P]
May 2003: JMEPA Working Group formed to conduct a feasibility study on the FTA. [S]
October 2003: Working Group feasibility study published.
January 2004: First round of FTA negotiations. [N]
May 2005: FTA negotiations concluded after ten rounds of talks. [C]
December 2005: FTA signed. Both sides intend to have the agreement enter into force by the third quarter of 2006.

Proposed in 2003

46.   *US–CACM FTA (CAFTA)*

January 2002: President Bush announced his intention to negotiate an FTA with the Central American Common Market (CACM) group of countries (Costa Rica, El Salvador, Guatemala, Honduras and Nicaragua) in a speech before the Organization of American States.
October 2002: The Bush Administration notifies Congress that it intended to begin CAFTA negotiations in January 2003.
January 2003: The US and the CACM group formally propose to commence FTA talks later that month. First round of FTA negotiations. [P] [N]
December 2003: FTA negotiations concluded after nine rounds of talks, although without Costa Rica coming to an agreement with the US at this time.
January 2004: Costa Rica concludes its CAFTA negotiations with the US. [C]

May 2004: CAFTA formally signed.
August 2004: The Dominican Republic joins the CAFTA arrangement.
February 2005: All sides sign two additional agreements designed to complement and facilitate the implementation of CAFTA's environmental provisions.
January 2006: Deadline missed for FTA entering into force.

47. Taiwan–Guatemala FTA

March 2003: Formally proposed. [P]
May 2004: Statement by the Taiwan Government confirming that both sides still intend to negotiate an FTA.
December 2004: Both sides sign an 'FTA Negotiating Framework' and plan to commence negotiations in March 2005 with the aim of concluding talks by June 2005.
March 2005: First round of FTA negotiations. [N]
September 2005: FTA negotiations concluded after five rounds of talks. [C]
January 2006: FTA comes into force. [F]

48. Thailand–US FTA

October 2002: Both sides sign a trade and investment framework agreement (TIFA).
May 2003: The US announces that Thailand, Indonesia and the Philippines are at the top of its list of future potential FTA partners in Asia.
June 2003: Formally proposed at the 2003 APEC Trade Ministers Meeting. [P]
October 2003: FTA scoping study is initiated. [S]
February 2004: The Bush Administration officially notifies US Congress of its intention to open FTA negotiations with Thailand.
June 2004: First round of FTA negotiations. [N]
January 2006: Sixth round of FTA negotiations. Thailand chief negotiator, Nit Pibulsongkram, resigns citing political pressures as the reason. This mainly related to both the lack of progress in the talks and mass public demonstrations against the FTA.

49. Macao–China Closer Economic Partnership Agreement (MCCEPA)

June 2003: Formally proposed. First round of FTA negotiations also start this month. [P] [N]
October 2003: FTA negotiations concluded after and signed. [C]
January 2004: FTA enters into force. [F]

50. Japan–Indonesia Economic Partnership Agreement (JIEPA)

June 2003: Formally proposed during a visit by Indonesia's President Megawati Sukarnoputri to Tokyo. Both sides agree to begin studies on an FTA or Economic Partnership Agreement. [P]
December 2004: Announcement that both sides will commence FTA negotiations in April 2005 (*VNA News*, 26.12.2004).
January 2005: The first FTA study meeting held between business executives, academics and government officials from both sides.
February 2005: Joint Study Group (JSG) launched. [S]
May 2005: JSG report published. Both sides sign a Strategic Investment Action Plan, which would allow Japanese investors to start investing in Indonesia's technology industry and was seen as a precursor to commencing FTA negotiations.
July 2005: First round of FTA negotiations. [N]
October 2005: Second round of FTA negotiations.

51. US–Panama FTA

June 2003: Formally proposed. [P]
April 2004: First round of FTA negotiations. [N]
December 2004: Sixth round of FTA negotiations.

52. Thailand–Peru FTA

October 2003: Formally proposed at the 2003 APEC summit. [P]
January 2004: First round of FTA negotiations. [N]
October 2004: FTA negotiations concluded after four rounds of talks. [C]
November 2005: FTA signed at the 2005 APEC Summit.
Mid-2006: FTA enters into force. [F]

53. China–Australia FTA

October 2003: Formally proposed, a planned two-year scoping study also initiated.
[P] [S]
August 2004: Announcement that the scoping study would be completed ahead of
schedule, by the middle of 2005, with a view to commencing negotiations soon
thereafter.
April 2005: Scoping study published.
May 2005: First round of FTA negotiations. [N]
August 2005: Second round of FTA negotiations.
November 2005: Third round of FTA negotiations.

54. US–Peru (Andean Community) FTA

November 2003: FTA formally proposed between the US and the Andean
Community (Peru, Columbia, Ecuador). [P]
May 2004: First round of FTA negotiations. [N]
November 2005: Andean Community break off negotiations at the 14th round of
talks owing to disagreements with the US over agriculture and IPR.
December 2005: Peru and the US conclude their FTA negotiations but outstanding
issues remain unresolved between the other two Andean Community members and
the US. [C – Peru–US]

Proposed in 2004

55. Singapore–Panama FTA

February 2004: Formally proposed. [P]
May 2004: First round of FTA negotiations. [N]
July 2004: Second round of FTA negotiations. Subsequent talks stalled after failure to
reach agreement on telecommunications, governmental procurement, transnational
financial services of Panamanian banks and the recognition of the Certificate of
Origin of the Free Zone of Colon.
April 2005: FTA negotiations concluded after three rounds of talks. [C]

56. South Korea–ASEAN FTA

October 2003: At the 2003 APT summit, South Korea and ASEAN agree to hold a
meeting of economic ministers starting in 2004 to discuss the prospects of an FTA
and other cooperative projects.

March 2004: Formally proposed. Both sides also announce the initiation of a Joint Study Group process. [P] [S]

November 2004: At the 2004 APT summit, an announcement is made that FTA negotiations will commence in early 2005, hoping to end by 2007 with the target of eliminating at least 80 percent of tariffs between both sides by 2009.

February 2005: First round of FTA negotiations. [N]

December 2005: FTA negotiations concluded after eight rounds of talks. FTA signed, although Thailand at this stage abstains because of concerns about access to South Korea's rice market. [C]

July 2006: FTA enters into force. [F]

57. New Zealand–China FTA

October 2003: Both sides agree to establish a Trade and Economic Co-operation Framework Agreement (TECFA) that could possibly lead to an FTA.

April 2004: Formally proposed, scoping studies also initiated. [P] [S]

May 2004: Both sides sign the TECFA.

November 2004: FTA scoping study published.

December 2004: First round of FTA negotiations. [N]

November/December 2005: Fifth round of FTA negotiations.

58. China–Chile FTA

March 2004: Both sides agree to establish a trade and economic framework agreement that could possibly lead to an FTA.

April 2004: Formally proposed, a scoping study is also initiated. [P] [S]

August 2004: Announcement that the FTA project was to be fast-tracked, with the completion of the study phase brought forward to October 2004.

January 2005: First round of FTA negotiations. [N]

October 2005: FTA negotiations concluded after five rounds of talks. [C]

November 2005: FTA signed at the 2005 APEC Summit.

59. Malaysia–Australia FTA

July 2004: Formally proposed. [P]

August 2004: Scoping study process initiated. [S]

May 2005: First round of FTA negotiations. [N]

August 2005: Second round of FTA negotiations.

60. Taiwan–Nicaragua FTA

August 2004: Formally proposed. [P]

September 2004: First round of FTA negotiations. [N]

April 2005: Fourth round of FTA negotiations.

61. South Korea–Canada FTA

November 2004: Formally proposed at the 2004 APEC summit. [P]

July 2005: First round of FTA negotiations. [N]

September 2005: Second round of FTA negotiations.

62. Singapore–Peru FTA

November 2004: Both sides propose an FTA at the 2004 APEC summit. Negotiations are planned to commence in the first quarter of 2005. [P]

December 2005: FTA negotiations not yet initiated.

63.   *Japan–ASEAN Comprehensive Economic Partnership (JACEP)*

January 2002: Japanese Prime Minister Junichiro Koizumi makes a visit to Southeast Asia where he outlines his vision for a Japan–ASEAN Comprehensive Economic Partnership (JACEP), though this does not at this stage include an FTA element.

March 2002: Second meeting held between the ASEAN Economic Ministers (AEM) group and Japan's Ministry of Economy, Trade and Industry (METI) to discuss JACEP terms of reference and agenda items. A JACEP Expert Group is established to undertake a scoping study. [S]

October 2002: JACEP Expert Group submits their report and recommend that the realisation of the JACEP should "include elements of a possible FTA."

November 2002: JACEP signed at the APT 2002 Summit. Aside from wide-ranging measures on economic co-operation, it could include a FTA element at its centre to be implemented within ten years. JACEP's elements to implemented through a series of bilateral agreements between Japan and ASEAN member states, and will thus involve separate bilateral FTA deals.

November 2004: FTA element with JACEP formally proposed at the 2004 APT Summit. An announcement made that FTA negotiations will commence in April 2005 and be concluded by April 2007. [P]

April 2005: First round of FTA negotiations. These run parallel to Japan's bilateral FTA negotiations with individual ASEAN member states, by this time with Thailand, Malaysia and the Philippines, and from July with Indonesia. [N]

December 2005: Both sides acknowledge that negotiations have made slow progress mainly due to differences over rules of origin, intellectual property rights and agriculture.

64.   *ASEAN–Australia–New Zealand (CER) FTA*

1999 and 2000: Informal discussions between Australia, New Zealand, Singapore and Thailand to establish an AFTA–CER link.

October 2000: At the ASEAN Economic Ministers Meeting at Chiang Mai, ASEAN reject a proposal for a ASEAN–CER free trade agreement or zone after Malaysia, Indonesia and the Philippines oppose the plan.

September 2002: Closer Economic Partnership signed in this month but does not include an FTA element.

April 2004: ASEAN Economic Ministers agree to propose FTA links with Australia and New Zealand, with a plan to officially propose an ASEAN–CER FTA at the next ASEAN summit in November.

September 2004: ASEAN Economic Ministers further endorse the FTA proposal.

November 2004: At the 2004 APT summit, ASEAN agree to initiate FTA talks with Australia and New Zealand in early 2005. [P]

February 2005: First round of FTA negotiations. [N]

August 2005: Second round of FTA negotiations.

Proposed in 2005

65.   *Malaysia–New Zealand FTA*

September 2004: Both sides agree to initiate FTA scoping studies. [S]

March 2005: FTA scoping study report published. FTA negotiations formally proposed. [P]

May 2005: First round of formal FTA negotiations. [N]

July 2005: Second round of formal FTA negotiations.
September 2005: Third round of formal FTA negotiations.

66.   *Japan–Brunei FTA*

December 2005: Formally proposed at the 2005 APT Summit. **[P]**

67.   *Japan–Vietnam FTA*

December 2005: Formally proposed at the 2005 APT Summit. Both sides agree to organise a conference in January 2006 to initiate the scoping study process. **[P]**

Appendix B: Scope and Schedules of Liberalisation of Selected Asia-Pacific FTAs: A Comparative Analysis

New Zealand–Singapore (ANZSCEP)

- The Agreement enters into force on 1 January 2001.
- Immediate elimination of *all* tariffs on date of entry into force of the Agreement.

Australia–Singapore (SAFTA)

- The Agreement enters into force on 30 November 2002.
- Immediate elimination of all tariffs on date of entry into force of the Agreement.

Japan–Singapore (JSEPA)

General

- The Agreement enters into force on 30 November 2002. At this time, 99 percent of bilateral trade duty-free under the Agreement. Prior to the JSEPA, only 65 percent of bilateral trade was duty-free. Ninety four percent of Singapore's total exports to Japan enter tariff-free under JSEPA compared to a previous 84 percent.

Agricultural products

- Many sensitive agriculture product items omitted. Those covered include products whose import tariff-rates are already bound at zero under the WTO, or products that are currently duty-free but are not bound at zero under the WTO.

Industrial products

- **Japan** to commence reduction of tariffs on *petrochemical* products from April 2006, leading to duty-free trade by 1 January 2010. In *plastics* products, Japan immediately to: reduce tariff-rates down to minimum rates (2.8 percent, 3.1 percent, 3.9 percent) for certain polymers of ethylene and styrene, and thereafter further reduce the rates by eight equal annual instalments to zero percent by 1 January 2010; reduce the tariff-rate for polypropylene to 6.5 percent from 1 January 2004 and thereafter further reduce the rate by six equal annual instalments to zero percent from 2005 to 2010.
- **Singapore** to immediately eliminate *all* tariff duties on imports from Japan.

US–Chile (USCFTA)

General

- The Agreement enters into force on 1 January 2004. At this time, 85 percent of bilateral trade to become tariff-free, with complete tariff-free trade established after 12 years.

- General liberalisation phase-in schedules used by both the **United States** and **Chile** involve transitional periods of: four years (*Category B*); eight years (*Category C*); ten years (*Category D*); 12 years (*Category E*); existing tariff-rates unchanged in Years 1 through 4, and are then reduced by an annual 8.3 percent rate from Year 5 through Year 8, by an annual 16.7 percent in Year 9 through Year 12 and then duty-free trade established at the beginning of that year (*Category G*); existing tariff-rates unchanged in Years 1 and 2, and are then reduced in eight equal annual stages with duty-free trade established at the beginning of Year 10 (*Category H*). Tariff-rates immediately eliminated for *Category A* products.
- In certain circumstances, the **United States** to use additional phase-in schedules: liberalisation starting Year 8 and ending Year 12 (*Category J*); liberalisation after two years (*Category K*); initial phase of tariff-rate reductions at five percent per annum up to Year 6 and thereafter from Year 7 at ten percent per annum ending at zero tariff-rates in Year 10 (*Category L*); immediate tariff-rate reductions in equal annual rates of reduction leading to zero tariff-rates by Year 10 (*Category M*).
- Similarly, in certain circumstances **Chile** to use its own additional phase-in schedules, these being: existing tariff-rates unchanged in Years 1 and 2, and then duty-free trade effective in Year 3 (*Category O*); tariff-rate reduction of 80 percent in Year 1, 90 percent in Year 2, and then duty-free trade effective in Year 3 (*Category P*); existing tariff-rates unchanged from Year 1 to Year 6, and in Year 7 these rates reduced by 3.3 percent, in Year 8 by 21.7 percent, in Year 9 by 40.0 percent, in Year 10 by 58.3 percent, in Year 11 by 76.7 percent, and then duty-free trade effective in Year 12 (*Category V*).

Agricultural products

- **United States** to gradually raise its quota limits for certain Chilean imports and thereafter allow tariff and quota free entry after: four years for beef (*Category B*); ten years for poultry (*Category D*); 12 years for dairy, sugar, avocados, and tobacco products (*Category E*). *Category B, C, D, E*, and *G* treatment on a number of non-quota product sectors, most notably certain dairy, vegetable, cereal and grain, fruit, conserved fruits and vegetables, nuts and fish products, wine and other alcoholic products. *Category J* treatment on certain dairy products.
- **Chile** to gradually raise its quota limits for certain US imports and thereafter allow tariff and quota free entry after four years for beef (*Category B*), and ten years for chickens and turkeys (*Category D*). *Category B, C, D, E, G, H* and *O* treatment on a number of non-quota product sectors, most notably certain dairy, vegetable, cereal and grain, fats and oils, sugar, cocoa, conserved fruits and vegetables and certain alcoholic products. *Category V* treatment on wine and certain other alcoholic products.

Industrial products

- **United States** to gradually raise its quota limits for certain Chilean imports and thereafter allow tariff and quota free entry after: two years for copper (*Category K*); eight years for tyres (*Category C*); ten years for hotel or restaurant chinaware (*Category D*). *Category B, C, D*, and *E* treatment on various non-quota product sectors, most notably: certain tobacco based products; petroleum oils; certain rubber, leather and woollen products; certain footwear and clothing items; certain ceramic and glass products; certain iron, steel, aluminium and other metal products; certain tools and utensil products; various watch and clock products. *Category L* treatment on certain footwear products, and *Category M* treatment on certain clothing products.

- **Chile**: *Category B, C,* and *D* treatment on various product sectors, most notably: certain industrial oils and chemicals; certain paint, soap and rubber products; certain footwear products; various millstone products and building materials; various ceramic, glass and optical equipment products; certain industrial machinery products. *Category P* treatment on certain fuels.

US–Singapore (USSFTA)

General

- The Agreement enters into force on 1 January 2004. At this time, the **United States** to remove tariffs on 78.7 percent of Singapore imports. After four years (i.e. by 1 January 2008) this total percentage will be raised to 92 percent.
- **United States** to use the following liberalisation phase-in schedules: *Category B,* in equal part reductions over four years; *Category C* as previous over eight years; *Category D* over ten years.
- **Singapore** to immediately eliminate tariffs on *all* imports originating from the US.

Agricultural products

- **United States** to gradually raise its quota limits for beef, cotton, dairy, peanuts, sugar and tobacco imports from Singapore, and thereafter allow tariff and quota free entry after ten years (*Category D*). In addition, *Category B, C* and *D* treatment on various product sectors, most notably certain live animal, cereal and grain, dairy, seafood, horticultural, vegetable, fruit, seed and nut products.

Industrial products

- **United States**: *Category B, C,* and *D* treatment on various product sectors, most notably: certain tobacco based products; various chemical, pharmaceutical and plastics products; certain wood, metal and glass products; certain footwear and clothing items; certain tools and utensil products; certain audio-video products; certain industrial equipment (inc. motors) products; various bicycle products and bicycle parts, various watch and clock products, and other miscellaneous manufactures.

Hong Kong–China (HKCCEPA)

General

- The Agreement enters into force on 1 January 2004.
- **Hong Kong** to continue applying zero tariff-rates to all imported goods of mainland China origin.
- **China** from 1 January 2004 to apply zero tariff-rates to the HTS list of 273 products originating from Hong Kong provided in Annex 1 of the Agreement (Stage 1). In Stage 2 of the Agreement, duty-free trade to apply to non-listed items (see below) no later than 1 January 2006. This particularly applies to extractive products and materials.

Agricultural products

- **China**: all agricultural products, including processed foods (except ice cream), to be liberalised in Stage 2 of the Agreement.

Industrial products

- **China**: liberalisation from Stage 2 of the Agreement applies to: alcohol and tobacco products; most mineral and precious stone products; soaps and other cleaning agents; explosives, various plastics, rubber, leather and wood products; certain textile, clothing and footwear products; most glassware products; various metals and metal products; tools and utensils; various industrial and power generating machinery; various office machine products and electrical equipment; various office machines and computers; transport vehicles and equipment; various watch and clock products, and other miscellaneous manufactures.

Services

- **China** offers preferential access to Hong Kong registered firms in 18 service industries, including accounting, advertising, construction, film production, health care, insurance, legal counselling, logistics, real estate, telecoms, tourism and transportation.

South Korea–Chile (KCFTA)

General

- The Agreement enters into force on 1 April 2004. **Chile** to immediately eliminate tariffs on 2,439 goods (42 percent of total) originating from South Korea, while **South Korea** to immediately eliminate tariffs on 9,740 goods (87 percent of total) originating from Chile. After ten years (i.e. by 2014), 97 percent of bilateral trade will be duty-free.
- General liberalisation phase-in schedules used by **South Korea** and **Chile** to begin with different reduced base tariff-rates from date of entry into force of the Agreement and thereafter reduced in most cases on an annual basis on the 1 January of the subsequent years.
- **South Korea** to use the following phase-in schedule categories: *Year 5*, base tariff-rate immediately reduced by 16.7 percent and thereafter in five equal annual stages with duty-free trade established 1 January 2009; *Year 7*, base tariff-rate immediately reduced by 12.5 percent and thereafter in seven equal annual stages with duty-free trade established 1 January 2011; *Year 9*, base tariff-rate immediately reduced by ten percent and thereafter in nine equal annual stages with duty-free trade established 1 January 2013; *Year 10*, base tariff-rate immediately reduced by 9.1 percent and thereafter in ten equal annual stages with duty-free trade established 1 January 2014; *Year 10-S (Seasonal)*, as *Year 10* but only applied from 1 November to 30 April of each year; *Year 16*, no tariff liberalisation until from 1 January 2011 when the base tariff-rate is reduced by ten percent and thereafter in nine equal annual stages with duty-free trade established 1 January 2020.
- **Chile** to use the following phase-in schedule categories: *Year 3*, base tariff-rate immediately reduced by 25 percent and thereafter in three equal annual stages with duty-free trade established 1 January 2007; *Year 5*, base tariff-rate immediately reduced by 16.7 percent and thereafter in five equal annual stages with duty-free trade established 1 January 2009; *Year 7*, base tariff-rate immediately reduced by 12.5 percent and thereafter in seven equal annual stages with duty-free trade established 1 January 2011; *Year 10*, base tariff-rate immediately reduced by 9.1 percent and thereafter in ten equal annual stages with duty-free trade established 1 January 2014; *Year 13*, no tariff liberalisation until from 1 January 2010

when the base tariff-rate is reduced by 12.5 percent and thereafter in nine equal annual stages with duty-free trade established 1 January 2017.

- For both **South Korea** and **Chile**, *Category E* items refer to those products not subject to tariff liberalisation, and *Year 0* to those subject to immediate tariff liberalisation.

Agricultural products

- **South Korea**: almost all agricultural product imports by sector from Chile subject to some degree of *Year 5*, *Year 7* or *Year 10* treatment. *Year 9* treatment on miscellaneous fruit juices. *Year 10-S* treatment on grapes. *Year 16* treatment on certain dried milk products, certain prepared food and fruit juice products. *Category E* treatment on 21 products, including rice, apples and pears. South Korea to also phase-in liberalisation in various tariff quota (TQ) schedules, i.e. TQ1 to TQ7. This applies to particular beef, poultry and dairy products, as well as mandarins, olives and plums.
- **Chile**: *Year 5* treatment on certain syrups. *Year 10* treatment on beef, rice, soya beans, peanuts, cooking oils, sugar, certain syrups. *Category E* treatment on certain wheat and cereal products.
- Both sides agreed to consider the further liberalisation of 373 agricultural products after the completion of the WTO's Doha Development Round of global trade talks, expected sometime in 2005.

Industrial products

- **South Korea**: *Year 5*, *Year 7* or *Year 10* treatment on: essential oils (e.g. from citrus) and certain gelatine products; various timber and certain wooden products (including prefabricated buildings); cathodes.
- **Chile**: *Year 3 to Year 10* treatment on: most industrial oils and gases; almost all chemicals; almost all paint and varnish products; most ink and dye products; graphite and carbon; plastics; most rubber products; animal skins (real and artificial); leather and leather products; printed material (e.g. books); woollen products; cotton yarns; almost all man-made fabrics and other textiles; most clothing and footwear products; millstone products and building materials; ceramic and glass products; most iron and steel products; most copper and aluminium products; tools and utensil products; almost all industrial, electrical and power generating equipment and parts; construction vehicles; various audio-visual products; certain automobiles and auto parts; most boats and ships; fishing equipment. *Year 13* treatment on most tyre products; certain rubber gloves; various manmade fabrics; various clothing and most footwear products; various iron and steel products; certain copper and aluminium products; various plumbing products; certain specialist vehicles, e.g. ambulances; various boats and ships; metal furniture; prefabricated buildings. *Category E* treatment on packaging ribbons; certain tyre products (e.g. aircraft); refrigerators; washing machines; certain industrial equipment products.

Thailand–Australia (TAFTA)

General

- The Agreement enters into force on 1 January 2005. At this time, **Australia** eliminates 83.2 percent of its tariffs, which account for 83.0 percent of current imports from Thailand. 12.9 percent of Australian tariffs phased down to zero over the period from entry into force to 1 January 2010. For 3.9 percent of Australia's tariff lines, Australia will phase its rates to zero in 2015. **Thailand** to immediately eliminate 49.4 percent of its tariffs, which account for 77.9 percent of current imports from Australia. 43.7 percent of Thailand's tariffs will be phased down to zero over the period from entry into force to 1 January 2010. For 6.9 percent of its tariff lines, Thailand will phase its rates to zero in the period 2015–2020. Thailand expands access for Australian imports under tariff-rate quotas (TRQs) over a transition period that varies according to the product, with the eventual elimination of all TRQ restrictions. Australia immediately eliminates any TRQ restrictions that it previously maintained.

Agricultural products

- For *meat products*, **Thailand** to: phase its 32 percent tariff for sheep meat to zero by 2010; immediately reduce its tariff on beef to 40 percent, down from 51 percent, and for beef offal to 30 percent, down from 33 percent, and phase these rates to zero by 2020; phase the current 33 percent tariff for pork to zero by 2020.
- For *dairy products*, **Thailand** to: immediately eliminate the current tariffs on infant formula (five percent), lactose (up to 20 percent), casein and milk albumin (ten percent), and phase the tariffs on butter fat, milkfood, yoghurt, dairy spreads and ice cream to zero by 2010; provide immediate additional quota for Australia of 2,200 tonnes for skim milk powder and 120 tonnes for liquid milk and cream, expanding by 17 percent at five-yearly intervals until 2025, when all tariffs and quotas will be eliminated; phase the tariffs for butter and cheese, other milk powders and concentrates to zero by 2020.
- For *grains and related products*, **Thailand** to: immediately eliminate the current tariffs on wheat (ad valorem equivalent of 12–20 percent), barley, rye and oats (ad valorem equivalents of up to 25 percent), and the tariff and tariff-rate quota on rice; immediately eliminate the tariffs on unroasted malt (ad valorem equivalent of 28 percent) and wheat gluten (31 percent), and phase the tariffs on wheat flour (32.6 percent) and starch (31 percent) to zero by 2010.
- For *fruit and vegetable products*, **Thailand** to: phase tariffs on most fresh fruit and vegetables (current rates mostly 33 percent or 42 percent) to zero by 2010. Tariffs on mandarins (42 percent) and grapes (33 percent) immediately reduced to 30 percent, and then phased to zero by 2015; immediately eliminate its tariffs on most tropical fruit; provide immediate additional quota for fresh potatoes, expanding yearly until 2020, when all tariffs and quotas will be eliminated; phase its 30 percent tariffs for processed potatoes to zero by 2015; immediately reduce tariffs on fruit juices and canned fruit from 30 percent to 24 percent and phase the tariff to zero by 2010.
- For *sugar products*, **Thailand** to: immediately provide an additional quota, expanding annually by ten percent, with tariff and quota free access by 2020.
- **Australia**, to confer tariff-free entry *all* Thai agricultural products from Day 1 of the Agreement (although a tariff of 2.5 percent (down from five percent) remained on canned tuna until its elimination in 2007.

Industrial products

- **Thailand** to immediately reduce tariffs on any industrial goods not subject to immediate elimination to a ceiling of no more than 20 percent (with the exception of small and medium passenger motor vehicles), before phasing to zero.

- In the *automotive sector*, **Thailand** to: immediately eliminate tariffs on large passenger motor vehicles (engine capacity of over 3000 cc) and goods vehicles, at 80 percent and 60 percent respectively when the FTA signed; immediately reduce an 80 percent tariff to 30 percent for other passenger motor vehicles before phasing this down by six percent each year to zero by 2010; immediately reduce tariffs on all automotive parts, components and accessories to a ceiling of 20 percent, and phased to zero by 2010; immediately reduce tariffs on engines from 30 percent to 15 percent. Australia to immediately eliminate tariffs on all passenger vehicles, off-road vehicles, goods vehicles and other commercial vehicles of Thai origin. Tariffs on 98 of the 146 tariff items covering automotive parts and components immediately reduced to five percent and then totally eliminated in 2010. Tariffs on the remaining 48 items to be immediately eliminated.
- In the *machinery and equipment sector*, **Thailand** to either immediately eliminate or phase to zero the tariffs on products from this sector by 2010, with the exception of three tariffs covering electric power boards, which will be eliminated in 2015.
- In the *steel sector*, **Thailand** to immediately halve its tariffs on flat-rolled steel products of interest to Australia, including hot-rolled coil (current tariff of ten percent), cold-rolled coil (12 percent) and coated steel (15 percent). Tariffs to then be eliminated in 2015, with the exception of most coated steel products for which the tariffs will be phased to zero in 2008. Australia to immediately eliminate current tariffs of five percent or less on most steel items but maintain its tariff of four percent for goods of Thai origin on eight selected tariff items until 2010, when the tariff will be eliminated.
- In the *textiles, clothing and footwear sector*, **Australia** to immediately reduce tariffs previously at 25 percent on 239 tariff items for apparel and certain finished textiles to 12.5 percent. This rate to be held until 2010, when it will be reduced to five percent, and then held until complete elimination in 2015. For textiles, clothing, leather items and related products, but excluding carpets, with tariffs previously at ten percent or 15 percent, the tariffs to be immediately reduced to five percent. This rate to be held until elimination in 2010. For textile yarns and other textile products with tariffs previously at five percent or below, the tariff to be immediately reduced to three percent and then reduced to two percent in 2006, one percent in 2007, and eliminated in 2008. For footwear, Australia to immediately reduce tariffs from 15 percent to nine percent, and then reduced to eight percent in 2008, five percent in 2009, and eliminated in 2010.
- In the *pharmaceuticals sector*, **Thailand** to phase previous tariffs of ten percent or 20 percent to zero in 2009. On products of specific interest, tariffs of ten percent will be halved immediately and eliminated in 2007.
- For *plastics products*, **Thailand** to: immediately reduce previous tariffs of 30 percent on plastic articles to 20 percent and phase to zero by 2010; immediately reduce the previous 30 percent tariff on miscellaneous plastic articles to 15 percent; phase the previous tariffs of up to 20 percent on polymers to five percent by 2008 and to zero by 2010. Australia to immediately eliminate tariffs of five percent or less on most plastics and chemicals items but maintain the tariffs of five percent on 71 selected tariff items until 2008, when Australia to eliminate all tariffs.
- For *alcoholic products*, **Thailand** to immediately reduce its 54 percent tariff on wine to 40 percent, and then phase the tariff to zero by 2015, and immediately reduce its tariffs of 60 percent to 30 percent for beer and spirits before phasing to zero by 2010.

Services

- **Thailand** will permit majority Australian ownership of mining operations, companies providing certain services (e.g. construction, education, management consultancy, hotels, maritime cargo) in all cases up to 60 percent, from the previous limit of 49.9 percent.
- **Thailand** will permit Australian companies that manufacture goods in Thailand to provide distribution services in relation to those goods without limitation of Australian equity, i.e. up to 100 percent, from the previous limit of 49.9 percent.

Australia–US (AUSFTA)

General

- The Agreement enters into force on 1 January 2005.
- **Australia** to use the following liberalisation phase-in schedules: *Category B*, where base tariff-rate is reduced in equal stages starting immediately and ending 1 January 2010 of the Agreement; *Category D*, where base tariff-rate is reduced in ten equal stages starting immediately and ending 1 January of Year 10 of the Agreement. *Category T1*, where base tariff-rate immediately reduced to three percent and remaining at this level until 1 January 2010, when duty-free trade established; *Category Tx*, where base tariff-rate immediately reduced to 5.5 percent and remaining at this level until 1 January 2010, when the rate will be further reduced to three percent until 1 January 2015, when duty-free trade effective; *Category T2*, where base tariff-rate immediately reduced to eight percent and remaining at this level until 1 January 2010, when the rate will be further reduced to three percent until 1 January 2015, when duty-free trade effective; *Category T3*, where base tariff-rate immediately reduced to 15.5 percent and remaining at this level until 1 January 2010, when the rate will be further reduced to eight percent until 1 January 2015, when duty-free trade effective; tariff-rates immediately eliminated for *Category A* products, and tariff-rates to remain at zero percent for *Category E* products.
- **United States** to use the following liberalisation phase-in schedules: *Category B*, in equal part reductions over four years; *Category C* as previous over eight years; *Category D* over ten years; *Category F*, over 18 years (agricultural products only); *Category G*, where base tariff-rate remains unchanged during Years 1 through 6, then reduced to 5.6 percent from 1 January of Year 7 and then by an additional 5.6 percent of the base rate on 1 January of each year thereafter through Year 12, and thereafter by an additional 11.1 percent of the base rate annually through Year 18, with duty-free effective on 1 January of Year 18 of the Agreement; *Category H*, where base tariff-rate remains unchanged during Years 1 through 8, then reduced to 6.7 percent from 1 January of Year 9 and then by an additional 6.7 percent of the base rate on 1 January of each year thereafter through Year 13, and thereafter by an additional 13.3 percent of the base rate annually through Year 18, with duty-free effective on 1 January of Year 18 of the Agreement; *Category I*, where base tariff-rates will remain unchanged; *Category T1*, where the base tariff-rate immediately reduced to three percent and remaining at this level until 1 January 2010, when duty-free trade established; *Category TX*, where if the base tariff-rate is greater than three percent but less than 5.5 percent the US to immediately apply a rate that is 0.9 percent of its base rate through 31 December 2009, and beginning 1 January 2010 the US to apply the lower of the rate that was in effect on 31 December 2009, or three percent, with duty-free trade effective on

1 January 2015; *Category T2*, where if the base tariff-rate is greater than three percent but less than eight percent the US to immediately apply a rate that is 0.9 percent of its base rate through 31 December 2009, and beginning 1 January 2010 the US to apply the lower of the rate that was in effect on 31 December 2009, or three percent, with duty-free trade effective on 1 January 2015; *Category T3*, where if the base tariff-rate is greater than three percent but less than 15.5 percent the US to immediately apply a rate that is 0.9 percent of its base rate through 31 December 2009, and beginning 1 January 2010 the US to apply the lower of the rate that was in effect on 31 December 2009, or eight percent, with duty-free trade effective on 1 January 2015; tariff-rates immediately eliminated for *Category A* products, and tariff-rates to remain at zero percent for *Category E* products.

Agricultural products

- **United States** to maintain its quota limits on Australian *sugar* imports at 87,000 tonnes per annum. For *dairy products*, the US to increase Australia's tariff quota in Year 1 by almost threefold, with subsequent growth in the quotas at an average yearly rate of five percent. No change to the US's above-quota tariff-rates on dairy imports from Australia subject to quotas (*Category I*). Full liberalisation by Year 18. For *beef products*, Australia's quota in the US market increased by 15,000 tonnes in Year 2, increasing to 70,000 tonnes by Year 18, and then effectively duty-free trade. In-quota tariffs eliminated immediately, and over-quota duties phased out from Years 9 to 18 of the Agreement (*Category H*). Other quota liberalisation arrangements for other quota-subjected products: peanuts, tobacco and cotton (*Category F*); avocadoes (*Category G*). For *tariff-only affected products*, US tariffs on the majority of agricultural products (including most lamb and sheepmeat, oranges, cut flowers and cotton seeds) set at zero from Day 1 of the Agreement, with further elimination of other tariffs phased in over periods of four, ten and 18 years (*Categories B, D* and *F*). Base tariff-rates unchanged for certain peanut, tobacco and chocolate products (*Category I*). Special differentiated tariff elimination schedules set for US imports of Australian *wine* from Year 1 through 10 of the Agreement, with duty-free trade effective 1 January of Year 11.
- **Australia,** to confer tariff-free entry *all* US agricultural products from Day 1 of the Agreement.

Industrial products

- **United States:** *Category B* treatment on certain chinaware, glassware, tools and utensils, ball bearing, camera and miscellaneous manufacture products. *Category C* treatment on certain rubber, ceramic, glassware, precious stone, electrical and optical products. *Category D* treatment on certain footwear, ceramic and glassware products. *Categories T1, TX, T2* and *T3* treatment on almost all textile, clothing and footwear products (*TX* and *T3* on most clothing and footwear products).
- **Australia:** *Category B* treatment on certain chemical products and certain motor vehicles. *Category D* to certain footwear products. *Categories T1, TX, T2* and *T3* treatment for most textile, clothing and footwear products (*T3* to many clothing and footwear products). *Category Tx* treatment on lamps and lighting fittings.

Appendix C: Thematic Content of Asia-Pacific FTAs

Thematic Content	East Asia centred											Oceania centred						United States centred				
	JSEPA	JAFTA	JMEPA	KSFTA	KOFTA	ACEFTA	TBR CEPA	MR CEPA	CCFTA	TPSEPA		ANZER CER	ANZ CER	PICTA	SAFTA	TAFTA	TNZCEP	NAFTA	USCFTA	USAFTA	AUSFTA	TPPFTA
	2001	2004	2005	2004	2005	2004	2002	2003	2005	2005		1983	2000	2001	2002	2004	2004	1994	2003	2004	2004	2003
Miscellaneous headings																						
Accession clause	•	•	•		•	•	•	•				•	•	•	•	•		•	•	•	•	•
Disputes settlement mechanism	•		•	•		•	•	•				•	•	•	•	•		•	•	•	•	•
e-commerce															•	•			•	•	•	
Environment clause										•		•						•			•	
Labour clause																				•	•	
Movement of natural persons	•		•	•	•	•	•	•	•	•		•	•	•	•	•		•	•	•	•	•
Periodic review (whole agreement)	5 yrs	yrs	5 yrs	1 yr	1 yr	2 yr	1 yr	1 yr	3 yrs			yns	2 yr	5 yrs	2 yr	5 yrs	5 yrs	1 yr	1 yr	1 yr	1 yr	1 yr
Rules of origin (regime-wide only)												•	•					•				
Rules of origin (product-specific included)	•	•	•	•	•	•	•	•	•	•		•	•	•	•	•	<	•	•	•	•	•
Sanitary and phytosanitary measures	•	•	•	•	•	•	•	•	•	•		•	•	•	•	•		•	•	•	•	•
Services trade	•	•	•	•	•	•	•	•	•	•		•	•	•	•	•		•	•	•	•	•
TBTs, safeguards, regulatory conformity	•	•	•	•	•	•	•	•	•	•		•	•	•	•	•		•	•	•	•	•
Behind the border market access/rights																						
Competition policy	•	•	•	•	•	•			•			•	•	•		•		•	•	•	•	•
Financial sector (liberalisation)	•	•	•	•				•												•	•	
Government procurement	•	•	•	•			•	•				•	•			•		•	•	•	•	•
Intellectual property (rights emphasis)	•	•	•	•	•		•	•				•	•			•		•	•	•	•	•
Investment (rights emphasis)	•	•	•	•			•	•				•	•			•		•	•	•	v	•
Privatisation	•		•									•	•			•		•	•	•	•	•
Telecommunications (market access emphasis)	•	•	•										•									
Economic co-operation																						
Agriculture/primary industry co-operation	•	•	•	•	•		•		•													
Broadcasting co-operation							•															
Economic co-operation (general chapter)	•	•	•	•	•		•	•	•	•				•								
Education/HRD co-operation	•	•	•	•	•																	
Energy industry co-operation		•	•	•					•													
Entertainment industry co-operation		•	•					•														
Environment co-operation	•	•	•	•	•				•													
Financial sector (co-operation)	•	•	•	•	•		•															
Information technology co-operation	•	•	•	•			•		•	•												
Intellectual property (co-operation emphasis)	•								•	•												
Investment (co-operation emphasis)	•	•	•				•	•	•	•		•										
Science and technology co-operation	•	•	•	•					•	•												
SME co-operation	•	•	•	•	•		•		•	•												
Telecommunications (co-operation emphasis)	•	•	•	•	•				•	•												
Tourism industry co-operation	•	•	•	•	•		•	•	•	•												

Notes: HRD (human resource development), SME (small and medium sized enterprises) TBTs (technical barriers to trade). Period review row gives details of how often whole agreement reviews are undertaken, and 'yns' denotes 'year-period not stated' under whole agreement review provisions. * Denotes a side letter agreement or understanding on a thematic content issue. < Denotes a relatively limited application of product-specific rules of origin (see Appendix E).

Sources: Original FTA texts.

Appendix D: Bilateral Trade Flows in the Asia-Pacific, 2004 in US$ millions

	Australia	Brunei	Canada	Chile	China	Costa Rica	El Salvador	Guatemala	Hong Kong	Indonesia	Japan	Macao	Malaysia	Mexico	New Zealand	Nicaragua	Panama	Peru	Philippines	Singapore	South Korea	Taiwan	Thailand	United Sates	Vietnam
Australia		536	2,649	209	20,760	13	8	11	3,928	4,555	29,790	40	5,888	751	9,805	4	5	91	1,158	7,909	10,546	5,637	4,848	22,265	2,308
Brunei	536		7	1	276				62	315	1,920		346	1	142			1		660	695	15	435	461	2
Canada	2,649	7		1,202	19,566	208	35	228	2,976	1,100	16,406	68	1,809	10,620	754	60	56	460	795	1,219	5,884	3,953	1,716	438,391	434
Chile	209	1	1,202		5,208	114	67	171	376	238	4,675	478	243	1,905	56	5	110	1,286	70	98	2,571	616	268	8,562	58
China	20,760	276	19,566	5,208		616	159	542	172,456	11,095	168,069	1,882	22,530	11,237	2,945	109	1,143	1,754	9,320	29,144	84,708	78,324	16,316	207,588	6,811
Costa Rica	13		208	114	616				247	11	575		207	920	3	285	251	20	32	110	144	106	35	6,789	2
El Salvador	8		35	67	159			902	71	5	130		10	389	16	242	127	19	4	13	70	1	17	4,523	2
Guatemala	11		228	171	542		902		103	15	381		33	941	24	215	172	79	2	28	650	138	37	5,898	2
Hong Kong	3,928	62	2,976	376	172,456	247	71	103		2,258	41,904	1,023	9,693	844	614	41	313	117	5,886	203,579	19,992	26,113	6,898	42,028	1,714
Indonesia	4,555	315	1,100	238	11,095	11	5	15	2,258		24,886	12	5,983	475	480	4	36	47	1,391	12,084	8,410	4,094	5,144	13,191	1,028
Japan	29,790	1,920	16,406	4,675	168,069	575	130	381	41,904	24,886		249	28,104	2,111	4,816	1	70	3,183	801	16,569	27,461	67,078	35,138	189,975	7,023
Macao	40		68	478	1,882				1,023	12	249		27		5	6	1	14	12	78	74	194	27	1,586	15
Malaysia	5,888	346	1,809	243	22,530	207	10	33	9,693	5,983	28,104	27		2,111	855	6	39	211	4,404	41,467	9,846	3,685	11,327	39,012	1,751
Mexico	751	1	10,620	1,905	11,237	920	389	941	844	475	2,111		2,111		480	211	259	490	520	1,904	4,426	3,685	966	271,973	45
New Zealand	9,805	142	754	56	2,945	3	16	24	614	480	4,816	5	855	480		1	1		361	1,038	1,470	987	626	5,399	167
Nicaragua	4		60	5	109	285	242	215	41	4	1	6	6	211	1		23	12	1				8	1,605	
Panama	5		56	110	1,143	251	127	172	313	36	70	1	39	259	1	23		149	11				33	1,825	10
Peru	91	1	460	1,286	1,754	20	19	79	117	47	3,183	14	211	490		12	149		12				46	6,323	22
Philippines	1,158		795	70	9,320	32	4	2	5,886	1,391	801	12	4,404	520	361	1	11	12		7,092	4,676	5,442	3,007	16,069	1,136
Singapore	7,909	660	1,219	98	29,144	110	13	28	203,579	12,084	16,569	78	41,467	1,904	1,038				7,092		12,219	12,705	12,821	39,611	4,629
South Korea	10,546	695	5,884	2,571	84,708	144	70	650	19,992	8,410	27,461	74	9,846	4,426	1,470				4,676	12,219		17,156	5,522	73,047	4,319
Taiwan	5,637	15	3,953	616	78,324	106	1	138	26,113	4,094	67,078	194	3,685	3,685	987				5,442	12,705	17,156		6,583	57,942	2,386
Thailand	4,848	435	1,716	268	16,316	35	17	37	6,898	5,144	35,138	27	11,327	966	626	8	33	46	3,007	12,821	5,522	6,583		23,898	6,688
United Sates	22,265	461	438,391	8,562	207,588	6,789	4,523	5,898	42,028	13,191	189,975	1,586	39,012	271,973	5,399	1,605	1,825	6,323	16,069	39,611	73,047	57,942	23,898		6,688
Vietnam	2,308	2	434	58	6,811	2	2	2	1,714	1,028	7,023	15	1,751	45	167		10	22	1,136	4,629	4,319	2,386	6,688	6,688	

Notes: Figures for total bilateral trade between trade partners. Owing to discrepancies in the trade statistics published by bilateral trade partners concerning their bilateral trade flows, figures from both partners have been aggregated and then halved.

Source: IMF Direction of Trade Statistics Yearbook 2005.

Appendix E: Rules of Origin (RoO) Regimes in Asia-Pacific FTAs

FTA	Product-Specific Aspects			De minimis (%)	Regime-Wide Aspects			
	Value Content Calculation		Calculation basis (%)		Roll-up	Cumulation		Duty Drawback
	IC (%)	RVC (%)				Bilateral	Diagonal	
ANZCER	50		Factory cost	2	Yes	Yes	Yes (full)	Yes
AFTA		40	Value of content	No	No	Yes	No	Yes
ACFTA		40	Value of content	No	No	Yes	No	Yes
ISFTA	40	60	Transaction value	No	Yes	Yes	No (except OP)	No
ANZSCEP		40	Factory cost	No	Yes	Yes	No (except selected OP)	No
PICTA		40	Factory cost	2	Yes	Yes	Yes (full)	No
SAFTA		30–50	Factory cost	2	Yes	Yes	No (except OP)	No
AUSFTA		30–65	30–35 build-up, 35–65 build-down	10 (exceptions in ch 1–21; 7% applied in TCF sector)	Yes	Yes	No (except OP and NC)	No
USMFTA		30–60	30–35 build-up, 45–60 build-down	10 (exceptions in ch 1–24; 7% applied in TCF sector)	Yes	Yes	No (except selected OP and NC)	No
KCFTA		30–45	30–35 build-up, 45 build-down	8 (ch 50–63 except TCF; 7% applied in TCF sector)	Yes	Yes	No	No
TPFTA		30–50	Transaction value	10 (exceptions in ch 1–24; 7% applied in TCF sector)	Yes	Yes	No	No
HKCCEPA		30	Transaction value	No	No	No	No	No
JMFTA		30 (or 55 & 60)	Transaction value	10 (exceptions in ch 16–27; 7% applied in TCF sector)	No	Yes	No	No
TAFTA		40–55	Transaction value	No	No	Yes	No	No
KSFTA		45–55	Transaction value	10 (exceptions in ch 1–24; 8% applied in TCF sector)	No	Yes	No (except OP)	No
ENZCEP		50 (or 55 & 60)	Transaction value	10	No	Yes	No	No
TPSEPA		50 (or 60 & 65)	Transaction value	10	No	Yes	No (except OP)	No
COFTA		40–50	Value of content	8	No	Yes	No	No
NAFTA		50–60	Net cost, 50 transaction value	7 (exceptions in industrial and agri-products; 9 exceptions in agri-products and TCF sectors)	No (except automotive)	Yes	No	Yes (but small and limited)
US-Chile		35–45	35 build-up, 45 build-down	10 (exceptions in agri-products, industrial products; 7 exceptions in agri-products and TCF sectors)	Yes	Yes	No	No
US-CACM		35–45	35 build-up, 45 build-down	10 (exceptions in agri-products, industrial products; 7 exceptions in agri-products and TCF sectors)	Yes	Yes	Yes in ch with small and limited	No
Mexico–Costa Rica		41.66–50	41.66 net cost, 50 transaction value	7 (except in ch 1–24 and TCF; 8% in TCF sector)	Yes	Yes	No	No after 7 years
Mexico–Chile		40–50	40 net cost, 50 transaction value	8 (exceptions in industrial and agri-products; exceptions in industrial and agri-products and TCF sectors)	Yes	Yes	No	No
Canada–Chile		50–60	40 net cost, 50 transaction value	9 (exceptions in industrial and agri-products; exceptions in industrial and agri-products and TCF sectors)	Yes	Yes	No	No
Other								
PESC (EU)	50–40		Ex-works price	10	Yes	Yes	Yes (but limited except diagonal)	No
EU–Chile	50–30		Ex-works price	10	Yes	Yes	No	No after 4 years
EU–Mexico	50–30		Ex-works price	10	Yes	Yes	No	No after 2 years
EU–South Africa	50–30		Ex-works price	15	Yes	Yes	Yes (but limited with ACP and SACU)	No

Notes: IC (import content), DC (domestic content). Regarding the calculation basis for product-specific RoOs, the 'build-up' method is: RVC = (VOM/AV) x 100, and the 'build-down' method: RVC = [(AV – VNM)/AV] x 100, where VOM is the value of originating materials inputed into production, AV is the adjusted value, VNM is the value of non-originating materials inputed into production; the 'net cost' method is RVC = [(NC – VNM)/NC] x 100, and the transaction value (or export or customs value) method is: RVC = (TV – VNM/TV) x 100, where NC is the net cost of the good, TV the transaction value of the good. OP (Outward Processing), ISI (Integrated Sourcing Initiative), PESC (Pan-European System of Cumulation), ch (chapter subheadings), CS (chapter subheadings), TCF (textiles, clothing, footwear), ACP (Africa, Caribbean, Pacific), SACU (Southern Africa Customs Union).

Sources: Estevadeordal and Suominen (2003, 2005), FTA texts.

References

ACIL Consulting (2003) A Bridge Too Far? *An Australian Agricultural Perspective on the Australia/United States Free Trade Area Idea*, report for the Rural Industries Research and Development Corporation, Canberra.

Aggarwal, V.K. and Ravenhill, J. (2001) 'Undermining the WTO: The Case Against Open Sectoralism', *Asia Pacific Issues*, No. 50 (February), East–West Centre.

American Sugar Alliance/ASA (2003) *US Sugar Industry: Status and Challenges*, presented at the American Farm Bureau Federation, Sugar Advisory Committee, 22 February, Dallas.

Amsden, A. and Hikino, T. (2000) 'The Bark is Worse than the Bite: New WTO Law and Late Industrialisation', *Annals of American Political and Social Science*, Vol 570(July), pp. 104–14.

Anderson, J.E. and van Wincoop, E. (2004) 'Trade Costs', *Journal of Economic Literature*, Vol 42(3), pp. 691–751.

Andriamananjara, S. (1999) 'On the Size and Number of Regional Integration Arrangements: A Political Economy Model', *World Bank Working Paper Series No. 2117*, World Bank, Washington DC.

Andriamananjara, S. (2000) 'Regionalism and Incentives for Multilateralism', *Journal of Economic Integration*, Vol 15(1), pp. 1–18.

Andriamananjara, S. (2003) 'On the Relationship Between Preferential Trading Agreements and the Multilateral Trading System', presented at the *PECC Trade Forum*, 22–23 April, Washington DC.

Antkiewicz, A. and Whalley, J. (2005) 'China's New Regional Trade Agreements', *World Economy*, Vol 28(10), pp. 1539–57.

Aoki, M. (2004) 'New Issues in FTAs: The Case of Economic Partnership Agreements Between Japan', presented at the *APEC Study Centres Consortium Meeting*, Vina del Mar, Chile, 26–29 May.

Asia–New Zealand Foundation (2003) *Annual Report 2002/03*, Asia–New Zealand Foundation, Wellington.

Asia Pacific Economic Co-operation/APEC forum (2002) *Toward the Shanghai Goal: Implementing the APEC Trade Facilitation Action Plan*, APEC Secretariat, Singapore.

Asia Pacific Economic Co-operation/APEC forum (2004) 'Best Practice for RTA/FTAs in APEC', submitted at the *16th APEC Ministerial Meeting*, Santiago, Chile, 17–18 November.

Asia Pacific Economic Co-operation/APEC forum (2005a) 'Implementing the APEC Best Practice for FTAs/RTAs in APEC', paper presented by the Chilean delegation, *APEC Third Trade Policy Dialogue on FTAs*, Jeju, South Korea, 29 May.

Asia Pacific Economic Co-operation/APEC forum (2005b) 'PECC Recommendations for Building on the "Best Practice" Guidelines on RTAs/FTAs in APEC', paper presented by PECC, *APEC Third Trade Policy Dialogue on FTAs*, Jeju, South Korea, 29 May.

Augier, P., Gasiorek, M. and Tong, C.L. (2005) 'The Impact of Rules of Origin on Trade Flows', *Economic Policy*, Vol 43, pp. 567–624.

Bagwell, K. and Staiger, R.W. (2004) 'Multilateral Trade Negotiations, Bilateral Opportunism and the Rules of GATT/WTO', *Journal of International Economics*, Vol 63, pp. 1–29.

Balassa, B. (1961) *The Theory of Economic Integration*, Irwin, Boston MA.

Baldwin, R.E. (1997) 'The Causes of Regionalism', *World Economy*, Vol 20(7), pp. 865–88.

Baldwin, R.E. (1999) 'A Domino Theory of Regionalism', in J. Bhagwati, R. Krishna and A. Panagariya (eds), *Trading Blocs: Alternative Approaches to Analysing Preferential Trade Agreements*, MIT Press, Cambridge MA.

Baldwin, R.E. (2004) 'The Spoke Trap: Hub and Spoke Bilateralism in East Asia', *CNAEC Research Series*, No. 04/02, Korea Institute for International Economic Policy, Seoul.

Beeson, M. and Islam, I. (2005) 'Neo-Liberalism and East Asia: Resisting the Washington Consensus', *Journal of Development Studies*, Vol 41(2), pp. 197–219.

Berger, M.T. (1999) 'APEC and its Enemies: The Failure of the New Regionalism in the Asia-Pacific', *Third World Quarterly*, Vol 20(5), pp. 1013–30.

Bergsten, C.F. (1994) 'Sunrise in Seattle', *International Economic Insights*, Vol 5(1), pp. 18–20.

Bergsten, C.F. (2000) *Back to the Future: APEC Looks at Subregional Trade Agreements to Achieve Free Trade Goal*, speech given at PBEC luncheon, Washington DC, 31 October.

Bergsten, C.F. (2001) 'Brunei: A Turning Point for APEC?', *International Economics: Policy Briefs*, No. 01-1, Institute for International Economics, Washington DC.

Bhagwati, J. (1968) 'Trade Liberalisation Amongst LDCs, Trade Theory, and GATT Rules, in J.N. Wolfe (ed.) *Value, Capital and Growth: Essays in Honour of Sir John Hicks*, University of Edinburgh Press, Edinburgh.

Bhagwati, J. (1993) 'Regionalism and Multilateralism: An Overview', in J. De Melo and A. Panagariya (eds) *New Dimensions in Regional Integration*, Cambridge University Press, Cambridge.

Bhagwati, J. (1995) 'US Trade Policy: The Infatuation with Free Trade Areas', in J. Bhagwati and A. Krueger (eds) *The Dangerous Drift to Preferential Trade Agreements*, AEI Press, Washington DC.

Bilal, S. (2003) 'North-South Agreements: Integrating Developing Countries into the World Trading System?, presented at the *Seminar on RTAs and the WTO*, 14 November, WTO Secretariat, Geneva.

Bisley, N. (2004) 'Asia-Pacific Regionalism and Preferential Trade Agreements: The Australian Case', *International Relations of the Asia-Pacific*, Vol 4(2), pp. 239–64.

Bohara, A.K., Camargo, A.I., Grijalva, T. and Gawande, K. (2005) 'Fundamental Dimensions of US Trade Policy', *Journal of International Economics*, Vol 65, pp. 93–125.

Bond, E., Riezman, R.G. and Syropoulos, C. (2004) 'A Strategic and Welfare Theoretic Analysis of Free Trade Areas', *Journal of International Economics*, Vol 64, pp. 1–27.

Bond, E. and Syropoulos, C. (1996) 'The Size of Trading Blocs, Market Power and World Welfare Effects', *Journal of International Economics*, Vol 40, pp. 411–37.

Borrus, M., Ernst, D. and Haggard, S. (eds) (2000) *International Production Networks in Asia: Rivalry or Riches?* Routledge, London.

Braga, C., Primo, A., Safadi, R. and Yeats, A. (1994) 'NAFTA's Implications for East Asian Exports', *World Bank Policy Research Working Paper*, No. 1351, World Bank, Washington DC.

Breslin, S. and Higgott, R. (2000) 'Studying Regions: Learning from the Old, Constructing the New', *New Political Economy*, Vol 5(3), pp. 333–52.

Brown, D.K., Deardorff, A.V. and Stern, R.M. (2003) 'Multilateral, Regional and Bilateral Trade: Policy Options for the United States and Japan', *The World Economy*, Vol 26, pp. 803–28.

Cadot, O., de Melo, J. and Olarreaga, M. (2001) 'Can Bilateralism Ease the Pains of Multilateral Trade Liberalisation?', *European Economic Review*, Vol 45(1), pp. 27–44.

Cai, K.G. (2001) 'Is a Free Trade Zone Emerging in Northeast Asia in the Wake of the Asian Financial Crisis?, *Pacific Affairs*, Vol 74(1), pp. 7–24.

Calder, K.E. (1988) 'Japan's Foreign Economic Policy Formation: Explaining the Reactive State', *World Politics*, Vol 40(July), pp. 517–540.

Capling, A. (2001) *Australia and the Global Trade System: From Havana to Seattle*, Cambridge University Press, Cambridge.

Centre for International Economics/CIE (2001) *Economic Impacts of an Australia–United States Free Trade Area*, CIE, Canberra.

Centre for International Economics/CIE (2004a) *Economic Analysis of AUSFTA: Impact of the Bilateral Free Trade Agreement with the United States*, CIE, Canberra.

Centre for International Economics/CIE (2004b) *The Australia–Thailand Free Trade Agreement: Economic Effects*, CIE, Canberra.

Cheng, J. (2001) 'Sino-ASEAN Relations in the Twenty-First Century', *Contemporary Southeast Asia*, Vol 23(3), pp. 420–51.

Cheong, I. (2002) *Korea's FTA Policy: Focusing on Bilateral FTAs with Chile and Japan*, Discussion Paper 02-02, Korea Institute for International Economic Policy, Seoul.

Cho, S.J. (2003), 'Towards Synergistic Building Blocks: Social Regulations under RTAs and Their Ramifications to the Global Trading System', presented at the *Seminar on RTAs and the WTO*, 14 November, WTO Secretariat, Geneva.

Coe, D.T., Helpman, E. and Hoffmaister, A.W. (1997) 'North-South R&D Spillovers', *Economic Review*, Vol 39(6), pp. 859–70.

Collie, D. (1997) 'Bilateralism is Good: Trade Blocs and Strategic Export Subsidies', *Oxford Economic Papers*, Vol 49, pp. 504–20.

Colvin, J. (2004) *The Costs of Competitive Liberalization*, column article (22 November), Centre for American Progress, Washington DC.

Cooper, C.A. and Massell, B.F. (1965) 'Toward a General Theory of Customs Unions for Developing Countries', *Journal of Political Economy*, Vol 73(5), pp. 461–76.

Corbey, D. (1995) 'Dialectical Functionalism: Stagnation as a Booster to European Integration', *International Organisation*, Vol 49, pp. 253–84.

Crawford, D. (2000) 'Chinese Capitalism: Cultures, the Southeast Asian Region and Economic Globalisation', *Third World Quarterly*, Vol 21(1), pp. 69–86.

Daquila, T.C. and Huy, L.H. (2003) 'Singapore and ASEAN in the Global Economy: The Case of Free Trade Agreements', *Asian Survey*, Vol 43(6), pp. 908–28.

Das, D.K. (2001) *Regional Trading Agreements and the Global Economy: An Asia-Pacific Perspective*, Centre for International Development, Harvard University, Cambridge MA.

Deardorff, A.V. and Stern, R.M. (1994) 'Multilateral Trade Negotiations and Preferential Trading Agreements', in A.V. Deardorff and R.M. Stern (eds) *Analytical and Negotiating Issues in the Global Trading System*, University of Michigan Press, Ann Arbor.

Dee, P. (2004) *The Australia–United States Free Trade Agreement: An Assessment*, report undertaken for the Senate Select Committee on AUSFTA, Canberra.

Dee, P. and Gali, J. (2003) 'The Trade and Investment Effects of Preferential Trading Arrangements', presented at the *14th Annual East Asian Seminar on Economics*, Taipei, 5–7 September.

Dent, C.M. (2001) 'Singapore's Foreign Economic Policy: The Pursuit of Economic Security', *Contemporary Southeast Asia*, Vol 23(1), pp. 1–23.

Dent, C.M. (2002) *The Foreign Economic Policies of Singapore, South Korea and Taiwan*, Edward Elgar, Cheltenham.

Dent, C.M. (2003a) 'Transnational Capital, the State and Foreign Economic Policy: Singapore, South Korea and Taiwan', *Review of International Political Economy*, Vol 10(2), pp. 246–77.

Dent, C.M. (2003b) 'Networking the Region? The Emergence and Impact of Asia-Pacific Bilateral Free Trade Agreement Projects', *The Pacific Review*, Vol 16(1), pp. 1–28.

Dent, C.M. (2005a) 'Taiwan and the New Regional Political Economy of East Asia', *China Quarterly*, Vol 182, pp. 385–406.

Dent, C.M. (2005b) 'Bilateral Free Trade Agreements: Boon or Bane for Regionalism in East Asia and the Asia-Pacific?', *European Journal of East Asian Studies*, Vol 4(2), pp. 287–314.

Dent, C.M. (2006a) 'The New Economic Bilateralism in Southeast Asia: Region-Convergent or Region-Divergent?, *International Relations of the Asia-Pacific*, Vol 6(1), pp. 81–111.

Dent, C.M. (2006b) 'Economic Security', in A. Collins (ed.) *Contemporary Security Studies*, Oxford University Press, Oxford.

Dent, C.M. and Huang, D. (eds) (2002) *Northeast Asian Regionalism: Learning from the European Experience*, Curzon Press, London.

Department of Foreign Affairs and Trade (Australia)/DFAT (1997) *In the National Interest: Australia's Foreign and Trade Policy*, DFAT, Canberra.

Department of Foreign Affairs and Trade (Australia)/DFAT (2003) *Advancing the National Interest: Australia's Foreign and Trade Policy*, DFAT, Canberra.

De Santis, H. (2005) 'The Dragon and the Tigers: China and Asian Regionalism', *World Policy Journal*, Vol 22(2), pp. 23–36.

Desker, B. (2004) 'In Defence of FTAs: From Purity to Pragmatism in East Asia', *The Pacific Review*, Vol 17(1), pp. 3–26.

Deutsch, K.W. (1957) *Political Community and the North Atlantic Area. International Organization in the light of Historical Experience*, Princeton University Press, Princeton N.J.

Dieter, H. (1997) 'APEC and WTO: Collision or Co-operation?', *Pacific Review*, Vol 10(1), pp. 19–38.

Dieter, H. and Higgott, R. (2003) 'Exploring Alternative Theories of Economic Regionalism: From Trade to Finance in Asian Co-operation?', *Review of International Political Economy*, Vol 10(2), pp. 430–54.

Dobson, W. (2001) 'Deeper Integration in East Asia: Regional Institutions and the International Economic System', *World Economy*, Vol 24(8), pp. 995–1018.

Dosch, J., Connors, M. and Davison, R. (2004) *The New Global Politics of the Asia-Pacific*, Routledge, London.

Drifte, R. (1998) *Japan's Foreign Policy for the 21^(st) Century: From Economic Superpower to What Power?*, MacMillan, Basingstoke.

Economist Intelligence Unit (2004) *Country Profile: Thailand, 2004/05*, EIU, London.

Eminent Persons Group (1995) *Third Report: Implementing APEC's Vision*, APEC Secretariat, Singapore.

Estevadeordal, A. (2002) 'RTAs in the Americas', presented at the *PECC Trade Forum*, 17–19 May, Lima.

Estevadeordal, A. and Suominen, K. (2003) 'Rules of Origin in the World Trading System', presented at the *Seminar on RTAs and the WTO*, 14 November, WTO Secretariat, Geneva.

Estevadeordal, A. and Suominen, K. (2005) 'Mapping and Measuring Rules of Origin Around the World', presented at the *International Workshop on Identifying and addressing Possible Impacts of FTAs/RTAs Development on APEC Developing Member Economies, Hanoi, 28–30 June*.

294   *References*

Ethier, W.J. (1998) 'The New Regionalism', *Economic Journal*, Vol 108(July), pp. 1149–61.

Fawcett, L. and Hurrell, A. (1995) *Regionalism in World Politics*, Oxford University Press, Oxford.

Feinberg, R.E. (2003) 'The Political Economy of United States' Free Trade Arrangements', *World Economy*, Vol 26(7), pp. 1019–40.

Feridhanusetyawan, T. (2005) 'Preferential Trade Agreements in the Asia-Pacific Region', *IMF Working Paper Series*, WP/05/149, International Monetary Fund, Washington DC.

Findlay, C. (2002) 'Walking and Chewing Gum at the Same Time: Australia's Free Trade Area Strategy', *Australian Journal of Agricultural and Resource Economics*, Vol 46(4), pp. 605–17.

Findlay, C., Piei, M.H. and Pangestu, M. (2003) 'Trading with Favourites: Risks, Motives and Implications of FTAs in the Asia-Pacific', presented at the *PECC Trade Forum*, 22–23 April, Washington DC.

Finger, J.M. (2002) *The Doha Agenda and Development: The View from the Uruguay Round*, Asian Development Bank, Manila.

Frankel, J.A. and Wei, S.J. (1997) 'The New Regionalism and Asia: Impact and Options', in N.P. Rao and A. Panagariya (eds) *The Global Trading System and Developing Asia*, Oxford University Press, Oxford.

Freund, C.L. (2000) 'Spaghetti Regionalism', *International Finance Discussion Papers*, No. 680, Board of Governors of the US Federal Reserve System.

Frydenlund, J.E. (2002) 'The Erosion of Freedom to Farm', *Backgrounder Report No. 1523*, Heritage Foundation, Washington DC.

Gamble, A. and Payne, A. (eds) (1996) *Regionalism and World Order*, Macmillan, Basingstoke.

Gehrels, F. (1956) 'Customs Unions from a Single-Country Viewpoint', *Review of Economic Studies*, Vol 49, pp. 696–712.

General Accounting Office (2004) *International Trade: Intensifying Free Trade Negotiating Agenda Calls for Better Allocation of Staff and Resources*, GAO report number GAO-04-233, Washington DC.

Gordon, B.K. (2003) 'A High Risk Trade Policy', *Foreign Affairs*, Vol 82(4), pp. 105–11.

Goyal, S. and Joshi, S. (1999) 'Bilateralism and Free Trade', *Econometric Institute Report No. 9953*, Erasmus University, Rotterdam.

Hettne, B. and Inotai, A. (1994) *The New Regionalism: Implications for Global Development and International Security*, World Institute for Development Economics Research, United Nations University, Helsinki.

Hettne, B., Inotai, A. and Sunkel, O. (eds) (1999) *Globalism and the New Regionalism*, MacMillan, London.

Hettne, B. and Soderbaum, F. (2000) 'Theorising the Rise of Regionness', *New Political Economy*, Vol 5(3), pp. 457–74.

Holst, D. and Weiss, J. (2004) 'ASEAN and China: Export Rivals or Partners in Regional Growth', *World Economy*, Vol 27(8), pp. 1255–74.

Hufbauer, G. and Schott, J. (1993) 'Regionalism in North America', in K. Ohno (ed.) *Regionalism and its Impact on Developing Countries*, Institute of Developing Economies, Tokyo.

Hughes, C.W. (2000) 'Japanese Policy and the East Asian Currency Crisis: Abject Defeat or Quiet Victory?', *Review of International Political Economy*, Vol 7(2), pp. 219–53.

Hughes, C.W., Hook, G.D., Gilson, J.A. and Dobson, H. (2001) *Japan's International Relations: Politics, Economics and Security*, Routledge, London.

Hund, M. (2003) 'ASEAN Plus Three: Towards a New Age of Pan-East Asian Regionalism? A Sceptic's View', *Pacific Review*, Vol 16(3), pp. 383–417.

Hurrell, A. (1995) 'Regionalism in Theoretical Perspective' in L. Fawcett and A. Hurrell (eds) *Regionalism in World Politics: Regional Organisation and International Order*, Oxford University Press, Oxford.

International Monetary Fund/IMF (2005) *Asia-Pacific Regional Outlook*, International Monetary Fund, Washington DC.

Irwin, D.A. (1993) 'Multilateral and Bilateral Trade Policies in the World System: An Historic Perspective', in J. De Melo and A. Panagariya (eds) *New Dimensions in Regional Integration*, Cambridge University Press, Cambridge.

Jayasuriya, K. (1994) 'Singapore: The Politics of Regional Definition', *The Pacific Review*, Vol 7(4), pp. 411–20.

Jayasuriya, K. (ed.) (2004) *Asian Regional Governance: Crisis and Change*, Routledge, London.

Johnson, C. (1996) *Japan: Who Governs? The Rise of the Developmental State*, W.W. Norton Publishers, New York.

Johnson, H.G. (1965) *The World Economy at the Crossroads: A Survey of Current Problems of Money, Trade, and Economic Development*, Clarendon Press, Oxford.

Kagami, M. (2003) 'ASEAN–Japan Comprehensive Economic Partnership and Japan's FTAs with Other Countries including Korea and Mexico', presented at the *JEF/SIIA International Symposium*, Singapore, 7–8 March.

Katzenstein, P.J. (1997) 'Introduction: Asian Regionalism in Comparative Perspective', in P.J. Katzenstein and T. Shiraishi (eds) *Network Power: Japan and Asia*, Cornell University Press, Ithaca.

Katzenstein, P.J. (2000) 'Regionalism and Asia', *New Political Economy*, Vol 5(3), pp. 353–68.

Keidanren (1999) *Report on the Possible Effects of a Japan–Mexico Free Trade Agreement on Japanese Industry*, Keidanren, Tokyo.

Keidanren (2000) *Urgent Call for Active Promotion of Free Trade Agreements: Toward a New Dimension in Trade Policy*, Keidanren, Tokyo.

Kemp, M.C. and Wan, H.V. (1976) 'An Elementary Proposition Concerning the Formation of Customs Unions', *Journal of International Economics*, Vol 6(1), pp. 95–7.

Kennedy, P. (1988) *The Rise and Fall of the Great Powers*, Fontana, London.

Keohane, R.O. (1990) 'Multilateralism: An Agenda for Research', *International Organisation*, Vol 45(4).

Khor, M. (2005) 'Developing Countries Warned Against WTO-Plus Issues and Rules in FTAs', *South North Development Monitor*, Third World Network, 31 August 2005.

Kikuchi, T. (2002) 'East Asian Regionalism: A Look at the ASEAN Plus Three Framework', *Japan Review of International Affairs*, Vol 16(1), pp. 1–23.

Kimura, F. and Ando, M. (2004) 'The Economic Analysis of International Production/ Distribution Networks in East Asia and Latin America: The Implications of Regional Trade Arrangements', presented at the *APEC Study Centres Consortium Meeting*, Vina del Mar, Chile, 26–29 May.

Koh, T. and Lin, C.L. (2004) *The United States–Singapore Free Trade Agreement: Highlights and Insights*, Institute of Policy Studies, Singapore.

Krauss, E.S. (2004) 'The US and Japan in APEC's EVSL Negotiations: Regional Multilateralism and Trade', in E.S. Krauss and T.J. Pempel (eds) *Beyond Bilateralism: The US– Japan Relationship in the New Asia-Pacific*, Stanford University Press, Stanford.

Kreinen, M. (1992) 'Multilateralism, Regionalism and Their Implications for Asia', paper presented at the *Conference on Global Interdependence and Asia-Pacific Co-operation*, Hong Kong, 8–10 June.

Krishna, K. (1998) 'Regionalism and Multilateralism: A Political Economy Approach', *Quarterly Journal of Economics*, Vol 113(1), pp. 227–51.

Krishna, K. and Krueger, A. (1995) *Implementing Free Trade Areas: Rules of Origin and Hidden Protection*, National Bureau of Economic Research, Working Paper No. 4983.

Krueger, A.O. (1997) 'Free Trade Areas Versus Customs Unions', *Journal of Development Economics*, Vol 54(1), pp. 506–19.

Krugman, P. (1991) 'Is Bilateralism Bad?', in E. Helpman and A. Razin (eds) *International Trade and Trade Policy*, MIT Press, Cambridge MA.

Krugman, P. (1993) 'Regionalism Versus Multilateralism: Analytical Notes', in J. De Melo and A. Panagariya (eds) *New Dimensions in Regional Integration*, Cambridge University Press, Cambridge.

Krumm, K. and Kharas, H. (eds) (2004) *East Asia Integrates: A Trade Policy Agenda for Shared Growth*, World Bank, Washington DC.

Lee, J.W. and Park, I. (2005) 'Free Trade Areas in East Asia: Discriminatory or Non-Discriminatory?', *World Economy*, Vol 28(1), pp. 21–48.

Lipsey, R.G. (1957) 'The Theory of Customs Unions: Trade Diversion and Welfare', *Economica*, Vol 24, pp. 11–32.

Lloyd, P.J. (2002) 'New Bilateralism in the Asia-Pacific', *The World Economy*, Vol 25(9), pp. 1279–96.

Lloyd, P.J. (2003) 'The Case for Free Trade and the Role of RTAs', presented at the *Seminar on RTAs and the WTO*, 14 November, WTO Secretariat, Geneva.

Lloyd, P.J, and MacLaren, D. (2005) 'Gains and Losses from Regional Trading Agreements', *Economic Record*, Vol 80, No. 251, pp. 445–67.

Low, L. (2003) Singapore's Bilateral Free Trade Agreements: Architectural and Institutional Issues, presented at the *PECC Trade Forum*, 22–23 April, Washington DC.

MacDuff, D. (2002) 'APEC After Shanghai: Which Path Forward', *International Journal*, Vol 57(3), pp. 439–57.

MAFF (2002) *Japan's Agricultural, Forestry and Fishery Industries, and Free Trade Agreements*, MAFF, Tokyo.

MAFF (2004) *What is Multifunctionality of Agriculture?*, http://www.maff.go.jp/soshiki/kambou/joutai/onepoint/public/ta_me.html MAFF, Tokyo (accessed September 2004).

Mansfield, E.A. and Milner, H.V. (eds) (1998) *The Political Economy of Regionalism*, Columbia University Press, New York.

Mansfield, E.A. and Milner, H.V. (1999) 'The New Wave of Regionalism', *International Organisation*, Vol 53(3), pp. 587–627.

Marchand, M.H., Bøås, M. and Shaw, T.M. (1999) 'The Political Economy of New Regionalisms', *Third World Quarterly*, Vol 20(5), pp. 897–910.

Mathis, J.H. (2003) 'Systemic Issues in the CRTA', presented at the *Seminar on RTAs and the WTO*, 14 November, WTO Secretariat, Geneva.

McCleery, R. (1993) 'Modelling NAFTA: Macroeconomic Effects', in K. Ohno (ed.) *Regionalism and its Impact on Developing Countries*, Institute of Developing Economies, Tokyo.

McKibbin, W.J., Lee, J.W. and Cheong, I. (2004) 'A Dynamic Analysis of a Korea–Japan Free Trade Area: Simulations with the G-Cubed Asia-Pacific Model', *International Economic Journal*, Vol 18(1), pp. 3–32.

Meade, J.E. (1955) *The Theory of Customs Unions*, North Holland, Amsterdam.

Medalla, E.M. and Lazaro, D.C. (2004) *Exploring the Philippine FTA Policy Options*, Philippine Institute for Development Studies, Policy Notes No. 2004–09, Makati City.

Michaely, M. (1965) 'On Customs Unions and the Gains from Trade', *Economic Journal*, Vol 75, pp. 577–83.

Mikanagi, Y. (1996) *Japan's Trade Policy: Action or Reaction?*, Routledge, London.

Miller, C., Reed, G. and Talerngsri, P. (2004) 'Foreign Direct Investment and Vertical Integration of Production by Japanese Multinationals in Thailand', *Journal Of Comparative Economics*, Vol 32(4), pp. 805–21.

Milner, H. (1992) 'International Theories of Co-operation Among Nations: Strengths and Weaknesses', *World Politics*, Vol 44 (April), pp. 466–96.

Ministry of Economy, Trade and Industry (Japan)/METI (2001) *Promotion of Economic Partnership*, METI, Tokyo.

Ministry of Economy, Trade and Industry (Japan)/METI (2005a) *White Paper on International Economy and Trade 2005: Towards a New Dimension of Economic Prosperity in Japan and East Asia*, METI, Tokyo.

Ministry of Economy, Trade and Industry (Japan)/METI (2005b) *Japan's Policy on FTAs/EPAs*, METI, Tokyo.

Ministry of Foreign Affairs (Japan)/MOFA (2004) *Basic Policy Towards Further Promotion of Economic Partnership Agreements*, 21 December 2004, MOFA, Tokyo.

Ministry of Foreign Affairs and Trade (New Zealand)/MFAT (2002) *A US–Australia Free Trade Agreement: A Qualitative Assessment of the Business Impacts on New Zealand*, MFAT, Wellington.

Ministry of Foreign Affairs and Trade (New Zealand)/MFAT (2005) *Trans-Pacific Strategic Economic Partnership Agreement: National Interest Analysis*, MFAT, Wellington.

Ministry of International Trade and Industry (Japan)/MITI (1998) *White Paper on International Economy and Trade 1998*, MITI, Tokyo.

Ministry of International Trade and Industry (Japan)/MITI (1999) *White Paper on International Economy and Trade 1999*, MITI, Tokyo.

Murray, W.E. and Challies, E. (2004) New Zealand and Chile: Partnership for the Pacific Century?, *Australian Journal of International Affairs*, Vol 58(1), pp. 89–103.

Nabers, D. (2003) 'The Social Construction of International Institutions: The Case of ASEAN + 3', *International Relations of the Asia-Pacific*, Vol 3, pp. 113–36.

Nagai, F. (2002) 'Thailand's FTA Policy: Continuity and Change Between the Chuan and Thaksin Governments', in J. Okamoto (ed.) *Whither Free Trade Agreements? Proliferation, Evaluation and Multilateralisation*, IDE-JETRO, Japan.

Narlikar, A. (2003) *International Trade and Developing Countries: Bargaining Coalition in the WTO*, Routledge, London.

National Federation of Farmers/NFF (2004) *Submission to the Joint Standing Committee on Treaties Regarding the Proposed Australia–US Free Trade Agreement*, NFF, Canberra.

Ng, F. and Yeats, A. (2003) 'Major Trade Trends in East Asia: What are their Implications for Regional Co-operation and Growth?', *World Bank Policy Research Paper Series*, No. 3084, World Bank, Washington DC.

Nixon, C. (2000) 'CER: The Cornerstone of New Zealand's Trade Policy', *NZ Trade Consortium Working Paper No. 10*, NZ Trade Consortium, Wellington.

Nixon, C. and Yeabsley, J. (2002) *New Zealand's Trade Policy Odyssey: Ottawa, via Marrakech and On*, Research Monograph 68, New Zealand Institute of Economic Research, Wellington.

Noland, M. (1994) 'Asia and the NAFTA', in Y.S. Kim and K.S. Oh (eds) *The US–Korea Economic Partnership*, Ashgate Publishers, Aldershot.

OECD (2001) *Multifunctionality: Toward an Analytical Framework*, OECD, Paris.

Ogita, T. (2003) 'Japan as a Late-Coming FTA Holder: Trade Policy Change for the Asian Orientation', in J. Okamoto (ed.) *Whither Free Trade Agreements? Proliferation, Evaluation and Multilateralisation*, IDE-JETRO, Japan.

Okamoto, J. (ed.) (2004) *Trade Liberalisation and APEC*, Routledge, London.

Olds, K., Kelly, P., Kong, L., Yeung, H. and Dicken, P. (eds) (1999) *Globalisation and the Asia-Pacific*, Routledge, London.

Otto, C. (2000) 'International Regimes in the Asia-Pacific: The Case of APEC', in J. Dosch and M. Mols (eds) *International Relations in the Asia-Pacific: New Patterns of Power, Interest, and Co-operation*, St. Martin's Press, New York.

Oye, K.A. (1992) *Economic Discrimination and Political Exchange: World Political Economy in the 1930s and 1980s*, Princeton University Press, Princeton.

Pacific Economic Co-operation Council/PECC (2003a) 'PECC Position on Agriculture Negotiation', paper presented by the PECC Agriculture Trade Study Group, *PECC Focus Workshop on Trade*, 1 September 2003, Brunei Darussalam.

Pacific Economic Co-operation Council/PECC (2003b) *Proposals for an APEC Common Understanding on RTAs*, PECC Secretariat, Singapore.

Panagariya, A. (1999) 'The Regionalism Debate: On Overview', *The World Economy*, Vol 22(3), pp. 477–511.

Panagariya, A. (2000) 'Preferential Trade Liberalisation: The Traditional Theory and New Development', *Journal of Economic Literature*, Vol 37(2), pp. 123–45.

Pangestu, M. and Gooptu, S. (2004) 'New Regionalism: Options for East Asia', in K. Krumm and H. Kharas (eds) *East Asia Integrates: A Trade Policy Agenda for Shared Growth*, World Bank, Washington DC.

Petri, P.A. (1993) 'The East Asian Trading Bloc: An Analytical History', in J.A. Frankel and M. Kahler (eds) *Regionalism and Rivalry: Japan and the United States in Pacific Asia*, University of Chicago Press, Chicago.

Phillips, N. (2004) *The Southern Cone Model: The Political Economy of Regional Capitalist Development in Latin America*, Routledge, London.

Poon, J. (2001) 'Regionalism in the Asia-Pacific: Is Geography Destiny?, *Area*, Vol 33(3), pp. 252–60.

Powers, K. (2004) 'Regional Trade Agreements as Military Alliances', *International Interactions*, Vol 30, pp. 373–95.

Productivity Commission (2004) *Restrictiveness Index for Preferential Rules of Origin*, Productivity Commission, Canberra.

Prusa, T.J. (2005) '2004 Trade Policy Review: The United States', *World Economy*, Vol 28(9), pp. 1263–75.

Rafael, V.L. (1999) 'Regionalism, Area Studies and the Accidents of Agency', *American Historical Review*, Vol 104(4), pp. 1208–20.

Rajan, R.S., Sen, R and Siregar, R. (2001) *Singapore and Free Trade Agreements: Economic Relations with Japan and the United States*, ISEAS, Singapore.

Rapkin, D. (2001) 'The US, Japan, and the Power to Block: The APEC and AMF Cases', *Pacific Review*, Vol 14(3), pp. 373–410.

Ravenhill, J. (2000) 'APEC Adrift: Implications for Economic Regionalism in Asia and the Pacific', *Pacific Review*, Vol 13(2), pp. 319–33.

Ravenhill, J. (2001) *APEC and the Construction of Pacific Rim Regionalism*, Cambridge University Press, Cambridge.

Ravenhill, J. (2002) 'A Three Bloc World? The New East Asian Regionalism', *International Relations of the Asia-Pacific*, Vol 2(2), pp. 167–95.

Ravenhill, J. (2003) 'The New Bilateralism in the Asia-Pacific', *Third World Quarterly*, Vol 24, No. 3 (2003), pp. 299–318.

Riezman, R. (1999) 'Can Bilateral Trade Agreements Help Induce Free Trade?', *Canadian Journal of Economics*, Vol 32(3), pp. 751–66.

Rose, C. (2004) *Sino-Japanese Relations: Facing the Past, Looking to the Future?*, RoutledgeCurzon, London.

Ruggie, J.G. (1993) 'Multilateralism: The Anatomy of an Institution', in J.G. Ruggie (ed.) *Multilateralism Matters: The Theory and Praxis of an Institutional Form*, Columbia University Press, New York.

Ruland, J. (2000) 'ASEAN and the Asian Crisis: Theoretical Implications and Practical Consequences for Southeast Asian Regionalism', *Pacific Review*, Vol 13(3), pp. 421–52.

Salazar-Xirinachs, J.M. (2001) 'Implications of Proliferating Sub-Regional Trade Agreements: Lessons from the Latin American Experience', presented at the *PECC Trade Policy Forum*, Bangkok, 12–13 June.

Santos-Paulino, A.U. (2005) 'Trade Liberalisation and Economic Performance: Theory and Evidence for Developing Countries', *World Economy*, Vol 28(6), pp. 783–821.

Schiff, M. and Winters, L.A. (2003) *Regional Integration and Development*, World Bank, Washington DC.

Schott, J.J. (2001) *Free Trade Agreements: The Cost of US Non-Participation*, testimony before the Sub-Committee on Trade, House Committee on Ways and Means, Washington DC, 29 March.

Schott, J.J. (ed.) (2004) *Free Trade Agreements: US Strategies and Priorities*, Institute for International Economics, Washington DC.

Scollay, R. (2003) 'Asia-Pacific RTAs as Avenues for Achieving APEC's Bogor Goals', *PECC Focus Workshop on Trade*, 1 September 2003, Brunei Darussalam.

Scollay, R. (2004) 'Preliminary Assessment of the Proposal for a Free Trade Area of the Asia-Pacific (FTAAP)', issue paper for the *APEC Business Advisory Council (ABAC)*, presented 8th August.

Scollay, R. and Gilbert, J.P. (2001) *New Regional Trading Arrangements in the Asia-Pacific*, Institute for International Economics, Washington DC.

Sen, R. (2004) *Free Trade Agreements in Southeast Asia*, Institute of Southeast Asian Studies, Singapore.

Sohn, C.H. and Yoon, J. (2001) *Korea's FTA Policy: Current Status and Prospects*, Discussion Paper 01-01, Korea Institute for International Economic Policy, Seoul.

Stroper, M. (1997) *The Regional World: Territorial Development in a Global Economy*, Guilford Press, New York.

Stubbs, R. (2000) 'Signing on to Liberalisation: AFTA and the Politics of Regional Economic Co-operation', *Pacific Review*, Vol 13(2), pp. 297–318.

Stubbs, R. (2002) 'ASEAN Plus Three: Emerging East Asian Regionalism?', *Asian Survey*, Vol 42(3), pp. 440–55.

Tabaiwalu, P. (2005) 'A Summary of Regional Trade Agreements Among Developing Countries: The Case of the Pacific Island Countries', presented at the *APEC Workshop on RTAs/FTAs and Developing Member Economies*, Hanoi, 28–30 June.

Terada, T. (2001) 'Directional Leadership in Institution-Building: Japan's Approach to ASEAN in the Establishment of PECC and APEC', *The Pacific Review*, Vol 14(2), pp. 195–220.

Terada, T. (2003) 'Constructing an East Asian Concept and Growing Regional Identity: From EAEC to ASEAN+3', *The Pacific Review*, Vol 16(2), pp. 251–77.

Thangavelu, S.M. and Toh, M.H. (2005) 'Bilateral WTO-Plus Free Trade Agreements: The WTO Trade Policy Review of Singapore', *World Economy*, Vol 28(9), pp. 1211–28.

Tongzon, J.L. (2005) 'ASEAN–China Free Trade Area: A Bane or Boon for ASEAN Countries', *World Economy*, Vol 28(2), pp. 191–210.

United Nations Conference on Trade and Development/UNCTAD (2004) 'Swimming in the Spaghetti Bowl: Challenges for Developing Countries Under the New Regionalism', *Policy Issues in International Trade and Commodities Study Series*, No. 27, UNCTAD, Geneva.

Urata, S. and Kiyota, K. (2003) 'The Impact of an East Asia FTA on Foreign Trade in East Asia', *NBER Working Paper Series*, No. 10173, National Bureau of Economic Research.

van Wolferen, K. (1988) *The Enigma of Japanese Power: People and Politics in a Stateless Nation*, MacMillan, London.

Viner, J. (1950) *The Customs Union Issue*, Steven and Sons, London.

Wade, R.H. (2003) 'What Strategies are Viable for Developing Countries Today? The World Trade Organisation and the Shrinking of "Development Space"', *Review of International Political Economy*, Vol 10(4), pp. 621–44.

Wallace, W. (1994) *Regional Integration: The West European Experience*, The Brookings Institution, Washington DC.

Wang, Z. and Coyle, B. (2002) 'APEC Open Regionalism and its Impact on the World Economy: A Computable General Equilibrium Analysis', *World Economy*, Vol 25, pp. 563–89

Weiss, L., Thurbon, E. and Mathews, J. (2004) *How to Kill a Country: Australia's Devastating Trade Deal with the United States*, Allen and Unwin, Crows Nest.

Wendt, A. (1992) 'Anarchy is What States Make of It: The Social Construction of Power Politics', *International Organisation*, Vol 46(2), pp. 391–425.

Wesley, M. (2001) 'APEC's Mid-Life Crisis? The Rise and Fall of Early Voluntary Sectoral Liberalisation', *Pacific Affairs*, Vol 74(2), pp. 185–204.

Westhoff, F.H., Yarbrough, B.V. and Yarbrough, R.M. (1994) 'Preferential Trade Agreements and the GATT: Can Bilateralism and Multilateralism Co-exist?', *Kyklos*, Vol 47(2), pp. 179–95.

Winham, G.R. (1992) *The Evolution of International Trade Agreements*, University of Toronto Press, Toronto.

Wong, J. and Chan, S. (2003) 'China–ASEAN Free Trade Agreement: Shaping Future Economic Relations', *Asian Survey*, Vol 43(3), pp. 507–26.

Wonnacott, R.J. (1996) 'Trade and Investment in a Hub-and-Spoke System versus a Free Trade Area', *World Economy*, Vol 19(3), pp. 237–52.

World Bank (2005) *Global Economic Prospects 2005: Trade, Regionalism and Development*, World Bank, Washington DC.

World Trade Organisation/WTO (2000) *Mapping of Regional Trade Agreements: Background Note by the Secretariat*, WTO Secretariat, Geneva.

World Trade Organisation/WTO (2001) *Chair's Report to the Trade Negotiating Committee*, Document TN/RL/6, Negotiating Group on Rules, WTO Secretariat, Geneva.

World Trade Organisation/WTO (2002a) *Coverage, Liberalisation Process and Transitional Provisions in Regional Trade Agreements*, Committee on Regional Trade Agreements, Document WT/REG/W/46, WTO Secretariat, Geneva.

World Trade Organisation/WTO (2002b) *Rules of Origin Regimes in Regional Trade Agreements*, Committee on Regional Trade Agreements, Document WT/REG/W/45, WTO Secretariat, Geneva.

World Trade Organisation/WTO (2002c) *Negotiating Group on Rules Summary Report, November 2002*, Document TN/RL/M/5, WTO Secretariat, Geneva.

World Trade Organisation/WTO (2003a), 'The Changing Landscape of RTAs', Regional Trade Agreements Section, prepared for the *Seminar on RTAs and the WTO*, 14 November, WTO Secretariat, Geneva.

World Trade Organisation/WTO (2003b) *Adjusting to Trade Liberalisation: The Role of Policy, Institutions and WTO Disciplines*, WTO Secretariat, Geneva.

World Trade Organisation/WTO (2005a), 'The Changing Landscape of Regional Trade Agreements', *WTO Discussion Paper Series*, No. 8, WTO Secretariat, Geneva.

World Trade Organisation/WTO (2005b), *The Future of the WTO: Addressing Institutional Challenges in the New Millennium*, WTO Secretariat, Geneva.

World Trade Organisation/WTO (2005c) *Report by the Chairman of the Trade Negotiations Committee, November 2005*, Negotiating Group on Rules, Document TN/RL/15, WTO Secretariat, Geneva.

Yamazawa, I. (1998) *APEC's Progress Toward the Bogor Target: A Quantitative Assessment of the 1997 IAP/CAP*, PECC Japan Committee, Tokyo.

Yamazawa, I. (ed.) (2000) *Asia Pacific Economic Co-operation (APEC)*, Routledge, London.

Yanai, A. (2001) *Reciprocity in Trade Liberalisation*, IDE APEC Study Centre Working Paper, Series 00/01, No. 2, Tokyo.

Yang, Z. (2004) 'China's FTA Developments', presented at the *APEC Study Centres Consortium Meeting*, Vina del Mar, Chile, 26–29 May.

Yi, S. (1996) 'Endogenous Formation of Customs Unions Under Imperfect Competition: Open Regionalism is Good', *Journal of International Economics*, Vol 11(2), pp. 153–77.

Yoshimatsu, H. (2003) 'Japanese Policy in the Asian Economic Crisis and the Developmental State Concept', *Journal of the Asia-Pacific Economy*, Vol 8(1), pp. 102–25.

Yoshimatsu, H. (2005) 'Japan's Keidanren and Free Trade Agreements', *Asian Survey*, Vol 45(2), pp. 258–78.

Zissimos, B. and Vines, D. (2000) 'Is the WTO's Article XXIV a Free Trade Barrier?', *CSGR Working Paper No. 49/00*, University of Warwick, Coventry.

Zoellick, R. (2001a) 'The United States, Europe and the World Trading System', remarks before the Kangaroo Group, 15 May, Strasbourg.

Zoellick. R. (2001b) 'American Trade Leadership: What is at Stake?', remarks before the Institute for International Economics, 24 September, Washington DC.

Index